Election Polls, the News Media, and Democracy

Paul J. Lavrakas
Ohio State University

Michael W. Traugott
University of Michigan

CHATHAM HOUSE PUBLISHERS
SEVEN BRIDGES PRESS, LLC
NEW YORK • LONDON

Seven Bridges Press, LLC
135 Fifth Avenue, New York, NY 10010

Publisher: Robert J. Gormley
Managing Editor: Katharine Miller
Production Supervisor: Melissa A. Martin
Cover Design: Inari Information Services, Inc.
Production Services: Linda Pawelchak/Lori Clinton
Printing and Binding: Versa Press, Inc.

Library of Congress Cataloging-in-Publication Data

Lavrakas, Paul J.
    Election polls, the news media, and democracy / Paul J. Lavrakas, Michael W. Traugott.
    p.   cm
    Includes bibliographical references and index.
    ISBN 1-889119-16-4
    1. Public opinion—United States.   2. Public opinion polls.   3. Election
forecasting—United States.   4. Press and politics—United States.   I. Traugott, Michael W.
II. Title.

HN90.P8 L38 2000
070.4′493247′0973—dc21
                                                                                      99-056614

Manufactured in the United States of America
10   9   8   7   6   5   4   3   2   1

To our children,
Nikolas J. Lavrakas
Elisabeth and Christopher Traugott,
For their love and friendship

Contents

Preface

The use and importance of political polling in the United States has grown considerably in the last two decades of the twentieth century. Polls, especially those widely disseminated by the news media, are interesting to political elites and average citizens alike. They also appear to be drawing the ire of growing numbers of political partisans and others. For example, in 1998 and early 1999, many political conservatives criticized the public polls when they reported a solid majority support for keeping President Clinton in the White House. The source of much of the blame was some Republicans, who apparently were frustrated by the failing effort to remove Bill Clinton from his presidency because they thought these polls were playing a role in keeping him in office. Conservative Clinton critics just could not believe that these public polls, which were being reported in the media at least weekly, were accurate—and considerable rhetoric was aimed at trying to undermine their validity in the public's eye.

Criticism of the role of polls in a democracy—both thoughtful and not—is not a recent phenomenon. However, as the use of polls has grown and they have become a more prominent feature in election news and other political coverage, the amount and tenor of the criticism that they are overused and harm democracy have increased considerably. What seems clear to us, as close observers of the way election polls are used in the United States, is that there is room for improvement in the reporting of polls and a great need for a better public understanding of the strengths and limitations of polls.

Within this evolving political climate, we have worked together for more than a decade to try to educate poll users and poll consumers about the methods of good (valid) polls and the ways that poll-based information can enhance democracy. We have done this through teaching at our respective universities and other speaking opportunities, research we have done together and separately, and our professional service, in particular with the American Association for Public Opinion Research. We are convinced that there is a great deal of misunderstanding about how polls can be used to help democratic processes and that unless corrected, this misunderstanding will grow and further erode the potential of polls to enhance the functioning of our democracy.

This edited volume is the fourth book on which we have collaborated. It brings together both practitioners and scholars who are experts in the conduct of election polls and the media's use of them. Like its predecessors, this book explains how polls are conducted and used during major election contests, in particular the 1996 American election for president, how the current methods and usage can be improved, and why these changes are needed.

Many people helped this book become a reality. First and foremost, we express our appreciation to the authors of the respective chapters: it is their expertise in this field and their own commitment to improving the polling enterprise that makes this book important. Martha Kayler of the now-defunct Northwestern University Survey Lab played an important role in initially contacting the authors and helping to secure their agreement to write their chapters. Jessica Banks, Lillian Diaz-Castillo, and Judy Essig of the Ohio State University Center for Survey Research helped with many and varied editorial tasks. At Chatham House, thanks go to publisher Bob Gormley for his support, understanding, and patience; as well as to Katharine Miller and Linda Pawelchak for their considerable editorial acumen. The Communications Studies Department at Northwestern University provided Lavrakas support for his early work on the book, as did the School of Journalism and Communication and the Center for Survey Research at Ohio State University during the past three summers. Part of Traugott's research effort was supported by a grant from The Pew Charitable Trusts and by the Department of Communication Studies at the University of Michigan.

Paul J. Lavrakas, Columbus, Ohio
Michael W. Traugott, Ann Arbor, Michigan

Contributors

SANDRA BAUMAN is a senior research executive based in the New York office of Wirthlin Worldwide, an international public opinion and marketing research firm. During her ten-year background in research, Dr. Bauman has designed and managed numerous projects for corporate and nonprofit clients in the areas of employee communications and commitment, corporate image and brand positioning, strategic marketing, and customer satisfaction and loyalty. Prior to joining Wirthlin Worldwide, Dr. Bauman's experience included working for Roper Starch Worldwide as a project director and for Voter News Service as exit poll manager, both in New York. From 1990 to1994, Dr. Bauman was the assistant manager of the Northwestern University Survey Laboratory in Evanston, Illinois. In addition to research studies, her responsibilities included managing the telephone research center and coordinating the quarterly student assessments of courses and teachers at Northwestern. She also taught undergraduate courses on the topics of public opinion, mass media, and interpersonal communication. Dr. Bauman began her career as a reporter and editor for several daily newspapers. She holds a B.A. from Drake University and an M.S. and a Ph.D. from Northwestern University.

LEO BOGART is a columnist for *Presstime* magazine. For many years, he was the executive vice president and general manager of the Newspaper Advertising Bureau. Earlier Dr. Bogart directed public opinion research for the Standard Oil Company (New Jersey) [now Exxon], marketing research for Revlon, Inc., and account research services for McCann Erickson, Inc. He holds a doctorate in sociology from the University of Chicago and has taught at New York University, Columbia University, and the Illinois Institute of Technology. He has been president of the American and World Associations for Public Opinion Research, the Society for Consumer Psychology, the Market Research Council, and the Radio and Television Research Council. Among his books are *Polls and the Awareness of Public Opinion; Commercial Culture: The Media System and the Public Interest; Cool Words, Cold War; Preserving the Press; Press and Public; The Age of Television; Strategy in Advertising;* and *Project Clear: Social Research and the Desegregation of the U.S. Army.*

MIKE CURTIN is president, associate publisher, and former editor of *The Columbus Dispatch.* He has been with the newspaper for twenty-five years, and he covered state and local politics and government for eighteen years. His beats have included Columbus City Hall, Franklin County government, the Ohio General Assembly, and local and state politics. In 1985, Curtin became the paper's chief political writer and director of *The Dispatch Poll.* In October 1994, he became the paper's executive managing editor. He was promoted to editor in December 1995 and associate publisher in July 1998. He was named president in January 1999. He is the author of *The Ohio Politics Almanac,* published in February 1996 by Kent State University Press. He is a Columbus native and a graduate of the Ohio State University School of Journalism.

ROBERT P. DAVES is director of polling and news research at the *Star Tribune* in Minneapolis, Minnesota. He directs the newspaper's *Minnesota Poll* and serves as an internal consultant on public journalism and computer-assisted reporting projects. Daves has worked in newspapers as a reporter, copy editor, and news editor before his training in public opinion research. During two decades of polling experience, he has conducted national, state, and local polls for newspapers nationwide. Prior to joining the *Star Tribune,* he was a research manager at the *Charlotte Observer,* where he conducted polling and market research in the newspaper, health care, and financial industries. He earned an M.A. in journalism at the University of North Carolina at Chapel Hill and a B.S. in sociology (magna cum laude) from Western Carolina University. The topics of his other book chapters on polling range from how news organizations use polls to methods of allocating undecided respondents in preelection polls.

MURRAY EDELMAN is editorial director of Voter News Service, a pool of ABC, CBS, CNN, FOX, NBC, and the Associated Press, where he has the responsibility for conducting the exit polling and estimating the outcome of elections. He did similar work for a prior pool of the networks called Voter Research and Surveys. Before that, he was associated with CBS News, where he developed new methods of vote projections, pioneered the use of exit polls for vote analysis, and managed the CBS News/*New York Times* poll. Dr. Edelman is vice president/president-elect of the American Association of Public Opinion Research (AAPOR). He received his doctorate from the University of Chicago.

MICHAEL KAGAY is News Surveys Editor at the *New York Times.* He heads the department that designs, conducts, and analyzes public opinion polls for the newspaper, as well as the paper's half of *Times/*CBS News polls. Prior to joining the *Times* in 1987, he was vice president and division head at Louis Harris and

Associates in New York City. For five years at Harris, he directed large-scale surveys on public policy and social issues for the firm's foundation clients. Prior to that, he was a faculty member for ten years at Princeton University, where he taught the university's courses on public opinion and polling. He earned his Ph.D in political science at the University of Wisconsin—Madison. He was a National Science Foundation postdoctoral fellow at the University of Michigan's Institute for Social Research. During 1998 and 1999, Kagay served as national president of AAPOR, the American Association for Public Opinion Research.

MEE-EUN KANG completed her Ph.D. in mass communication at the University of Michigan. Her dissertation focused on the impact of polls on the attitudes of those exposed to the results and combined a secondary analysis of survey data with an experiment. She served as a postdoctoral scholar at the Institute for Social Research. After leaving Michigan, she was an assistant professor in the Department of Communication at Cleveland State University. Dr. Kang recently accepted a position as assistant professor in the School of Communication at Sookmyung University in Seoul, Korea. She earned her M.A. from the School of Journalism at Ohio State University.

GERALD M. KOSICKI earned his Ph.D. in mass communications from the University of Wisconsin–Madison and is associate professor and director of graduate studies at the School of Journalism and Communication at Ohio State University. He is also senior faculty associate with the OSU Center for Survey Research, where he is coprincipal investigator on the *Buckeye State Poll,* a monthly survey of Ohioans in partnership with the *Columbus Dispatch* and WBNS-TV. He is the author of many scholarly articles and book chapters about mass communication and public opinion that have appeared in such journals as *Communication Research; Journal of Communication, Political Behavior, Political Communication;* and *Journalism and Mass Communication Quarterly.*

JON KROSNICK was the winner of the Erik H. Erikson Early Career Award for Excellence and Creativity in the Field of Political Psychology. He is professor of psychology and political science at Ohio State University. From 1996 to 1997, he was a fellow at the Center for Advanced Study in the Behavioral Sciences at Stanford University. Dr. Krosnick is coauthor of *Introduction to Survey Research and Data Analysis* and of *Designing Great Questionnaires: Insights from Psychology.* He has written more than eighty articles on methods to maximize the quality of data collected through surveys, on how public attitudes on political issues are formed and changed, and on the social and cognitive forces shaping political activism and voting behavior. Dr. Krosnick has served on the editorial boards of the *Journal of Personality and Social Psychology, Journal of Experimental Social Psychology,* and *Public Opinion Quarterly.* Dr. Krosnick serves on the Board of Overseers of the National Election Study. He has lectured on survey questionnaire design at the U.S. General Accounting Office, the U.S. Census Bureau, the U.S. Internal Revenue Service, the Office of National Statistics of the United Kingdom, and other academic and nonacademic organizations.

PAUL J. LAVRAKAS is professor of journalism and communication, of public policy and management, and of sociology in the College of Social and Behavioral Sciences at Ohio State University. Dr. Lavrakas is director of OSU's Center for Survey Research, where he also serves as principal investigator of the *Buckeye State Poll.* He served on the faculty of Northwestern University from 1979 to 1996. Since the early 1980s, a main focus of his scholarship and teaching has been survey research methods. His book *Telephone Survey Methods: Sampling, Selection, & Supervision* has been used extensively by telephone survey researchers for the past two decades. In addition, he is co-editor of two previous books on election polls and the news media: *Polling and Presidential Election Coverage* and *Presidential Polls and the News Media.* He also is coauthor of *The Voter's Guide to Election Polls.* Dr. Lavrakas served on AAPOR's Executive Council from 1995 to 1999. He earned his doctorate in applied social psychology from Loyola University of Chicago in 1976.

JESSE F. MARQUETTE is professor of political science and director, Institute for Policy Studies at the University of Akron. He received his Ph.D. in political science from the University of Florida in 1971. His academic research interests are concentrated in public opinion and voting behavior with special emphasis on models of vote choice and mobilization. His publications have appeared in many of the major journals of political science, including the *American Political Science Review, American Journal of Political Science, Journal of Politics, Political Behavior,* and *Public Opinion Quarterly.* As founding director of the Institute for Policy Studies, Dr. Marquette has a continuing applied research interest in survey methods and data quality issues.

DANIEL M. MERKLE is senior polling analyst at ABC News, where he conducts and reports on election and nonelection polls. Previously he was director of surveys at Voter News Service, a pool of ABC, CBS, CNN, FOX, NBC, and the Associated Press, where he oversaw the methodological aspects of the exit polls that are used by the media to analyze the vote and make election projections. Dr. Merkle is the author of numerous conference papers and articles on survey research methodology and public opinion, including such topics as survey non-response, the impact of incentives, respondent selection methods, the impact of polls on the public, how poll consumers evaluate poll results, deliberative polling, and exit poll methodology. He received his M.A. and Ph.D. in communication studies from Northwestern University.

PHILIP MEYER holds the Knight Chair in, and is professor of, journalism and mass communication at the University of North Carolina at Chapel Hill. As a working journalist, he was a pioneer in the use of computer-based social science research methods as reporting tools and has written extensively on media ethics and professional problems. These interests sprang from a long newspaper career that he began by delivering papers for the *Clay Center (Kansas) Dispatch* in 1944 and ended on the corporate staff of Knight Ridder in 1981. His longest posting was to the Knight Ridder Washington Bureau (1962–1978). His formal education was at Kansas State (B.S., 1952), North Carolina (M.A., 1963), and Harvard (Nieman Fellow, 1967). At Harvard, he was introduced to quantitative methods in social science, and he applied those techniques to coverage of the Detroit riot while on temporary assignment with Knight Ridder's *Detroit Free Press* in the summer of 1967. That work helped the staff of the *Free Press* win the 1968 Pulitzer Prize for general local reporting and contributed to legitimizing the concept of precision journalism. Meyer currently consults for *USA Today* and writes an occasional column of media criticism as a member of its Board of Contributors.

DEBORAH POTTER is executive director of NewsLab, a nonprofit television news laboratory in Washington, D.C., which works with local TV stations on better ways of telling complex, nonvisual stories. The project is an initiative of the Park Foundation in association with the Columbia University Graduate School of Journalism. Potter is a journalist and educator who spent sixteen years as a correspondent for CBS News and CNN. She covered the White House, State Department, Congress, national politics, and the environment. She later hosted the PBS series *In the Prime*. Her teaching experience includes three years on the faculty of the Poynter Institute in St. Petersburg, Florida, and a year as assistant professor at American University in Washington, D.C. Potter is frequently quoted in newspapers and interviewed on television and radio, and she often moderates panel discussions and teleconferences. She is the coauthor of *The Poynter Election Handbook: New Ways to Cover Campaigns*. Her work has been published by the *Harvard International Journal of Press/Politics, The Christian Science Monitor, St. Petersburg Times, National Civic Review, RTNDA Commu-*

nicator, and *News Photographer.* She has a B.A. from the University of North Carolina at Chapel Hill and a master's degree from American University.

ELIZABETH C. POWERS is a Ph.D. candidate in the interdepartmental program in mass communication at the University of Michigan. Since beginning her studies at Michigan, she has focused her research on how news reports influence public opinion about social issues such as welfare and crime. She has coauthored articles on news processing; the most recent appeared in *Communication Research.* Although she was born in the Midwest, she has spent most of her life in Texas and received her bachelor's (Texas Woman's University) and master's (University of North Texas) degrees there before joining the program at the University of Michigan.

VINCENT PRICE is associate professor in the Annenberg School for Communication and a faculty associate of the Annenberg Public Policy Center at the University of Pennsylvania. He completed his doctorate at Stanford University and was formerly chair of the Department of Communication Studies and faculty associate with the Center for Political Studies at the University of Michigan. Price has published extensively on mass communication and public opinion, social influence processes, and political communication. He is the editor of *Public Opinion Quarterly,* one of the field's leading journals, and has served as a guest editor for *Communication Research* and *Political Communication.* His book *Public Opinion* has been published in several languages and used in graduate and undergraduate courses throughout North America, Europe, and Asia. The recipient of numerous awards for his teaching and research, Price is a peer reviewer for more than two dozen journals, academic organizations, publishers, and funding agencies in communication, psychology, and political science.

MICHAEL W. TRAUGOTT is professor and chair of the Department of Communication Studies at the University of Michigan, as well as a senior research scientist in the Center for Political Studies at the Institute for Social Research. A political scientist by training, he focuses his research on campaigns and elections, the uses of polls in journalism, and survey methods. He has written extensively in all three areas. He is coauthor of *The Voter's Guide to Election Polls* and co-editor of *Presidential Polls and the News Media.* He has served as a consultant to several news organizations for their election coverage, most recently as an analyst for Voter News Services. He is the current president of the American Association for Public Opinion Research. Dr. Traugott has earned degrees in political science from Princeton University (B.A.) and the University of Michigan (M.A. and Ph.D.).

PENNY S. VISSER is an assistant professor at Princeton University with a joint appointment in the Department of Psychology and the Woodrow Wilson School of Public and International Affairs. She received her Ph.D. in social psychology from Ohio State University in 1998. Her research focuses primarily on the structure and function of attitudes, including the dynamics of attitude formation and change, the impact of attitudes on thought and behavior, the antecedents and consequences of attitude strength, and issues associated with attitude measurement. Her work has appeared in journals such as *Public Opinion Quarterly, American Political Science Review, Journal of Personality and Social Psychology, Personality and Social Psychology Review, Personality and Social Psychology Bulletin, British Journal of Social Psychology*, and in a number of edited volumes.

Introduction

CHAPTER 1

Why Election Polls Are Important to a Democracy: An American Perspective

Paul J. Lavrakas and Michael W. Traugott

Polling has been a part of American elections and election news coverage since the early 1800s. Early straw polls, with unscientific "samples" of whoever happened to attend a political rally or was present in a public place, represented journalists' earliest interests in directly measuring and reporting public opinion about candidate preferences (cf. Frankovic 1998; Herbst 1995; Mann and Orren 1992). Journalists recognized that it was newsworthy to report which candidate had greater support among which segments of the public, even if they did not well understand the unreliable nature, and thus the severe limitations, of these early polls.

Why, within the democratic society of the United States—with its First Amendment protections for freedom of speech—should polling information be popular among and deemed newsworthy by the members of the "free press"?

Is it at all surprising that election polling as a formal mechanism to measure public opinion developed and began to take hold in a relatively new democracy that, at least in theory, placed so much value on the equality of voting rights of the "common man"? Straw polls in the early 1800s served a *vox populi* function even if early journalists did not explicitly recognize this or conduct them primarily for this reason. In retrospect, as Herbst (1995) notes, these early "people's" polls "were a means of citizen expression during [election] campaigns, and a starting point for discourse among voters" (p. 28). Although this may be an overly romanticized view of how news about straw polls was actually "used" by the nineteenth-century American citizenry, it seems more certain that poll-based election news was highly valued by nineteenth-century American journalists for several reasons.

First, polls gave journalists a means of writing about the *popular will and sentiment* by providing information that was gathered directly and in the aggre-

3

gate from relatively large groups of citizens. As James Bryce noted at the time, the nineteenth-century American press clearly served "as an index and mirror of public opinion" (1891, 265). This polling information had at least the aura, if not the reality, of being representative of the public. Second, as the United States grew in size and population, and as the twentieth century unfolded, polling techniques became formalized and systematic. Pollsters such as George Gallup, Archibald Crossley, and Elmo Roper were able to provide their media sponsors with more information about larger geographic segments of the public on a more timely basis (cf. Cantril, 1991). Third, the technological advances of the last 25 years made it possible to gather this information even more rapidly, thus allowing the media to report it ever more quickly (cf. Frankovic, 1994). For these reasons alone it is not surprising that at the end of the twentieth century, election polls became a central feature in election news coverage and, thus, of the American democratic milieu.

But the motivation for America's free press to use election polls was not simply the relative ease with which the data could be collected and analyzed. A fourth reason journalists were attracted to this information was that it allowed them a quasi-objective, *proactive* role in the news-making process. We recognize that the news media have always "made" news, not merely reported it, unlike some critics of the media and their use of election polls, especially ones that media sponsor or conduct (e.g., Salmon and Glasser 1998; Von Hoffman 1980). To us this conclusion seems unassailable because of the simple fact that the media are constantly awash in much more information than they can ever report. As such, they are constantly "making news" by actively exercising their own news judgments about which stories to cover, with what amount of prominence, and which stories to ignore. When the media gather and report poll-based election information, they are making news that should in theory, and we believe often does in practice, contribute to the democracy within which the media operate. By conducting polls and reporting on poll-based information to represent the public's opinions, preferences, and intentions, journalists are behaving in a quintessential "Fourth Estate" manner. This is information that comes from a qualitatively unique source that is independent of the media's other political sources such as elected officials and other politicians, their campaign staffers and supporters, lobbyists, and other special interest groups—and this is another reason polling information appeals to journalists.

When the media report on methodologically sound election polls, they make perhaps their single greatest contribution to democracy. In doing this, they send the *symbolic message* that it is the will and preferences of the entire population of individual citizens that the polity exists to serve, symbolized nowhere better than by a good-quality survey's representative sample of the public. Reporting on majority and minority public preferences is important because the continuous presentation of the opinions and intentions of representative segments of the public through election polls and other political surveys reinforces the purpose of the democracy and the reality that elected leaders ultimately need majority public support for their policies and practices. As long as public polls about citizens' political preferences and intentions are conducted and reported freely, there is little possibility that elected politicians could completely flaunt the will of the public for any length of time.

Another important contribution that media-sponsored election polls make to a democracy is to provide the news media with an independent way to know, and thus be able to report, the thoughts and intentions of the citizenry. These polls provide information that is intended to be widely disseminated; thus, they empower the media to *speak for the people*. No one else has more power and legitimacy to act in this manner than a respected news organization when it reports the results of a high-quality opinion poll of the citizenry. Such polls allow reporters to know about majority and minority opinion preferences, even if these opinions appear unwise from a more "knowledgeable" elite perspective (cf. Yankelovich 1991).

Take, for example, the role of the public polls of 1998 and early 1999 that showed consistent and strong majority support for keeping President Clinton in office. This news about the will of the majority of Americans reduced the strength of the congressional Republicans and bolstered the congressional Democrats in the House impeachment and Senate trial processes (cf. Morin 1999; Schneider 1999). Had this information about the public's preferences been unavailable to Congress and to the American people, there would no doubt have been a much higher probability that Congress would have removed the president from office or that he would have resigned before being required to leave office.

This is one of the important ways the news media fulfill their "watchdog" function to determine if elected officials are out of sync with the larger public they purport to serve. It also gives the public a *direct voice* in the nation's political discourse. Despite a lack of evidence that many in the public recognize or appreciate that the media can and do serve these functions for them in a democracy, we believe that these roles of the media are highly consistent with the real workings of a successfully functioning democratic system. That is, in accord with Aristotelian thinkers about American democracy such as James Bryce and John Dewey, we strongly believe that our nation functions better when journalists and the organizations for which they work help the public serve as an active "check and balance" on the workings of the formal government (cf. Glynn et al. 1999). For example, when elected officials and candidates for office are made aware of public sentiment toward a policy issue and find this information being widely disseminated by the news media, they are "put on notice" that their own policy stances can and will be scrutinized. In this way, the media actively and powerfully affect the direction and tenor of the public discourse that evolves around various political issues.

Other critical thinkers about democracy, from Plato through Walter Lippman, have lamented that the majority of the citizenry is generally ill-informed on many policy issues and thereby appears ill-equipped to play any meaningful, positive role in political discourse. However, we side more with the view most recently articulated by Yankelovich (1991) that the mass public in a democracy, even with its lack of detailed knowledge of many issues, can nevertheless be "wise" on many matters—and in ways not often immediately apparent because, in part, their policy attitudes are difficult to ascertain and understand with traditional, purely rational theories and methods. If one values the equality of all citizens—including their right to hold and articulate their own opinions and beliefs and to act in any legal manner they choose—then it is difficult to dismiss the importance of using quality polls to measure and report the public's preferences regardless of whether or not certain elites may agree with the "wisdom" manifest in those mass preferences.

With this said, it is also necessary to emphasize the special responsibility the media have both to gather accurate poll data and to report the results accurately (a topic that receives greater attention in Chapter 14). Because this type of information has the power to affect democratic processes, it is paramount that the media (1) be confident they are releasing information that accurately reflects the public's opinions and intentions, (2) have analyzed their data to find the most newsworthy results, and (3) have reported on these accurately (cf. Lavrakas and Traugott 1995; Traugott and Lavrakas 1999; Traugott and Means 1995).

We also believe that the information election polls produce serves other democracy-enhancing functions. First, the information from election polls that enters the public sphere immediately becomes an important form of "political capital." Because this happens to some extent regardless of whether or not the information is accurate, it increases the need for accurate public polls. When the media report "horse-race findings" showing which candidate is leading before a primary or general election or when they report other poll findings about the public's awareness levels and evaluations of candidates and their policy positions, they are providing an important measure of a candidate's viability. We can think of few better ways that public accountability for candidates and their policy stances can be achieved than by the routine reporting of election polls. Some have lamented the decline in the relative importance of political parties in the candidate selection and support processes during the past few decades. However, anyone who values the "wisdom of the public"—what Yankelovich (1991) calls "public judgment"—should be pleased that "closed-door deals" alone no longer can determine which candidates will win their party's nominations for prominent political offices.

Another important way election polls enhance American democracy takes place immediately after major national elections. Mostly unrecognized by both the public and many elites, current Election Day exit polls give the news media the power to frame or interpret the meaning of an election. Unlike in previous campaigns, when no timely source of reliable information was available to explain "why" the electorate voted as it did, the exit polls conducted by the Voter News Service empower journalists to explain the underlying motivations of the citizenry that led to an election's outcomes. In this way, the media serve American democracy by thwarting the efforts of political "spin doctors" to put their own self-serving interpretations on an election's "mandate." At the national level, for example, one needs only to wait a day or two after a November presidential election to learn in detail from the *New York Times* what the national exit polls showed were the "why's and wherefore's" of the public's vote. The significance of this role further reinforces the need for exit polls to be accurate and for the media to report accurately on their findings.

Another valuable role that election polls play in a democracy is the heightened interest they can create among citizens about an upcoming election during the months and weeks preceding Election Day (cf. Meyer 1989). The sports metaphors routinely used to report horse-race poll findings in election news stories resonate with many news consumers. In fact, it may well be that the public interest generated by horse-race coverage helps to draw some members of the public into more complex election news coverage, including issue-related news. This, however, can be a double-edged sword: Whereas the public may find preprimary and preelection poll predictions interesting news up to a point, they quickly complain if this type of news grows too large, especially close to Election Day. Exactly when this point is reached and what constitutes "too much" horse-race attention across different election contexts remains to be understood. But this potential problem notwithstanding, election polling news that focuses on who is ahead and who is behind has become an anticipated part of the election news stream among most of the citizenry. Imagine the public hue and cry if news organizations stopped reporting such information.

One failing that the media have yet to address adequately is the negative effect preelection polls may have on registered voters and thus, in theory, on democracy. This problem concerns the tendency for a proportion of the American public to abstain from voting simply because they have concluded that their own vote will not matter in an election whose outcome is a foregone conclusion according to the preelection polls. Lavrakas, Holley, and Miller (1991), in study-ing the effects of preelection polling on the 1988 presidential election, concluded that at least 10 percent, and possibly as many as 20 percent, of people who were registered but did not vote (between 2.5 and 5 million Americans) opted out pri-marily because they expected a Bush victory over Dukakis as had been predicted by all the preelection polls in the month preceding the election. Of equal inter-est, this research also indicated that had this subset of registered nonvoters actu-ally voted in 1988, the outcome of the presidential election would have been nearly identical to what actually occurred. When the media report preelection poll results in an unrestricted fashion, as is their right in the United States, we believe they also should shoulder some responsibility for the unintended but potentially negative consequences of this news. For example, recognizing that pre-election poll predictions can dampen the likelihood of some citizens' voting when a major contest is lopsided, the media bear a special responsibility to encourage the public to vote.

For those who believe that more information is better than less, then both private and public election polls provide valuable strategic information to can-didates and the public (cf. Hickman 1991; Meyer 1989). In deciding how best to plan their campaigns, public and private polls help candidates make informed decisions about the various strategies they will use. We think that to some extent these polls, especially the public ones, help to place "boundaries" on what will be acceptable policy stances for those who aspire to elected office. To the extent that election polls, including ones that focus on the horse race, speak to a can-didate's viability, these polls provide the voting public, journalists, and potential campaign supporters with strategic information useful for their own behaviors. For partisan voters in a primary season, poll standing may be one the few acces-sible pieces of information that plays an important role in helping them decide which of their party's candidates to support. For journalists, poll-based infor-mation helps in deciding how to allocate among the candidates such limited resources as reporters' time, travel budgets, and space and airtime. Finally, cam-paign support from partisans can take many forms, including making financial contributions. Election polls, especially during the primary season, help poten-tial supporters make more informed judgments about the wisdom of voluntar-ily supporting a particular candidate with a contribution or helping with a "get out the vote" drive (cf. Mutz 1995; Perloff 1998; Traugott 1992).

Of course, many scholars and others disagree with our view about the poten-tial for polls and the media's use of them to enhance contemporary democracy in the United States. These criticisms can be summarized under four general head-ings. First, there are those who question the construct validity of the data gathered by polls as not truly representing "public opinion" or the individual attitudes often measured in polls. Second, there are questions about the external validity (generalizability) of opinion polls because of allegedly flawed methods used to draw samples and gather data. Third, there are arguments that the opinion-polling enterprise actually harms democratic processes by replacing public deliberation with the dissemination of private opinions, thereby alienating citizens further from a sense that their voices are being heard. Finally, some argue that the quality of the news reported by journalists has suffered because some have become "lazy" and rely too much on poll results to cover political news.

Blumer (1948) articulated a position that has served as a rallying point for many recent critics of opinion polls and the media's use of them (e.g., Herbst 1993; Salmon and Glasser 1998). However, we find fault with these "antipoll" views at a very basic level. Blumer criticized the polling enterprise of the first half of the twentieth century because, in part, it generated "data" that purported to represent public opinion without offering any evidence that such data actually represented anything that approximated what "public opinion" actually is. Strange though it may seem, in his essay Blumer did not venture a clear definition of what he thought "public opinion" was, other than arguing that it was not the information that opinion polls generate. Many who use Blumer's 1948 essay to support their own critiques of opinion polling have not appeared to be bothered by this missing element of Blumer's argument, nor do they offer their own definition of "public opinion."

The thrust of Blumer's argument is that public opinion in a society is not an aggregation of individual-level expressions of "private opinion," although this is what he believes opinion polls do. In making this argument, Blumer, we believe, took much too narrow a view of how opinions are communicated within a free society, possibly because he could not have anticipated the effects of the telecommunications revolution of the last part of the twentieth century. Much like the "'invisible' dark matter" astronomers now believe accounts for much of the mass in the universe, most manifestations of what public opinion actually is are, we believe, "invisible" to most attempts to measure them. That is, citizens *qua* individuals express their opinions in many direct and indirect ways. As such, the effects of these expressions on the public and private deliberations that occur in a democracy, from the level of elected officials down to small informal groups of friends and neighbors, are hopelessly complicated and impractical to measure in any comprehensive manner. We also believe, however, that the best way to capture this complexity is to ask individual citizens about their opinions and behaviors in good-quality opinion polls. We are not arguing that opinion polls are the end-all and be-all of representing "public opinion"; that is, we do not believe they are a sufficient condition. But good-quality polls of the citizenry are necessary to understand what public opinion is under the simple, yet broad, conceptualization to which we subscribe: the expression of individual- and group-level opinions by all citizens within a society, regardless of their position or roles within that society.

We also believe that many critics of election polling and polls more generally miss the mark on two other important counts. First, they appear locked into an overly romanticized (i.e., theoretical) view of how democracy ideally *should* work rather than accepting how it *does* work. Since much of this antipolling rhetoric uses a utopian standard for how citizens should behave in a well-functioning democracy, it is not surprising that the critics find many shortcomings in how democracy is practiced. With this predisposition serving as the lens through which their view of opinion polling is filtered, it is also not surprising that they find much to fault in the opinion-polling enterprise. Second, critics of opinion polls have misdirected their criticism to the polls themselves rather than to those agents and organizations that may imperfectly use these manifestations of public opinion. More criticism should be targeted at those reporters and editors who misuse the information that polls provide rather than at the polls themselves. Although we believe that polls are a valuable but limited indicator of public opinion, we also want the media to improve their treatment of these polls in news making, and that is one of our explicit motivations in compiling this volume.

In sum, we believe strongly that election polls *can and do* aid democratic processes, especially in a society with unrestricted freedom of speech such as the United States. They do this by the following means:

- Sending a continuous symbolic message that the opinions of "everyone" matter, not simply those of elites and other special interests

- Empowering the media to serve as an independent watchdog on politicians and resisting other would-be spokespersons for the public or for so-called election mandates

- Empowering the media to speak on behalf of the public and thereby helping to fulfill their responsibilities as the Fourth Estate

- Empowering politicians and their supporters, interest groups, journalists, and the public alike with information about candidate viability so that each group can make more informed judgments about how this knowledge might affect their respective future behaviors

- Raising the public's interest in political campaigns, although this has a potential downside if too much horse-race reporting occurs

Purpose and Contents of This Book

This book is the latest in an informal "series" (cf. Lavrakas and Holley 1991; Lavrakas, Traugott, and Miller 1995) and shares three goals with its predecessors:

- First, it adds rich description of how journalists and media organizations use election polls, especially during the 1996 presidential election year.
- Second, it reports on the effects of election polling and poll-based news coverage on those who are exposed.
- Third, it makes recommendations, both broad and mundane, about how to improve election poll quality and the media's use of the information contained in these polls.

Chapters for this book were invited from many individuals, including election-polling scholars as well as practitioners, who have spent a considerable portion of their professional lives using or doing research on election polls and how the news media report on them. The content of the book generally follows the key points we have advanced earlier in this chapter. In succession, the sections show how news organizations inform (or misinform) the public by reporting on information gathered through political opinion polls, illustrate the methods contemporary journalists use when they report on election polls, discuss issues related to the real and perceived quality (accuracy) of election polls, and provide critiques of several controversial issues related to election polling in the 1990s.

The organization of the book proceeds in distinct sections. Following this introductory chapter, the book continues with three chapters that address the media use of polls in covering major political news in the mid-1990s. In Chapter 2, Michael R. Kagay, long-time editor of news surveys for the *New York Times*, explains the "story" of why Bill Clinton won and why Bob Dole lost the 1996 election. He reports in detail the findings of various types of election polls the *Times* conducted for its 1996 campaign coverage and how the polls were used as news. As Kagay notes,

> In the 1990s public opinion for many news-gathering organizations has become its own beat—to be covered with regularity and thoroughness like other beats, except that a team [of staffers] with polling skills is necessarily involved. This is especially true for presidential elections, when the reporting of an occasional poll at a few key junctures of the political campaign has evolved within some news organizations into a year-long (or longer!) program of polling aimed at covering all phases of the campaign cycle.

The chapter is filled with excellent examples of the complex and creative ways that the *Times* deploys its election polls. Kagay provides specific advice for planning the use of polls in the larger news coverage of an election, including a caution that "because long-term, middle-run, and short-lived forces can each affect the [election] outcome, it is important to build in [polling] devices to measure all three types of factors." He also points to areas of polling accuracy that need improvement, including the way one identifies a "probable electorate."

Chapter 3, by Daniel M. Merkle and Murray Edelman of the Voter News Service (VNS), provides a critical review and evaluation of the 1996 exit polls the authors conducted for their media sponsors and other media clients. As they note, "Exit polls play an important role in the media's coverage of elections by providing accurate and timely information that allows them to report on the main stories of any election—Who won? How and why did it happen? What does it mean?" Merkle and Edelman explain various aspects of the methodologies that were used to conduct the 1996 national exit polls and that generated the data so highly valued by the media. As part of this, they explain their recent efforts to improve exit poll data quality. In terms of measurement error, they review changes in how issues, candidate qualities, and "grab bag" items in their questionnaires were measured in the 1996 exit polls. Where it was not possible to make methodological changes, they attempted to gain a better understanding of these sources of error and the strengths and limitations of the resulting data. In terms of nonresponse error, the authors use their unique and extensive database to show that the response rate at the sampled precinct level is *uncorrelated* with the magnitude of the error in the vote estimates in precincts. Exit polls with relatively high response rates tended to be just as accurate as those with lower response rates in predicting the election winner's margin of victory at the level of the sampled precinct. They also report the surprising results of an experimental study in which they found that their successful efforts to increase response rates actually backfired by significantly increasing the bias in the vote estimates.

The authors also explain the need to understand how best to deal with "early voting" and its impact on the accuracy of future exit polls. As the authors note,

> A new and growing concern for exit pollsters is the increasing potential for coverage error. In the past, there was little possibility of coverage error in exit polls because very few people voted early. The rapid increase in early voting rates in some states is a relatively new phenomenon that will only continue in coming years. The challenge in this area will be to balance the significant extra costs of interviewing these voters by telephone with the benefits that are gained in terms of decreasing [the likelihood of] coverage error.

Next, in Chapter 4, Michael Traugott and Elizabeth Powers, a communication studies scholar, present an important case study about a major news story from 1994 that illustrates the serious problems that can arise when "naïve" and time-stressed journalists report on other people's polls (cf. Frankovic 1999). Using the Contract with America and related claims about majority public opinion that were made by the Republican leaders and pollster Frank Luntz in 1994, the chapter highlights the problems with the news coverage. It also provides explicit examples of how journalists can conduct independent validation of such claims about the public's opinions, much as they would check the facts in claims made by political leaders in interviews. Traugott and Powers's critique is based on an original content analysis of news coverage of the Contract. They provide a chronology of how the story unfolded, an explanation of why the claims about majority public preferences were actually unfounded, and how public reaction to key elements of the Contract could have been, but was not, verified had reporters used a number of publicly available data sources. The authors note that the purpose of their chapter is "[not] to draw attention to the specious claims about public support for the Contract." Rather, their purpose is to use the case study to illustrate ways that journalists who report on public opinion can utilize modern news-gathering procedures that do not involve any additional cost, time, or access to resources with which any computer-literate journalist is not already familiar. In this way, reporters can produce more informed stories, as well as reduce the likelihood of misrepresenting public opinion to their mass audience.

The next part of the book includes three chapters that focus on recent trends in how election polls are used by media organizations and how they are reported by the journalists who write the news stories. A new approach to covering public affairs news, including election campaigns, emerged in the 1990s. This is the so-called public or civic journalism movement that advocates the need for journalists to look to the citizenry to set at least a part of their organization's news agenda—namely, using a nontraditional "bubble up" approach, rather than relying entirely on a traditional "top-down" elite agenda-setting perspective. Chapter 5 focuses on the use of election polls in a large-scale public journalism project during the 1996 presidential campaign. Here public opinion and journalism scholars Phil Meyer and Deborah Potter of the Poynter Institute for Media Studies present their original research conducted across twenty-one newspaper markets in 1996. Meyer and Potter start by reviewing the applied theory behind public journalism and the evolution of its goal to make news, such as election coverage, more relevant to the local citizenry. Quoting David Broder, they note that "if reporters spent more time with voters, [journalists] would have clearly in our heads what the voters' concerns are. Then it might be possible to let their agenda drive our agenda for covering the campaign." On the basis of their extensive research, Meyer and Potter conclude Chapter 5 by suggesting five "guiding principles" for journalists in their use of polling information in election campaign coverage: (1) keep the horse-race polls, but do not make them the center of coverage; (2) deemphasize the referendum model of election reporting, which tends to show merely where the majority stands and implies that nothing more needs to be said about the election; (3) concentrate on special populations, comparing the attitudes and intentions of various demographic subgroups, thereby helping citizens of different views better understand each other; (4) do not use polls as a substitute for news judgment; and (5) do not limit issue coverage to the election campaign.

Chapter 6 focuses on another innovation in reporting that occurred during the 1996 news coverage of the Clinton-Dole-Perot race. Here journalism scholars and survey researchers Jerry Kosicki and Paul Lavrakas report on a project they conducted with Michael Winerip, a *New York Times* reporter and literary journalist, as part of his year-long series, *An American Place*. This series covered the 1996 election through the lens of one "typical" American community (Stark County, Ohio) and included more than forty news stories in the *Times* in 1996, many of which ran on page one. The chapter explains how the literary journalist learned to incorporate the types of quantitative information that comes from public opinion survey research, such as preelection polls, into his highly qualitative approach to reporting on public opinion. Chapter 6 also discusses how social scientists can better serve reporters in both gathering newsworthy quantitative data and conducting sophisticated yet timely and news-relevant analyses with these data. Although much has been written about the virtues of so-called precision journalism (cf. Meyer 1991), there are relatively few detailed examples of its deployment. Thus, this chapter illustrates how survey research can further a reporter's news agenda in ways beyond mere reporting of frequencies and crosstabs. Furthermore, Kosicki and Lavrakas discuss several important trends in journalism and political reporting and make suggestions for the improved use of polling by the news media.

In Chapter 7, communication scholars and market opinion researchers Sandra L. Bauman and Paul J. Lavrakas present a condensed version of the lead author's dissertation, which focused on reporters' use of causal explanation in interpreting election polls in printed newspaper stories. This study is based upon a detailed content analysis of a probability sample of 225 election poll articles drawn from five prestigious daily newspapers during the 1988 and 1992 election campaigns. The authors note that

in presenting public opinion poll results to their audiences, journalists usually try to explain and interpret the results rather than merely describe them. This *interpretive role* is not new to American journalism; histori-cally, presenting the answers to the 'why' questions has been as important as answering the more descriptive 'who, what, where, and when' ques-tions. Studies have shown that to a majority of journalists, the interpre-tive role is more dominant than that of information disseminator.

Thus, it is not surprising that this research documents the great extent to which reporters include explicit "cause and effect" conclusions to explain and interpret the election polls results they are reporting. A total of 85 percent of the news stories contained at least one causal explanation connected to a reported poll finding, and the majority of these were in the reporter's own "voice" (i.e., not from another quoted source).

The authors conclude that

from a journalistic standpoint, we consider this to be a positive finding, given the importance of the media in bringing the election campaign to the public and enhancing public deliberation on candidates and issues. . . . They are not merely presenting numerical findings from the polls; rather, they strive to put these numbers in context and to concentrate on the meaning of the findings for the public, the candidates, and the cam-paign itself.

However, "from a social science standpoint, the presence of unsupported causal attributions can be highly disturbing. Since most surveys cannot provide true evi-dence of causality, [thus, what are merely] correlational relationships may likely be misreported as causal relationships." The chapter also provides a review of the "attribution theory" literature as applied to the interpretations that journalists often make, thus putting the findings about poll stories into a broader theoret-ical perspective.

Following this is another part with three chapters that address various aspects of the accuracy of election polls, including how election poll accuracy can be improved in predicting election outcomes.

In Chapter 8, political communication scholars and survey researchers Michael W. Traugott and Mee-Eun Kang present their own original research that looks at public interest in polls during the 1996 election year. This research employs a secondary analysis of a 1996 Gallup national survey to investigate factors that explain differing levels of public interest in and satisfaction with polls, as well as the public's assessment of the quality of poll performance and their attitudes about network election night projections. The chapter begins with a review of past literature on how the American public evaluates opinion polls, how polls are reported in the American media, and what is known about the American public's knowledge of polling methods. From their findings, Traugott and Kang conclude that "public confidence in polls remains high. The public is attentive to polls, especially in an election year, even if they do not have a strong a priori interest in them." These relatively high approval levels of polls exist despite the public's low levels of knowledge about polling methods and their less than positive perceptions about the general accuracy of polls. The authors note that their findings raise an important question: Does the public value polls for some reason[s] other than the quality of the information they contain? They suggest that polls may be valued because the public recognizes their function in representing public opinion to the elite decision-makers in a democracy.

Chapter 9, by journalist and pollster Rob Daves of the *Minneapolis Star Tribune*, addresses how pollsters ascertain respondents' "likelihood to vote" and discusses various approaches pollsters use to model the "probable electorate" in preelection polls. Daves starts by reviewing what went "right" and what went "wrong" in the 1996 polls' predictions for the Clinton-Dole-Perot outcome. Then he provides a historical perspective on how pollsters have approached the technical aspects of the "art and science" of predicting election outcomes. Here he discusses the need to estimate the expected turnout for the election of interest, focusing in detail on screening methods and the use of a "cutoff index." Daves then returns to the 1996 presidential election and discusses various schemes that were used to identify the probable electorate. He has a section that explains the challenges reporters face in writing news stories that report results (e.g., election predictions) that come from the complex statistical estimates pollsters make. Chapter 9 concludes with a section that looks to the future and discusses how pollsters can try to make, and journalists can try to report, better election predictions. Throughout the chapter, Daves uses examples from the surprise election of Jesse Ventura in the 1998 gubernatorial election in Minnesota.

Chapter 10 is a collaboration by political psychologists Penny S. Visser and Jon A. Krosnick, academic pollster Jesse F. Marquette, and Michael F. Curtin, editor and associate publisher of the *Columbus Dispatch*. This chapter presents a great deal of original research meant to improve election forecasting that should be of special interest to pollsters and to journalists who work closely with horse-race polls. These authors had previously chronicled the remarkable accuracy of the *Dispatch*'s preelection mail polls during the past two decades (Visser et al. 1996), with its average error of only 1.6 percentage points. The authors explain that the superior accuracy of the *Dispatch*'s mail survey has been related to (1) larger sample sizes, (2) sampling from registered voters' lists, (3) not asking about undecided opinions and thus not allocating undecided sentiment, and (4) asking only horse-race questions, thus mirroring an actual election ballot.

In presenting their new research that uses a large database of telephone and mail polls for statewide and local races and referenda from 1980 to 1997, Visser and her colleagues note that "both [modes] manifest a bias toward overpredicting the winner's margin of victory, though the mail surveys manifested this less than the telephone surveys did." They show that one way to offset this bias is to "allocate undecided respondents randomly to various candidates or referendum responses." Other suggestions from their research address questionnaire formatting and the choice of the response alternative in horse-race items presented to respondents. In drawing their conclusions, they note that some run contrary to those presented in Crespi's (1988) seminal work on election poll accuracy.

The next part of the book includes three chapters that focus on various controversial issues in election polling. The 1996 campaign saw attention in the United States given to the National Issues Convention (NIC), a $4 million deliberative polling "experiment" organized by University of Texas political scientist James Fishkin. In Chapter 11, public opinion scholar Vincent Price reviews and comments on this major demonstration and evaluation project for "deliberative democracy"—one "designed to measure not simply top-of-the-head opinions but fully informed, thoughtful opinions forged in the heat of careful public debate." In doing this, Price examines concerns about contemporary public opinion and polling that motivated the development of the deliberative poll. He notes Walter Lippman's criticism that democracy, in theory and in practice, asks too much of its citizens and more than they can deliver. Price notes the linkages between this view of American democracy and more contemporary critics of the media's heavy usage of traditional opinion polls to portray public opinion. He reviews the implementation of the NIC in advance of the 1996 presidential primaries, including some of the controversy that surrounded its design and results. In theory, the deliberative poll was "conceived of as a new tool for popular decision making, intended to inject fully informed public choice directly into the political process." Price provides a critical perspective on whether or not it met its goals. Chapter 11 concludes by speculating about the future of deliberative polling in light of Price's views on the costs and benefits of the technique.

Chapter 12, a second contribution by Michael W. Traugott and Mee-Eun Kang, addresses the use of "push polls" as *negative persuasion strategies*. They explain that push polling is a relatively new campaign technique designed to move voters away from one candidate toward another—one that has been adopted by candidates, political parties supporting a candidate, and organized interest groups supporting a candidate or an issue. Initially push polling was developed and employed with some success in presidential campaigns, but it has increasingly been used in contests for smaller constituencies, referenda, and initiatives. The technique has raised alarms among advocates of good government and fair campaign practices as well as in the survey research industry, with the latter fearing that the technique will contribute further to already declining response rates among the public. Traugott and Kang explain the difficult defin- itional issues involved in differentiating unethical push polls from legitimate strategic polling. The latter technique tests various persuasive themes with respon- dents to see which might work best in a future advertising campaign to win voters' support, but it does this in an ethical way. The authors use several exam- ples from the 1996 elections to illustrate these differences.

Chapter 12 also presents a conceptual framework for thinking about push polls that includes four dimensions that define the "context" for push polls: (1) the nature of partisanship, (2) the type of contest, (3) the geographical scope of the campaign, and (4) the type of push poll sponsor. The chapter concludes with a discussion of possible responses to unethical push polls, including legislative efforts to prohibit them, a renewed call for a journalistic focus on disclosure standards when reporting poll results, and increasing the public's awareness of and willingness to report push polls.

Chapter 13 by Leo Bogart, public opinion scholar and widely respected former senior researcher of the American newspaper industry, focuses on the 1996 election campaign, dissects the role that preelection polls played that year, and explains why many misstated the presidential vote. Setting the context for his cri- tique of poll performance, Bogart notes that "the news media often misrepresent or misinterpret polls either because they take them too literally or because, at the other extreme, they underestimate their technical complexity." He believes it is important for journalists and other poll consumers to understand that

> (1) projections from election surveys are uncertain because many people change their minds and some who say they will vote don't, (2) all surveys are subject to errors that go beyond the laws of chance, and (3) survey statistics arise from a series of professional judgments; just because they come out of a computer does not make them right.

Throughout the chapter, Bogart identifies various factors that can contribute to election poll accuracy and inaccuracy, most of which are linked to the foci of the earlier chapters in the book. He discusses them as they apply to the 1996 polling experience; in doing this he also recalls the historical record where appro- priate. In addition to the public polls the media conduct or sponsor, Bogart dis- cusses "hidden polls" and notes that

> of the approximately $200 million spent on election polls in 1996, only a fraction went for the public surveys made to be published or broadcast.

Many more confidential polls were done privately to test the waters, appraise candidates' chances, and assess the strengths and weaknesses of reputations and policies. They were not merely a source of political intelligence; when favorable findings were leaked to the press, they were actively used as a campaign tool.

Bogart concludes with the warning that "journalists and the public should pay less attention to the inexact art of election forecasting and more to the sinister implications of [hidden] political marketing."

Concluding the book in Chapter 14, Paul Lavrakas and Michael Traugott present their perspective on challenges and opportunities that will be faced by election polling and the media in the twenty-first century. They argue that the decade of the 1990s has seen various forms of political polls used more often, and with greater political effects, than ever in history. They believe that as a result, it has never been more important to American democracy that (1) pollsters gather accurate data and do so ethically, (2) journalists know how to use poll-based information accurately and in ways that enhance and expand their news judgments, (3) news organizations report poll-based information in non-superficial ways, and (4) the public and so-called experts alike become more discerning consumers of the poll-based information to which they are exposed.

Lavrakas and Traugott predict that the power of the polls to affect varied political issues and outcomes and their credibility will certainly be attacked in future years, and the frequency and the strength of these attacks are likely to grow as well. The authors believe that to withstand these attacks, pollsters and the news organizations that fund these polls must build their own capacity to respond quickly and adequately; and to do this they recommend that pollsters conduct better polls and anticipate the types of criticism likely to be directed toward them.

They also argue that in addition to improving the quality and public credibility of election polls, there is a need for reporters and editors to become more sophisticated users of the information election polls generate, including the need to recognize the effects this information has on their own news judgments (cf. Morin 1999). The authors conclude by explaining the need for at least a significant portion of the public—significant in size and/or in influence—to become better educated in interpreting election polls to know what to expect from quality polls and from the use of poll-based information by the media. Only in this way, the authors believe, can the demands of the "news marketplace" spur media organizations to support high-quality polling and work to report polling results accurately and in a newsworthy and democracy-enhancing manner.

PART I

Media Use of Polls in Covering Major Political News in the Mid-1990s

Continuing Evolution in the Use of Public Opinion Polls by the *New York Times:* The 1996 Presidential Election Experience

Michael R. Kagay

In the past quarter century, public opinion polling in the United States has shifted from just two or three publicly syndicated polls available to the media to a situation today in which a dozen or more national polls are available, many of them operated by the news-gathering organizations themselves.

For the close observer of public opinion, this proliferation of polls has been a boon. More polling agencies mean more publicly available information about what Americans are thinking and saying; more competition among pollsters to gather that information better, faster, or smarter; and a sped-up learning curve regarding new events and unfamiliar issues. Any poll that misunderstands a subject or uses poorly worded questions is swiftly outmoded by another poll from a polling organization using a more adequate approach.

At the same time, during the past quarter century the methods used by pollsters have also changed—from mainly face-to-face interviewing then to mainly telephone interviewing today, from paper-and-pencil questionnaires transferred to punchcards then to computer-assisted questionnaires now, and from clustered samples then to more purely random samples now. Polling still involves a conversation between two human beings, but even that may eventually change as the Internet develops in the future.

The ways of presenting the findings from polls have also evolved. Twenty-five years ago, for instance, newspapers often used graphics for decorative purposes to break up the grayness of type on a page. Today graphics are frequently used for their power to communicate information, to show patterns, to turn data into meaning.

In the 1990s, public opinion has become its own beat for many news-gathering organizations—to be covered with regularity and thoroughness like other beats, except that a team with polling skills is necessarily involved. This is especially true for presidential elections, when the reporting of an occasional poll at a few key junctures of the political campaign has evolved within some news organizations into a year-long (or longer!) program of polling aimed at covering all phases of the campaign cycle.

This chapter describes how one news organization approached the 1996 presidential election campaign, how it developed its program of polling, and what it learned (and reported) in the process.

The *Times*'s Program of Polling in 1996

Throughout 1996, the *New York Times* used public opinion polls to aid its reporters, editors, and readers in understanding how the American public was reacting to the personalities, issues, and events of the presidential election campaign. The polls included six major types in 1996:

1. Frequent national telephone polls to measure how voters' perceptions and attitudes shifted, or persisted unchanged, as the primary and general election campaigns developed over the months. Because campaigning began earlier than usual in this election cycle, the series of polls lasted from August 1995 until early November 1996.

2. Statewide exit polls of voters leaving voting places on primary Election Day in states having major Republican presidential primaries from February through the end of March. These polls allowed us to interpret voters' choices in the internal contest for the Republican nomination.

3. Polling of delegates to both the Republican National Convention and the Democratic National Convention to compare and contrast the two parties' activists with each other and with each party's rank-and-file voters.

4. A poll of business leaders, CEOs, and other top corporate officers across the country to gauge how this constituency, usually reliably Republican, was reacting to the issues and personalities of the campaign.

5. Two local polls, one in the spring and the other in the fall, in Stark County, Ohio, to test how the national campaign was playing out in a typical locality in a battleground state to which the *Times* had assigned a reporter for an entire year.

6. A national exit poll of voters leaving voting stations across the country on Election Day in November, including additional exit polling in sev-

eral key states in each region. These polls permitted us to document the sociology and the psychology of the final vote in 1996.

Other polling designs were occasionally also employed. For instance, CBS News conducted a "panel" survey for the presidential television debates, calling back after a debate the same respondents interviewed shortly before the debate to see if any minds were changed. And further designs yet were available but not used in 1996. For instance, we have sometimes conducted "tracking" polls, with independent daily samples, to capture day-to-day change in some swiftly moving situation. Obvious tracking situations did not arise in 1996, although in retrospect a tracking poll might have been useful for our final preelection polling (more on that later).

The telephone polls were conducted mainly with our television polling partner, CBS News. The exit polls we analyzed were conducted by Voter News Service, the consortium created by ABC News, CBS News, CNN, NBC News, the Associated Press, and Fox News. The two polls of Stark County, Ohio, were a collaboration by the *Times* with the Northwestern University Survey Lab and the Ohio State University School of Journalism.

The *Times* polls and *Times*/CBS News polls were used in several ways. First, they formed the basis of 22 news articles in the *Times* that relied heavily on polling data, usually accompanied by graphs and tables presenting detailed results. Second, they were incorporated to a lesser extent in an additional 105 articles in the paper that cited one or more particular poll findings. Third, they were used in freestanding graphics on a number of occasions. And fourth, they indirectly helped to inform the reporting and editing during the election year by permitting reporters and editors to check hunches about how the campaign was progressing, to test the claims of politicians, pundits, and other pollsters, and generally to avoid being manipulated. (The exit polls by Voter News Service figured in additional articles after each primary election.)

The *Times* has been involved in conducting its own public opinion polls by telephone since late 1976. In 1996, as in earlier years, the questionnaires were developed jointly with CBS News from topics suggested by correspondents, editors, or producers in both organizations, then winnowed and refined by the two organizations' polling directors and their staffs. CBS News drew the samples of telephone numbers, using the GENESYS system developed by Marketing Systems Group of Philadelphia. The *Times* oversaw the field work, including the recruiting, training, and monitoring of interviewers. Interviewing is performed using the CASES system for computer-assisted telephone interviewing, developed by the Survey Lab at the University of California, Berkeley; the system is located at CBS News. CBS News also performed the initial data processing. Once the data were ready, each news organization had independent access to the data sets, and each interpreted and reported its findings independently. Thus, each

Times/CBS News telephone poll received two simultaneous but independent analyses by separate research teams. The actual data sets of these polls have been archived at the Roper Center for Public Opinion Research at the University of Connecticut and in the Inter-university Consortium for Political and Social Research at the University of Michigan.

In 1996, as in five previous presidential election years, the *Times* conducted a systematic program of polling research designed to cover the American public's responses to the campaign. We viewed the campaign as a 15-month-long process in which would-be leaders could make their appeals to the electorate and during which the voters could take the measure of those who would lead. Our polls were designed to find out what the public learned and concluded.

Drawing on examples from these polls, the following sections discuss our major goals in this program, many of the particular polling devices we employed, and some of the most important conclusions we reached. At each point we also indicate the headline, byline, and publication date of the articles in the newspaper that reported our findings and conclusions. The chapter is organized in sections according to the use we made of polls.

Understanding the Public Mood

As election year 1996 approached, the *Times* used several polling devices to inform its reporters, editors, and readers about the public's mood. These allowed us to probe both the strengths and the vulnerabilities of Bill Clinton as he sought a second term as president.

A Continuing Referendum on the Incumbent's Stewardship

Throughout the president's tenure in office, the *Times*/CBS News Poll regularly tracked his job performance rating with the question, "Do you approve or disapprove of the way Bill Clinton is handling his job as president?" Introduced by the Gallup poll in the 1930s, this question provides a continuing public referendum on an incumbent's stewardship between elections. Two other questions are more specific—rating the president's handling of foreign policy and his handling of the economy.

For much of Bill Clinton's first three years, his overall job performance rating fluctuated around the 43 percent of the popular vote he received in the three-way election of 1992. Table 2.1 shows our readings for the two-year period from autumn 1994, when the 1994 midterm congressional election campaign took place (and Republicans captured the House of Representatives for the first time in more than 40 years), through early November 1996. For the first half of this period every reading is between 38 and 48, or within plus or minus 5 percentage points of his 43 percent (1992) electoral share. But starting in December 1995, Clinton rose above the 50 percent threshold considered crucial for an incumbent (especially incumbents in two-way contests). By contrast, George Bush in his reelection campaign year never rose above the 50 percent approval level, spending most of 1992 in the high 30s and low 40s. Richard L. Berke, the *Times*'s national political correspondent, reported Clinton's ratings rebound in his front page article on 14 December 1995 under the headline "Clinton's Ratings Over 50% in Poll as G.O.P. Declines."

The three or four months leading up to Clinton's December 1995 breakthrough saw the federal budget standoff, with Clinton's veto of the Republicans' budget bill, the temporary shutdown of the federal government, and Republican

TABLE 2.1   A CONTINUING REFERENDUM ON BILL CLINTON'S STEWARDSHIP

	PERCENTAGE APPROVING OF THE WAY BILL CLINTON IS HANDLING . . .		
DATES OF POLL	His Job as President	Foreign Policy	The Economy
8–10 September 1994	42	32	46
16–17 October 1994	44	47	39
29 October–1 November 1994	43	49	37
27–28 November 1994	40	42	39
6–9 December 1994	38	36	41
2–3 January 1995	42	44	41
22–25 February 1995	45	47	47
1–4 April 1995	42	36	38
4–6 May 1995	44	39	42
4–6 June 1995	48	35	—
5–9 August 1995	45	36	41
22–25 October 1995	48	41	41
9–11, December 1995	51	41	47
18–20 January 1996	47	50	44
22–24 February 1996	52	46	45
10–11 March 1996	54	47	—
31 March–2 April 1996	48	43	42
31 May–3 June 1996	51	52	46
20–23 June 1996	53	51	49
11–13 July 1996	54	50	51
3–5 August 1996	58	—	—
16–18 August 1996	51	47	46
2–4 September 1996	57	53	55
10–13 October 1996	58	51	55
27–29 October 1996	54	—	—
30 October–2 November 1996	56	51	57

Note: Based on all adults in 26 nationwide polls by the *New York Times* and CBS News. Three questions were asked: "Do you approve or disapprove of the way Bill Clinton is handling his job as president?" "Do you approve or disapprove of the way Bill Clinton is handling foreign policy?" and "Do you approve or disapprove of the way Bill Clinton is handling the economy?"

efforts to trim Medicare spending. During this period, according to Dick Morris in his book *Behind the Oval Office*, the Clinton camp and the Democratic National Committee also had begun an expensive and continuous television campaign, broadcasting messages criticizing the Republicans' budget-cutting proposals and promoting Clinton's alternative balanced budget proposals. Adam Clymer, the *Times*'s chief congressional correspondent, analyzed the way the public was beginning to respond to all these developments in his page one article on 26 October 1995, "Americans Reject Big Medicare Cuts, A New Poll Finds."

Clinton's more specific ratings on handling foreign policy and the economy allowed us to look beneath the surface and make some further distinctions. During the period of the rebound in Clinton's overall rating, these more particular ratings lagged behind. In foreign policy Clinton's rating spent much of his term in the 30s and 40s; it was only by June 1996 that Clinton consistently gained a foreign policy rating over 50 percent—and even then just barely over. When it came to handling the economy, Clinton's rating spent most of his term in the 40s; it was only in fall 1996 that he scored consistently in the mid-50s. Even though, objectively, the economy had improved during his tenure, subjectively Americans either did not see much improvement or else they did not give credit for it to Clinton until quite late in the game.

Charting the Dynamics of the Campaign Year

We approached 1996 as a 15-month-long cycle of events that could potentially take some surprising turns. We therefore tried to design a program of polling research that would be responsive to events, flexible in nature, and, we hoped, adequate to the task. A major part of that task would be to capture the dynamics of public perceptions about the candidates. That, in turn, required frequent polls with many time-series questions to be asked again and again. One device we used to record the shifts and the continuities of 1996 was to ask registered voters whether their opinion of each of the major candidates was "favorable," "not favorable," or "undecided" or if they had "not heard enough yet" to form an opinion.

A useful feature of the favorable-unfavorable format is that it does not require respondents to choose between or among candidates. A respondent can express favorable feelings toward all, some, or none of the candidates. Each candidate, in effect, is in a contest with himself to generate more favorable than unfavorable impressions in the electorate's mind. This feature is especially useful early in a campaign cycle when voters may be much more familiar with some candidates than with others. In addition, by offering respondents two ways to admit that they have not yet formed an opinion about a candidate, this question format provides a good measure of "nonopinion" about each candidate, allowing us to track the degree of "crystallization" at any given moment and its pace as public opinion becomes more informed and firms up over time.

Republican Voters' Image of Bob Dole before and during the Primaries

Our earliest use of this device was from August 1995 through March 1996 to examine how Republican voters felt about the candidates seeking their party's nomination. We asked this series of questions on a frequent basis, starting with nine Republican candidates, gradually dropping names as particular Republican candidates withdrew.

The results consistently showed that only Bob Dole evoked a positive balance of sentiment among rank-and-file Republicans. Although he took some hits from his opponents during the primaries, Dole consistently had a surplus of favorable over unfavorable feelings of at least 20 percentage points among Republican registered voters. Patrick Buchanan, in contrast, consistently stimulated more negative than positive feelings among his own party's members. Republicans' opinion of Steve Forbes was initially evenly split, but it turned sharply unfavorable by February.

Richard L. Berke reported on the favorable and unfavorable images of nine Republican hopefuls in his article inside the paper of 30 October 1995, headed "Poll Finds G.O.P. Primary Voters Are Hardly Monolithic." R. W. Apple Jr., the *Times*'s Washington bureau chief, examined how images of the major Republican candidates changed as the primary season unfolded with Bob Dole's lackluster victory in Iowa and his loss in New Hampshire to Patrick J. Buchanan, in Apple's front page article of 27 February 1996, "Social Issues Give Buchanan Boost, A New Poll Finds." A graphic accompanying this article showed the August-to-February trends from the favorable-unfavorable questions among registered Republicans.

All Registered Voters' View of Bob Dole: A Different Story

By contrast, among *all* registered voters, Bob Dole had a negative balance of opinion throughout much of the 15-month campaign cycle. As Table 2.2 shows, the last time Dole had a statistically clear positive image among all voters was August 1995. By autumn and early winter 1995, registered voters had become evenly split on Dole; the slightly negative balance of opinion at that time was within the polls' margin of sampling error. But by January of election year 1996, voter opinion had clearly turned negative, with a surplus of unfavorable over favorable opinion in double digits. His two best showings after that, when voter

TABLE 2.2   REGISTERED VOTERS' SHIFTING OPINION OF BOB DOLE

DATES OF POLL	FAVORABLE OPINION (%)	NOT FAVORABLE OPINION (%)	NET BALANCE: FAVORABLE MINUS NOT FAVORABLE	UNCRYSTALLIZED OPINION: UNDECIDED OR NOT HEARD ENOUGH YET
5–9 August 1995	32	25	+7	42
22–25 October 1995	27	29	–2	44
9–11 December 1995	26	31	–5	43
18–20 January 1996	24	35	–11	40
22–24 February 1996	23	42	–19	34
10–11 March 1996	25	35	–10	40
31 March–2 April 1996	37	36	+1	28
31 May–3 June 1996	29	35	–6	36
20–23 June 1996	27	35	–8	38
11–13 July 1996	20	38	–18	41
3–5 August 1996	22	39	–17	37
REPUBLICAN PARTY CONVENTION				
16–18 August 1996	29	32	–3	37
DEMOCRATIC PARTY CONVENTION				
2–4 September 1996	29	36	–7	34
10–13 October 1996	29	41	–12	30
17–20 October 1996	28	43	–15	28
27–29 October 1996	29	43	–14	27
30 October–2 November 1996	30	43	–13	26

Note: Based on registered voters in 14 *New York Times*/CBS News polls, two CBS News polls (10–11 March and 27–29 October), and one *New York Times* poll (20–23 June). The question was: "Is your opinion of Bob Dole favorable, not favorable, undecided, or haven't you heard enough about Bob Dole yet to have an opinion?"

opinion was merely evenly split, occurred in early April, when he clinched the Republican nomination after numerous primary victories, and again in mid-August just after the Republican National Convention at which Dole officially received that nomination. For most of the fall campaign in 1996, among the electorate as a whole Dole suffered from a double-digit balance of opinion on the negative side.

Registered Voters' Shifting Opinion of Bill Clinton

Table 2.3 presents the image of Bill Clinton over the 15-month election cycle for all registered voters. In August 1995 the public was evenly divided on Clinton: The net balance of 2 percentage points more favorable than unfavorable is

TABLE 2.3 REGISTERED VOTERS' SHIFTING OPINION OF BILL CLINTON

DATES OF POLL	FAVORABLE OPINION (%)	NOT FAVORABLE OPINION (%)	NET BALANCE: FAVORABLE MINUS NOT FAVORABLE	UNCRYSTALLIZED OPINION: UNDECIDED OR NOT HEARD ENOUGH YET
5–9 August 1995	42	40	+2	19
22–25 October 1995	45	35	+10	20
9–11 December 1995	45	38	+7	17
18–20 January 1996	47	38	+9	15
22–24 February 1996	47	39	+8	14
10–11 March 1996	50	34	+16	16
31 March–2 April 1996	50	38	+12	12
31 May–3 June 1996	48	33	+15	18
20–23 June 1996	47	32	+15	20
11–13 July 1996	40	31	+9	26
3–5 August 1996	43	34	+9	22
REPUBLICAN PARTY CONVENTION				
16–18 August 1996	42	36	+6	20
DEMOCRATIC PARTY CONVENTION				
2–4 September 1996	46	33	+13	20
10–13 October 1996	47	36	+11	16
17–20 October 1996	49	34	+15	16
27–29 October 1996	46	37	+9	15
30 October–2 November 1996	46	37	+9	16

Note: Based on registered voters in 14 *New York Times*/CBS News polls, two CBS News polls (10–11 March and 27–29 October), and one *New York Times* poll (20–23 June). The question was: "Is your opinion of Bill Clinton favorable, not favorable, undecided, or haven't you heard enough about Bill Clinton yet to have an opinion?"

within the poll's margin of sampling error. By autumn 1995 he had widened that net balance a bit more in his favor and carried a modestly favorable image into campaign year 1996. Clinton improved his image further in late winter and early spring while his would-be Republican opponents attacked each other in the Republican primaries. His image balance dipped a bit in summer, just before and after the Republican National Convention, when his opponents had the spotlight. It then rebounded after the Democratic National Convention, and he carried a positive image into the fall campaign. Only at the very end of the campaign was there another dip; Clinton's final preelection image was 9 percentage points more positive than negative.

We reported on the favorable-unfavorable images of both Bill Clinton and Bob Dole several times during the campaign year, presenting graphics that tracked the measures over time. For example, Richard L. Berke examined these image trends in his front page article on 5 June 1996, "Poll Indicates Stable Ratings for President," and again toward the end of the campaign in his page one article on 16 October 1996, "As Dole Weighs Tougher Image, Poll Finds He Already Has One."

Registered Voters' Opinion of Ross Perot

Throughout the 15-month campaign cycle Ross Perot consistently had a negative image among all registered voters. During much of that time his negatives exceeded his positives by 30 or 40 percentage points. As compared with his first independent campaign for president in 1992, when voter reactions to Perot seemed volatile—as he publicly contemplated running, then was in, then out, then back in again—by his second campaign in 1996 the electorate's opinion of the Texas billionaire seemed to have jelled or stabilized, and with a negative cast. In general, as shown in Table 2.4, public views of Perot were about twice as negative during 1996 as in 1992.

TABLE 2.4   REGISTERED VOTERS' SHIFTING OPINION OF ROSS PEROT IN 1996 COMPARED TO 1992

DATES OF POLL	1996 FAVORABLE OPINION (%)	1996 NOT FAVORABLE OPINION (%)	1996 NET BALANCE: FAVORABLE MINUS NOT FAVORABLE	1992 NET BALANCE: FAVORABLE MINUS NOT FAVORABLE
5–9 August 1995	28	38	−10	NA
9–11 December 1995	20	56	−36	NA
22–24 February 1996	24	48	−24	+8
31 March–2 April 1996	21	46	−25	+12
11–13 July 1996	18	45	−27	−8
3–5 August 1996	15	48	−33	−17
REPUBLICAN PARTY CONVENTION				
16–18 August 1996	16	59	−43	−19
DEMOCRATIC PARTY CONVENTION				
2–4 September 1996	11	60	−49	−18
10–13 October 1996	12	58	−46	−17
17–20 October 1996	15	55	−40	−3
27–29 October 1996	15	51	−36	−18
30 October–2 November 1996	17	51	−34	−18

Note: Based on registered voters in 11 *New York Times*/CBS News polls, and one CBS News poll (27–29 October) in 1995 and 1996. Figures for 1992 are from nearest comparable poll date. The question was: "Is your opinion of Ross Perot favorable, not favorable, undecided, or haven't you heard enough about Ross Perot yet to have an opinion?"

Putting Major Campaign Events into Perspective

An additional use of polling by the *New York Times* in 1996 was to put events into perspective and to make abstract processes more concrete. Here are two examples.

A Composite National Republican Party Primary Electorate

During 1996 the *Times* analyzed voting patterns in many individual state primary elections, utilizing exit polls that Voter News Service conducted. In our week-to-week polling analysis during the primary season, we were interested both in what was new or unique about each state's primary and in the underlying patterns that were common across states. But the news necessarily emphasized the individual victories, near misses, and solid defeats of the various candidates and the resulting impact on political "momentum" from state to state over time. Somewhat less prominence was given to the recurrent patterns that emerged. As soon as it was clear that Bob Dole had clinched his party's nomination, therefore, it seemed useful to remind our reporters, editors, and readers of some of the voting patterns that had persisted across both time and geography in the Republican primary contests.

To synthesize a national Republican primary electorate for 1996, Table 2.5 combines vote totals and exit poll percentages from 28 states where exit polls were conducted in Republican primaries from February through the end of March. Each state influences the total table according to its share of all votes cast. A graphic containing these results ran inside the paper of 31 March 1996, with Richard L. Berke's article, "Polls Find Far Right Doesn't Define G.O.P. Vote."

Bob Dole won 55 percent of all votes cast in these 28 Republican primaries, Patrick Buchanan won 23 percent, Steve Forbes won 13 percent, and all other Republican hopefuls won 9 percent. Dole won support across a broad swath of Republican subgroups. He did particularly well with older primary voters, those who called themselves moderates or only somewhat conservative, and those who had voted for George Bush in 1992. He also did well with those who regularly thought of themselves as Republicans (many Republican primaries were open, so that some independents and even a few Democrats participated).

Pat Buchanan did well among those Republican primary voters who called themselves very conservative and those who wanted a constitutional ban on abortion in their party's platform. Mr. Buchanan managed to attract support in the 20 to 30 percent range across a wide array of Republican subgroups. He clearly tapped feelings of economic anxiety that touched many groups.

Steve Forbes did particularly well with those Republican primary voters who voted for Ross Perot in 1992, and he came close to Buchanan among those with postgraduate education, but Forbes lagged behind Buchanan in virtually every other subgroup.

TABLE 2.5   THE PRIMARIES AS A WHOLE THROUGH MARCH: HOW REPUBLICANS IN THE FIRST 28 STATES VOTED

PORTION OF PRIMARY VOTERS (%)	VOTING GROUP	PERCENTAGE OF EACH GROUP VOTING FOR			
		Dole	Buchanan	Forbes	Others
100	Total, 28 states through March	55	23	13	9
10	18–29 years of age	52	25	12	11
30	30–44	50	25	12	11
28	45–59	52	24	13	11
32	60 or older	65	18	10	7
3	No high school diploma	49	24	8	19
20	High school graduate	57	27	9	7
30	Some college	54	24	11	11
27	College graduate	55	20	13	12
19	Postgraduate education	39	12	10	39
	Those who voted in 1992 for:				
66	George Bush	63	20	9	6
13	Ross Perot	38	29	20	13
12	Bill Clinton	40	24	16	20
75	Republican	61	21	10	8
21	Independent	41	28	15	16
4	Democrat	29	29	11	31
21	Very conservative	44	38	9	9
37	Somewhat conservative	59	20	11	10
33	Moderate	59	16	13	12
7	Somewhat liberal	53	19	14	14
2	Very liberal	45	19	10	26
38	Favoring a constitutional ban on abortion in the party platform	49	35	7	9
57	Those not favoring such a plank	58	18	15	12
43	Trade creates more jobs in state	61	14	11	14
39	Trade costs more jobs in state	49	34	8	9
56	Buchanan is too extreme	71	5	13	11
41	Buchanan is not too extreme	35	47	10	8
(11.9)	TOTAL VOTES (millions)	(6.6)	(2.7)	(1.5)	(1.1)

Note: This table, which constructs a composite Republican primary electorate for the nation, combines vote totals and exit poll percentages from 28 Republican primary states through March 1996. Vote totals are from secretaries of state. Exit polls were conducted by Voter News Service. Some questions were not asked in all 28 states. There was no exit poll conducted in Nevada. Each state influences the total table according to its share of all votes cast through the end of March.

Although the *Times* had constructed synthetic national primary electorates for the Democrats in several past presidential election years, this was the first time we have been able to do so for the Republicans (since it requires contested primaries for at least a few months).

The Spectrum of Political Choice

The quadrennial gathering of party activists in the Democratic and Republican National Conventions provided an opportunity to examine the spectrum of political views in American politics—at least that part of the spectrum contained within the two major party coalitions. Candidates may sometimes hide or misrepresent their views on controversial issues, but delegates to the two party conventions are usually candid in revealing where they individually stand and, collectively, where their party stands.

The *Times* and CBS News polled both Republican delegates and Democratic delegates and asked many of the same questions that we had asked of rank-and-file voters of each party in the national polls we conducted during the summer. These questions ranged from the ideological labels used to describe themselves, to their preferred scope of government, to their positions on contentious social issues such as abortion, affirmative action, and organized prayer in public schools.

This enabled the *Times* to construct a graphic comparing and contrasting the party activists with each other and with three groupings of the public on these issues. A larger version of Table 2.6 (including additional demographic data) appeared in the paper on 26 August 1996, with an article by James Bennet under the headline "Clinton, Setting Out for Chicago, Denounces G.O.P."

A remarkable clarity is evident in Table 2.6 as we move, left to right, from Democratic delegates to Democratic voters, to the entire electorate including independents, then to Republican voters, and then to Republican delegates. On many items the two major party coalitions in 1996 had politically distinct positions, with Democrats taking the more liberal position and Republicans the more conservative. The contrast is strongest between the two sets of convention delegates, for whom differences of 50 points, 60 points, or even 70 points are encountered. This shows that party activists are more ideologically consistent or homogeneous than are their rank-and-file voters. Even among the grassroots followers of each party, differences of 20 points to 30 points separate the two groups of voters on a number of issues. Polarization was sufficient on enough issues in 1996 that clearly distinguishable choices were available for any voter who was looking for them.

It is also interesting to pause on a few issues in the table that break the pattern, that is, on issues on which opinion does not march neatly along as we look from left to right across the table. On whether the government should do more to promote traditional values, the two sets of convention delegates differ by about 30 percentage points, but the three groupings of voters cluster together in the middle without any significant differentiation. A different pattern occurs on whether organized prayer should be permitted in the public schools: The two

**TABLE 2.6   A SPECTRUM OF POLITICAL VIEWS: CONVENTION DELEGATES
AND VOTERS ON THE ISSUES**

	DEMOCRATIC DELEGATES	DEMOCRATIC VOTERS	ALL VOTERS	REPUBLICAN VOTERS	REPUBLICAN DELEGATES
POLITICAL PHILOSOPHY					
Very liberal	15	7	4	1	0
Somewhat liberal	28	20	12	6	0
Moderate	48	54	47	39	27
Somewhat conservative	4	14	24	36	31
Very conservative	1	3	8	17	35
GOVERNMENT SHOULD DO MORE TO					
Solve the nation's problems	76	53	36	20	4
Regulate the environment and safety practices of businesses	60	66	53	37	4
Promote traditional values	27	41	42	44	56
SOCIAL ISSUES					
Favor a nationwide ban on assault weapons	91	80	72	62	34
Necessary to have laws to protect racial minorities	88	62	51	39	30
Affirmative action programs should be continued	81	59	45	28	9
Abortion should be permitted in all cases	61	30	27	22	11
Children of illegal immigrants should be allowed to attend public school	79	63	54	46	26
Organized prayer should be permitted in the public schools	20	66	66	69	57

Note: Based on *New York Times*/CBS News polls of 509 delegates to the Democratic National Convention conducted 8–22 August 1996, and with 1,310 delegates to the Republican National Convention conducted 15 July to 8 August. Figures for voters are based on nationwide *New York Times*/CBS News polls conducted in June and August.

parties' delegates differ by 30 to 40 percentage points, but all three groups of voters are more in favor of school prayer than *either* set of delegates.

Analyzing Key Factors in the Campaign

During the 1996 election cycle the *Times* often used polling to give its reporters, editors, and readers insights into how the campaign was shaping up. We viewed the electorate as being influenced by forces of three different types—some of long duration, some of middling permanence, and some of short-lived intensity. We made polling efforts to study each type in order to explain *why* the election was developing as it was. The examples that follow include one factor from each category.

Long-Term Party Identification

"Party identification" is the electorate's underlying partisan allegiance or proclivity. It normally changes only gradually as generations enter or exit the population or as long-term secular developments such as industrialization, suburbanization, or population migration work their social and political consequences. Only rarely does party identification undergo more rapid shifts, typically accompanying some great historic discontinuity such as the Civil War or the Great Depression.

Therefore, the balance of party loyalty exerts a long-term force on any given election year, constraining the election, even if not fully determining it. Typically it gives one party a starting advantage, which the party must then work to keep or expand, while it gives the other party an initial disadvantage that the party must work to overcome.

The *Times* and CBS News measure party identification in every poll we conduct, using the question originated by the National Election Studies at the University of Michigan: "Generally speaking, do you usually consider yourself a Republican, a Democrat, an independent, or what?" Table 2.7, based on 284,001 respondents in 213 of our national polls, pools our data within each year and shows the party allegiance of Americans annually from 1976, the first full year of *Times*/CBS News national polling, through the end of 1997. For purposes of analysis we have divided the respondents into two age groups: the youngest group comprised of individuals age 18 to 29 at the time of the poll, and the older group consisting of everyone age 30 or older at the time of the poll.

During the two decades leading up to the 1996 election, the long-term Democratic advantage that had existed since the Great Depression and the New

TABLE 2.7 **SHIFTS IN PARTY IDENTIFICATION FOR TWO AGE GROUPS, 1976–1997**

PERCENTAGE OF EACH AGE GROUP IDENTIFYING WITH EACH PARTY

	18 TO 29 YEARS OLD			30 YEARS AND OLDER		
YEAR	Republican	Democratic	Democratic Advantage	Republican	Democratic	Democratic Advantage
1976	16	34	+18	23	41	+18
1977	17	34	+17	21	41	+20
1978	16	36	+20	21	42	+21
1979	19	32	+13	23	42	+19
1980	20	37	+17	24	44	+20
1981	25	30	+5	25	39	+14
1982	24	32	+8	23	41	+18
1983	23	34	+11	24	42	+18
1984	28	31	+3	26	40	+14
1985	32	28	−4	29	39	+10
1986	30	28	−2	28	39	+11
1987	34	31	−3	28	41	+13
1988	31	31	0	28	39	+11
1989	37	28	−9	30	39	+9
1990	33	26	−7	28	37	+9
1991	35	28	−7	29	37	+8
1992	31	29	−2	29	37	+8
1993	29	31	+2	28	38	+10
1994	33	27	−6	28	36	+8
1995	30	28	−2	30	36	+6
1996	29	33	+4	29	38	+9
1997	27	32	+5	30	36	+6

Note: Based on 213 polls by the *New York Times* and CBS News, which have been pooled for each year, totaling 284,001 respondents. Independents and those who do not know are not shown. The question was: "Generally speaking, do you usually consider yourself a Republican, a Democrat, an independent or what?"

Deal seemed to be in the process of dissolving. The Republicans, once the minority party with a disadvantage of up to 20 percentage points in allegiance by the public, appeared to have been closing the gap. In the second Reagan administration the Republican deficit in party identification among people age 30 and older was reduced from 20 points to the midteens, and then during the Bush years it was reduced further to high single digits. Among the youngest group of Americans—the 18- to 29-year-old age group, who are normally the most open or vulnerable to the changing tides of politics—the trend was even more dramatic. The Republican deficit, near 20 points in the late 1970s, withered away completely by the mid-1980s, and Republicans actually predominated among this younger age group by single-digit levels.

During the Clinton years, however, this long-term trend seems to have stalled. The Republican momentum ran out as the election of a Democratic president at least delayed further Democratic erosion. Among people over age 30 a Democratic advantage ranging from 6 to 10 percentage points seems to be persisting under Clinton. And among the youngest group of voters, loyalty seems to be making at least a temporary comeback for the Democrats. Another interpretation for the younger generation is that their party loyalty may be fluctuating around a roughly even split between the two parties—a few points pro-Republican one year, a few points pro-Democratic the next year—as if the two parties were in equilibrium. (With such huge samples, not much sampling error is involved.)

The division of party loyalty in the nation served as a backdrop to the 1996 election campaign. As the election approached, the Democrats clung to a marginal advantage in the long-term force of party loyalty, but it wasn't nearly the size it once was. The Republicans remained at some disadvantage, but the deficit they needed to make up or overcome was much less than it once had been.

Since party identification is by definition a long-term and fairly slow moving factor, it is a particular challenge to make it newsworthy at any given moment. We found two occasions during 1996 to use our findings about party identification to explore newsworthy political trends over time: first, among younger versus older Americans and, second, among male versus female Americans. A chart illustrating the material in Table 2.7 (from 1976 through 1995) was published in the 30 March 1996 edition of the *Times* as a freestanding graphic adjacent to an article about political participation by young people. The 20-year time-series data were presented graphically again, this time broken down by gender instead of by age, as part of a page one article on 21 April 1996 by Robin Toner, "With G.O.P. the Issue, 'Gender Gap' Is Growing Wider."

A Middle-Term Factor: The Economy

The link between the condition of the national economy and the vote on Election Day is an example of a middle-term factor the *Times* examined in 1996. "Middle-term"—or perhaps "middle-run"—seems an appropriate designation, since the economy can change more rapidly than a long-term factor such as party loyalty, but not nearly so fast as some of the truly short-term factors in the campaign such as the candidates' personal images, to be discussed later.

The *Times* and CBS News measure the public's economic perceptions in every poll we do, using the question: "How would you rate the condition of the national economy these days? Is it very good, fairly good, fairly bad, or very bad?" Table 2.8 presents fourteen readings we took from January to November

TABLE 2.8   THE PUBLIC'S VIEW OF THE ECONOMY DURING 1996
COMPARED WITH 1992

| | PERCENTAGE SAYING THE NATIONAL ECONOMY IS "VERY GOOD" OR "FAIRLY GOOD" | |
	1996 Polls	1992 Polls Nearest the Same Date
18–20 January 1996	51	21
22–24 February 1996	53	17
10–11 March 1996	NA	17
31 March–2 April 1996	56	19
31 May–3 June 1996	55	24
20–23 June 1996	60	—
11–13 July 1996	61	21
3–5 August 1996	63	—
16–18 August 1996	62	21
2–4 September 1996	69	20
10–13 October 1996	72	19
17–20 October 1996	67	23
27–29 October 1996	70	23
30 October–2 November 1996	70	23

Note: Based on all adults in polls by the *New York Times* and CBS News during two election years. The question was: "How would you rate the condition of the national economy these days? Is it very good, fairly good, fairly bad, or very bad?" Entries are the sum of "very good" plus "fairly good."

during Clinton's reelection year 1996, compared to readings taken at the nearest comparable date during George Bush's reelection year 1992.

Table 2.8 leaves no doubt that 1996 had a very different economic climate as compared to 1992. In winter and spring 1996 the public's evaluation of the economy ("very good" plus "fairly good") was about 30 percentage points more positive than it had been in 1992. By summer 1996 that increased to 40 points more rosy than in 1992. And by the end of the campaign the economic mood of the public was almost 50 points sunnier in 1996 than in 1992.

The public's evaluation of the economy had hardly budged during all of 1994 and 1995 and the first half of 1996, hovering just a few points above 50 percent saying "very good" or "fairly good." But during summer 1996 more people finally started seeing some improvement. Americans were feeling better about the economy than at any time in the previous eight years, and they were giving Bill Clinton at least some of the credit. Richard L. Berke analyzed this development in his front page article on 6 September 1996, "Majority Give Clinton Credit on Economy, Poll Finds." The page one graphic tracing the public's economic perceptions from 1991 through 1996 is a good example of how a middle-term factor that is measured on every poll but that hadn't moved for a few years can at last begin to shift and have a major impact on politics. It also confirms the value of asking certain key questions on every poll, even though they are not reported at the time, but only at some later date when an important shift eventually happens.

Another graphic, included with the jump of Berke's article inside the paper, confirmed the link between economic perceptions and the vote. Electorates in the United States as well as other countries have been observed in the past to reward or punish incumbent governments on the basis of economic performance. In 1996 American voters acted as if they were doing just that. Those who pronounced the economy "very good" or "fairly good" in the September poll preferred Clinton by 57 percent to 30 percent for Dole. In contrast, those who judged the economy "fairly bad" or "very bad" preferred Dole by 50 percent to 31 percent for Clinton. Thus, each candidate was getting the economic constituency he "ought" to get. It was just that about 70 percent of the electorate saw the economy as good, whereas only under 30 percent saw it as bad. So the advantage in total "votes" in this preelection poll went to Clinton.

That link between the economy and the vote was also apparent in real votes on Election Day. The 16,359 respondents leaving voting stations across the country in the exit poll conducted by Voter News Service were asked, "Which one issue [of seven offered] mattered most in deciding how you voted for president?" Table 2.9 shows the answers, cross-tabulated by actual vote. More voters cited the economy and jobs (21 percent) than any other issue offered (Medicare/Social

TABLE 2.9   THE PRIORITY OF SEVEN POLICY ISSUES: WHAT MATTERED MOST ON ELECTION DAY

PERCENTAGE OF ALL VOTERS WHO FALL INTO EACH CATEGORY (% ADD VERTICALLY)	ISSUES	PERCENTAGE OF VOTERS IN EACH CATEGORY WHO VOTED FOR (% ADD HORIZONTALLY)		
		Clinton	Dole	Perot
21	Economy/Jobs	61	27	10
15	Medicare/Social Security	67	26	6
12	Education	78	16	4
12	Federal Budget Deficit	27	52	19
11	Taxes	19	73	7
7	Crime/Drugs	40	50	8
4	Foreign Policy	35	56	8

Note: Based on questionnaires completed by 16,359 voters leaving polling places in 300 precincts nationwide on Election Day, conducted by Voter News Service. The question was: "Which one issue mattered most in deciding how you voted for president?"

Security was next at 15 percent). And those who cited either economy/jobs or Medicare/Social Security voted strongly for Bill Clinton. Note that most of the issues on which Bob Dole scored strongest did not rank as high as these top two themes.

What of Bob Dole's centerpiece policy issue—a 15 percent cut in federal income taxes? On Election Day, as shown in Table 2.9, Dole won 73 percent of the votes of those who cited taxes as the issue that mattered most to them, but the size of the group to whom taxes mattered most was only 11 percent of all who cast ballots—too small to tip the balance in Dole's favor, given all the other factors involved. Our polling also showed considerable public skepticism about the 15 percent tax cut plan. Many Americans doubted that it was the right thing for the country during a time of budget deficits, and many also doubted that Dole could actually deliver it in any case.

Short-Term Personal Images of the Candidates

Much journalistic activity is invested in assessing the effects of shorter-term phenomena that occur during the course of any campaign. These include the propaganda and advertising efforts of each side, major speeches and issue appeals by the candidates, performances in face-to-face (or at least side-by-side) television debates, and unanticipated events that happen along the campaign trail. These shorter-term factors occupy so much attention because they are new since the last news story or since the previous poll, and because they are most likely to account for any week-to-week or month-to-month fluctuations in the images and standings of the candidates.

Shorter-term effects are also what any campaign organization can exert the most control over. A campaign organization cannot do much about the long-term forces it faces or the middle-term conditions it must contend with, except to try to exploit them when favorable and, when unfavorable, to attempt to deflect blame or divert people's attention to more promising subjects. But campaigns spend enormous sums trying to create, and then to reinforce, positive images of their candidate and negative images of their opponents.

Table 2.10 displays some of the personal images of Bill Clinton and Bob Dole that the *Times* and CBS News tracked during fall 1996. When a question was asked in several polls, the results shown are from the poll nearest the election. The table shows that Bill Clinton succeeded in being perceived, as he sought to be, as the candidate who cares about the needs and problems of ordinary Americans. Although Democratic candidates traditionally benefit from this image, reinforcing it was what much of the defense of Medicare and other

TABLE 2.10   SOME IMAGES OF CLINTON AND DOLE IN THE FALL CAMPAIGN

PERCENTAGE WHO SAY	REGARDING CLINTON	REGARDING DOLE
CLINTON ADVANTAGES		
The candidate is addressing the issues that matter to me[a]	57	41
The candidate cares about the needs and problems of people like me[b]	65	49
The candidate is spending more time explaining what he would do if elected, rather than attacking his opponent[a]	69	18
The candidate is a "moderate"[a]	37	23
DOLE ADVANTAGES		
The candidate shares the moral values most Americans try to live by[c]	55	70
The candidate has more honesty and integrity than most people in public life[a]	31	43
MUTUAL STRENGTHS		
The candidate has made it clear what he wants to accomplish in the next four years as president[a]	58	51
MUTUAL WEAKNESSES		
The candidate can be trusted to keep his word as president[a]	46	49
If he is elected president, my taxes would increase[c]	44	40

Note: Based on three *New York Times*/CBS News polls during the fall campaign: (a) 30 October–2 November, (b) 17–20 October, and (c) 10–13 October. When a question appeared in two or more polls, the results from the poll nearest the election appear in the table. Note that each question was asked separately about Clinton and Dole, so that each candidate's image can range between zero and 100 on each item.

middle-class entitlements against attacks from the Republicans in Congress was all about. Also, significantly, more voters viewed Clinton than Dole as a "moderate"—a major goal in Clinton's move to the center during his second two years in office after the Republicans took control of Congress. Clinton's image as a moderate was reinforced, for instance, by his acceptance of the goal of a balanced budget in 1995 and by his signing of the welfare reform bill during summer 1996. Clinton also succeeded in being perceived as the candidate addressing issues that matter and the candidate spending more time explaining his goals, rather than attacking his opponent.

For his part, Bob Dole succeeded, as he sought to, on the "ethics" or "character" dimension. More voters said of Dole than of Clinton that he shares the moral values most Americans try to live by and that he has more honesty and integrity than most people in public life. What is of significance on the ethics dimension is that Dole did not overwhelm Clinton in the public's perception. A majority of 55 percent still said Clinton shared the country's moral values. And, perhaps in an example of public cynicism toward all politicians, neither Dole nor Clinton gained a majority thinking either candidate had above-average honesty and integrity.

In an example of a mutual strength, both Clinton and Dole succeeded in being perceived as making clear what he wanted to accomplish in the following four years. But, in an example of a mutual weakness, neither Clinton nor Dole succeeded in convincing a majority that his word could be trusted as president. Also, perhaps as a result of widespread cynicism, substantial minorities perceived each man as likely to increase taxes; this was particularly unfortunate for Dole, whose central campaign appeal was a promise to reduce taxes by 15 percent.

The *Times* published our examination of these perceived traits of the candidates at several junctures during the campaign year. In the spring, for instance, Richard L. Berke analyzed them in his front page article on 7 April 1996, "New Poll Finds Strength for Dole on Personal and Political Traits." During the summer, in his 20 August 1996 page one article, "Poll Shows Dole Slicing Away Lead Clinton Had Held," Berke compared a number of Bob Dole's perceived traits in our polls taken before versus after the Republican National Convention. And in the autumn, Berke compared some key perceptions of Dole in our polls taken before versus after the last televised debate between the two major party candidates, in his 22 October 1996 front page article, "Aggressive Turn by Dole Appears to Be Backfiring."

On Election Day these and other perceived candidate traits were clearly connected to the actual vote. The 16,359 respondents leaving voting stations across the country were asked in the exit poll conducted by Voter News Service, "Which one candidate quality [out of six listed] mattered most in deciding how you voted for president?" Table 2.11 shows the answers, cross-tabulated by the actual vote of each group. No single perceived trait dominated the ranking of those that mattered most. Dole was the overwhelming choice of those who cited honesty and trustworthiness, and although that theme tied as the most frequently cited of the six choices, the size of the group citing that theme was 20 percent of all voters, not enough by itself to put Dole over the top. Moreover, out of the six it was the only theme that Dole clearly won. Clinton was the strong choice of those who cited a candidate's vision for the future; that group was 16 percent of all voters. Clinton was also the strong favorite of those who cited that their candidate was in touch with the 1990s and that he cared about people like the respondent. On the two remaining themes Clinton and Dole were tied.

**TABLE 2.11   THE PRIORITY OF SIX CANDIDATE QUALITIES: NO SINGLE FACTOR
DOMINATED ON ELECTION DAY**

PERCENTAGE OF ALL VOTERS WHO FALL INTO EACH CATEGORY (% ADD VERTICALLY)	CANDIDATE QUALITIES	PERCENTAGE OF VOTERS IN EACH CATEGORY WHO VOTED FOR (% ADD HORIZONTALLY)		
		Clinton	Dole	Perot
20	He shares my view of government	41	46	10
20	He is honest and trustworthy	8	84	7
16	He has a vision for the future	77	13	9
13	He stands up for what he believes in	42	40	16
10	He is in touch with the 1990s	89	8	4
9	He cares about people like me	72	17	9

Note: Based on questionnaires completed by 16,359 voters leaving polling places in 300 precincts nationwide on Election Day, conducted by Voter News Service. The question was: "Which one candidate quality mattered most in deciding how you voted for president?"

Documenting Voter Decision Making and the Outcome of the Election

At the end of the longer than usual 1996 presidential campaign cycle, as the electorate rendered its judgment on the men who sought to lead the nation, the *Times* used public opinion polling to document voter decision making and to record who voted for whom. We also measured how the public evaluated the 1996 campaign itself compared to past campaigns.

A Campaign That Engaged Fewer Voters

Only a minority of registered voters called the 1996 campaign "interesting" (42 percent), whereas a majority called it "dull" (54 percent). That was a sharp reversal from four years earlier when 80 percent judged the 1992 campaign as interesting. The 1996 level is very like that measured in the Bush-Dukakis contest of 1988, when 42 percent also called it interesting.

As a consequence of the reduced engagement, public attention to the 1996 campaign never reached the level it did in the 1992 campaign. As Table 2.12 illustrates, in our final preelection poll in 1996, when public interest reached the year's peak, only 46 percent of registered voters said they were paying "a lot of attention" to the campaign. Four years earlier, at the end of the 1992 campaign, 69 percent said they were paying a lot of attention. Again, 1996 looks like the Bush-Dukakis campaign of 1988, when attention at the end was 45 percent.

TABLE 2.12   REGISTERED VOTERS PAYING "A LOT OF ATTENTION" TO THE CAMPAIGN

DATES OF POLL	PERCENTAGE PAYING "A LOT OF ATTENTION" TO 1996 CAMPAIGN	NUMBER OF REGISTERED VOTERS IN 1996 POLL	ATTENTION LEVEL NEAREST SAME DATE IN 1992	1988
18–20 January 1996	20	867	20	15
22–24 February 1996	31	994	30	27
10–11 March 1996	30	969	33	34
31 March–2 April 1996	26	1,035	35	34
31 May–3 June 1996	24	977	33	—
20–23 June 1996	26	948	39	—
11–13 July 1996	31	743	40	24
3–5 August 1996	30	900	—	26
16–18 August 1996	34	856	45	33
2–4 September 1996	35	978	50	29
10–13 October 1996	42	1,126	54	39
17–20 October 1996	40	1,149	61	31
27–29 October 1996	40	872	67	—
30 October –2 November 1996	46	1,519	69	45

Note: Based on registered voters in 11 *New York Times*/CBS News polls, two CBS News polls (10–11 March and 27–29 October), and one *New York Times* poll (20–23 June) during 1996. Figures from 1992 and 1988 are from nearest comparable poll date. The question was: "How much attention have you been able to pay to the 1996 presidential campaign—a lot, some, not much, or no attention so far?"

One reason for the reduced interest and engagement in 1996 was that the stakes of the election may have seemed lower to many voters. The economy had improved, so there was not the urgency for change many voters had felt four years earlier. And voters are often willing to stick with the incumbent, a known and tested quantity, if they lack good reasons—such as severe recession, high inflation, or an unpopular war—to take a chance on a new and untried person to replace the sitting president.

But another reason for the reduced interest and engagement in the 1996 election must surely lie with the nature of the campaign itself. The Dole organization could never seem to get traction with any of the issues it raised or the tactics it tried. Polls by many different polling agencies constantly showed Clinton ahead of Dole in what looked for much of the year like a potential blowout or landslide, so the contest seemed oddly static, lacking the excitement that greater competitiveness can generate. And for his part, Bill Clinton's strategy was aimed at the middle class and the middle-of-the-road voters; he was trying to reassure voters, not to issue stirring appeals to traditional Democratic constituencies like the poor, or blacks, or labor unions that might have raised the temperature of the campaign and energized people.

In addition, Ross Perot's independent campaign for the White House seemed to have had less political voltage in 1996 compared to four years earlier. In 1992 the novelty and quirkiness of his campaign, which seemed to many like a potential wild card, probably helped to raise the excitement of that year's contest. Throughout 1996 Perot never drew the level of support he had at times generated four years earlier.

As a result of all these factors, voter turnout in 1996 dropped below the level of 1992, even below the level of 1988, to the lowest level since the 1920s (when women entered the electorate and took some years getting into the habit of voting, thus pulling down the overall turnout figure for a few years). Robin Toner examined the lower interest levels, the prospect for reduced voter turnout, and each party's fears about the potential partisan consequences in her page one article on 27 October 1996, "Parties Pressing to Raise Turnout as Election Nears."

Voter Dissatisfaction with the Tone and Content of the Campaign

Although the public found the tone of the 1996 campaign somewhat less negative than usual, their reaction was not a ringing endorsement: A majority of voters said 1996 was "about the same as usual" in this regard. Table 2.13 presents these findings.

TABLE 2.13   VOTERS EVALUATE PRESIDENTIAL CAMPAIGNS IN 1996, 1992, AND 1988

	VIEWS OF REGISTERED VOTERS IN		
	1988	1992	1996
"Would you be more likely to describe the (year) presidential campaign as interesting or dull?"			
Interesting	42	78	42
Dull	52	20	54
"Compared with past presidential campaigns, do you think the campaign has been more positive this year, more negative this year, or about the same?"			
More positive	7	27	28
More negative	61	29	16
About the same	28	40	54
"With [names of candidates for president] running for president this year, are you satisfied choosing among them, or would you want other choices?"			
Satisfied	34	49	50
Want other choices	64	48	48

Note: Based on registered voters in *New York Times*/CBS News polls in October or early November before Election Day—two polls in each year. When a question was asked in more than one poll in a given year, the reading nearest to Election Day is shown.

Moreover, almost half the voters in 1996 said they were not satisfied in choosing among the three candidates running for president and wished there were "other choices." This was the same level as in 1992, but in 1988 an even higher proportion of voters preferred having additional choices. There may be something inherently confining about the choices produced by a two-party system that inevitably frustrates many voters and compromises their preferred policies—even in years such as 1996 and 1992 when an independent candidate actually offers a third alternative.

Richard L. Berke reported on public evaluations of the 1996 campaign in his front page article on 16 October 1996, "As Dole Weighs Tougher Image, Poll Finds He Already Has One."

Head-to-Head Trial Heats

The measurement of the "horse race" has always been a secondary consideration in polls sponsored by the *Times*. Our first priority has always been to measure the public's reactions to issues, personalities, and events and to plumb the public's political perceptions and attitudes. But we did include trial heat questions on most of our 1996 polls to chart the tentative decisions voters were coming to as the campaign progressed. Table 2.14 reports the results of our three-way trial heats among Clinton, Dole, and Perot, as well as the results of our two-way trial heats between just Clinton and Dole (useful in case Perot dropped out of the race, but also to discern whom Perot's participation helped or hurt more).

From February through August the results are based on all registered voters. From September through November the results have been weighted to reflect a "probable electorate." As explained in the "Method Box" that accompanied most major poll articles, this technique uses responses to questions dealing with voter registration, past voting history, attention to the campaign, and intention to vote as a measure of respondents' probability of voting in the presidential election. The technique weighted registered respondents from 0.11 to 0.89 according to their likelihood of actually turning out to vote on Election Day. In practice over the years, the technique has had the effect of reducing the Democratic candidate's share slightly and/or boosting the Republican candidate's share slightly because Republican voters are more likely to turn out than are Democrats.

All year long in 1996, as in previous election years, when the *Times* reported trial heat results, it made a practice of not allocating undecided voters who, in answer to a subsequent question, said they "leaned" toward one of the candidates. When CBS News reported trial heats, it usually allocated those self-described leaners. This accounts for occasional slight discrepancies between figures broadcast by CBS News and those published by the *Times*.

Table 2.14 shows the candidate preference of voters throughout the 15-month campaign cycle. The most striking feature is that Clinton maintained a double-digit lead over Dole throughout calendar year 1996. The only time Dole was close to Clinton at all was at the beginning of the cycle in August 1995, when he tied Clinton in a three-way trial heat and actually led him in a two-way trial heat. After the budget standoff, the two shutdowns of the federal government, and the Republican assaults on Medicare in Congress, Dole's early competitiveness simply disappeared. It is tempting to conclude that the presidential contest was pretty much set in place by the time calendar year 1996 began.

Another striking aspect of Table 2.14 is the stability of the standings across the entire autumn phase of 1996. Although individual voters may have switched back and forth or wavered, and although many voters said they might yet change their minds, the net outcome of all the individual decisions resulted in very stable aggregate standings for Clinton and Dole. In five successive polls by the *Times* and CBS News taken after 1 September, the preference of the "probable electorate" for Bill Clinton stood within plus or minus 3 percentage points of 52 percent (in three-way trial heats). In the same five polls, the preference of the "probable electorate" for Bob Dole remained within plus or minus 2 points of 35 percent. Graphics showing trend lines for the whole 15-month period were published with our final preelection poll analysis in a page one article by Richard L. Berke on Monday, 4 November 1996, "After a Long Trip, Election Arithmetic Has Gone Nowhere."

Final Preelection Estimates

In the final *Times*/CBS News poll, conducted on Thursday, 30 October, to Saturday, 2 November, the standings were at 50 percent of the "probable electorate" preferring Bill Clinton, 34 percent preferring Bob Dole, and 8 percent preferring Ross Perot, with 7 percent undecided or favoring other candidates. These were the figures reported by the *Times* in the paper of Monday, 4 November 1996, in Richard L. Berke's article, just cited.

CBS News broadcast slightly different figures after allocating leaners. When respondents who said they leaned toward one candidate or another were allocated, the figures for the "probable electorate" became 53 percent for Clinton, 35 percent for Dole, and 9 percent for Perot, with 3 percent undecided or favoring other candidates. These are the figures CBS News broadcast.

Actual Outcome Compared with the Polls

On Election Day, 5 November 1996, the actual outcome of the balloting across the country, was 49 percent of the popular vote for Bill Clinton, 41 percent for

TABLE 2.14   VOTERS' PREFERENCES FOR PRESIDENT IN TRIAL HEATS, BOTH THREE-WAY
AND TWO-WAY

| | THREE-WAY TRIAL HEATS | | | | TWO-WAY TRIAL HEATS | | |
DATES OF POLLS	Prefer Bill Clinton (%)	Prefer Bob Dole (%)	Prefer Ross Perot (%)	Clinton's Advantage over Dole	Prefer Bill Clinton (%)	Prefer Bob Dole (%)	Clinton's Advantage over Dole
5–9 August 1995	35	34	23	+ 1	42	48	–6
22–25 October 1995	44	34	17	+10	50	43	+7
9–11 December 1995	44	32	16	+12	52	40	+12
18–20 January 1996	NA	NA	NA	NA	51	40	+11
22–24 February 1996	NA	NA	NA	NA	54	36	+18
10–11 March 1996	NA	NA	NA	NA	53	36	+17
31 March–2 April 1996	44	33	18	+11	49	39	+10
31 May–3 June 1996	48	32	16	+16	54	35	+19
20–23 June 1996	51	31	13	+20	54	34	+20
11–13 July 1996	49	27	16	+22	54	34	+20
3–5 August 1996	58	28	10	+30	56	34	+22
REPUBLICAN PARTY CONVENTION							
16–18 August 1996	49	37	8	+12	50	39	+11
DEMOCRATIC PARTY CONVENTION							
2–4 September 1996	51	37	5	+14	55	39	+16
10–13 October 1996	53	36	5	+17	57	38	+19
17–20 October 1996	55	33	5	+22	NA	NA	NA
27–29 October 1996	51	35	7	+16	NA	NA	NA
30 October–2 November 1996	50	34	8	+16	NA	NA	NA

Note: Based on registered voters in fourteen *New York Times*/CBS News polls, two CBS News polls (10–11 March and 27–29 October), and one *New York Times* polls (20–23 June). Beginning with the poll of 2–4 September, the respondents were weighted to reflect a "probable electorate." This technique uses responses to questions dealing with voter registration, past voting history, intention to vote in 1996, and attention paid to the campaign as a measure of the probability of particular respondents voting in November 1996. Not shown are those who were undecided, some of whom, in answer to a subsequent question, said they currently leaned toward one candidate or another. (Note that CBS News normally adds the leaners to the initially decided, so trial heat figures released by CBS News usually differ slightly from those released by the *New York Times*.)

The three-way trial heat question, beginning with the September poll was: "If the 1996 presidential election were being held today, and the candidates were Bill Clinton for president and Al Gore for vice president, the Democrats, and Bob Dole for president and Jack Kemp for vice president, the Republicans, and Ross Perot for president and Pat Choate for vice president, the Reform Party candidates, would you vote for Clinton and Gore, for Dole and Kemp, or for Perot and Choate?" In earlier polls the vice-presidential candidates were not mentioned.

"NA" denotes three polls early in 1996 when the three-way trial heat was not asked, and three polls near the end of the campaign when the two-way trial heat was not asked.

The two-way trial heat question, beginning with the September poll, was: "What if Ross Perot were not running? If the 1996 presidential election were being held today, would you vote for Bill Clinton for president and Al Gore for vice president, the Democratic candidates, *or* would you vote for Bob Dole for president and Jack Kemp for vice president, the Republican candidates?" In earlier polls the vice-presidential candidates were not mentioned. The introduction "What if Ross Perot were not running?" was also not used in earlier polls.

Bob Dole, 8 percent for Ross Perot, and 2 percent for other candidates. That represented an 8-point margin of victory for Clinton, up slightly from his 6-point victory over George Bush in 1992, and about equal to Bush's 8-point victory over Michael Dukakis in 1988.

The *Times*'s final preelection estimate, then, was within 1 point of Clinton's actual vote, and within 1 point of Perot's actual vote, but 7 points under Dole's actual vote. Three of those points could simply be the result of sampling error, but that leaves another 4 points attributable to other factors. What were they? Two factors loom large: (1) the timing of the final interviewing, which may not have captured a last-minute gain for Dole; and (2) the workings of the "probable electorate" technique in 1996, which may not have been sufficiently ruthless in squeezing out nonvoters in a year when turnout would plunge.

Timing and Swing. Evidence for a late shift that benefited Bob Dole is presented in Table 2.15. It shows ten polling organizations' final results, ordered by the date of the midpoint of their interviewing period. The two polls whose final interviews were centered on 26 October measured Dole's support at 34 and 35 percent, respectively. The one poll with interviews centered on 29 October put Dole's support at 36 percent. The *Times*/CBS News poll, with interviewing centered on 31 October, found Dole's support at 34 percent (the *Times*) and 35 percent (CBS News). After this date, every later poll found somewhat more support for Dole than we did. The one poll with interviews centered on 1 November put Dole at 36 percent. The four polls centered about 2 November put Dole at 37, 38, or 39 percent. And the one poll that went the latest, with interviewing centered on 3 November, put out two estimates based on two different likely voter methods that found Dole with 36 percent or 40 percent support, respectively.

The implied lesson: Later was better in 1996, and the *Times* and CBS News stopped interviewing slightly too soon. At the end of the contest, Bob Dole launched a final 96-hour round-the-clock campaign leading up to Election Day that may have changed a few minds or rallied more of the Republican faithful to come out to vote or to "come home" to their traditional political party. From the evidence it appears that polls that conducted more of their interviewing during that last 96 hours fared slightly better. Also at the end of the campaign, Republican charges that the Democrats had taken illegal campaign contributions from Indonesian businessmen were widely publicized and may also have been having some impact over the final weekend.

Further evidence of a late swing to Dole is contained in Table 2.16, from the Election Day exit poll by Voter News Service. The 16,359 voters leaving polling stations nationwide were asked, "When did you finally decide who to vote for in the presidential election?" The results showed that those voters who decided in the final three days split more to Dole than to Clinton by about

TABLE 2.15   TEN FINAL PREELECTION POLLS: TIMING AND RESULTS

MIDPOINT OF INTERVIEWING	POLL	CLINTON	DOLE	PEROT	UNDECIDED OR OTHER	CLINTON ADVANTAGE	PEOPLE SAMPLED
Saturday							
26 October	*Los Angeles Times*	51	34	12	3	17	1,112 LV
	Washington Post	51	35	10	4	16	1,480 LV
Tuesday							
29 October	Hotline/						
	Battleground	45	36	8	11	9	1,000 RV
Thursday							
31 October	*New York Times*/ CBS News						
	No. 1: *N.Y. Times*	50	34	8	7	16	1,513 PE
	No. 2: CBS News	53	35	9	3	18	1,513 PE
Friday							
1 November	Pew Research Center	49	36	8	7	13	1,211 LV
Saturday							
2 November	ABC News	51	39	7	3	12	703 LV
	Harris	50	38	8	3	12	1,339 LV
	NBC/*Wall Street Journal*	49	37	9	5	12	1,020 RV
	Reuters/Zogby	44	37	7	12	7	1,200 LV
Sunday							
3 November	Gallup/CNN/ USA Today						
	No. 1	49	36	9	6	13	1,573 PV
	No. 2	48	40	6	6	8	1,448 LV
AVERAGE OF LAST 7 POLLS THAT CONDUCTED AT LEAST SOME INTERVIEWS IN FINAL WEEKEND		49	37	8	6	12	
ACTUAL ELECTION RESULTS		49	41	8	2	8	

Note: The polls are ordered according to the midpoint of the interviewing period, the date by which approximately half of the interviews would have been completed. In computing the average results at the bottom of the table, only the last seven polls are used because at least part of their interviews were conducted during the final Saturday, Sunday, or Monday before Election Day. The first three polls, which finished their interviewing before the final weekend started, are excluded from calculating the average results on the grounds that they deliberately refrained from polling until the very end. To facilitate comparison, the figures shown are before any allocation of undecided voters. This is necessary because some polling organizations allocate undecided voters, but others do not. In computing the average of the seven polls, when an organization released two sets of results, each was counted as one-half of that poll's findings. Gallup No. 1 is based on probable voters; Gallup No. 2 is based on a more strictly defined group of likely voters. *NYT*/CBS No. 2, CBS News's version, includes those who said they leaned toward a candidate; *NYT*/CBS No. 1, the *Times*'s version, leaves leaners among the undecided. Full field dates were the *Los Angeles Times* (24–27 October), the *Washington Post* (23–30 October), Hotline/Battleground (28–31 October), *NYT*/CBS (30 October–2 November), Pew (31 October–3 November), ABC News (2–3 November), Harris (1–3 November), NBC/*WSJ* (2–3 November), Reuters/Zogby (1–3 November), Gallup/CNN/*USAT* (3–4 November).

The organizations defined the nature of the population sampled in somewhat different ways. Key to the type of people sampled: LV = likely voters; PV = probable voters; RV = all registered voters; PE = probable electorate.

3 percentage points. Those who said they decided in the last week split toward Dole over Clinton by an even larger 12 percentage points.

A comparison of the "internals" (cross-tabulations) of that Election Day exit poll with the final preelection *Times*/CBS News telephone poll suggests at least part of what was happening. In the final preelection poll the loyalty to Dole by self-identified Republicans was significantly *less* than the loyalty to Clinton by self-identified Democrats. Seventy-two percent of Republicans supported Dole, whereas 84 percent of Democrats supported Clinton; that left more "headroom" or potential for Dole to improve if he could successfully call unenthusiastic Republicans and Republican-leaning independents to "come home"—no doubt a major goal for the final 96-hour marathon push by the Dole campaign.

When the same cross-tabulation is performed on the Election Day exit poll, it appears that the effort succeeded in part. In that poll 80 percent of self-identified Republicans actually voted for Dole, whereas 84 percent of self-identified Democrats voted for Clinton. So, although Clinton's success in keeping Democratic support remained unchanged, Dole increased his success among Republicans from 72 percent to 80 percent. Bob Dole also increased his support among independents—from 29 percent in the preelection telephone poll to 35 percent in the Election Day exit poll; Clinton, in contrast, remained fairly steady among independents. Some of the last-minute swing to Dole probably also came from voters who pronounced themselves "undecided" in the final preelection polling. This pattern is fairly familiar (though not universal) in contests that pit a challenger against an incumbent, for undecided voters to break at least slightly in favor of the challenger at the end.

The value of polling up to the last minute had also been the lesson of the 1980 campaign, when late shifts helped Ronald Reagan and worked against

TABLE 2.16   WHEN VOTERS DECIDED HOW TO VOTE: BOB DOLE BENEFITED FROM LATE DECIDERS

PERCENTAGE OF ALL VOTERS WHO FALL INTO EACH CATEGORY (% ADD VERTICALLY)	VOTER'S TIME OF DECISION	PERCENTAGE OF VOTERS IN EACH CATEGORY WHO VOTED FOR (% ADD HORIZONTALLY)		
		Clinton	Dole	Perot
11	In the last three days	35	38	22
6	In the last week	35	47	17
13	In the last month	47	36	13
69	Before that	53	41	5

Note: Based on questionnaires completed by 16,359 voters leaving polling places in 300 precincts nationwide on Election Day, conducted by Voter News Service. The question was: "When did you finally decide who to vote for in the presidential election?"

Jimmy Carter. But in the three campaigns in between—1984, 1988, and 1992—no last-minute swings had actually occurred.

Yet there must be another factor at work. Table 2.15 shows that *all* the final polls underestimated Bob Dole's strength to at least some extent. None of the ten final polls measured Dole's support either at or above the 41 percent share of the popular vote he received. Normally we expect polls as a group to bracket, or straddle, the true result—with some a bit high, some a bit low, and some right on the mark. That is, we expect the truth to be found not in any one poll but amid the preponderance of polls. Indeed, the seven final polls that included at least some interviewing during the final weekend do bracket or straddle Clinton's true vote as well as Perot's true vote. But they all underestimate Dole's by varying amounts (albeit some of them within the margin of sampling error). When that occurs, one must look elsewhere for the rest of the story.

The author reviewed the performance of the final preelection polls in an article inside the paper of 15 December 1996, under the headline "Experts Say Refinements Are Needed in the Polls." (Note that after allocating leaners, some polling organizations also went on to assign the remaining undecided voters, each polling group according to its own formula, and usually improved their estimates further. Because not all polls did this, however, the table looks at each poll's results *before* any final massaging of the undecided in order to keep the figures comparable.)

Squeezing Out Nonvoters. Evidence that the *Times*/CBS News poll's "probable electorate" technique was inadequate in squeezing out nonvoters in a year when turnout would plunge is presented in Table 2.17. The effects of five levels or degrees of "squeezing" are shown in the table, which was constructed for an internal postmortem at the *Times* after the election.

When No Squeeze is applied at all and the trial heat results in our final preelection poll are based on all adults (100 percent of the sample), Clinton held a 24-point advantage over Dole. When the Mildest Squeeze is applied, looking only at registered voters (77 percent of the sample), Clinton's advantage shrank to 17 percentage points. When the Actual Squeeze (what we actually used) is applied, using the probable electorate weighting (60 percent of the sample), Clinton's advantage was only slightly reduced to 16 percentage points. When a Tighter, Better Squeeze was applied, looking only at the top two levels of the probable electorate categories (49 percent of the sample, approximating the actual voter turnout in 1996), Clinton's advantage drops to 10 percentage points; that is close to his actual margin of victory (which was 8 percentage points). Finally, when a Totally Ruthless Squeeze is applied, looking only at registered voters who say they will definitely vote and are paying a great deal of attention to the campaign (33 percent of the sample, approximating the turnout at an off-year con-

TABLE 2.17 EFFECTS OF FIVE WAYS OF SQUEEZING THE FINAL PREELECTION POLL FOR LIKELY VOTERS

PERCENTAGE OF SAMPLE CAPTURED IN EACH SQUEEZE		PERCENTAGE OF EACH CATEGORY WHO PREFERRED			CLINTON ADVANTAGE
		Clinton	Dole	Perot	
NO SQUEEZE					
100	All adults	53	29	10	+24
MILDEST SQUEEZE					
77	All registered voters	50	33	8	+17
ACTUAL SQUEEZE USED					
60	Probable electorate weighting	50	34	8	+16
A TIGHTER, BETTER SQUEEZE					
49	Top two levels of probable electorate only	48	38	7	+10
TOTALLY RUTHLESS SQUEEZE					
33	Registered voters who say they will definitely vote and are paying a lot of attention	51	38	5	+13

Note: Based on the final preelection *New York Times*/CBS News poll with 1,919 adults conducted 30 October–2 November 1996. "Probable Electorate" is explained in the notes to Table 2.14.

gressional election that draws each party's hardcore loyalists), Clinton's advantage goes back to 13 percentage points.

Clearly a somewhat tighter, rather than a looser, squeeze was needed in 1996.

In the 1988 and 1992 elections, the degree of squeeze had not made much difference. That was because the candidate preferences of likely voters versus unlikely voters were almost identical in each of those elections. But with a 6-percentage-point drop in turnout in 1996 that did not uniformly affect both parties, the degree of squeeze suddenly made a big difference. The candidate preferences of likely voters versus unlikely voters in 1996 were very different from each other, and where one drew the line (or how one set the weights) mattered greatly.

The degree of closeness of final preelection poll estimates to the actual outcome of an election constitutes a natural "acid test" of the methods used in opinion polls and creates a highly visible and powerful built-in incentive for pollsters to constantly refine and improve their techniques.

Confirming National Patterns in a Battleground Locality:
Stark County, Ohio

In most election years the *Times* and CBS News prefer to conduct statewide telephone polls in key states around the country to see how national patterns are playing out in battleground localities. In 1996 this confirmatory function was performed by two unusual polls, one in spring and the other in fall, conducted in Stark County, Ohio.

The *Times* had assigned a correspondent, Michael Winerip, to spend the entire election year there (based in Canton, Ohio), reporting on how the issues, candidates, and campaigning were viewed by grassroots Americans living in a typical community in a swing state. By the end of the year Winerip would write between 30 and 40 articles for the paper.

The two Stark County polls were a collaboration with the Northwestern University Survey Laboratory and the Ohio State University School of Journalism—and, in particular, with Professors Paul J. Lavrakas and Gerald Kosicki. Chapter 6 of this book describes this joint venture of journalism and academia from their perspective.

From the *Times*'s perspective, this polling partnership was unprecedented. It was truly useful in support of Winerip's unusual year-long reporting mission. He talked personally with countless individuals throughout the county and developed a fine feel for the "voices" of various segments of the community. But the two polls enabled him to represent the views of the entire county statistically and to know the relative size of the various segments whose voices he reported on.

The Stark County polls asked many of the same questions that had already been asked nationwide by the *Times*/CBS News poll. That enabled Winerip to compare and contrast Stark County with the nation, putting his local findings in context. And it enabled the *Times*'s polling department to test whether patterns identified in our national polls were also playing out similarly in an individual locality that had been deliberately selected as a microcosm of the country.

Also from our point of view, it was very useful to collaborate with university-based survey researchers, who necessarily have somewhat different goals and different theoretical and methodological perspectives. The interaction was immensely productive. We appreciated all the resources they put into the two joint polls, all their hard work in conducting those polls, and their professional collegiality throughout the partnership.

Findings from Stark County, Ohio, did indeed confirm the national patterns. Clinton led Dole throughout spring and autumn. The economy was a major explanatory factor. And Bob Dole failed to catch fire with either the "character" issue or his 15 percent tax cut. Likewise, the final Stark County poll also somewhat underestimated Dole's ultimate electoral strength, but it identified the same softness of Dole's strength among Republicans—and therefore the same "headroom" or potential to call Republicans to "come home" at the end—as we identified in our national polls. Michael Winerip reported these findings in the spring in "Backers of Bush in '92 Are Turning to Clinton," inside the paper of 27 May 1996, and in the autumn in "Ohio County Reluctantly Tilts toward Clinton," inside the paper of 28 October 1996.

Who Voted for Whom: The "Portrait of the Electorate"

Use of polling by the *Times* in 1996 came to a climax when we analyzed the Election Day exit polls conducted by Voter News Service, both nationally and in key states. Results of these polls informed several articles and graphics in the Wednesday and Thursday papers. In the paper of 6 November 1996, these included the two front page pieces by Richard L. Berke and R. W. Apple Jr., under the banner headline "Clinton Elected to a 2d Term with Solid Margins across U.S.; G.O.P. Keeps Hold on Congress," as well as James Bennet's inside piece devoted entirely to the exit polls, "Voter Interviews Suggest Clinton Was Persuasive on Path of U.S."

The *Times*'s most intensive use of polling data appeared in the Sunday paper of 10 November 1996, when we printed the "Portrait of the Electorate," traditionally known as the Supertable, that for the first time grew to be a full page wide and a full page deep, showing how 120 different subgroups of the population voted in the presidential elections of 1972, 1976, 1980, 1984, 1988, 1992, and 1996. Table 2.18 presents much of the Supertable.

Our objective in preparing and publishing the Supertable is to share with readers some of the rich exit poll data that we pore over on election night and during the days afterward, much of which would otherwise never make it into the newspaper.

The Supertable invites the reader to pursue his or her own analysis of the vote. One can compare different groups with each other within a given election (vertically), or compare the same groups over time (horizontally), or both. For instance, when comparing the votes of men versus women, one can see that a "gender gap" of 11 percentage points existed in 1996, with women giving the Democratic candidate a greater share of their vote than men did. At the same time one can see that although a similar gap of 6 to 8 points also existed in the four previous contests, it reached its largest magnitude in 1996.

In the demography of the 1996 vote one can still discern the faint outlines of the old New Deal coalition. Clinton did particularly well in big cities, among lower-income Americans, less-educated people, union voters, Catholics, Jews, and liberals, as well as blacks. But the continuing news is that Clinton also did

TABLE 2.18 PORTRAIT OF THE ELECTORATE

% of vote in 1996		1980			1984		1988		1992			1996		
		Reagan	Carter	Anderson	Reagan	Mondale	Bush	Dukakis	Cinton	Bush	Perot	Clinton	Dole	Perot
100%	TOTAL VOTE	51	41	7	59	40	53	45	43	38	19	49	41	8
48	Men	55	36	7	62	37	57	41	41	38	21	43	44	10
52	Women	47	45	7	56	44	50	49	45	37	17	54	38	7
83	White	56	36	7	64	35	59	40	39	40	20	43	46	9
10	Black	11	85	3	9	90	12	86	83	10	7	84	12	4
5	Hispanic	33	59	6	37	62	30	69	61	25	14	72	21	6
1	Asian	—	—	—	—	—	—	—	31	55	15	43	48	8
17	18–29 years old	43	44	11	59	40	52	47	43	34	22	53	34	10
33	30–44 years old	55	36	8	57	42	54	45	41	38	21	48	41	9
26	45–59 years old	55	39	5	60	40	57	42	41	40	19	48	41	9
24	60 and older	54	41	4	60	39	50	49	50	38	12	48	44	7
35	Republicans	86	9	4	92	7	91	8	10	73	17	13	80	6
26	Independents	55	30	12	63	36	55	43	38	32	30	43	35	17
39	Democrats	26	67	6	25	74	17	82	77	10	13	84	10	5
20	Liberals	25	60	11	28	70	18	81	68	14	18	78	11	7
47	Moderates	49	42	8	53	47	49	50	47	31	21	57	33	9
33	Conservatives	73	23	4	82	17	80	19	18	64	18	20	71	8
23	From the East	47	42	9	53	47	50	49	47	35	18	55	34	9
26	From the Midwest	51	41	7	58	41	52	47	42	37	21	48	41	10
30	From the South	52	44	3	64	36	58	41	41	43	16	46	46	7
20	From the West	53	34	10	61	38	52	46	43	34	23	48	40	8
6	Not a high school graduate	46	51	2	50	50	43	56	54	28	18	59	28	11
24	High school graduate	51	43	4	60	39	50	49	43	36	21	51	35	13

Some college education	27	55	35	8	61	38	57	42	41	37	21	48	40	10
College graduate or more	43	52	35	11	58	41	56	43	44	39	17	47	44	7
College graduate	26	—	—	—	—	—	62	37	39	41	20	44	46	8
Postgraduate education	17	—	—	—	—	—	50	48	50	36	14	52	40	5
White Protestant	46	63	31	6	72	27	56	33	33	47	21	36	53	10
Catholic	29	50	42	7	54	45	52	47	44	35	20	53	37	9
Jewish	3	39	45	15	31	67	55	64	80	11	9	78	16	3
Union household	23	44	49	6	46	53	42	57	55	24	21	59	30	9
Family income is:														
Under $15,000	11	43	49	7	45	55	37	62	58	23	19	59	28	11
$15,000–$29,999	23	53	39	7	57	42	49	50	45	35	20	53	36	9
$30,000–$49,999	27	59	32	8	59	40	56	43	41	38	21	48	40	10
Over $50,000	39	64	26	10	69	30	62	37	39	44	17	44	48	7
Over $75,000	18	—	—	—	—	—	—	—	36	48	16	41	51	7
Over $100,000	9	—	—	—	—	—	65	32	—	—	—	38	54	6
Family's financial situation is:														
Better today	33	37	55	7	86	14	—	—	24	61	14	66	26	6
Same today	45	46	47	7	50	50	—	—	41	42	17	46	45	8
Worse today	20	66	25	8	15	85	—	—	60	14	25	27	57	13
Size of place:														
Population over 500,000	10	—	—	—	—	—	37	62	58	28	13	68	25	6
Population 50,000 to 500,000	21	—	—	—	—	—	47	52	50	33	16	50	39	8
Suburbs	39	55	35	9	61	38	57	42	41	39	21	47	42	8
Population 10,000 to 50,000	9	—	—	—	—	—	61	38	39	42	20	48	41	9
Rural areas	21	55	39	5	67	32	55	44	39	40	20	44	46	10

TABLE 2.18 (CONTINUED)

% of vote in 1996		1980			1984		1988		1992			1996		
		Reagan	Carter	Anderson	Reagan	Mondale	Bush	Dukakis	Clinton	Bush	Perot	Clinton	Dole	Perot
9	First time voters	—	—	—	61	38	51	47	46	32	22	54	34	11
49	Congressional vote: For the Democratic candidate	22	69	7	23	76	27	72	74	11	15	84	8	7
49	For the Republican candidate	83	11	5	93	7	82	17	10	72	18	15	76	8
43	Previous Presidential vote: For the Democratic candidate	29	63	6	18	82	7	92	83	5	12	85	9	4
35	For the Republican candidate	83	11	6	88	11	80	19	21	59	20	13	82	4
12	For Wallace/ Anderson/Perot	—	—	—	27	69	—	—	—	—	—	22	44	33
66	Married	—	—	—	62	38	57	42	40	41	20	44	46	9
34	Unmarried	—	—	—	52	47	46	53	51	30	19	57	31	9

Note: Data for 1996 were collected by voter News Service based on questionnaires completed by 16,627 voters leaving 300 polling places around the nation on Election Day. Data for 1992 were collected by Voter Research and Surveys based on questionnaires completed by 15,490 voters. Data for 1980 through 1988 were based on surveys conducted by the *New York Times* and CBS News: 11,645 in 1988; 9,174 in 1984, and 15,201 in 1980. Data for 1972 and 1976 were based on surveys conducted by CBS News, with 15,300 voters in 1976 and 17,595 in 1972. . . . .

Those who gave no answer are not shown. Dashes indicate that a question was not asked or a category was not provided in a particular year.

Marjorie Connelly prepared the 1996 Supertable, as she has for the past several presidential elections.

relatively well, as he did in 1992, among independents, moderates, middle-income groups, and suburbanites—groups that Democratic candidates have had trouble capturing in some previous elections. Clinton also managed to split the South evenly with Dole, just as he had four years earlier with George Bush.

Another important contributing factor to the Clinton reelection victory was that he won as much loyalty from Democratic voters as Dole did from Republican voters. Before the Clinton years the pattern had been for self-described Republicans to be more loyal to their party, whereas self-described Democrats experienced somewhat more defections to the enemy camp.

Also still apparent in the 1996 Supertable are the outlines of the traditional Republican coalition. Bob Dole did particularly well among white Protestants, higher-income voters, conservatives, and college graduates (though not among those with postgraduate training).

Ross Perot did his best among independents, who are less tied to the major parties and who were also Perot's biggest backers four years earlier.

Testing Hunches and Claims

In addition to contributing directly to news articles, our polling allowed reporters and editors to check hunches, to test claims, and to avoid being manipulated. Two examples follow.

Why Didn't Whitewater, "Ethics," and "Character" Play a Bigger Role?

Toward the end of his campaign against Bill Clinton, Bob Dole began to ask Americans "Where's the outrage?," to indicate his disbelief that the public would not penalize Clinton for his accumulating scandals—Whitewater-related matters, the FBI file controversy, the Paula Jones lawsuit alleging sexual harassment, and campaign contributions by Indonesian businessmen. Our hunch was that the public at that time saw many of these "ethics" accusations as partisan attacks during an election campaign and discounted them accordingly. We made several efforts at testing this hunch. Tables 2.19 and 2.20 present the evidence that we examined.

In preelection telephone polls, majorities or pluralities said that allegations of Clinton's ethical problems did not affect their vote, that Republican charges that the Democrats took illegal campaign contributions from Indonesian businessmen were just election year politics as usual, and that they were withholding judgment on whether the Clintons did anything wrong in connection with Whitewater.

**TABLE 2.19 ETHICS AND CHARACTER AS ELECTION ISSUES:
THREE TESTS BEFORE THE ELECTION**

PERCENTAGE OF REGISTERED VOTERS WHO FALL INTO EACH CATEGORY (% ADD VERTICALLY)	ISSUES	PERCENTAGE OF REGISTERED VOTERS IN EACH CATEGORY WHO PREFERRED (% ADD HORIZONTALLY)		
		Clinton	Dole	Perot
	How much do the allegations of ethical problems in Bill Clinton's personal life matter to you in deciding how to vote—have they caused you to change your vote, or are they one factor among many, or don't they affect your vote?[a]			
8	Changed vote	4	71	15
36	One factor	29	55	8
54	Don't affect	72	15	6
	Do you think Bill and Hillary Clinton did or did not do anything wrong in connection with Whitewater, or don't you know enough about it to say?[b]			
40	Did wrong	24	64	8
13	Did not do wrong	95	1	9
43	Don't know enough	72	13	4
	Do you think this [Republican charges that the Democratic Party took illegal campaign contributions from Indonesian businessmen] is a serious issue, or is this election year politics as usual? [c]			
35	Serious issue	27	65	6
62	Election politics as usual	61	22	7

Note: Based on two *New York Times*/CBS News polls and one CBS News poll: (a) 30 October–2 November; (b) 17–20 October; and (c) the CBS News poll of 27–29 October.

In the Election Day exit poll by Voter News Service, a majority of actual voters (58 percent) said their candidate's "position on the issues" was more important for their vote decision than was his "personal character and values" (38 percent). The exit poll also showed that voters were split on whether Bill Clinton is "honest and trustworthy" (41pecent yes, 54 percent no), but that whereas Clinton got almost nine out of ten of the votes of those who said yes, Bob Dole got only about seven out of ten of the votes of those who said no. When it came to Whitewater, about twice as many voters thought Clinton had not been telling the truth as those who saw truth telling. But whereas Clinton got nine out of ten of the votes of those who saw truth telling, Bob Dole got only about six out of ten of the votes of those who saw lying.

TABLE 2.20   ETHICS AND CHARACTER AS ELECTION ISSUES: THREE MORE TESTS
ON ELECTION DAY

PERCENTAGE OF ALL VOTERS WHO FALL INTO EACH CATEGORY (% ADD VERTICALLY)	ISSUES	PERCENTAGE OF VOTERS IN EACH CATEGORY WHO VOTED FOR (% ADD HORIZONTALLY)		
		Clinton	Dole	Perot
	Which was more important in your vote for president today?			
58	His position on the issues	69	20	8
38	His personal character and values	18	71	10
	Regardless of how you voted today, do you think Bill Clinton is honest and trustworthy?			
41	Yes	88	6	4
54	No	18	67	12
	In explaining Whitewater and other matters under investigation, do you think Bill Clinton has			
33	Told the truth	89	6	4
60	Not told the truth	24	62	13

Note: Based on questionnaires completed by 16,359 voters leaving polling places in 300 precincts nationwide on Election Day, conducted by Voter News Service.

We concluded that the public was discounting the ethics charges because of the partisan atmosphere of an election year. In our June poll, for instance, 84 percent of respondents said that when Republicans in Congress criticized the president about Whitewater-related matters, they were doing so because they were "looking for political gain" rather than because they "cared about ethics." We published these analyses as part of several articles over the course of the campaign. One example is Richard L. Berke's article inside the paper of 26 June 1996, headed "Clinton Lead Is Unaffected by Troubles."

Did the Public Prefer Divided Control of Government?

Toward the end of the 1996 election year, as it became apparent that the Dole campaign was failing to generate sufficient steam, some Republicans campaigning for Congress urged the voters to maintain Republican control of Congress in order not to give President Clinton a "blank check" in his second term. Our hunch was that this appeal resonated with enough voters to be effective. Moreover, another hunch we had was that Clinton was favored by voters in the first place because he represented a counterbalancing force vis-à-vis the Republican Congress. The public may have wanted no blank check in Republican hands, either. We made several efforts to test these hunches. Table 2.21 shows the kind of evidence we examined.

In our final preelection poll we asked respondents to suppose Bill Clinton were reelected, and then we asked them whether in that event it would be better to elect a Democratic Congress to increase the power of President Clinton, or better to elect a Republican Congress to limit the power of President Clinton. Registered voters in the poll split 40 percent for a Democratic Congress and 50 percent for a Republican Congress that could check Clinton. We concluded that a majority of the public did prefer divided control of government in such a situation.

We also found, however, that by an even bigger margin the public preferred Clinton as a check on the Republicans. In the same poll we asked respondents to suppose the Republican Party continued to control Congress and then asked them whether in that event it would be better to elect a Republican president to increase the power of Republicans in Congress, or better to reelect President Clinton to limit the power of Republicans in Congress. In this scenario, registered voters in the poll split just 33 percent for a Republican president and 54 percent for reelecting Clinton. We concluded that although many voters did want a Republican Congress as a check on Clinton, even more voters wanted Clinton as a check on the Republicans.

TABLE 2.21 HOW MUCH PUBLIC SENTIMENT FOR DIVIDED CONTROL OF GOVERNMENT?

IN THE FINAL PREELECTION TELEPHONE POLL
Suppose Bill Clinton is reelected president after the 1996 election: Would it be better to elect a Democratic Congress to increase the power of President Clinton, or would it be better to elect a Republican Congress to limit the power of President Clinton?

>   Democratic Congress   40
>   Republican Congress   50

Suppose the Republican Party continues to control Congress after the 1996 elections—would it be better to elect a Republican president to increase the power of Republicans in Congress, or would it be better to reelect President Clinton to limit the power of the Republicans in Congress?

>   Republican president   33
>   Reelect Clinton   54

AND IN THE ELECTION DAY EXIT POLL
If Bill Clinton is reelected, would you rather have the U.S. Congress controlled by

>   The Democrats   44
>   The Republicans   49

Note: Based on registered voters in the *New York Times*/CBS News final preelection telephone poll of 30 October–2 November, and on questionnaires filled out by 16,359 voters leaving polling places in 300 precincts nationwide on Election Day, conducted by Voter News Service.

Among actual voters in the Election Day exit poll conducted by Voter News Service, it was also apparent that the electorate favored divided control, but by a smaller margin. When asked whether they would rather have the U.S. Congress controlled by the Democrats or by the Republicans if Bill Clinton were reelected, 44 percent preferred the former, whereas 49 percent preferred the latter. And, in that exit poll, 11 percent of voters said they actually voted for a president of one major party and a congressperson of the other party, in other words, for divided government. (This figure does not include Perot voters.)

Adam Clymer reported some of this analysis of the public's desire for partisan checks and balances in his page one article on 23 October 1996, "G.O.P. Pushes Congress Strategy That Shuns Dole."

Conclusion

Lessons Learned or Reaffirmed

The overarching polling lesson reaffirmed by the *Times*'s experience in 1996 is that any program of opinion research must be designed so that it is responsive, flexible, and adequate to its task. Because the election is a year-long (or longer) process, it is necessary to design a series of polls (covering 15 months this time) that can track the individual phases of the electoral cycle. Because public reactions to personalities, issues, and events can change during the year, it is important to repeat a core of trend questions in poll after poll to capture the dynamics of the campaign. Because long-term, middle-run, and short-lived forces can each affect the outcome, it is important to build in devices to measure all three types of factors. Because American presidential elections are in the end decided by fifty separate state elections, it can be important to poll in some of the crucial battleground states to see how national patterns are playing out in different locales. Because last-minute swings in voter preference sometimes occur, as they appear to have done in 1996, it is important to poll as close as is practical to Election Day with preelection polling, then to document actual voter decision making through exit polling on Election Day itself, and then to be prepared to call back the preelection respondents afterward in the event there are unexplainable surprises in the election outcome. Because voter turnout can be critical, as it was in 1996, it is important to develop (and to improve) ways of estimating the likelihood that individuals will vote. Because nonvoters were actually a majority of the voting age population in 1996, it is important to find ways to hear their voices, too. And because the quality of the polling data is crucial to all subsequent interpretation and reporting, it is important to invest in properly drawn samples, high-quality interviewing, and an experienced staff for question writing and data analysis. Finally, when it comes to the ultimate reporting of poll results, it is a boon and a pleasure to have so many fine correspondents, editors, and graphic artists on one's team!

Steps for the Future

For the *Times*/CBS News poll, in particular, our experience in 1996 revealed the need to improve on the "probable electorate" model of voter turnout we had used since 1980. It works well in most presidential election years, but it performed inadequately this year when voter turnout seriously dropped and when voters and nonvoters held distinctly different candidate preferences. We plan to use state elections in 1997 and 1998 and the national congressional elections in 1998 to test various improvements, as well as potential substitute models, to identify likely voters in the future.

The *Times*/CBS News poll also plans to reinstate ways to deal better with possible last-minute shifts at the end of a campaign. In some previous election years, for example, we have used a "tracking" design in our final preelection polling, with independent daily samples, to register any day-to-day shifts that might occur. In retrospect, that design might have proved useful in 1996. In other years CBS News has gone on polling by itself after the final joint poll, since the network can still broadcast last-minute results on the air the night before Election Day.

For the polling profession more generally, 1996 was a good year. Most polls had final results quite close to the actual election outcome, and most successfully identified the underlying dynamics of the campaign. Many polls could also use some further refinements, however. As one example, a better job could have been done by all, first, in anticipating the last-minute surge for Bob Dole and in understanding how it might (and did) happen and, second, in communicating that information to readers and viewers of polling reports, many of whom were somewhat taken by surprise in 1996.

No doubt improvements will be made. Because final preelection polling results are so visible and can quickly and easily be compared to the official outcome of an election, the polling profession has a built-in self-correcting tendency. When lessons are there to be learned, pollsters have every incentive to learn them.

Author's Note

Many thanks to the staff members of the News Surveys Department at the *Times* who initially computed, checked, and organized most of the numerical data presented in this chapter and who contributed mightily to the paper's polling analysis during 1996: Janet Elder, Marjorie Connelly, Deborah Hofmann, Steve Gleason, and Brian Strub. The correspondents and reporters who most frequently wrote the poll articles in 1996 brought to the polling effort a seemingly endless supply of ideas, hypotheses, and insightful interpretations: R. W. Apple Jr., James Bennet, Adam Clymer, Robin Toner, and especially the national political correspondent, Richard L. Berke. It was also a pleasure working with the editors most frequently involved with our 1996 polling: Soma Golden Behr, Dean Baquet, William Schmidt, and Andrew Rosenthal. Also many thanks to our partners in telephone polling, our colleagues at CBS News: Kathleen Frankovic, Cheryl Arnedt, Martin Plissner, and Dotty Lynch. And, as always, we much appreciated the exit polling expertise of Murray Edelman and his staff at Voter News Service. None of these individuals necessarily agrees with all the interpretations in this chapter.

CHAPTER 3

A Review of the 1996 Voter News Service Exit Polls from a Total Survey Error Perspective

Daniel M. Merkle and Murray Edelman

Exit polls play an important role in the media's coverage of elections by providing accurate and timely information that allows them to report on the main stories of any election—Who won? How and why did the outcome happen? What does it mean? The demand for accuracy in the exit polls is very high. Exit poll data are used in statistical models, in addition to past and current vote data, to project election winners. The goal is to make the correct projections at poll closing time, or as soon thereafter as the data allow. After the winner is known, the coverage focuses on how and why a particular candidate won or lost and on the meaning of the election outcome. The answers to these questions are based primarily on exit polls because they provide a wealth of data about what issues were important to the outcome of the election and how various groups voted.

Throughout the 1988 election, each of the broadcast networks (ABC, CBS, and NBC) conducted its own exit polls and made its own projections on election night. In 1990 these broadcast networks and CNN formed Voter Research and Surveys (VRS) to conduct one set of exit polls in an effort to cut costs. In 1993 VRS merged with the News Election Service (NES), a media pool that collected and tabulated the vote on Election Day. The result of that merger was Voter News Service (VNS). Now a pool of ABC, the Associated Press, CBS, CNN, FOX, and NBC, VNS is the main source of exit poll data in the United States, providing data to its six member organizations and approximately 100 television stations, newspapers, magazines, and radio stations.[1]

This chapter reviews the 1996 VNS exit polls, beginning with a description of the methodology used to conduct these polls and a discussion of their accuracy. This discussion is followed by a detailed review of the types of potential exit poll error and some of the research we have conducted on them.

Exit Poll Methodology

Conducting nationwide exit polls is a huge undertaking. For the 1996 general election, VNS conducted fifty-two separate exit polls—one in each state and the District of Columbia—as well as a national exit poll. In all, 147,081 voters were interviewed at 1,468 precincts across the country. The VNS exit polls were conducted using a two-stage sampling design. In the first stage, a stratified, systematic sample of precincts was selected in each state, proportionate to the number of votes cast in a previous election. The national sample of 305 precincts was selected from the state samples, proportionate to the number of votes cast in the 1992 presidential election. In the second stage, interviewers systematically selected voters as they exited polling places on Election Day, using a sampling interval based on the size of the precinct and the expected turnout at that precinct. The interval was computed so that approximately 100 interviews were completed in each precinct.

All interviewers were hired and extensively trained by VNS. One interviewer was assigned to each precinct in the sample, and backup interviewers were also hired in case any of the primary interviewers were not able to report to work on Election Day. Interviewers were instructed to work with a polling place official to determine the best place to stand. Interviewers approached the selected voter, showed the questionnaire, and using a set script, asked the voter to fill it out. The self-administered questionnaires were one or two sides of a standard piece of paper, depending on the newsworthiness of the races in the state. After the voter filled out the questionnaire, he or she placed it in a "ballot box."

Interviewers took a 10-minute break from interviewing each hour to tally the responses to the vote questions and to tally the refusals and misses. Interviewers called VNS three times during the day to report their data. In local time, the first call was around 9:00 A.M., the second around 3:00 P.M.; the last call was made shortly before poll closing. During each call, the interviewer reported the vote and nonresponse tallies and read in the question-by-question responses from a subsample of the questionnaires. This subsampling is carried out so that we can use the responses from the vote questions from the full sample in each precinct (i.e., the 100 interviews) for the projection models without having to spend interviewer and operator time reading in each questionnaire. In 1996, 70,119 of the 147,081 questionnaires were subsampled, and the data for all questions were read into our system.

Accuracy of the 1996 Exit Polls

Given the widespread usage of VNS exit polls on Election Day, accuracy is critical. A significant error can lead to an incorrect election projection that is seen by millions of people. An error quickly becomes apparent as the poll results are compared with the actual vote returns as they come in. This is in contrast to most polls and surveys for which the population values are never known. Because of this, those who conduct election polls, both preelection and Election Day polls, are often subjected to serious public criticism when their polls are off the mark and even sometimes when they are not (e.g., Ladd, 1996).

Table 3.1 displays VNS's 1996 national estimate throughout Election Day from checkpoints of our data files. These horse-race numbers are the ones that are displayed on VNS national survey screens throughout the day. These screens present the rounded numbers to avoid implying any more precision than the data deserve. Early tabulations that imply what the election outcome might be are not broadcast until the evening, but they do affect the way newspeople formulate their stories for election night and frame the meaning of the election.

The 1:26 P.M. checkpoint is the first time we had an estimate from all four regions of the country. This is made up of exit poll data mainly from the morning call. Later checkpoints incorporate data from the afternoon and evening calls. Then, as the actual votes are reported throughout the evening, they are incorporated with the exit poll data in our national estimate. As seen in Table 3.1, the estimates were stable throughout the day. Because the data in the table are

TABLE 3.1   ACCURACY OF THE 1996 NATIONAL EXIT POLL ESTIMATES (IN PERCENTAGES)

	CLINTON	DOLE	PEROT	CLINTON MINUS DOLE	ESTIMATE MINUS ACTUAL
Actual Result[a]	49	41	8	8	—
Estimates:					
1:26 P.M.	49	42	7	7	−1
2:40 P.M.	49	42	7	7	−1
3:54 P.M.	49	42	8	7	−1
5:36 P.M.	49	42	8	7	−1
7:54 P.M.	49	41	8	8	0
9:27 P.M.	50	40	9	10	2
10:50 P.M.	50	40	8	10	2
12:06 A.M.	50	40	8	10	2
2:40 A.M.	49	42	7	7	−1

[a]Source of actual election outcome from Barone and Ujifusa (1997).

rounded, it is not possible to say whether the differences between the estimates and the actual results are attributable to rounding or to real differences. In any case, the estimate is quite accurate throughout the day and gives no hint of a serious bias. By 8:00 P.M. when the final call is in for a large majority of the polling places, the estimate is exact.

In some past elections there has been a Democratic bias (i.e., an overstatement of support for Democratic candidates) in the exit polls. For example, in the 1992 exit polls Clinton's support was overstated by about 2.5 percentage points.[2] This bias has virtually disappeared in recent elections. In the 1994 and 1998 general elections, there was no bias in the exit polls, and the 1996 bias was less than half the size of the 1992 bias, as Clinton's vote was overstated by only 1 percentage point.

The Total Survey Error Framework

Many users of polls and surveys are aware of sampling error, which reflects the possible fluctuation in the estimates because they are based on samples drawn from a larger population. In media accounts, this is often referred to as the "margin of error." Too often poll consumers interpret the margin of error as a measure of the total error in a survey. But there are other harder-to-quantify sources of nonsampling error that should not be ignored.

Exit polls are designed to represent the electorate voting on a given day. A number of questions, relating to the different types of nonsampling error, could be asked when evaluating that representation. What is the impact of the voters who do not cooperate with the request to fill out the questionnaire? Are they different in a systematic way from voters who do respond (i.e., nonresponse error)? Did all voters have an opportunity to be chosen in the sampling process? What is the impact of absentee or early voters who did not go to the polling place (i.e., coverage error)? Does the questionnaire have limitations? Could a finding be an artifact of the way a question is asked (i.e., measurement error)?

Given the widespread usage of VNS exit polls and the obvious need for accuracy, considerable effort has been spent studying such questions in order to better understand the sources of exit poll error, with the ultimate goal being to minimize errors. The sections that follow use the Total Survey Error (TSE) framework (cf. Groves 1989; Lavrakas 1993) to discuss the potential types of exit poll errors and some of the research we have conducted on them. Groves (1989) distinguishes between four types of survey error: sampling error, nonresponse error, coverage error, and measurement error.

Sampling Error

Sampling error is the most straightforward type of survey error because, unlike the three types of nonsampling error discussed later, it can be quantified using statistical techniques. The size of the sampling error is a function of the sample size, the population size, and the variability in the population. Most media polls randomly select respondents from telephone households and compute the margin of error under the assumption of simple random sampling.[3] However, an exit poll uses a much more complicated sampling design. It is first a sample of precincts and then a sample of voters within the precincts. The sampling error in exit polls is larger for characteristics that are clustered or disproportionately found in some precincts. If the distribution of a characteristic is roughly the same across all precincts, then the sampling error is close to the simple random sampling case. The more a characteristic is clustered, or varies across the precincts, the larger the sampling error for that characteristic. For example, candidate vote and political opinion items are highly clustered, whereas the percentage male or female is fairly similar across precincts.

The increase in exit poll sampling error is measured by the "design effect," a statistical expression that relates the variance in a complex survey to simple random sampling. We have estimated the exit poll design effect for the vote and related opinion items to be approximately 1.7, but obviously this will vary by question and by state. A design effect of 1.7 translates into a 30 percent increase in the sampling error computed under the assumption of simple random sampling. Items that are more highly clustered, such as the percentage Hispanic or the percentage gay, will have somewhat larger design effects.

Table 3.2 compares the sampling error for various sample sizes for simple random sampling and for exit polls. The table shows that using the sampling error computed under the assumption of simple random sampling can significantly underestimate an exit poll's sampling error for clustered items with small sample sizes. For example, for samples of 100 respondents, the sampling error for simple random sampling is 9.8 percentage points versus 12.8 points for most exit poll variables. At much larger sample sizes, such as 15,000, the differences are less dramatic: 0.8 for simple random sampling versus 1.0 for the exit poll.

It is important that analysts take into consideration the complexity of the sampling design when performing tests of statistical significance on exit poll data. This means using properly computed measures of the margin of error that take into account the design effect. Those who analyze exit poll data using statistical software should also be cautious. When using exit poll data, the statistical tests in commonly used statistical software packages will be too liberal because they are based on the assumption that simple random sampling was used to

TABLE 3.2   SAMPLING ERROR—SIMPLE RANDOM SAMPLING VERSUS
EXIT POLL

SAMPLE SIZE	SIMPLE RANDOM SAMPLING (PERCENTAGE)	EXIT POLL— CLUSTERED (PERCENTAGE)
100	9.8	12.8
250	6.2	8.1
500	4.4	5.7
750	3.6	4.7
1,000	3.1	4.0
1,500	2.5	3.3
2,000	2.2	2.9
2,500	2.0	2.6
5,000	1.4	1.8
7,500	1.1	1.5
10,000	1.0	1.3
12,500	.9	1.1
15,000	.8	1.0

Note: The "Exit Poll—Clustered" column is computed using a design effect of 1.7.

collect the data. Using this software on exit poll data will increase one's chances of committing a Type I error, that is, concluding there is a statistically significant relationship in the data when there is not.

Nonresponse Error

As with any survey, some sampled voters who were selected to fill out the exit poll questionnaire will not do so. There are two types of nonrespondents in exit polls: refusals and misses. A refusal occurs when a sampled voter is asked to fill out the questionnaire and declines. A miss is when the interviewer is unable to ask a sampled voter to fill out the questionnaire. This can occur when the interviewer is too busy to approach the voter or when the voter does not pass the interviewer. Most of the nonresponse in exit polls is attributable to refusals rather than misses. In 1996 VNS's average statewide refusal rate was 33 percent and the average miss rate was 10 percent.[4]

The presence of nonresponse in a sample survey does not necessarily mean there is nonresponse error. The magnitude of nonresponse error is a function of the proportion of nonrespondents and how different nonrespondents are from the respondents (cf. Groves and Couper 1998). Survey methodologists have devoted considerable effort in recent years exploring ways to improve survey response rates under the assumption that a higher response rate will lead to lower survey error. Although this assumption makes sense theoretically, it can rarely be tested because the population values needed to compute error measures are often not known. The VNS exit polls provide a unique opportunity to look at how survey nonresponse is related to survey error.

Who Are the Nonrespondents?

In many surveys it is difficult to obtain information on nonrespondents. Because exit polls are conducted in person, it is possible to obtain basic demographic information about nonrespondents. Interviewers for VNS keep track of nonrespondents on a worksheet. Interviewers code whether the nonrespondent was a refusal or a miss, as well as the nonrespondent's gender, race, and age (from observation). The information on these three variables is used in a nonresponse adjustment on Election Day.

As seen in Table 3.3, there was minimal nonresponse bias in 1996 for gender or race as respondents and nonrespondents were quite similar on these two characteristics.[5] Consistent with previous elections, however, there was a significant nonresponse bias for age in 1996, with older voters being less likely to fill out the questionnaire; 19 percent of respondents were age 60 or older, versus 29 percent of nonrespondents. The age difference between respondents and nonrespondents, and the fact that this is a consistent finding in our exit polls, highlights the importance of conducting a nonresponse adjustment for age.

TABLE 3.3   A COMPARISON OF 1996 EXIT POLL RESPONDENTS AND NONRESPONDENTS (IN PERCENTAGES)

	ALL (N = 132,996)	RESPONDENTS (N = 72,772)	NONRESPONDENTS (N = 60,224)
GENDER			
Male	47.4	46.6	48.4
Female	52.6	53.4	51.6
RACE			
White	85.2	84.4	86.1
Nonwhite	14.8	15.6	13.9
AGE			
18–29	16.7	17.6	15.7
30–59	60.0	63.8	55.5
60+	23.3	18.7	28.8

Note: The figures in this table were computed by summing the cases across all states and are not weighted to form a national estimate.

Education and Nonresponse

Another way to look at the representativeness of the exit polls is to compare them to other surveys of voters such as the Current Population Survey (CPS) conducted by the Census Bureau after the election. As seen in Table 3.4, the 1996 VNS national exit poll and the CPS are quite similar on all of the demographic characteristics except education. Mitofsky and Edelman (1995) reported similar results after the 1992 election.

TABLE 3.4   DEMOGRAPHIC CHARACTERISTICS OF THE 1996
ELECTORATE: VNS NATIONAL EXIT POLL VERSUS
THE CURRENT POPULATION SURVEY
(IN PERCENTAGES)

	VNS	CPS	DIFFERENCE
AGE			
18–29	17.1	14.9	2.2
30–44	32.9	31.8	1.1
45–59	26.3	26.5	−0.2
60+	23.7	26.7	−3.0
RACE			
White	83.0	82.5	0.5
Black	10.1	10.6	−0.5
Hispanic	4.5	4.7	−0.2
Other	2.4	2.2	0.2
GENDER			
Male	47.9	46.6	1.3
Female	52.1	53.4	−1.3
EDUCATION			
No HS degree	6.3	10.7	−4.4
HS degree	23.6	30.5	−6.9
Some college	27.1	21.2	5.9
Associate's degree		8.2	—
College graduate	25.6	19.3	6.3
Postgraduate study	17.4		—
Advanced degree		10.1	—
INCOME			
<15K	11.4	14.3	−2.9
15K–30K	22.7	19.9	2.8
30K–50K	27.4	25.4	2.0
50K–75K	20.6	21.2	−0.6
>75K	17.9	19.2	−1.3

Note: Table adapted from Popkin and McDonald (1998).

One critic has taken this difference on education between the two surveys as evidence of a nonresponse bias related to education in the exit polls. Teixeira (1998), using the 1996 VNS and CPS data, noted that the proportion of college graduates in the exit poll was 43 percent, versus 29 percent in the CPS. Teixeira argued that the reason for this difference is a "chronic bias" in the exit polls because "the highly educated are much more willing to fill out survey forms in polling places" (pp. 82–83).

Popkin and McDonald's (1998) review of this issue calls into question Teixeira's claim that the VNS exit polls overstate education because of nonresponse bias. First, Popkin and McDonald point out the very obvious difference in education response categories used by VNS and CPS. Eight percent of voters in 1996 had an associate's degree, but the VNS question does not have that category. In his analysis Teixeira does not consider these people to be college educated, but it is likely that most of the associate's degree holders check the college degree category in the exit poll, rather than the alternative category which is "some college, but no degree."

Popkin and McDonald also point out that the CPS has its own measurement problems. First, unlike exit polls, which sample voters right after they have voted on Election Day, the CPS is a household survey conducted after the election. Second, vote in the CPS is reported by the respondent for all household members. Third, one in twelve reported voters in the CPS did not actually vote but reported doing so because of social desirability. According to Popkin and McDonald, this misreporting of voting results in an overreport of the lower-education categories. Although more educated nonvoters are more likely to overstate voting, there are so many more nonvoters in the lower-education categories that the net result of the false reporting is an overstatement of the proportion of less-educated voters in the CPS.

Further, Popkin and McDonald point out that if the educational differences between the exit polls and the CPS were attributable to nonresponse bias, one would expect differences in other demographic items, especially income, which is highly correlated with education. But the differences between the two surveys for income and the other demographic variables are minimal and easily attributed to sampling error and measurement error (Table 3.4). Popkin and McDonald conclude that these results "strengthen the case that the exit poll samples are representative of voters. How can a sample be substantially more educated without being either an older or richer one?" (p. 29).

Another way to explore this question is to look at the relationship between precinct response rates and education. If voters with more education are more likely to participate in the exit polls, then it should be the case that precincts with a greater proportion of college-educated voters would have higher response rates and those with less-educated voters would have lower response rates. Conducting this analysis on the 1996 exit poll data, we find no support for this hypothesis. There is no correlation between a precinct's response rate and the percentage with postgraduate study ($r = .02$, $p = $ n.s.), the percentage of college graduates ($r = -.04$, $p = $ n.s.), the percentage of high school graduates ($r = -.02$, $p = $ n.s.), or the percentage who did not complete high school ($r = .02$, $p = $ n.s.).

This review of Teixeira's (1998) criticism illustrates the danger of failing to take into account significant differences in survey methodology when using the results of one survey to discount the results of another. Although the discrepancy between the VNS and CPS education distributions has not been fully explained, a good part of it can be attributed to the questions used rather than to nonresponse bias. However, this debate also raises an important question about VNS's measurement of education. Whereas the VNS "college graduates" category likely includes many people with two-year associate's degrees, this may not fit with the common usage of the term *college graduate*. If so, this would be a form of measurement error. This could be resolved either by being more clear in the reporting of this category or by revising the question.

Response Rates and Survey Error

A unique aspect of the VNS exit polls is that they make it possible to look at the relationship between survey response rates and survey error using a very large number of cases because response rates and error measures can be computed on a precinct-by-precinct basis.[6]

On Election Day, VNS gathers the actual vote in each exit poll precinct to be used in the projections. These data are also used to compare the actual vote to the exit poll results in each precinct. In our evaluations of exit poll error, we operationalize error in two ways. First, we subtract the Dem-Rep difference (i.e., the Democratic vote percentage minus the Republican vote percentage) in the exit poll in each precinct from the actual Dem-Rep difference for the main race in that state.[7] This is used to compute the "signed error," which is simply the actual Dem-Rep difference minus the exit poll Dem-Rep difference for each precinct. Second, the "absolute error" is the absolute value of the signed error.

The main issue when considering nonresponse error is the extent to which response rates are correlated with the error. The general hypothesis is that lower response rates will lead to more survey error. Contrary to conventional wisdom, however, the 1996 data show no relationship between response rates and error.[8] At the precinct level, response rates are not correlated with the signed error ($r = -.05$, $p = $ n.s.) and are only slightly correlated with the absolute error at the bivariate level ($r = -.13$, $p < .05$).[9] However, much of the relationship between response rates and the absolute error is spurious because the precinct's sample size is affected by the response rate and the absolute error is affected by the sample size. This correlation becomes insignificant (statistically and practically) when controlling for the precinct's sample size ($r = -.05$, p = n.s.). We also conducted this analysis using state-level response rates and error. Similar to the precinct-level data, there is no relationship between response rates and the signed error ($r = .14$, p = n.s.) or the absolute error ($r = -.06$, p = n.s.).[10]

Experimenting with Response Rates and Error

Another way to study nonresponse and survey error is to conduct an experimental study. We conducted such a study as part of our coverage of the New Jersey and New York City general elections in 1997 (Merkle et al. 1998). The study was designed to measure the impact of an incentive and a change in the interviewer's approach to the voter. It was hypothesized that the experimental manipulations would increase response rates and decrease survey error.

As our incentive, we used a VNS pen that had the logos of the VNS member organizations on it (cf. Willimack et al. 1995). We also used a colorful folder that fit over the right half of the questionnaire pads to better standardize the interviewer's approach and to stress key pieces of information that we hypothesized would lead to compliance.

A total of 80 precincts were randomly selected, 44 in New Jersey and 36 in New York City. These precincts were then randomly assigned to one of three conditions:[11]

1. *Folder Condition.* The interviewers in these precincts were given questionnaire pads with the color folders.
2. *Folder and Pen Condition.* The interviewers in these precincts used the same color folders and also offered VNS pens to voters as an incentive for filling out the questionnaire.
3. *Traditional Condition.* The interviewers followed the standard VNS interviewing procedures, approaching voters without the color folder and without the pen.

Judging from the interviewers' reactions, having the pens as an incentive was quite positive. Interviewers said they liked using the pens because the voters reacted favorably to them and they helped gain respondent cooperation. Some believed having the pens made their task easier in that they felt more comfortable asking voters to fill out the questionnaire because they were able to offer something in return. Contrary to the interviewers' reactions and our expectations, the hypothesis that the pen would increase the response rate was not supported. The average response rate was basically the same in the Folder and Pen Condition (55 percent) and the Folder Condition (54 percent) ($t = .25$, p = n.s.). This was somewhat surprising in that Willimack and others (1995) found that a pen incentive increased the response rate by 5 percentage points even though the pen was sent to the sampled household a few weeks in advance. In our study, the actual respondents were offered the pen at the time of the interview request, which should have increased its effectiveness. The hypothesis that the pen would decrease survey error was also not supported. The Folder and Pen Condition and the Folder Condition did not differ significantly in terms of the signed error or the absolute error.

Because the Folder Conditions were not significantly different from each other, we combined them to test the impact of the Folders versus the Traditional method. The data suggest that the Folder Conditions had the hypothesized impact on response rates. The response rate was 5 percentage points higher in the combined Folder Conditions compared with the Traditional method, although this difference does not quite reach the traditional level of statistical significance ($t = 1.23$, $p = .11$, one-tailed test). Since it was hypothesized that the main effect of the folders would be on gaining respondent cooperation, it is also informative to look at the refusal rate. Most of the increase in the overall response rate in the Folder Conditions is the result of a decrease in refusals rather than in misses. The refusal rate was 4 percentage points lower in the Folder Conditions ($t = 1.25$, $p = .11$, one-tailed test).

Although the slight increase in response rates is a good sign, the important question is, What impact did this manipulation have on survey error? Contrary to what we hypothesized, the signed error was actually larger in the Folder Conditions than in the Traditional Condition, even though the Folder Conditions had a higher response rate. The Folder Conditions had a large Democratic bias (8 percentage points on the difference) whereas the Traditional had a small Republican bias (2 percentage points on the difference) ($t = 2.33$, $p < .05$). The Folder and Traditional Conditions did not differ significantly in terms of the absolute error.

Most of the studies that explore ways to increase response rates ignore the bigger issue of how increasing the response rate will affect survey error. The Folder Conditions appear to have had a small effect on response rates, increasing them by 5 percentage points. More important, however, the Folder Conditions had a much larger signed error than the Traditional Condition. In other words, if one were to look just at the response rate as the measure of survey quality, the procedures used in the Folder Conditions would appear to be an improvement. However, instituting a change in methodology to use these procedures based on the likelihood of improving the response rate, without information about the effect on survey error, would have been a mistake in this case.

Coverage Error

Noncoverage occurs when elements of the population have no chance (i.e., zero probability) of being included in the sample. Exit polls are used to measure the characteristics and opinions of voters in a given election. Noncoverage can occur in exit polls for several reasons. First, some voters will have no chance of being sampled if they vote prior to Election Day through absentee or early voting. Second, some voters will have no chance of being selected if an exit poll is conducted through only part of the day. As with nonresponse error, coverage error is a function of the proportion of voters who have a zero probability of being included in the sample and the difference between those who have a chance of being selected and those with a zero probability of being selected.

Absentee and Early Voting

The main coverage issue that exit polls face is the growing trend toward absentee and early voting. Exit polls, which interview voters at their polling places on Election Day, miss absentee or early voters who cast their ballots prior to Election Day. Traditionally citizens have been able to vote by absentee ballot only if they have a condition that makes it difficult for them to go to the polls on Election Day. These conditions include illness, a handicap, advanced age, or being out of town on Election Day. Some states have abolished these restrictions, making it possible for all citizens to vote before Election Day either by mailing in an absentee ballot or by going to an early voting location to cast a ballot.[12] The trend toward early voting has been increasing in recent years as it has become more accessible and as more voters are discovering its ease and convenience. Twelve percent of voters nationally voted early in 1996.

The potential for noncoverage bias in exit polls is minimal in the many states where the proportion of early voters is relatively small. However, the rate of absentee or early voting is increasing dramatically in some states, with a third or more voting early. Obviously, the potential for noncoverage bias is greater in states with a larger proportion of early voters. In 1996 VNS decided to conduct telephone surveys of early voters to improve the representativeness of the exit polls in states with a large proportion of early voters. Telephone surveys were conducted in the four states where we expected the highest proportion of early voters: California, Oregon, Texas, and Washington.[13] These four states put no restrictions on early voting, and each had a relatively large proportion of early voters in recent elections.[14] In 1996 Oregon had the highest proportion of early voters, with about one-half voting early, compared with approximately one-third in Texas and Washington and one-fifth in California (Table 3.5). Because of changes in early voting rules, Oregon and Washington had very large increases in early voting from 1992, whereas California's and Texas's levels were more similar to 1992.

The telephone survey data were used by VNS in two ways on Election Day. First, the vote estimates from the telephone polls were combined with the vote estimates from the exit polls to be used in the projection of winners. This is important because not only are early voters not represented in the exit poll data, but in some states many of the absentee ballots are not counted until well after Election Day. For example, in 1996 Washington counted absentee ballots after Election Day as long as they were postmarked on or before Election Day. In Oregon in 1996 early voting ballots had to be received by 8:00 P.M. on Election Day to be counted, but the tabulation of the early ballots was not completed until the Friday after Election Day. The second way the telephone data were used was by combining the raw data from the telephone surveys with the exit poll data for all questions (i.e., the vote, demographics, and issue questions) for analysis purposes. The 1996 election was the first time that VNS included data from early voters in its exit poll files.[15]

The telephone data, in conjunction with the exit polls in these states, enable us to compare the characteristics of early voters and Election Day voters. These comparisons provide information about the potential coverage biases in exit polls that result from not including early voters. Consistent with previous elections, early voters and Election Day voters differed significantly in terms of age, with older respondents being much more likely to vote early (Table 3.6). Obviously the ease and convenience of voting early is a benefit to those who have a difficult time going to the polls on Election Day.

The other demographic variables do not show consistent differences across the states. Early voters and Election Day voters were not significantly different in terms of race. For gender, women were more likely to vote early in Washing-

TABLE 3.5   **PROPORTION OF EARLY VOTERS: 1992 VERSUS 1996 (IN PERCENTAGES)**

STATE	1992	1996
California	17	20
Oregon	14	48
Texas	33	32
Washington	18	36

TABLE 3.6 COMPARISON OF EARLY VOTERS AND ELECTION DAY (ED) VOTERS (IN PERCENTAGES)

	CALIFORNIA		OREGON		TEXAS		WASHINGTON	
	Early ($N = 414$)	ED ($N = 2868$)	Early ($N = 414$)	ED ($N = 1323$)	Early ($N = 410$)	ED ($N = 2013$)	Early ($N = 416$)	ED ($N = 1479$)
GENDER								
Male	45	48	45	49	52[a]	47[a]	44[b]	50[b]
Female	55	52	55	51	48	53	56	50
AGE								
18–29	13[c]	18[c]	13[d]	20[d]	14[e]	19[e]	16[f]	17[f]
30–44	26	32	23	35	26	37	24	37
45–59	24	25	26	26	27	26	24	27
60+	38	25	38	18	33	18	36	19
RACE								
White	80	75	94	93	69	72	88	88
Black	5	7	1	2	9	10	2	4
Hispanic	9	12	1	2	19	16	3	2
Other	6	6	3	3	3	2	7	6
INCOME								
<30K	30	27	45	40	37[g]	30[g]	42[h]	29[h]
30K–50K	26	25	29	30	27	26	32	30
50K–75K	20	24	15	19	19	22	16	24
>75K	23	24	11	11	17	22	11	16
PARTY ID								
Democrat	36[i]	43[i]	39	40	35[j]	37[j]	27[k]	36[k]
Republican	40	37	37	33	30	41	30	31
Ind./Other	24	20	24	28	35	22	43	32
IDEOLOGY								
Liberal	15[l]	24[l]	20	21	13[m]	16[m]	15[n]	23[n]
Moderate	43	46	48	47	37	43	49	49
Conservative	42	31	32	32	50	41	36	27
PRESIDENTIAL VOTE								
Clinton	46[o]	52[o]	48	47	43[p]	44[p]	54	51
Dole	43	37	41	37	52	47	38	36
Perot	6	7	7	11	4	8	6	9
Other	6	3	4	5	<1	1	3	4

Note: Distributions with the same superscript are significantly different at $p < .05$. The Oregon results for president were computed by subtracting the vote totals for the Election Day voters (as collected by VNS on Election Day) from the vote totals for all voters reported by the Oregon secretary of state (i.e., early voters plus Election Day voters). The Texas results for president are the actual vote data from the Texas secretary of state, and therefore there is no sampling error for this variable. The results for California and Washington are from VNS's telephone and exit polls.

ton, whereas men were more likely to vote early in Texas. There were not significant differences for gender in California and Oregon. For income, early voters in Texas and Washington were more likely to have lower incomes, whereas the income distributions of early voters and Election Day voters in California and Oregon were quite similar.

One of the major issues for election analysts is whether early voters and Election Day voters differ politically. In Oregon, there were no major differences between early and Election Day voters on party identification, ideology, or the vote (Table 3.6). In California, Texas, and Washington, however, the findings for these three political variables indicate a general tendency for early voters to be more Republican and conservative, although these partisan differences varied somewhat by state. In California, early voters tended to be less Democratic in terms of party identification, and they were more ideologically conservative. In the vote for president, early voters in California were more likely to support Dole than were Election Day voters. In Texas, early voters were more likely to say they were independents and conservatives but less likely to say they were Republican. In the vote for president, early Texas voters were more Republican. In Washington, early voters were more likely to be independents and conservatives and less likely to be Democrats. There were no significant differences in the vote for president in Washington.

These data show that early voters can be quite different from Election Day voters, but that these differences are not inevitable. As more states relax the restrictions for voting early, the proportion of early voters will only increase. When early voters and Election Day voters differ, exit polls that interview only Election Day voters will have a noncoverage bias. This bias increases as the difference between early and Election Day voters increases and as the proportion of early voters increases.

We can use the data presented earlier to explore what the noncoverage bias would have been in these four states had we not conducted telephone surveys of early voters. Table 3.7 compares the age distributions of Election Day voters with all voters (i.e., early voters and Election Day voters combined, with each group weighted to its correct proportion). In each of the four states, older voters would have been underrepresented if the telephone surveys of early voters were not included. The noncoverage bias is not large in California even though early voters were much older than Election Day voters (as shown in Table 3.6) and 20 percent of voters voted early. This indicates that noncoverage bias is not as much of a problem in states with a relatively small proportion of early voters unless there are extreme differences between early voters and Election Day voters. The largest noncoverage bias would have been observed in Oregon, where those 60 and over would have been underestimated by 9 percentage points. In Oregon,

TABLE 3.7   **POTENTIAL COVERAGE ERROR FOR AGE: ELECTION DAY VOTERS (ED) VERSUS ALL VOTERS (IN PERCENTAGES)**

	CALIFORNIA		OREGON		TEXAS		WASHINGTON	
AGE	ED	All	ED	All	ED	All	ED	All
18–29	18	17	20	17	19	17	17	16
30–44	32	31	35	30	37	34	37	32
45–59	25	25	26	26	26	26	27	26
60+	25	28	18	27	18	23	19	25

almost half of all voters voted early. This highlights the importance of conducting surveys of early voters to supplement the exit poll data in those states with a substantial proportion of early voters.

The partisan makeup of early voters was also different from that of Election Day voters in California, Texas, and Washington in 1996, with the politically conservative being more likely to vote early. Partisan differences are not inevitable, however, as early voters and Election Day voters in Oregon did not differ on the partisan measures. It is also important to keep in mind that the composition of the electorate that votes early is not necessarily static in a given state across time. For example, although previous elections in Texas showed no partisan differences between early voters and Election Day voters, in 1996 early voters tended to be more conservative. One factor that can influence the composition of the early voting electorate is partisan activity designed to mobilize voters (Oliver 1996; Stein and Garcia-Monet 1997). Any assumptions about the partisan makeup of the early voting electorate based on past elections in a state could be invalidated by different levels of effort to mobilize supporters by one or both of the major parties.

Interviewing throughout the Day

A less costly way to conduct an exit poll would be to interview during part of the day, as is done in some local exit polls, but this could result in a coverage bias if the vote patterns differ throughout the day. Because VNS interviews voters throughout the day at each precinct, such noncoverage is not a problem with our exit polls. However, VNS exit polls are used earlier in the day by journalists as an aid in planning their election coverage that evening. It is therefore helpful to discriminate between trends that will stand up at the end of the night and those that are an artifact of the time of day. Table 3.8 displays the composition of the national electorate from each wave of data in 1996. On Election Day, analysts would be

TABLE 3.8 COMPOSITION OF THE 1996 NATIONAL ELECTORATE THROUGHOUT
THE DAY (IN PERCENTAGES)

	ALL (16,637)	MORNING CALL (N = 4,791)	AFTERNOON CALL (N = 5,109)	EVENING CALL (N = 6,737)
GENDER				
Male	48	52	46	46
Female	52	48	54	54
EDUCATION[a]				
HS or less	30	28	32	29
Some college	27	26	27	28
College grad	26	25	25	26
Postgrad study	17	21	16	16
AGE				
18–29	17	11	18	21
30–44	33	32	28	38
45–59	26	29	24	27
60+	24	29	30	15
PRESIDENTIAL VOTE				
Clinton	49	47	50	50
Dole	41	43	41	38
Perot	8	8	8	9
Other	2	2	1	2
HOUSE VOTE				
Democrat	49	47	51	50
Republican	49	51	48	48
Other	2	2	2	2

[a]The sample sizes for Education are about half of those listed above because education was on
only two of the four versions of the questionnaire.

looking at cumulative data, and so the displayed differences would be more muted,
but the table does suggest some differences in voting patterns by the time of day.

From this table, it can be seen that men and those with a postgraduate education tend to vote in the morning. Age shows the largest difference by time of
day, with older people voting earlier. The proportion of 18- to 29-year-old voters
is twice as large in the evening than in the morning; and at the evening call, the
proportion of those 60 years of age and older decreases to half of what it was
during the morning and afternoon. In terms of the vote for president and the
House, earlier voters were more Republican and later voters more Democratic.

Although differences on the vote questions between first-call respondents and all respondents were not large in 1996 (i.e., only 2 percentage points on the Democratic and Republican candidates), it is important to keep in mind that larger differences are possible for any given state or race. For example, in 1998 in Minnesota the demographic variables showed fairly similar trends by the time of day, with men, those with more education, and older voters being more likely to vote early (Table 3.9). For the gubernatorial vote question, however, the differences by time of day were much more pronounced than for the presidential vote in 1996. Supporters of Jesse Ventura, the Reform Party candidate, increased throughout the day from 29 percent at the morning call, to 35 percent at the afternoon call, to 43 percent at the evening call. The later turnout of Ventura voters resulted in his final vote percentage being underestimated by 8 percentage points at the first call.

For any given election, it is difficult to predict when the vote will vary significantly by the time of day. For this reason, it is important for those conducting exit polls to interview throughout the day and for those analyzing exit polls early on Election Day to recognize that the results may change as more data are collected.

TABLE 3.9 COMPOSITION OF THE 1998 MINNESOTA ELECTORATE THROUGHOUT THE DAY (IN PERCENTAGES)

	ALL (N = 1,526)	MORNING CALL (N = 377)	AFTERNOON CALL (N = 456)	EVENING CALL (N = 693)
GENDER				
Male	50	56	45	50
Female	50	44	55	50
EDUCATION				
HS or less	32	26	36	32
Some college	24	24	23	24
College grad	27	29	24	28
Postgrad study	18	22	17	15
AGE				
18–29	17	12	15	21
30–44	34	28	31	40
45–59	29	34	27	28
60+	20	27	28	11
GUBERNATORIAL VOTE				
Ventura	37	29	35	43
Coleman	34	37	35	32
Humphrey	28	32	30	24
Other	1	1	1	1

Measurement Error

Measurement error encompasses the remaining types of error not accounted for by sampling, nonresponse, or noncoverage (cf. Biemer et al. 1991). This section discusses two types of measurement error having to do with the exit poll questionnaires: response category order effects and question format.

Response Category Order Effects

As is well known by survey researchers, the format and wording of a question can significantly affect the results. After the 1992 election, Mitofsky and Edelman (1995) reported order effects for two exit poll questions that asked respondents to select from a list the issues that mattered most in their vote and the candidate qualities that mattered most. The two split-ballot experiments found a significant primacy effect in that items placed at the top of the list were chosen more often than items at the bottom (cf. Krosnick and Alwin 1987; Rasinski, Mingay, and Bradburn 1994).

As a result of the 1992 experiments, we altered the form of the questions in 1996. The 1996 issue question asked, "Which•one issue mattered most in deciding how you voted for president?" In 1992 respondents were asked, "Which one or two issues mattered most in deciding how you voted?"[16] Also, in 1996 each question had only seven response options, whereas in 1992 there were nine. Similar changes in format and wording were made to the candidate qualities question.

In 1996 we conducted a split-ballot experiment similar to that in 1992, in which the order of the response options was reversed. For the 1996 issues list, only one item, "Federal Budget Deficit," showed a meaningful difference between the forms (Table 3.10). This item was 6 percentage points higher when it was at the top of the list than when it was at the bottom of the list. The other items on this list showed a difference of 3 percentage points or less. These findings are quite different from those in 1992, which had three items with large differences of 8 percentage points or more.

The candidate qualities list showed a similar pattern between the two years. In 1996 the largest difference was on "Honest and Trustworthy" (4 percentage points), which was near the middle of the list (Table 3.11). All the other differences were 3 percentage points or less. This is in contrast to 1992, when three items showed differences of 7 percentage points or more.

What accounts for the virtual disappearance of order effects in 1996? The lists of issues are certainly different in the two years, but not different enough to account for the diminished order effects. Most of the issues are the same, with the notable difference that "Family Values" and "Abortion" are in the 1992

TABLE 3.10   RESPONSE CATEGORY ORDER EFFECTS: ISSUES QUESTION

1996 EXIT POLL
Which one issue mattered most in deciding how you voted for president?

ISSUE[a]	VERSION ONE (*N* = 4,185)	VERSION TWO (*N* = 4,203)	DIFFERENCE
Foreign policy	4	3	1
Medicare/Social Security	16	13	3
Taxes	12	10	2
Crime/Drugs	7	6	1
Economy/Jobs	20	21	−1
Education	10	13	−3
Federal budget deficit	9	15	−6

1992 EXIT POLL
Which one or two issues mattered most in deciding how you voted?

ISSUE[a]	VERSION ONE (*N* = 4,416)	VERSION TWO (*N* = 3,920)	DIFFERENCE
Health care	24	15	9
Federal budget deficit	25	17	8
Abortion	13	11	2
Education	12	13	−1
Economy/Jobs	41	44	−3
Environment	4	7	−3
Taxes	12	17	−5
Foreign policy	7	9	−2
Family values	10	20	−10

Note: The 1992 data are reprinted from Mitofsky and Edelman (1995).
   [a]Order on Version One of the questionnaire.

list but not the 1996 list. The candidate qualities lists are less comparable between the two years, but it is difficult to point to specific items that could account for the change in the magnitude of the effects from 1992 to 1996. As with the issues lists, it is difficult to come up with an explanation for the primacy effects related to the content of the qualities list.

Another explanation is that the length of the lists is shorter in 1996 than in 1992. However, during the 1992 primaries the second author (Murray Edelman) experimented with shorter lists and found order effects similar to those observed for the 1992 general election. A more likely explanation is the form of the question. In 1996, when respondents were asked to select only one response, they may have been more likely to look over the entire list before making their choice. In 1992, when respondents could select up to two responses, they may have chosen an acceptable response early on before going through the entire list,

TABLE 3.11   RESPONSE CATEGORY ORDER EFFECTS: CANDIDATE QUALITIES
QUESTION

1996 EXIT POLL
Which one candidate quality mattered most in deciding how you voted for president?

QUALITY[a]	VERSION ONE (N = 4,185)	VERSION TWO (N = 4,203)	DIFFERENCE
He shares my view of government	20	20	0
He stands up for what he believes in	14	12	2
He cares about people like me	11	8	3
He is honest and trustworthy	18	22	−4
He is in touch with the 1990s	9	11	−2
He has a vision for the future	15	16	−1

1992 EXIT POLL
Which one or two candidate qualities mattered most in deciding how you voted for president?

QUALITY[a]	VERSION ONE (N = 4,416)	VERSION TWO (N = 3,920)	DIFFERENCE
Has the right experience	22	15	7
Will bring about needed change	40	32	8
Is my party's candidate	5	5	0
Cares about people like me	14	13	1
Is honest and trustworthy	14	14	0
Has the best plan for the country	21	28	−7
Would have good judgment in a crisis	14	19	−5
His choice of vice president	7	10	−3
Has strong convictions	13	15	−2

Note: The 1992 data are reprinted from Mitofsky and Edelman (1995).
    [a]Order on Version One of the questionnaire.

knowing they still had the opportunity to select one more response. This finding suggests that self-administered questions that allow for multiple responses may be subject to larger primacy effects than those that ask respondents to select only one response.

Question Format

Another change that VNS decided to make to its questionnaires in 1996 was to stop using a question format called the "grab bag." This question asked respondents to check all that applied to them from a list of up to nine items, including Currently employed, Currently married, Someone in household belongs to a labor union, Of Hispanic descent, and Gay/lesbian/bisexual. This format is a way to measure the voting behavior of many diverse groups in a single question while saving the cost of inputting a piece of data for each item. More important, since the questionnaire is of limited size and must serve many needs, there is not the space to ask each of these questions individually.

The main problem with this question format is that because it is a long list, respondents do not always check every item that applies to them. The result, then, is an underestimate of the percentage of voters having each of these characteristics. For many years VNS had suspected that these were underestimates and cautioned users of these questions not to use them to estimate the incidence of each group but, rather, to use the data to describe how each group voted.

Results from a split-ballot experiment conducted by VNS in 1994 gave us an indication of just how different the results from the grab bag can be compared with asking a standard question. On one version of the national questionnaire, respondents were asked this question: "Do you consider yourself part of the religious right political movement?" The response categories for this question were yes and no. On the second version, this item was included as part of the grab bag. The grab bag asked, "Which of the following apply to you: (Please check all that apply)." The third item on this list was "Part of the religious right political movement." The marginal results for the two types of questions were quite different. For the grab bag question, 6 percent said they were part of the religious right, versus 19 percent for those who answered the full question.

In 1996 VNS decided to no longer use the grab bag because of the methodological limitations associated with it. Instead of using the grab bag list, VNS decided to use separate yes and no questions to ask about the items that have normally been part of the grab bag, knowing that only a few of the usual items could be used. This change reduces the measurement error in the data for 1996 and beyond. It is important to keep in mind, however, that any trend comparisons between the grab bag and the full questions are problematic. Because the grab bag tends to underestimate population values, any comparisons ignoring the change in methodology will lead to the incorrect conclusion that certain subgroups are voting in greater proportions. For example, some analysts have made a big deal of the increase in gay turnout from 2 percent in 1992 to 5 percent in 1996 (e.g., Bailey 1998). Similarly, a "big story" after the 1998 elections was the dramatic increase in turnout among voters who live in union households, from 14 percent in 1994 to 22 percent in 1998. In both of these examples, most or all of the increases can be attributed to the different question formats.

Conclusion

This chapter has discussed our efforts to understand the various types of exit poll error and to improve the accuracy of these polls. We have adopted the TSE framework, which moves beyond the common focus on sampling error to also include measurement error, nonresponse error, and coverage error. In some instances we have been able to decrease survey error by changing the methods that are used. For example, our explorations of measurement error have led to changes in how issues, qualities, and grab bag items are measured in the exit polls. When it has not been possible to make methodological changes, we have attempted to gain a better understanding of these sources of error and, thus, of the strengths and limitations of exit poll data.

One area in which exit polls have yielded unique insights is nonresponse error. With response rates declining over the years, nonresponse error has become an important concern among survey researchers in general. It is easy for critics to cite polling's relatively high nonresponse rates in their efforts to discredit polling in general or the results of a specific poll (e.g., Huffington 1998). Such an attack equates the mere existence of nonresponse with nonresponse error and assumes that surveys with higher nonresponse rates necessarily have more error. At least in the case of exit polls, this is not so. Knowing the response rate tells us nothing about the magnitude of the error in the vote estimates. Exit polls with relatively high response rates tend to be just as accurate as those with lower response rates. In the case of our experimental study, we found that our manipulation designed to increase response rates significantly increased the bias in the vote estimates.

Although nonresponse error has been and will remain a concern, a new and growing concern for exit pollsters is the increasing potential for coverage error. In the past, there was little possibility of coverage error in exit polls because very few people voted early. The rapid increase in early voting rates in some states is a relatively new phenomenon that will only continue in coming years. The challenge in this area will be to balance the significant extra costs of interviewing these voters by telephone with the benefits that are gained in terms of decreasing coverage error.

Notes

1. The Associated Press was a member of NES when it was merged with VRS in 1993. FOX joined VNS in 1996.
2. These estimates are computed by comparing the exit poll results in each precinct with the vote from that precinct as described in more detail below.
3. For ease of presentation, this section equates sampling error with the margin of error, which is calculated as the standard error multiplied by 1.96.
4. Refusal rates are computed as refusals/(completed questionnaires + refusals + misses), and miss rates are computed as misses/(completed questionnaires + refusals + misses).

5. Note, however, that although the differences between respondents and nonrespondents for gender and race are statistically significant (given the enormous sample sizes), they are not practically significant.
6. Response rates are computed as follows: completed questionnaires/(completed questionnaires + refusals + misses).
7. In presidential years the presidential race is used, and in nonpresidential years the race with the highest turnout is used.
8. We also checked for a variety of nonlinear relationships between the error measures and response rates and found none.
9. The sample size for the precinct-level correlations is 1,215.
10. The sample size for the state-level correlations is 47.
11. We decided to use this three-group experimental design instead of the more common four-group, two-by-two design because we did not see a scenario where we would use the pen incentive without the folders. Therefore, we did not see a need to have a treatment group to test this possibility, given the small sample sizes with which we were working.
12. In this section we use the term *early voting* to refer both to mailing in or dropping off an absentee ballot and to going to an early voting location prior to Election Day to cast a ballot.
13. Voter News Service hired Leitner/Braun Research to conduct the telephone surveys in Oregon, Texas, and Washington. The Field Institute conducted the survey in California. Interviews were conducted the week before the election with just over 400 voters in each state who either had already voted early or were very likely to do so.
14. Early voting in California, Oregon, and Washington is conducted by mail ballot, and in Texas voters have the option of voting at special polling locations during the three weeks before Election Day.
15. In 1992 VRS conducted telephone surveys of early voters in California and Texas, but the data from these surveys were not combined with the exit poll data in the system.
16. Note that even though "president" was not mentioned in the 1992 question, it was placed directly under the presidential vote question.

CHAPTER 4

Did Public Opinion Support the Contract with America?

Michael W. Traugott and Elizabeth C. Powers

Most of the poll-based reporting about American politics consists of stories organized around surveys that news organizations commission or conduct themselves. Sometimes, however, stories are offered to news organizations by interest groups or individuals because they believe that public consumption of the information they want disseminated will be enhanced by the credibility of an independent source such as a newspaper or network evening news show. When such stories are "shopped" around to news organizations, the availability of polling data related to the content may increase the likelihood that journalists will see the information as newsworthy and will run the story.

The danger for journalists—and ultimately for their readers and viewers—is that such stories, promoted by interest groups, are prompted by strategic goals. The sources have a policy or legislative interest they want satisfied, and they are invoking public opinion and the credibility of the media in support of these interests. Many journalists are untrained or inadequately trained to make an appropriate independent evaluation of such information when it is offered. Their gullibility or susceptibility to these influences compromises the quality of the stories they eventually produce.

An interesting example of such a strategy occurred with the Republican Party's development of the Contract with America as an organizing device for its 1994 congressional campaign. Republican officials and strategists designed the Contract as a unifying theme for the fall campaign in an attempt to nationalize their effort to gain control of the U.S. House of Representatives. At the elite level of the Republican Party, they produced a document that all their candidates could support by eliminating any controversial items that could divide Republicans, such as abortion or health care reform. When the roll out of the Contract was near, they promoted it to journalists with the claim that each of its ten "reforms" was supported by at least 60 percent of the American public. Although this claim was widely reported in the media across the entire campaign period, it was not true.

Eventually the main proponent of the claim—Frank Luntz, the Republican pollster and strategist—was censured by the American Association for Public Opinion Research (AAPOR) for a violation of its Standards for Disclosing Information about the Methodology of Public Polls because he refused to provide any supporting data to back up the claim (Morin 1997). But by then the election was long over, the Republicans had secured their first majority in the House since 1954, and the Contract with America had entered the folklore of effective winning campaign strategies.

This episode provides an interesting case study of how political strategists can take advantage of unwary and untrained journalists in order to frame a campaign by invoking public support for their agenda through (alleged or implied) polling data. In the 1994 elections, the Republican Party developed an effective strategy around a carefully crafted document that became the centerpiece of both a national advertising campaign and a series of events designed to produce news coverage favorable to its candidates. Some journalists in Washington and around the country were duped and misled by Republican strategists' claims of widespread public support, and content analysis shows that their reports of support became as central a part of reporting on the Contract as the details of the vague policy proposals it contained. After Election Day, there was extensive reporting on the role of the Contract in the campaign, the meaning of the Republicans' victory, and the nature of their mandate. Some *postelection* reporting was critical of the way public support of the Contract had been invoked (Balz 1994; Duncan 1995; Greve 1995a, 1995b). But virtually all the *preelection* reporting was based upon acceptance of the Republican claim of broad public support for the Contract.

In this chapter, we focus on available resources and appropriate techniques that political reporters could have used to validate the claims about public support for the Contract during the campaign, when it became a framing device for the news coverage. This case study is intended to raise issues about and discuss alternatives for reporting styles and practices when polling data are provided by political activists and strategists. What alternatives do reporters have for verifying their claims when potentially biased parties invoke public opinion for their cause? What standards should they use to evaluate polling information? And how should their behavior in these instances differ from what they would do in the cases of political reporting that proliferate when a partisan from one side makes a charge or claim about the other?

The Contract with America and the 1994 Elections

In summer 1994 political observers were comfortable in predicting that if the 1994 midterm elections were like any of the others during the twentieth century, the Republicans were likely to pick up seats in the U.S. House of Representatives. The incumbent president's party had lost seats in every "off year" election since the Civil War, with the exception of 1934. In August, after several primaries had determined who most of the opponents in the fall House races would be, the consensus estimate was that the Republicans would pick up 20 to 25 seats. Virtually no analysts at that time expected them to take control of the House for the first time since 1954 (Cook 1994).

Political scientists have developed models that predict off-year losses of congressional seats in the House with increasing precision (Campbell 1993). Although these models differ in some details, all models share two common elements—a measure of the president's popularity and a measure of recent changes in Americans' economic well-being. In theoretical terms, a midterm congressional election is a referendum on the incumbent president. Public opinion is a key factor in these models, represented by a measure of the president's approval rating in a summer Gallup poll. For most of 1994 Clinton's approval rating had been steadily declining, from 58 percent in January to 39 percent in August (Bowman and Ladd 1994). An aggregate-level measure of individuals' prosperity, typically the change in per capita disposable income in the second quarter of the year, is also present in all the models. In summer 1994 evaluations of the performance of the economy were improving, but they were obviously not highly correlated with the public's evaluation of Clinton's handling of his job as president.

Both sides in the campaign were aware of the historical trend in midterm elections. The Democratic Party was trying to minimize its likely losses, but the Republican Party began to develop a concerted strategy to maximize its potential gains. In a bold and unusual move, party leaders organized an attempt to nationalize the campaign against the president and his party with a strategy that much more resembled a parliamentary campaign in Europe than recent American congressional elections (Raasch and Tumulty 1994). The Contract with America became the focal point for that effort.

The Contract was a construct of political elites cast in terms of mass support—to appeal both to the public and to the journalists who would cover the campaign. It consisted of ten "common-sense reforms" the Republican Party proposed to bring to the floor of the House for a vote within the first 100 days of a newly elected Congress it controlled. When the Republican leadership met earlier in the year in Maryland, the idea for developing a positive agenda around which to organize the campaign was hatched. For much of the first two years of the Clinton administration, the Republicans had defined their role as the "loyal opposition" by consistently opposing Democratic legislative initiatives without offering any of their own. Their own research suggested that their prospects in the midterm elections would be enhanced if they could produce and promote a Republican legislative agenda.

The selection of ten items for the Contract was arbitrary and credited to Newt Gingrich, the minority leader at the time (Balz 1994). Specific items were included because they would be attractive to Republican voters, but any item such as abortion or health care reform that would divide Republicans was eliminated. Feasibility was also a criterion, so the flat tax did not make it into the Contract because the leadership did not believe it could be dealt with in the first 100 days. The Republicans started with a long list of items, and Luntz prepared a questionnaire for all Republican incumbents and most of the newly selected challengers to complete to indicate their preferences and support for specific policy issues. In the end, sixty-seven seriously considered reforms had to be reduced to ten, and language adopted that "promised" a vote on the ten issues within 100 days but not that each reform would become law within that time frame.

As part of the development of their strategy, the Republican leadership also designed an event that was likely to be newsworthy and generate coverage as well as an advertising campaign to promote the Contract to the electorate. For this "mediality" (Boorstin 1964), the Republicans decided to organize a ceremony on the steps of the Capitol, where Republican candidates would actually "sign" the Contract. This event, designed for good visuals that would be attractive to television news organizations, took place on 27 September; more than 300 Republican candidates were present. The second part of the strategy was to place an ad in *TV Guide* two weeks before the election. *Reader's Digest* was also considered as a venue, but the lead time to produce and submit the ad was shorter for *TV Guide*. The leadership also believed that the issue of *TV Guide* containing the ad would be consulted more frequently, at least in the week it was current. The content of the ad is reproduced in Figure 4.1.

The Republicans also carefully developed a roll-out strategy for the Contract. The elected leadership and party strategists participated in highlighting the Contract itself and the Capitol steps event whenever and however they could. Their goal was to maximize news coverage, and one way they accomplished this was to make key individuals available to reporters for interviews. Some columnists known to have Republican sympathies were briefed in advance so they could produce pieces that coincided with the news coverage of the signing ceremony (cf. Will 1994). Luntz (1994) himself prepared an op-ed piece for the *Wall Street Journal* for 27 September, and he participated in background briefings for reporters at various organizations in advance of the signing ceremony, most notably at a one-hour

A campaign promise is one thing. A signed contract is quite another. **That's why Republican House candidates have pledged, in writing, to vote on these 10 common-sense reforms.**

Contract with America

We've listened to your concerns, and we hear you loud and clear. On the first day of Congress, a **Republican House** will:

- Force Congress to live under the same laws as every other American
- Cut one out of every three congressional committee staffers
- Cut the congressional budget

Then, in the first 100 days, we will vote on the following bills:

1. **Balanced budget amendment and line-item veto:** It's time to force the government to live within its means and to restore accountability to the budget in Washington.
2. **Stop violent criminals:** Let's get tough with an effective, believable and timely death penalty for violent offenders. Let's also reduce crime by building more prisons, making sentences longer and putting more police on the streets.
3. **Welfare reform:** The government should encourage people to work, *not* to have children out of wedlock.
4. **Protect our kids:** We must strengthen families by giving parents greater control over education, enforcing child support payments and getting tough on child pornography.
5. **Tax cuts for families:** Let's make it easier to achieve the American Dream, save money, buy a home and send the kids to college.
6. **Strong national defense:** We need to ensure a strong national defense by restoring the essential parts of our national security funding.
7. **Raise the senior citizens' earning limit:** We can put an end to government age discrimination that discourages seniors from working if they choose.
8. **Roll back government regulations:** Let's slash regulations that strangle small businesses, and let's make it easier for people to invest in order to create jobs and increase wages.
9. **Common-sense legal reform:** We can finally stop excessive legal claims, frivolous law suits and overzealous lawyers.
10. **Congressional term limits:** Let's replace career politicians with citizen legislators. After all, politics shouldn't be a lifetime job.

After these ten bills, we'll tackle issues such as common-sense health care reform, tax rate reductions and improvements in our children's education.

FIGURE 4.1   THE CONTRACT WITH AMERICA

session with the Associated Press on 22 September (Drinkard, personal communication, 19 May 1997; Lawrence, personal communication, 19 September 1997). This was a crucial event because of the central role that wire service stories play in the production of subsequent news. Luntz told Associated Press reporters at the briefing that "each item in the Contract is supported by 60 percent of the American public; they are high priority items." This was duly reported in the main wire service story on 27 September, the day of the signing (Drinkard 1994). This quotation was then picked up in most of the succeeding coverage, and the claim was repeated by other political elites, including Gingrich.

A great deal of research obviously went into the design of the Contract, the production of the advertising, and the testing of public reactions to both. In a common procedure, Republican strategists such as Ed Goeas conducted focus groups to assess possible television ads in support of the Contract, and Luntz used focus groups to hone the *TV Guide* ad (Balz 1994). But focus groups are not representations of public opinion in the same way that surveys with probability samples of the electorate are. The clear intent of Luntz's claim to reporters that "each of the ten items on the list had registered at least 60 percent public approval in polls" was to suggest that survey data showed wide public support for each of the reforms (Drinkard 1994; Raasch and Tumulty 1994). Within the next news cycle, Newt Gingrich (Turner 1994) and local Republican candidates were citing this same level of public support for the Contract (Best 1994). Even though Luntz had not explicitly cited such support in his own *Wall Street Journal* article, he was on record affirming it in news articles the same day (Turner 1994).

Reporting on Public Opinion

News organizations gather more news than they can use in any single production cycle, and they select the actual stories that go into one of their products by applying a set of agreed-upon norms, often referred to as "criteria of newsworthiness." These involve such familiar elements as novelty, conflict, and the involvement of familiar figures. Editors and producers are also looking for stories with high impact on their audience, and they are always concerned with their factual content. Increasingly, news organizations are also interested in stories that relate to the interests of their readers and viewers. This "public journalism" movement reflects a concern about appropriate content as well as a sensitivity to declining numbers of readers and viewers.

Polls and survey results are inherently attractive to journalists because they fulfill many of the demands of newsworthiness: "They are topical, relate directly to issues in the news, are up-to-the moment" (Paletz et al. 1980). Poll results provide a ready-made snapshot of current opinion on a topic of interest. Consequently, polls on all topics have proliferated since 1972 when news organizations began to develop their own polling operations (Ladd and Benson 1992). Campaign coverage is a staple of the news business because elections involve high impact, familiar figures and willing sources on either side who want to be quoted. The increase in polls by media organizations is especially evident during election years because they can be used to track changes in the candidates' relative standings. Poll results are increasingly being used as the main topic of news stories, rather than as supporting information, because the rise of media polling operations means that news organizations often have direct control over content and a direct financial stake in the production of the information.

The use of poll results is also attractive because they provide a seemingly neutral source of information. Neutrality—or more precisely "balance"—is a concept ingrained in all journalists through formal coursework and on-the-job training. "Getting the story right" requires such techniques as consulting more than one source and using authoritative sources. Polls have become an important adjunct to standard reportorial techniques because of a sense that the data are scientifically neutral if a poll has a representative sample and good questions were asked. They also counter the unrepresentative nature of other standard reportorial techniques such as "person on the street" interviews with just a few convenient citizens or interviews with political elites such as party leaders or strategists.

Unfortunately, it is not true that all polls are neutral. In the worst case, data can easily be distorted or even manipulated by biased sample selection or question-wording procedures. More important, interest groups are increasingly aware of the newsworthiness potential of poll results, and they often try to use this to their advantage. As Paletz and his colleagues (1980, 504) note, one of the ways organizations "insinuate their views into the press, to imply public support for their objectives, is to sponsor polls which are then released to and reported in the media." But there are also inadvertent instances when media polls have reported diametrically opposed "findings" from separate polls on the same day, as an artifact of question wording. CNN/*USA Today* released results from a Gallup poll they commissioned showing Americans favored sending troops to Bosnia, based upon the following question wording:

> Now that a peace agreement has been reached by all the groups currently fighting in Bosnia, the Clinton administration plans to contribute U.S. troops to an international peace-keeping force. Do you favor or oppose that?
>
> | | |
> |---|---|
> | Favor | 46% |
> | Oppose | 40 |
> | Don't Know | 14 |

The results of the CBS News poll showed that Americans opposed troop deployment in Bosnia, based upon the following question:

Do you favor or oppose sending up to 20,000 U.S. troops to Bosnia, as part of a NATO peace-keeping force, to enforce this peace agreement between Bosnia, Serbia, and Croatia?

Favor	33%
Oppose	58
Don't Know	9

There is a subtle but useful distinction in the use of the terms *survey* and *poll*. Although polls and surveys share many common elements, they are generally commissioned by different types of organizations, and their results are used for different purposes. Both polls and surveys are methods of gathering information by asking people questions, and both usually rely on probability methods to ensure that the sample selected represents the population of interest (Traugott and Lavrakas 1999). Polls usually have a limited number of questions, and they are designed to obtain information on a topic of interest to a specific client. Polls can be conducted for a variety of reasons, from predicting the winner of an election to determining popular support for a particular public policy issue. They are usually conducted over a period of a few days. Sometimes poll results are provided to journalists as pegs for news stories; and sometimes journalists participate in the design and analysis of polls conducted for their own organization. Surveys, in contrast, often involve much longer questionnaires, designed to obtain information on a variety of topics, and they are most often used by academic researchers.

There are other forms of assembling information on what people think, usually far short of the representative methods of polls or surveys. The most common of these is to assemble focus groups, small homogeneous collections of citizens who sit together to talk about political issues of the day. Focus groups have a number of advantages for political strategists and even for news organizations (Traugott 1995). But because of their very size and the method of participant selection, they cannot be used to reflect or represent broader public opinion (Mitofsky 1998). One theory about the supporting data for the Luntz claim is that the results were based upon focus group conversations with selected individuals rather than polls with representative samples, but this issue could not be sorted out without additional information from Luntz.

Evaluating the quality of data obtained in polls and surveys presents a special problem for journalists, since formal training in interpreting these results is generally weak and inadequate. Journalists actually face two problems. First, they do not receive appropriate methodological training in journalism school or on the job that could make them good judges of the quality of survey data they see. Second, they do not receive training in alternative sources of public opinion data that can be used to conduct independent checks on the validity of such data. Despite the trends in the 1970s toward additional training in "precision journalism" (Meyer 1991), most reporters are ignorant of the resources available to help them in evaluating polls; as a result, they frequently default to the sponsor's interpretation of poll results. Changing the curriculum for the training of journalists is a long-term problem that should be addressed,[1] but there are other aids and techniques that could be employed in the short term.

Sources of Public Opinion Data

Two types of resources are readily available for journalists to use for guidance in reporting on polling data: standards from professional organizations on revealing the details about polling methods and general guides on evaluating and disseminating poll results. Both of the major professional organizations for public opinion researchers, the AAPOR and the National Council of Public Polls (NCPP), have developed standards that guide pollsters in disclosing the methodological details of a poll or survey so that consumers (including journalists) can evaluate the reliability and validity of the data being considered. These standards also allow journalists to determine if there is any systematic bias built into the polls.

There have also been several guides published (see Gawiser and Witt 1994; Traugott and Lavrakas 1999; Wilhoit and Weaver 1980; and Worcester 1987) that delineate what factors need to be considered in determining the quality of poll results. These guides help journalists analyze the content of polling data to which they are exposed and suggest how to present the material so that readers and viewers have the necessary information to evaluate the quality of the poll results being reported. Journalists must be able to identify bias in order to maintain standards of journalistic objectivity and fairness in reporting and to prevent interested parties from garnering unwarranted favorable news coverage.

Although many journalists may be familiar with sources of information about polls, almost none are familiar with sources of other data that they can use to corroborate data from the poll they are evaluating. Relatively little has been written on the topics, and those pieces that are relatively complete (Smith and Weil 1990) are based upon a publication environment rather than one in which resources are available relatively immediately on the Internet through various Web sites. This computer-based information is available from data archives, research centers, and media and polling organizations themselves. Some of these sites contain substantial holdings of American public opinion data in various forms. They provide critical information that permits journalists to make independent assessments of the reliability and validity of public opinion data collected or reported by others.

Some of the archives specialize in polls conducted by and for media organizations; others contain long-term trend data collections from academic survey organizations. This information is available in one or more of three different forms: data summaries in the form of tables and charts from individual or collections of polls or surveys; question databases that provide aggregate results (frequency distributions) from topical questions used by a variety of polling sources; and the actual computerized data files that allow users to perform their own statistical manipulations. Access to most of these sources is available on-line— through the World Wide Web and the Internet—and through subscriptions to services like Lexis-Nexis to which virtually every political reporter has access.

To verify poll results about general, long-term public policy issues, journalists have two major sources to tap into. The National Opinion Research Center (NORC) at the University of Chicago has been conducting the General Social Survey (GSS) since 1972.[2] The Center for Political Studies at the University of Michigan has been conducting a survey of the American electorate every two years since 1952, under the heading of the National Election Studies (NES). Each of these surveys employs probability sampling techniques and pays careful attention to question wording so that high-quality data are obtained in a consistent manner over time. The GSS is an "almost annual, omnibus personal interview survey of U.S. households" that first took place in 1972 (Davis and Smith 1992). The questions elicit attitudes on topics ranging from welfare to crime to satisfaction with hobbies. Nearly 600 of the questions have been repeated in several surveys to provide data on social trends and changes in attitudes. The NES offers more specialized data on voting, public opinion, and political participation, including a CD-ROM that contains all the survey data and documentation. The NES data collection includes time-series data from twenty-three biennial election studies, with a mix of repeated and new questions.[3] Although the NES provides a wealth of printed documentation for users, the material of most interest to journalists is probably the "Voter's Choice," an electronic publication on the NES Web site that includes detailed information on voter demographics by year and on other time series such as "trust in government" and "party identification."

Several centers also archive polls conducted by independent polling and media organizations. In addition to providing the raw data for analysis, these archives have created "question databases" that include information on who commissioned the poll, who conducted the poll, how the questions were worded, what method of interviewing was used (i.e., mail or telephone), and how the sample was selected. Most of these databases also include the frequency distribution or "marginals" containing the responses to each of the categories for the question, sometimes even for significant population subgroups such as gender or region.

Currently three major data archives provide such information. The largest social science data archive in the United States is located at the Inter-university Consortium for Political and Social Research at the University of Michigan (ICPSR).[4] The largest collection of polling data from commercial organizations is located at the Roper Center for Public Opinion Research at the University of Connecticut.[5] It also has the most extensive question database, available as "RPOLL" under the "CMPGN" library in Lexis-Nexis. This database is key-worded so a searcher can look for "welfare" or "welfare reform" and retrieve the distribution of opinion each time a polling organization such as CBS News and the *New York Times* or Gallup asked a question on the subject. The third location is the Institute for Research in Social Science, the archival home of the Louis Harris Data Center.[6] There are also other research centers that are developing their own Web sites and are including archives of their survey or poll results there. The best current example of such a site is that of the Pew Research Center for the People & the Press, where access to all of its surveys since 1995 can be found.[7] This site contains substantial content on contemporary public opinion and political attitudes.

Although most of these archives now have searchable databases available on the Internet, some of them are relatively new and would not have been available to journalists in 1994.[8] For our purposes, we want to look at what kinds of information a political reporter could have consulted during that congressional campaign. The central question is what sources were available to reporters so they could make an independent check on the validity of claims by Frank Luntz and other Republican leaders that "each item in the Contract is supported by 60 percent of the American public." Did reporters have to be at the mercy of Republican strategists, or could they have verified the truthfulness of this claim on their own? By extension, this examination will highlight a generally useful way that journalists can verify any claim about public opinion reported by individuals or special interest groups, especially those who might have an interest in promoting a particular version of contemporary public opinion.

Verifying Republican Claims of Public Support for the Contract with America

In order to make this a fair test of reporters' options in 1994, we analyzed only the data sources available at that time. In late summer of that year, three archival sources would have been accessible to most journalists: the Roper Center database, which was searchable through Lexis-Nexis; the GSS data at NORC through

1993; and the NES data at Michigan through 1992. Journalists could have tapped into any of these sources of public opinion data for a number of different purposes, representing a number of different story "pegs," in relation to the claims made by the Republicans in September. For example, they could have evaluated whether the Contract contained the items the American public considered important, as well as to see how much public support there was for several of the ten "reforms."

On the matter of salience or importance, pollsters frequently ask "What do you think is the most important problem facing this country today?" to get a general idea of what concerns the American public. Between 1 January 1994 and 28 September 1994, such a question was included in more than twenty-five polls.[9] In one version of the question used in some polls, the respondents were asked to indicate their preference from a specified list of problems offered to them; more often, the respondent's own free-form response to an open-ended question was recorded. Although the latter method creates a much longer list of "problems," it more appropriately reflects the range of public concerns. When the results from polls using this question are reported, they list the problems mentioned and the percentages of respondents naming that as their major concern.

In poll results from this nine-month period, the problem that was mentioned by the largest percentage of respondents was crime. In decreasing order of percentages, this was followed by health care, unemployment or other economic issues, and either drugs or moral problems and family values. A quick comparison of the list of public concerns with the list of items in the Republican Contract suggests that other than crime, the two do not share a common focus. Noting the difference between the Republicans' proposed legislative agenda and the public's sense of the most important problems facing the country might have enriched the early coverage of the Contract by revealing what later became evident—that the Contract was essentially contrived as a device to help focus public awareness on the differences between Republicans and Democrats, not necessarily to address the problems the public saw as most important.

Second, investigating these alternative data sources would also have illustrated the discrepancies in Republican leaders' claims that public support for each of the ten "reforms" was more than 60 percent. There are sound reasons why this would be the case. Many of these proposals, such as increasing defense spending, passing a balanced budget amendment, getting tough on crime, and reforming the welfare system have been a part of the national political discourse for many years. Enough time had passed for the public to have developed firmly held opinions about the issues, and information on the veracity of claims about the level of public approval for these items was readily available to journalists. But other issues were new to the public agenda, and attitudes on these issues would have been much more susceptible to the influence of such factors as question-wording effects. For some of the issues, such as term limits for members of Congress, public approval was as simple as the Contract suggests—the public was overwhelmingly in favor of term limits, and the results from several credible polls were available when the Contract was proposed. For other issues, though, available polling data would have suggested that the claim was completely unjustified or at least subject to interpretation based upon which questions were asked of what groups in the population. In the analysis that follows, selected "reforms" in the Contract that reflect these different possibilities are analyzed as illustrations of the way alternative data resources could have been used by journalists to obtain an independent check on the Republican claims.

Term Limits

In the Contract, the tenth proposed reform was "Congressional term limits: Let's replace career politicians with citizen legislators. After all, politics shouldn't be a lifetime job." This "reform" was not new. It had been supported in various forms by both parties, although the issue tended to garner more Republican than Democratic support. As recently as September 1994, Oklahoma voters had overwhelmingly passed a term-limit measure; in the 1992 election, term-limit measures were passed by voters in fourteen states; and in 1994, eight states had term-limit measures on the ballot (Barlow 1994).

To confirm that national public opinion mirrored what seemed to be universal support of term limits, journalists could have completed a quick search of the Roper database in Lexis-Nexis. Using the key words "term limits," a search would have revealed four questions from three studies released between July 1994 and September 1994 that contained questions relating to term limits. These questions were not worded exactly the same, as the length of term limits suggested varied. Despite the variations, in all four polls the proportion of respondents indicating that they favored term limits was well over 60 percent; in two of the polls, respondents saying they "strongly favored" or "favored" term limits for members of Congress was greater than 80 percent. So in this case, an independent check would have revealed that the Republican claim was justified.

Increasing Defense Spending

The eighth proposed "reform," which had been part of the public discourse for several decades, was "Strong national defense: We need to ensure a strong national defense by restoring the essential parts of our national security funding." The issue of spending on the military, a true "position" issue, had been one of the areas that ideologically separated Republicans and Democrats for many years. Because defense spending was a recurring issue, both the NES and the GSS asked questions about this topic during several different survey periods. By using the key terms "military" and "defense," a journalist would have found that both the GSS and the NES yielded trend data on public opinion on this topic. Although the phrasing of the questions in the NES and the GSS differs somewhat, responses to questions in both studies suggested that increased military spending did not enjoy the 60 percent support claimed by Republican leaders.

In the NES, respondents are asked to use a seven-point scale ranging from 1 ("greatly decrease") to 7 ("greatly increase") to indicate their own feelings about defense spending in response to the statement:

> Some people believe that we should spend much less money for defense. Others feel that defense spending should be greatly increased. Where would you place yourself on this scale, or haven't you thought much about this?

Since 1980, the percentage of individuals selecting a 5, 6, or 7 on this scale ranged between 17 and 61, with a clear trend reflecting declining support for increased spending. In 1994, during the congressional campaigns, the proportion of the sample giving these responses was 25 percent. These results are presented in Figure 4.2. Although the GSS words the questions a little differently and offers a different scale with response alternatives such as "too much money," "too little money," or "about the right amount," the results were similar. In 1994 only 16 percent said we were spending "too little" on "the military, armaments and defense," whereas 33 percent said we were spending "too much." Almost half

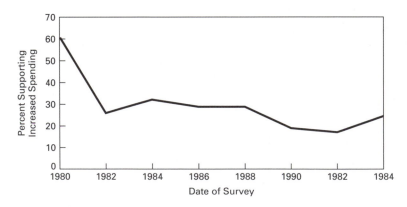

FIGURE 4.2 NES RESULTS ON DEFENSE SPENDING

of the respondents (47 percent) indicated they thought we were spending "about the right amount." Neither of these time series suggests that a majority of Americans supported increased funding for defense, never mind "at least 60 percent" as the Republicans suggested.

Welfare Reform

Although the American public does generally seem to support changes in welfare benefits, the reaction to concrete proposals for resolving these problems varies greatly. The effects of alternative question wording are evident in response to questions concerning particular policy measures for welfare reform. For instance, an April 1994 poll asked, "Would you oppose replacing the current welfare system with a completely new system to help poor people get off welfare, if that new system would cost the government more money in the next few years than the current system?" Sixty-eight percent of the respondents answered favorably. But when asked in the same Gallup poll conducted for *Time* and CNN, "Which of the following statements comes closer to your view? . . . The welfare system is fundamentally flawed and should be replaced with a completely new system. The welfare system may have problems which need to be fixed, but it should not be completely replaced," respondents overwhelming favored fixing the system (63 percent) as opposed to replacing it (36 percent). The high percentage approving replacement of the system in the first question could have been related to the implication that the replacement system would help recipients get off welfare rolls.

In May, Yankelovich and partners conducted an extensive survey of public attitudes toward the welfare system for *Time* and CNN. Overall, there was support for changes in the welfare system, including a significant majority (81 percent) who believed that the welfare system needed "fundamental" reform as opposed to only "minor" reform. These views are difficult to interpret, however, because when the questioning turned to specific proposals to replace the current system, three out of four respondents (74 percent) expressed support for a system that would "replace welfare with a system of guaranteed public jobs." Some policy analysts would argue about whether such a jobs program would not constitute a welfare system, at least in part. At the same time, a narrow majority of respondents (51percent compared to 42 percent) opposed "End increases in welfare payments to women who give birth to children while on welfare," a proposal essentially embodied in the third "reform" in the Contract. The point of these examples is to illustrate how complex the public's views about the welfare system are and the degree to which the measurements and the reporting of opinion reflect the specifics of the question asked. In this area, it was not clear that a majority of Americans supported all modes of welfare reform and penalizing mothers and their children.

Crime

For other elements of the Contract with America, such as addressing the problems of crime, public opinion is much more complex than the Contract "reform" suggests. The Contract proposed, "Stop violent criminals: Let's get tough with an effective, believable and timely death penalty for violent offenders. Let's also reduce crime by building more prisons, making sentences longer, and putting more police on the streets." This one reform really proposes several different ways to reduce violent crime, and each could be investigated independently in the same way, by looking at general opinions about the crime rate in the United States through queries of the GSS for indications of general public opinion about crime and of the RPOLL database in Lexis-Nexis for poll results that indicate opinions about specific proposals for dealing with criminals, violent or otherwise.

A number of sources provide information in the form of various questions that tap into general opinions about crime. These include measures of the salience of crime and the concerns that Americans have about it. This could be done through analysis of continuing mentions of crime as one of the "most important problems" facing the United States in the Gallup polls. In addition, several questions in the GSS provide an indication of how important Americans consider the crime issue to be. For example, more than 70 percent of the 1993 respondents agreed that "we're spending too little money on . . . 'halting the rising crime rate.' " These general indicators, however, do not translate into support for the specific proposals in the Contract.

Conclusion

The Republicans' development and implementation of the Contract with America was a very successful organizing strategy for their 1994 congressional campaigns, in part the result of their ability to persuade reporters that their "reforms" were widely supported by the American public. Although in large part true for some of the items, it was not true that "at least 60 percent of the American public" supported every one of their ten "reforms." After the election, while developing stories about how the new Republican majority could fulfill its obligations in the Contract, some journalists evaluated it more critically than they had during the campaign (Balz 1994; Duncan 1995; Greve 1995a). But meanwhile, the Republican Party had captured control of the House.

The purpose of this chapter has not been to draw attention to the specious claims about public support for the Contract. Rather, it has been to suggest ways that journalists who report on public opinion can make independent checks on claims about public support for policies. Competing claims are most likely to arise during campaigns, but they can also appear during heated policy dispute during a congressional session. Reporters do not have to rely upon different sources to supply them with quotations about alternative impressions or opinions about public opinion; there are several different ways that they can verify claims about public opinion by consulting a variety of computer-readable public opinion resources. They can do this by subject, as well as in terms of the most recent readings of opinion or by looking at a time series of repeated questions on a particular topic. These procedures involve no additional cost or access to resources any computer-literate journalist does not already have or could not master in a very short time.

In the end, using computerized data resources to verify facts is just a more modern form of applying the basic skills that successful journalists acquire during their early training. Especially when a partisan or special interest group invokes public support on its side, a prudent journalist would be wise to see whether other poll data are available on the same topic and what they indicate. This is the best way to contextualize current information in past measurements, to assess the potential impact of question wordings or order on the measure of interest, and to see whether opinions vary by significant subgroups in the population. This will produce more informed stories and reduce the likelihood of misrepresenting public opinion to a mass audience.

Notes

1. Elements of the journalism curriculum change continuously to accommodate technological developments, especially ways that computers can be applied to reporting. Most of this instruction involves enhanced search techniques across a wider range of sources than might otherwise be available (for example, see McGuire et al. 1997). But this is not the equivalent of training in a data collection methodology like survey research or polling.
2. The National Opinion Research Center (NORC) is located at the University of Chicago, 1155 East 60th Street, Chicago, IL 60637. Its telephone number is (773) 753–7500, and it has a Web page at http://www.norc.uchicago.edu. Information on the General Social Survey (GSS) is available through NORC (which conducts the survey), the Roper Center, and the Inter-university Consortium for Political and Social Research (ICPSR). The ICPSR also offers an on-line searchable question database for the GSS through their Web page http://www.icpsr.umich.edu.htm.
3. The National Election Studies is located in the Center for Political Studies at the University of Michigan, P.O. Box 1248, Ann Arbor, MI 48106–1248. Its telephone number is (313) 764–5494, and it has a Web page at http://www.umich.edu/~nes/.
4. The ICPSR is located at The University of Michigan, Institute for Social Research, P.O. Box 1248, Ann Arbor, MI 48106–1248. Its telephone number is (313) 764–8041, and it has a Web page at http://www.icpsr.umich.edu.htm. The ICPSR publishes an annual catalog that is also available in computer-read-

able form that covers the entire range of its archival holdings. In addition, it publishes a quarterly bulletin that describes newly released and updated ICPSR data holdings. Much of this information is also available through its Web site.

5. The Roper Center for Public Opinion Research can be contacted at P.O. Box 440, Storrs, CT 06268. Its telephone number is (860) 486–4440, and it has a Web page at http://www.ropercenter.uconn.edu. The Roper Center publishes a bimonthly magazine, *The Public Perspective*, that offers data on recent poll findings as well as articles and essays on public opinion topics and issues. The Roper Center also maintains POLL, the Public Opinion Location Library, a question database that is available directly from the Roper Center or through subscription services such as Lexis-Nexis (as RPOLL) and Dialog (as file 468).

6. The Institute for Research in Social Science, at the University of North Carolina at Chapel Hill, can be contacted at Manning Hall 026/CB#3355, Chapel Hill, NC, 27599. Its telephone number is (919) 962–4777, and it has a Web site at http://www.unc.edu/depts/irss/welcome.htm.

7. The Pew Research Center for The People & The Press can be contacted at 1150 18th Street, NW, Suite 975, Washington, DC 20036. Its telephone number is (202) 293–3126, and it has a Web site at http://www.people-press.org/.

8. The University of Kansas Department of Communication Studies maintains a World Wide Web listing of on-line survey research and public opinion centers. It ranks the sites from one to four stars, based on information content. The site also offers links to sites of related interest and is updated regularly. This makes it a good place to check for new data sources. Its Web site is located at http://www.ukans.edu/cwis/units/coms2/po/index.htm.

9. A query submitted through RPOLL in Lexis-Nexis for the period from 1 January to 28 September 1994 yielded more than 25 polls that had asked a close variation of this question. In almost all cases, the question wording was exactly the same. The question was asked more than once through this time period by different polling organizations that included Gallup, ABC News/*Washington Post*, the Wirthlin Group, Princeton Survey Research Associates, CBS News/*New York Times* and the *Los Angeles Times*, providing a rich record of what the American public thought were the most important problems facing the country.

PART II

Trends in Reporting on Election Polls

CHAPTER 5

Hidden Value: Polls and Public Journalism

Philip Meyer and Deborah Potter

To many who followed the way news media cover national election campaigns, the need for a course correction had been evident for some time. Coverage of the 1988 contest between George Bush and Michael Dukakis was a low point. Thoughtful news people decided that journalism was failing to connect the political elites—which by then included many journalists—to the public. Political reporting had degenerated into an insider's game of posturing and image manipulation in which citizens were excluded and their important concerns ignored.

The potential consequences for the democratic process were disturbing. A public indifferent to political campaigns would have little incentive to learn much about the issues, and even less to participate in elections. When a small minority of eligible voters actually chooses the nation's government, its legitimacy is threatened.

This concern was reinforced by critics from all sides of the news profession, including such important leaders as editor Davis "Buzz" Merritt (1995) of the *Wichita Eagle*; David Broder (1991), reporter and columnist for the *Washington Post*; the late James K. Batten (1989), chairman and CEO of Knight-Ridder; and Professor Jay Rosen (1994) of New York University.

A number of foundations, including the Pew Charitable Trusts and the Kettering Foundation, heard these complaints and began financing media experiments and symposia to try to repair the broken connection between citizens and leaders. These efforts were based on the common conviction among journalists that democracy in America depends on an informed public, and that a key function of the news media is to "facilitate the public discourse necessary to make the system work" (Miller 1994).

The foundations involved gave various names to what they were doing, most frequently "public journalism" and "civic journalism." (Most of the time, the two terms are interchangeable. To avoid choosing sides, we use the term *citizen-based journalism* in our research.) None defined the mission very clearly. A definition, Jay Rosen argued, would place limits on their efforts when what was more important was to try lots of different things to see what worked. "Public journalism," he said, "is what you find out when you try to do it."[1] The only consistent theme was that journalists should accept the responsibility for creating a good connection between policymakers and citizens, with the goal of making public life go well.

Traditional journalistic practice was a barrier to this approach. Broder noted that reporters and campaign consultants alike had always disclaimed any concern for the consequences of elections. The consultants' job was to get their candidates elected, and the journalists' job was to report the details of the process. Neither was supposed to care about what happened afterward. This detachment on the part of journalists allowed candidates to conceal their intentions on controversial issues and left voters in the dark about the possible consequences of their choices. If the public perceived that candidates were no more different than Tweedle-dum and Tweedle-dee, then voting for either one was a worthless exercise.

If reporters spent more time with voters, said Broder, "we would have clearly in our heads what the voters' concerns are. Then it might be possible to let their agenda drive our agenda for covering the campaign."

Public opinion research was involved in this effort in several ways for various reasons:

1. Polls, as Dr. George Gallup (1972) liked to argue, offer a continuing referendum that keeps public officials in touch with the views of citizens. So journalists sought to use polls in new ways to determine a voters' agenda and improve that referendum function.

2. Certain kinds of polls were viewed as part of the problem by public journalism advocates. Polls that focus on candidate standings might distract voters from substantive issues and make election campaigns too much like a spectator sport, dampening the public's interest in participating in the process. Some media managers used that rationale for cutting back on the use of candidate-standing or "horse-race" polls in 1996.[2]

3. Public journalism advocates expressed the hope that their efforts might increase political knowledge, trust in government, trust in people, and political participation.

These are factors that can be measured by survey research, so polls became a tool for evaluating the results of public journalism.

Covering Campaign '96

One of the more ambitious efforts to cover the 1996 presidential campaign took place in North Carolina, where more than a dozen news organizations—print and broadcast, commercial and public[3]—formed an unusual alliance. The project, called "Your Voice, Your Vote," was based on the principles of public or civic journalism and was designed to "let citizens, not the candidates, establish the issues in the campaigns."[4]

To do that, the partners paid for two statewide polls—one in January, before the spring primary, and the other in July. The polls' focus was exclusively on issues, to determine the priorities of North Carolina citizens. The January poll, for example, did not ask respondents about party affiliation, voter registration, or candidate support or recognition. Leaving that information out meant that stories based on the poll could not explore how partisanship affected the way voters ranked the issues or how their views of the issues were reflected in their choice of a candidate.

But editors said that first poll was designed to discover what issues mattered to all North Carolina voters. "We wanted to make sure we knew what was on people's minds," said Steve Riley, then state government editor at the *News & Observer* in Raleigh. "We gave them a little piece of the agenda" (Ready 1996). In retrospect, Riley said, "We were trying so hard to be non-traditional, we probably threw out some things we could have used" (personal interview, 8 April 1998).

Based on the results of those polls, the partners conducted lengthy, joint interviews with candidates in the two major statewide races that year—U.S. Senate and governor. They then wrote in-depth stories about issues that North Carolina residents identified as "very important." In the fall, the four issues selected were crime and drugs, taxes and spending, affordable health care, and education. Editors chose not to focus on four other issues that ranked almost as high in the survey: families and values, personal financial security, race relations, and the environment.

Stories written about the poll results, and grids indicating the candidates' positions on the issues, were published simultaneously in all six newspapers involved in the project. The stories ran over six Sundays before the primary and four Sundays before the November election. Television and radio coverage was timed to coincide with the print coverage.

The North Carolina media partners also worked together to sponsor candidate forums. Each partner independently produced additional coverage that amounted to a majority of its campaign content. But the existence of the alliance and its issues-oriented philosophy affected the tone of campaign coverage across North Carolina. The overall result? "Fewer reports on candidates' stump speeches and fewer standard polls," according to the *News & Observer*.

Newspapers in other parts of the United States made some ambitious solo efforts. Perhaps the paper that tried the hardest to do the most was the *Record* in Bergen County, New Jersey. From Labor Day through Election Day, the paper devoted a full page to citizen-based campaign coverage six days a week[5] under the heading "Campaign Central." There was plenty to write about. In addition to the presidential and congressional races, the state was holding its first election for U.S. Senate without an incumbent in fourteen years.

The stories on the "Campaign Central" page were selected based on public journalism criteria. These stories emphasized issues rather than campaign strategy; they gave voice to the concerns of citizens; they provided detailed information about the candidates; and they provided opportunities for citizens to participate in the campaign (Blomquist and Zukin 1997).

To determine which issues were most important to New Jersey voters, editors used the *Record* poll, which found that the top six issues in 1996 were job security, crime, education, programs for the elderly, welfare, and the environment. The *Record* explored the candidates' positions on those issues, among others, on the "Campaign Central" page. The newspaper's editorial board identified other issues for in-depth coverage, including immigration, IRS reform, and the future of the federal judiciary.

Unlike other public journalism efforts, the *Record*'s commitment did not extend to all of its campaign coverage. The paper continued to run more conventional "horse-race" stories about campaign strategy or candidate appearances elsewhere in the paper—sometimes on the front page or on the page next to "Campaign Central." This decision was based on the belief of *Record* editors "that they would be censoring the news to leave legitimate information about the campaign out of the paper solely because it did not conform to the public journalism model" (Blomquist and Zukin 1997, 29).

Both the North Carolina and Bergen County efforts were evaluated with survey research. The Pew Center for Civic Journalism sponsored a statewide telephone poll of registered voters in North Carolina, immediately after the election.[6] According to the survey, one in four voters was aware of the project, and those voters were more likely than others to feel better informed than in previous elections and to say they made voting decisions based on the candidates' positions on the issues ("Your Voice" 1996). But of the 25 percent who were aware of the project, only about half remembered "Your Voice, Your Vote" without being prompted. Twelve percent had to be prompted before they recognized the name of the project, barely above the noise level for name recognition in North Carolina, where 10 percent will say they recognize the name of a fictitious candidate.[7]

In Bergen County, a more sophisticated evaluation compared readers of the *Record* to readers of other newspapers before and after the election. With funding from the Pew Center for Civic Journalism, the newspaper designed a research project in which two telephone surveys of a random statewide sample, one before Labor Day and one after the election, were supplemented by four focus groups. The results indicate that the *Record*'s experiment had no substantial impact.

According to researchers David Blomquist and Cliff Zukin (1997), *Record* readers were no more interested in the campaign and no better informed than readers of other newspapers. They were not more likely to vote than other New Jersey residents, and they did not have more positive attitudes toward their newspaper.

"The experimental and control groups were the same prior to the election and were the same at the end of it," said Blomquist and Zukin (1997, 25). "Those exposed to the *Record* are not statistically different from those who read some other newspaper."

Why? The Pew Center report suggests that the *Record*'s public journalism effort was drowned out by negative advertising and mudslinging by candidates in what turned out to be an exceptionally nasty Senate campaign. But it also concedes that the impact of "Campaign Central" may have been blunted by the newspaper's decision to continue running more traditional campaign stories alongside its public journalism coverage: "Because the horse-race approach has dominated campaign coverage for so long, it may be that even modest amounts of it are enough to blind citizens to a change in focus," Blomquist and Zukin (1997, 29) said.

The fact that media effects do not constitute a "magic bullet" that is powerful, immediate, and universal has been known to public opinion researchers since the pioneering study by Paul Lazersfeld and his associates in Erie County, Ohio, in the presidential election campaign of 1940 (Lowery and DeFleur 1995, 69–92). Media do have effects, but they tend to be slow and selective.

Buzz Merritt, the founding editor of the public journalism movement, recognizes this. He is fond of quoting a Wichita friend, Balbir Mathur, head of a nonprofit organization that fights world hunger by planting trees. Mathur believes that meaningful cultural change must come slowly. "If this is important change," he told Merritt, "if it's really fundamental and you've only been at it for three or four years and you think you're seeing progress, then you're not asking all the right questions, and you're not looking in all the right places" (Merritt 1998, xi).

Evaluating the Coverage

Our own efforts at evaluation looked in many places at once. Rather than relying on a single-market case study, we made comparisons across twenty markets for the 1996 election (see Table 5.1).[8] We used an operational definition of citizen-based journalism that was based on specific media behaviors.

Our sample markets were selected to show variance. We wanted examples

TABLE 5.1 SAMPLE MARKETS

MARKET	NEWSPAPER	CIRCULATION	HOME-COUNTY PENETRATION
Atlanta, GA	*Atlanta Constitution*	308,000	25.6
Austin, TX	*American-Statesman*	181,000	44.7
Birmingham, AL	*Birmingham News*	168,000	15.1
Boston, MA	*Boston Globe*	471,000	30.2
Charlotte, NC	*Observer*	236,000	54.5
Chicago, IL	*Sun-Times*	496,000	21.5
Columbia, SC	*The State*	122,000	46.9
Des Moines, IA	*Register*	170,000	54.3
Grand Rapids, MI	*Grand Rapids Press*	139,000	54.5
Houston, TX	*Chronicle*	545,000	30.7
Little Rock, AR	*Democrat Gazette*	172,000	51.9
Minneapolis, MN	*Star Tribune*	394,000	48.8
New Orleans, LA	*Times Picayune*	260,000	50.9
Norfolk, VA	*Virginian-Pilot*	202,000	48.4
Portland, ME	*Press Herald*	75,000	50.0
Portland, OR	*Oregonian*	339,000	48.0
Raleigh, NC	*News & Observer*	151,000	42.9
Richmond, VA	*Times-Dispatch*	209,000	33.9
Rockford, IL	*Register Star*	74,000	54.9
Wichita, KS	*Wichita Eagle*	92,000	46.2

Source: Audit Bureau of Circulation, Circulation Data Bank, October 1996.

of both traditional and experimental coverage. Therefore we chose some newspapers because we expected them to be doing public journalism, based on their history, public statements by their managers, and their affiliation with nonprofit groups that were encouraging experimentation. We chose other papers for exactly the opposite reason—they had expressed no interest in doing things differently.

We developed the definition of citizen-based journalism by making a list of practices associated with that approach, mixing them with more traditional practices, and asking a sample of working newspeople in our twenty markets which ones they planned to apply in their coverage of the 1996 presidential and senatorial elections.

Names for our mail survey were obtained by calling each organization to obtain the names of five people who would be doing the most work on campaign coverage.[9] Each person received up to four mailings: a questionnaire, followed by a postcard reminder, then a second questionnaire to nonrespondents. It closed with a third questionnaire sent by certified mail to those who failed to respond to the earlier mailings.[10]

By looking at the pattern of these responses, we identified a list of seven practices that were so closely related as to define a single concept. They became our operational definition of citizen-based journalism:

1. Sponsor one or more public forums on issues

2. Use polls to establish the issues your coverage will focus on

3. Conduct focus groups with voters to establish their concerns

4. Form citizen panels to consult at different stages of the campaign

5. Seek questions from readers and viewers for use when interviewing candidates

6. Base reporting largely on issues developed through citizen contact

7. Provide information to help citizens become involved in the political process in ways other than voting

Respondents rated each practice on a 3-point scale on which 3 indicated belief that their organizations were "very likely" to do it, 2 meant that it hadn't been decided, and 1 indicated low likelihood of doing it. We obtained the averages within each organization and used them to construct a simple additive index of intent to practice citizen-based journalism. The average newspaper score was 2.23.[11] Table 5.2 shows the rankings of the twenty markets when only newspapers are considered.

TABLE 5.2   INDEX OF INTENT TO PRACTICE CITIZEN-BASED JOURNALISM

MARKET	CITIZEN-BASED RANK
Charlotte	3.00
Norfolk	2.89
Portland, OR	2.72
Portland, ME	2.71
Wichita	2.69
Minneapolis	2.66
Boston	2.64
Rockford	2.62
Raleigh	2.51
Columbia	2.37
Chicago	2.31
Des Moines	2.18
Richmond	2.14
Atlanta	2.03
Austin	1.93
Birmingham	1.79
New Orleans	1.71
Houston	1.44
Little Rock	1.20
Grand Rapids	1.00

The papers that fell into the top 10 in our survey in intent all had a history of concern with citizen-based reporting or community programs. Most of them have been associated in one way or another with nonprofit organizations that promote civic or public journalism.[12] Several have been involved in election-coverage partnerships with other media,[13] and some are owned by newspaper groups with a history of promoting community involvement.[14]

Aside from their history, the citizen-based newspapers were not substantially different from the other papers we studied based on two objective measures. The top 10 papers had slightly less circulation on average and higher home-county penetration, but these differences were too small to be significant.[15] Neither circulation nor home-county penetration had any predictive value.

Many of these citizen-based newspapers conducted high-profile efforts in 1996, often using survey research, to base their coverage on issues that mattered to their readers. The two North Carolina papers were part of "Your Voice, Your Vote." The *Minneapolis Star Tribune* conducted a statewide "deliberative poll" to establish citizens' concerns. The *Boston Globe* polled one representative community in New Hampshire as part of its "The People's Voice" project. The *Portland Press Herald* used a similar approach in a small town in Maine. The presence of these newspapers among the most citizen-based on our scale lends external validity to our measurement.

The remainder of our data collection consisted of these steps:

- A telephone survey of at least 50 citizens in each of the 20 markets[16]
- Content analysis of campaign coverage in a sample of 10 issues of each newspaper[17]
- A postelection telephone survey of citizens in each market[18]
- A follow-up mail survey of the journalists who had first been contacted in June[19]

In looking for effects of citizen-based journalism, we were guided by what its various practitioners and their academic supporters say are its possible benefits. In their view, citizen-based journalism results in more in-depth reporting on issues and creates better-informed citizens. So we established the following variables and hypotheses.

Political Knowledge. Citizens in counties with higher intent to practice citizen-based journalism (CBJ counties) should learn more about candidate's specific issue positions in the course of the campaign.

Trust in Media. Cynicism toward media should be less in the higher CBJ counties.

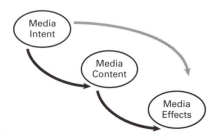

FIGURE 5.1   MODEL IMPLICIT IN THE DATA COLLECTION STRATEGY

Trust in Government. Trust might be greater in the high-CBJ counties—unless the drive toward greater citizen involvement is motivated by mistrust of government.

Social Capital. A long-term goal of citizen-based journalism is to improve community participation, which in turn requires a culture of reciprocal trust. So we might find greater social capital in the high-CBJ counties.

Participation. An effort to involve citizens in the election should lead to improved voter turnout in high-CBJ counties and more participation of other kinds, such as discussing the election with friends.

The model implicit in this data collection strategy is shown in Figure 5.1. Media intention is the first cause, and it leads to variations in content. These variations in content lead to variations in citizen attitudes and behavior. The three arrows show where we expect to find correlations. The strongest correlations should occur where the effects are most direct—along the shorter paths indicated by the darker arrows. We have the luxury of separating cause from effect because of the panel survey design (Figure 5.2).

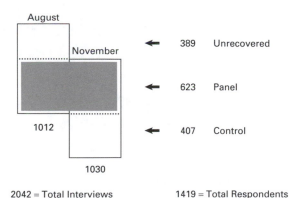

FIGURE 5.2   CITIZEN SURVEY

Effects on Content

The first question is whether the differences in intent discovered in our survey of media staff persons resulted in differences in content. Our pilot study in the Florida primary indicated that all eight newspapers contained similar coverage despite differing intentions. In the fall, however, the CBJ-intending newspapers had content that was visibly different in two important ways:

> *Newspapers with a high intent to practice citizen-based journalism had more stories that were mainly devoted to explanation of specific policy issues.*
> *And they had fewer stories containing any mention of horse-race polls.*

The *Portland Oregonian* had the most issue coverage, with 19 percent of its stories in the sampled newspapers devoted mainly to explaining issues. It was followed by the *Wichita Eagle* (18 percent) and the *Portland Press Herald, Charlotte Observer, Columbia State, Norfolk Virginian-Pilot* (all at 17 percent). At the other end of the spectrum, the *Little Rock Democrat Gazette* had the least issue coverage (3.5 percent). Figure 5.3 shows how issue content tends to increase with intent to do citizen-based journalism.[20]

Similarly, intent to do citizen-based journalism accurately predicts a low rate of stories referring to horse-race polls. The *Raleigh News & Observer* and *Charlotte Observer* had the fewest stories with any mention of poll results (11 percent), followed by *Portland Oregonian* (12 percent), and the *Wichita Eagle* (16 percent). At the other end of the scale, the *Grand Rapids Press* had the most stories mentioning horse-race polls (40 percent). Figure 5.4 shows how poll content tends to decrease with intent to do citizen-based journalism.[21]

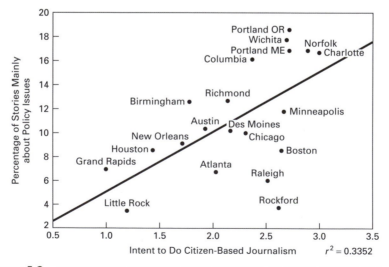

FIGURE 5.3   NEWSPAPERS THAT FOLLOWED THROUGH ON THEIR INTENTIONS

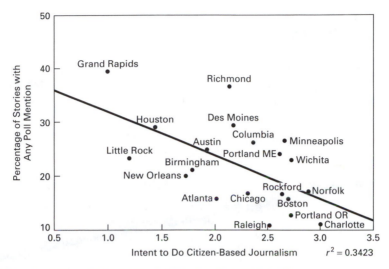

FIGURE 5.4   POLL MENTIONS IN CITIZEN-BASED JOURNALISM

These are not entirely overlapping effects because when we combine the high-issue and low-poll phenomena into a single variable,[22] we obtain even more powerful prediction (Figure 5.5).

What all this means is that the movement to change the way the media cover national elections was a real, behavior-modifying event and not just an

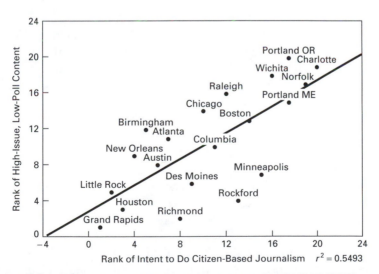

FIGURE 5.5   INTENT TO DO CITIZEN-BASED JOURNALISM BY HIGH-ISSUE, LOW-POLL CONTENT

empty resolution. Newspapers that promised reform actually delivered—downplaying horse-race polls and beefing up coverage of issues.

But they did not make some changes that might have been expected based on the theory of citizen-based journalism. A theoretical framework that puts citizens' interests ahead of those of candidates suggests that media should spend less time on conflict-oriented stories and on the strategic and tactical maneuverings of politicians. Although our twenty counties did vary on these dimensions, the variation was not related to their intent to practice citizen-based journalism.

Effects on Citizens

The next question was whether the difference in intent, which we found reflected in newspaper content, made any significant difference in the attitudes and behaviors of citizens. The design of the citizen survey is shown in Figure 5.2. For some analysis, we will rely on the 623 who were interviewed twice—the panel survey. In other cases, we will look at a cross-section at a single point in time to take advantage of the larger number of respondents.

Political Knowledge

Citizens in the ten markets that were high in intent to do citizen-based journalism learned more in the course of the campaign than citizens in the low-CBJ markets.

In August, the two groups had about the same knowledge of candidate issue positions. We asked respondents to volunteer answers to three questions: "Which candidate wanted a $1,500 tuition tax credit for middle-class Americans?" (Clinton), "Which candidate supported a balanced budget amendment to the Constitution?" (Dole), and "Which candidate wanted more restrictions on the purchase of firearms?" (Clinton).

In August, 20 percent of the citizens in the low-CBJ counties answered all three questions correctly, as did 21 percent of those in the high counties—statistically no difference at all.

Over the course of the campaign, both groups showed an increase in knowledge, but those in the high-CBJ counties gained more. By the November survey, 24 percent of those in low-CBJ counties had all the right answers, compared to 31 percent in the high counties. In other words, those whose media practiced citizen-based journalism gained 10 points, whereas their peers elsewhere gained only 4.

These comparisons are based on the full August and November samples. The fact that 623 were interviewed both times tends to suppress the differences in knowledge. That's because most of those interviewed in November had heard the questions before and were more likely to have thought about them and paid attention when the candidates discussed their stands on those issues. That tended to reduce the overall variance between the two groups, giving citizens in the low-CBJ counties a chance to get up to speed.

To eliminate that potential effect, we looked at the control portion of the November sample who had not heard the questions before. In November, we asked the same three August questions plus two new ones: "Which candidate proposed the antidrug slogan 'Just don't do it'?" (Dole) and "Do you happen to know if the polls called the presidential race correctly?" (yes). In the control group, the difference between the high-CBJ ten and the low ten is striking. Twice as many in the high-CBJ counties got all the answers right—21 percent versus 11 percent.

Because of a sampling fluke, the members of the November control sample in the high-CBJ markets were slightly better educated than those in the low-CBJ portion. So we sought to validate the CBJ advantage by controlling for differences in age and education and shifting to the market level for analysis. First, we ran a regression procedure with age and education predicting political knowledge as measured by the five-item November question. The regression residuals—which represent each person's knowledge after the effects of age and education are accounted for—were saved and aggregated to the market level. We plotted this adjusted measure of knowledge against the level of CBJ intent in the twenty counties (Figure 5.6).[23] In the plot, you can see the usual public journalism

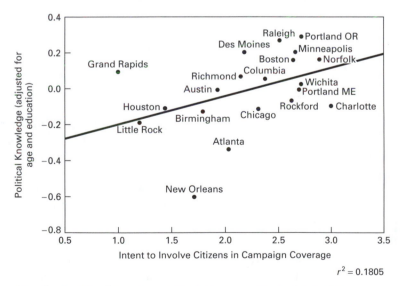

$r^2 = 0.1805$

FIGURE 5.6 **CITIZENS' POLITICAL KNOWLEDGE SCORES IN CBJ CITIES**

newspapers—including Portland, Oregon, Raleigh, Boston, and Norfolk in the high-knowledge upper-right-hand corner.

Our survey therefore supports those editors who believe that their techniques will improve voter knowledge. However, it contradicts the assumption that horse-race polls distract voters from the substance of the election and keep them from learning about the issues.

We tested this belief by comparing the gain in issue knowledge of people whose awareness of polls was high with those who had not followed the polls. We measured awareness of polls in August by asking people if they knew who was ahead (Clinton) and by how much (15 points, plus or minus 5). The poll-savvy people knew more about issues. Of those who answered both questions right in August, 40 percent answered all the issue questions right in November—compared to only 15 percent of those who knew nothing about the poll standings.

Of course, those poll-savvy people probably knew more and were more interested to begin with. So we used the portion of our sample that had been interviewed twice in order to control for prior issue knowledge as well as education. For good measure, we added another control: respondents' attention to the campaign based on their November self-reports. The multiple regression model revealed that even after the effects of education, attention, and prior knowledge were accounted for, awareness of the polls in August had a positive and significant effect on knowledge in November. For each 1-point increase in August poll knowledge, November issue knowledge went up by 0.175 points. Horse-race polls, by providing context for and arousing interest in the campaign, appear to help voters focus on the candidate issue positions (Meyer and Potter 1997).

Trust in Media

Citizens in the high-CBJ counties were less mistrustful of the media than those in low-CBJ counties.

Most of the people in our twenty-city sample are cynical toward their news media. We found this out by asking two questions (the percentages are based on the November survey):

Would you say the news media are run by a few big interests looking out for themselves or that they are run for the benefit of all the people? (A few big interests: 62 percent)

I'm going to mention some people or things that could be blamed for the way the political process works. I'd like you to tell me how much blame each of the following deserves: a lot, a little, or none at all. . . . How about the media? (A lot: 58 percent)

Combining these two questions by giving 1 point for each nontrusting answer, however, we found that citizens in the ten high-CBJ counties had the least mistrust, by 1.1 to 1.3 on the 0–2 scale. (If that seems small, think of it as 110 to 130 on a scale that goes to 200. The difference is statistically significant.) However, this difference was not the result of anything that happened during the general election campaign. The high-CBJ counties enjoyed the same lead in August, before the campaign began.

Two possible explanations are that

1. The high-CBJ counties have more citizens in the demographic groups that are likely to trust the media (e.g., older people, the better educated, and whites).

2. Media in the high-CBJ counties did not begin paying attention to citizen concerns with their coverage of the 1996 general election. Instead, their prior and ongoing attention to citizen involvement was a cause of their decision to practice citizen-based journalism in 1996.

We tested these hypotheses by ruling out their alternatives. Up to now, except for the special case of the November control sample, we have not been concerned about controlling for demographic differences. We have this luxury because we have been looking at the before-and-after comparisons of the 623-member panel. Each person is his or her own control as we look at differences between their answers in August and what they told us in November. But now we are interested in a phenomenon that does not change with time, and so we have to look at a cross-section of a single point in time. Now demographic differences can confound us.

The first step is to see if there are differences. We chose the November sample because it is more recent and might have campaign-created effects. We found that the ten high-CBJ markets were different in some respects from the ten low markets:

1. The high markets were slightly, but not significantly, better educated: Forty-five percent were college graduates, compared to 41 percent in the low markets.[24]

2. High-CBJ markets were a little bit younger. Twenty-two percent were 54 or older, compared to 27 percent in the low markets. The difference was not significant.[25]

3. Fewer nonwhites live in the high markets. The high ten were 82 percent white compared to 73 percent in the low ten. This is not a trivial difference and must be considered in any cross-sectional analysis.[26]

4. The high markets had weaker political party affiliation. Thirty-one percent identified themselves as independents, significantly more than the
25 percent in the low markets.[27]

So the high- and low-CBJ markets are different, but the differences do not
bias the sample in a uniform direction. Even so, we prefer to adjust for them.
Using the panel portion of the sample, we tested separately for mistrust in media
in both August and November using multiple regression to control for the effects
of education, age, and race. If demographic differences are the source of the CBJ
advantage, it should disappear with the introduction of these controls. It did
not. The effect of citizen-based journalism was statistically significant each time.
For each 1-point increase in the CBJ intent scale (the seven items mentioned earlier), media mistrust declined by 0.11 to 0.13 points (on the 0–2 scale).

As a further check, we added political party affiliation to the list of control
variables and used the entire November sample of 1,030. Media mistrust was
higher among nonwhites, older people, and Republicans. With all these factors
held constant, there remained a small effect for the CBJ level of the market.
Media mistrust declined by a tenth of a point on the 2-point scale for each 1-
point increase in CBJ intent. To see how this works at the market level, see
Figure 5.7.[28] Media bashing declines as citizen-based journalism increases, even
after the effects of party, age, race, and education have been filtered out. In the

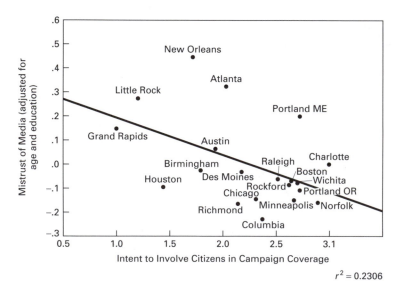

$r^2 = 0.2306$

FIGURE 5.7   LEVEL OF CITIZEN MISTRUST OF CBJ NEWSPAPERS

lower-right-hand corner, representing low mistrust and high citizen-based journalism, are the familiar names.

This connection is so important that it is worth remembering a key point that distinguishes this research from a single-snapshot survey. The variables that are correlated here come from two separate surveys of two separate populations: media workers on the one hand (the June intent survey) and citizens in the counties that they serve (the August-November panel surveys) on the other. Correlations in single-snapshot surveys are often redundant expressions of the same underlying variable. For example, people who report hearing of a CBJ effort and also report their personal approval of a news medium might, in each case, be expressing a preexisting friendly attitude or even an immediate desire to please the interviewer. This cannot be the case here because our key variables, media intentions and mistrust of media, are collected from different sources and by different methods.

Political Cynicism

Citizens in the high-CBJ markets were marginally less cynical than those in the low markets.

The theory of citizen-based journalism holds that greater attention to citizen concerns by the media can contribute to making "public life go well," as Buzz Merritt (1995) has argued. We found a trace of such an effect at the national level in the 1996 campaign. (Percentages are based on the full November sample.)

We measured political cynicism with these questions:

Would you say the government is pretty much run by a few big interests looking out for themselves or that it is run for the benefit of all the people? (Few big interests: 66 percent).

How much of the time do you think you can trust the government in Washington to do what is right—just about always, most of the time, only some of the time, or never? (Only some of the time or never: 72 percent)

Our additive scale awarded one point for the cynical answer in each case. Nonwhites, older citizens, and the less educated were the most cynical when the August poll was taken. These groups were still the most cynical at the end of the campaign, and they had been joined in their dour outlook by a fourth faction: Republicans. Forty-two percent of the self-described strong Republicans were in the high-cynicism group after the election, compared to 36 percent before.

The level of intent by the local media to practice citizen-based journalism had no effect in August and a small effect—in the expected direction with modest statistical significance—in November.[29]

Social Capital

Citizens in the high-CBJ counties had more trust in others—social capital—than those in the low counties, both before and after the election.

One often-expressed objective of citizen-based journalism is to increase the store of social capital, or the ability of members of a community to trust one another enough to engage in cooperative behavior. Why would we expect it to change in a political campaign? We really don't, but if the high-CBJ markets are doing things differently because of basically different and long-lasting attitudes toward a newspaper's role in the community, then they might have more social capital to begin with.

A straightforward measure of social capital is the standard battery of trust-in-people items that have been a staple of social science research for fifty years (percentages are based on the full November sample):

Generally, speaking, would you say that most people can be trusted or that you can't be too careful in dealing with people? (Can be trusted: 52 percent)

Would you say that most people try to be helpful or that they are mostly just looking out for themselves? (Try to be helpful: 65 percent)

Do you think most people would try to take advantage of you if they got a chance, or would they try to be fair? (Try to be fair: 68 percent)

Awarding 1 point for each trusting answer gives us a social capital scale with a range from zero to 3. Our panel was significantly more trusting after the election than before, but this was not because of anything that happened during the campaign or the way it was covered. Virtually all of the shift is explained by the reinterview effect. The November control sample gave answers much more like those of the August panel respondents than those of the November panel respondents. As people thought about these questions in the intervening three months, they expressed more trust.

Nevertheless, as in the case of trust in media, the high-CBJ counties had the most-trusting citizens—in August and November. In August, 32 percent of the citizens in the low-CBJ counties gave the most-trusting answers, compared to 44 percent in the high-CBJ counties. After the election, both groups grew in trust: to 39 percent in the low counties and 54 percent in the high counties.

Again, because the high and low counties have some differences in demographics, we need to use multiple regression to compare them on a level playing field. In August, we find significant or near-significant effects from education (better-educated people are more trusting), age (older folks trust more), and race (nonwhites are less trusting). With all these held constant, there is no additional effect from the presence of media with intent to do citizen-based journalism. All of what we thought we saw in the crosstabs was caused by background variables.

In November, after the election, with the same demographics held constant, we do find significantly more trust in the high-CBJ counties.[30]

What do our findings mean? Our tentative interpretation is that the effect of citizen-based journalism on social capital is potentially important and needs to be verified with further research.

Political Participation

There was no difference at all in political participation between citizens in the high-CBJ counties and those in the low counties.

In theory, citizen-based journalism should increase the rate of voter turnout and other forms of political participation. We found no such effects.

Participation was measured by asking citizens how closely they followed the presidential campaign, whether they tried to convince other people to vote a certain way, whether they attended political meetings, whether they had political discussions with friends, and whether they themselves voted. None of these had any visible relationship to the intent of their local media to practice citizen-based journalism.

Thus all the effects found thus far have been inside the citizens' heads. Citizen-based journalism has moved their attitudes but not their feet. In a more closely contested presidential election, this outcome might have been different.

Effect in Newsrooms

Journalists at high-CBJ papers spent more time planning and discussing their coverage, and they were more satisfied with the outcome.

Coverage plans in high-CBJ newsrooms were the result of significantly more advance planning and discussion than in the low markets. On a scale of 1 to 4 where 4 was "a lot" of preelection discussion and 3 was "some," the high-CBJ markets averaged 3.83, whereas the low markets were at 3.46 (see Figure 5.8).

Newspeople in the markets where citizen-based journalism was practiced generally gave themselves slightly higher marks for their campaign coverage than those in the traditional markets: an average of 4 on a 5-point scale compared to 3.8 for the traditionalists. The difference fell short of statistical significance.[31]

Asked to list the elements in their newspaper's best campaign story of the year, the CBJ journalists overwhelmingly chose issue explanation first (84 percent) and cited citizen voices as a close second (77 percent). Journalists at the more traditional papers scattered their choices widely, citing issue explanation the most (59 percent) and also mentioning citizen voices, campaign finance, and citizen proposals (48 percent each). When they were asked what elements should have been added to make their best story an ideal story, the traditional journalists most often selected "citizen voices" (33 percent). Few of the CBJ journalists were able to mention elements that would have improved their favorite story.

Asked how coverage should change in the next election, the traditional and CBJ groups expressed similar priorities. The CBJ people called for more stories explaining candidate proposals (averaging 7.5 on a 10-point scale) first and stories explaining all sides of the issues second. More "explainers" was the first choice of the traditional newspeople; their second choice was more monitoring of campaign contributions. Both groups voted for fewer stories based on horse-race polls.

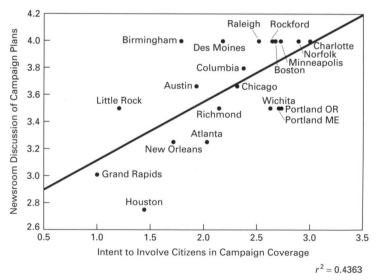

$r^2 = 0.4363$

FIGURE 5.8   AMOUNT OF NEWSROOM DISCUSSION ABOUT HOW TO COVER THE 1996 ELECTIONS

The two groups were well aware of the differences in their approaches. As a final means of validating the reality of citizen-based journalism as something that is new and different, we asked the newspeople to choose from a list of labels describing their approach to campaign coverage. The traditional journalists overwhelmingly selected "traditional journalism." The high-CBJ people, with equal clarity, chose "civic journalism" or "public journalism." There was no clear preference for one or the other of those two terms.

Effects of Content

When we designed this study, we expected to find that a newspaper's intentions would be reflected in its content, and we expected that content would have an effect on attitudes and behaviors. If our graphic model shown in Figure 5.1 is correct, we should find our strongest correlations between those variables that are closest together. That is, the link between intent and content and the link between content and attitudes should both be stronger than the link between intent and attitudes.

The first part of that supposition is true. The highest correlation link in this study is between intent and the high-issue, low-poll index of content. The correlation coefficient is .73, meaning that the intent measured in our initial survey explains more than half the variance in that combined measure of content.

But the second part is not true. Newspaper content explains hardly any of the attitude differences we found. To find any correlation at all, we had to separate the high-issue, low-poll index because its elements tend to work at cross-purposes. Having lots of issue stories does help people learn about the campaign, but depriving them of poll data can have the opposite effect by reducing their interest in the campaign.

When we looked at issue content alone, we found it had no effect at all on trust in government, social capital, or citizens' knowledge of the issues. Issue content did have a small but significant effect on just one variable: trust in media. With the usual demographics held constant, the more issue stories in the newspaper, the more the audience trusted the newspaper. This effect was marginally greater in November than in August. A mechanism for creating this effect is difficult to imagine. If a direct effect existed, we should find issue content increasing citizens' issue knowledge. But we don't. It seems likely to us that the effect is indirect; that papers with more issue stories are doing other things that relate to trust, and the issue count is only an intermediate variable.

In sum, election content as we measured it has very little to do with the effects that were so clear when we connected media intent to citizen attitudes. We will try to explain why in the following summary.

Summary and Conclusions

What ends up inside a citizen's head after an election campaign is related to what the media serving that citizen are trying to do. We found a connection between media intent and

1. Knowledge about candidate stands on issues
2. Trust in the media
3. Social capital
4. Trust in government

But we did not see a direct connection between the change in those variables and the content of the newspapers during the campaign. In other words, the causal path does not go clearly and consistently from intent through content as specified in the model. The prime cause of attitude change is evidently not media intent to cover the 1996 campaign in a certain way but something that has come before, something as yet undefined and undetected (at least by us). This antecedent appears to be causing both the media intent that we measured and the subsequent citizen effects.

This explanation fits with what we know about many of the news organizations we studied. The newspapers that expressed intent to do citizen-based journalism in June 1996 did not get the idea at just that minute. Either they were doing it already or something in their organizational culture made them ready for the citizen-based approach, and that something might already have had an effect on the community.

The fact that trust in media is higher in those counties in both the August and the November segments of our panel survey supports this notion. This prior cause may have made the high-CBJ counties more sensitive to the differences that existed in campaign coverage and thus may explain the August-to-November shifts that suggest the effects of citizen-based journalism in the campaign.

It is also possible that the communities themselves had certain qualities that provided fertile ground for citizen-based journalism to flourish. Yet the high-CBJ counties vary widely by location and population. The group includes both Portland, Oregon, and Portland, Maine, as well as Wichita and Minneapolis. Some of these cities are prosperous and growing rapidly; others are stable or even declining. It could be that despite their differences, these communities share a "civic culture" that distinguishes them from other American cities and that could have influenced the newspapers serving these communities to attempt a particular innovation.

It seems to us that citizen-based journalism involves a basic cultural change that affects both content and a newspaper's relationship to its community in ways we have not yet learned how to conceptualize, much less measure. The idea offers a fertile field for further research.[32]

The Theory and Practice of Public Journalism

The theoreticians who helped launch public journalism had a simple but ambitious goal: to save democracy by reconnecting citizens to public life (Rosen 1996). For practitioners, the question has been how to reach that goal. Many of them have tried similar steps, particularly in covering election campaigns, and our research shows they have had results. But in shifting the focus so heavily to citizens and away from candidates, critical information has been lost, and before the next election we recommend some fine-tuning.

The way many journalists tried to practice citizen-based journalism in the 1996 election campaign reflects a view of the democratic process that we think is flawed. It includes the following elements:

1. The majority is always right, and an elected representative should be obedient to the public's will.
2. Conflict is a destructive part of the democratic process.
3. Treating politics as a game makes it confusing and uninteresting.

If the majority is always right, then polls are most useful as referenda that can establish where the majority stands. But the referendum model has limitations. Polls rarely reveal concerns that have not already been widely discussed in the news media, and issue polls share the drawbacks of other types of surveys. They do not distinguish between considered judgment and superficial opinion, and they provide only a snapshot of what people think at a particular time.

Presenting poll results as a reflection of the majority's will and therefore as a guide for governance also overlooks a fundamental point. Democracy relies on representation instead of referenda for a very good reason. Voters want conflicting things. They want candidates who will give them more services and lower taxes. They seek a strong defense but prefer to avoid military service. They like the idea of less crime but want to spend less to fight it. A referendum cannot sort out all the conflicts; that is the job of representative government, with the executive and legislative branches negotiating and approving policies, and the judicial branch refereeing disagreements. Forcing candidates to commit to all their policy positions in advance, even if it could be done, would hinder the give-and-take that leads to resolution and compromise.

Conflict resolution is what representative democracy is about. The process is messy, uncertain, and dependent on the ability of people with different interests to understand one another and to base adjustments on that understanding. The traditional news convention of focusing on the most inflammatory statements of the most extreme participants in discussion works against that process by concealing the more moderate views of the meaningful majority. Coverage of civil rights in the 1960s and abortion rights in the 1990s fell into this trap and elevated advocates of violence to a far more visible level than was justified by their numbers.

Public journalism rightly seeks to break that convention and focus more attention on the rational middle, but in doing so it should not underplay conflict. Reporting of conflict has to be the first step in resolving it. The second step is getting different factions to understand one another.

The theory of public journalism as expressed by Merritt (1995) and Rosen (1994, 1996) and their intellectual predecessors like Jürgen Habermas requires news media to help different subgroups of the population to understand one another, and that can be done with polls that concentrate on subsets of the population—not concentrating on what the majority of voters want so much as on what could potentially unite different portions of the population. The better application of polls in public journalism is not in more referenda but in promoting discussion among groups.

Several CBJ newsrooms did this in 1996, sponsoring "deliberative" polls, which brought a representative sample of the population together to consider problems and solutions. The goal was to mimic the effectiveness of a New England town meeting, where people showed up not just to make their views known but to hear the view of others and perhaps adjust their own accordingly.

That same dynamic can apply with regard to horse-race polls. If voters know the relative standing of each candidate, they may change their minds about whom to support. This presumed "bandwagon" effect has long been a criticism of preelection polls. But providing information that changes minds is the function of democratic media. A rational voter should take into account what others, particularly others with shared interests, believe in forming his or her own beliefs. Rather than eliminate so-called horse-race polls, news organizations should make them more useful by showing how candidates' support rises and falls among competing subsets of the population.

Journalists have traditionally overemphasized campaign strategies and tactics, in part because of their fascination with the professionals who devise such tactics. But to ignore the posturing and maneuvering altogether, as some public journalism advocates would do, is also a mistake. If a candidate buys air time to attack gay rights because he knows that the same elderly voters who fear his stand on Medicare are also homophobic, shouldn't the public know that he is trying to build a wedge issue? Elections are a process not merely of referendum, but of coalition formation. And a citizen being invited into a coalition ought to be told the nature of it—if not by the candidate, then by the media.

Our twenty-market survey did not show consistently less coverage of conflict, tactics, or strategies among the high-CBJ papers, but in some individual cases editors did downplay these campaign coverage staples. In North Carolina, the two "Your Voice, Your Vote" papers in our sample, the *Charlotte Observer* and the *Raleigh News & Observer*, were below the median in their coverage of tactics, and the *Wichita Eagle* was particularly low.

Journalists in many public journalism projects appear to believe that what's needed to reconnect citizens to public life is more information. As David Blomquist of the *Bergen Record* put it, "If you hit the mule over the head with a big enough two-by-four, you can have results in the short run."[33] The Bergen project filled 54 full pages over nine weeks and used sophisticated graphics to tease readers into those pages, but it was all to no avail. Toward the end of the campaign, editors watching focus groups called to evaluate this massive effort were "stunned and somewhat shaken," according to Blomquist and Zukin: "In all three groups containing *Record* readers, it was clear that respondents were unfamiliar with the section, even after several sample pages were passed around the room. The frames through which respondents viewed the campaigns seemed to have been shaped mostly by the candidates' commercials. What little news coverage respondents remembered was largely an afterthought" (Blomquist and Zukin 1997, 9).

The New Jersey results validate what Daniel Yankelovich (1991) pointed out in a seminal work that inspired much of public journalism ideology: that the public can give its full attention—enough to go through the process of working through conflict and coming to a stable judgment—to no more than two or three issues at a time. A project that floods more information on many more issues into an already saturated environment appears doomed to have little meaningful impact.

Decades ago, publisher John S. Knight admonished his employees: "There is no excuse for a newspaper to be dull."[34] By turning so sharply away from the portrayal of politics as a spectator sport, many well-meaning practitioners of citizen-based journalism may have succeeded only in finding an excuse to be dull. The process of coalition formation, of give-and-take to reach compromises, of finding ways to get things done, is a wonderful, and in the end wholesome, spectator sport despite its messiness and frequent violations of fair play. Practitioners of citizen-based journalism should at least consider the possibility that avoidance of the game model contributes to dullness.

Some practitioners recognize as much. Tom Warhover, an editor at the *Norfolk Virginian-Pilot*, said his paper's decision in the early 1990s to stop using polls produced "pretty dull copy. . . . We moved too far to the citizen agenda and cut out the candidates." In 1996, his paper replaced the horse-race metaphor for election coverage with a job-search metaphor.[35] Voters were asked to imagine that they were interviewing people who wanted to work for them—an image that preserved the competitive aspect of the game model.

The excesses David Broder complained about in his 1991 Riverside lecture were real. His prescription was not nearly as radical as some of the responses, however. All he wanted was to "change the focus of our coverage. Moving away from our fascination with those political insiders and getting much closer to the voters would represent to me at least the possibility of a healthy change." That need is hardly controversial. The problem is finding the best way to do it.

Recommendations

Based on our research and that of others working in this field, we believe that polling can contribute to better election campaigns. We suggest five guiding principles:

1. *Keep the horse-race polls.* But do not make them the center of coverage. Do them frequently enough so that too much attention is not focused on any one poll. Resist the temptation to make headline news out of polls whose results are statistically insignificant. Keep poll results in the background like a scoreboard. Use tracking polls only for what they are, a limited measure of the campaign's shifting dynamics. And track trends among subgroups whose support is being contested, such as minorities, women, and old people.

2. *Deemphasize the referendum model.* Too often, polls as referenda are presented as though, by showing where the majority stands, they end the argument and nothing more needs to be said. Polls can be made more useful if they are done consistently over time to show the stability or lack of it in the majority view as conditions and opinions change.

3. *Concentrate on special populations.* In the 1960s national polls by *Newsweek* and local polls by Knight Newspapers illuminated the different factions of the civil rights movement for the benefit of both whites and blacks. Deliberative polling during the 1996 election helped to identify where citizens could find common ground. Helping citizens of different views understand one another is a generally underutilized application of polling.

4. *Do not use polls as a substitute for news judgment.* If the public can keep only two and one-half issues in mind at any given time, choosing the ones to emphasize is too important to be left to a poll. Knowing the public's current preoccupation can be helpful in deciding what to cover, and so issue polls remain a useful tool, but other factors that have not yet seeped into public awareness might be more important.

5. *Do not limit issue coverage to the election campaign.* Given the accompanying information overload, an election campaign is a bad time to help the public focus on anything except the contest itself. Accept that, and extend issue coverage beyond the election cycle, using polls to measure how opinions change. Improving the quality of public opinion should be a continuing preoccupation of the news media.

Notes

1. Remarks at AEJMC annual meeting, Chicago, 1 August 1997.
2. For example, Rolfe Neill, *Charlotte Observer*, op-ed, 1 December 1996; Al Hunt, on "Media Today," a Freedom Forum program, 14 March 1996.
3. The partners were the *Asheville Citizen-Times*, the *Charlotte Observer*, the *Fayetteville Observer-Times*, the *News & Observer* (Raleigh), the *News & Record* (Greensboro), the *Morning Star* (Wilmington), WBTV-TV (Charlotte), WGHP-TV (High Point), WLOS-TV (Asheville), WTVD-TV (Durham), WWAY-TV (Wilmington), and public television and public radio.
4. Memo from Rick Thames, public editor, the *Charlotte Observer*, to media partners, 1 February 1996.
5. The page did not run on Saturdays.
6. The poll, by Frederick Schneiders Research of Washington, D.C., was conducted 11–13 November 1996. Six hundred registered voters across North Carolina were contacted by telephone. The margin of error was +/– 4%.
7. In spring 1982, Carolina Poll, from the University of North Carolina at Chapel Hill School of Journalism, measured name recognition among 10 persons considered possible candidates for governor in 1984. To estimate the baseline noise level, "Philip Brown," a fictitious name, was included. Ten percent of the voting age sample reported recognizing the name. The data are archived at the Institute for Social Science Research in Chapel Hill.
8. Seeking to minimize possible confounding variables, we chose markets only in states with an election for the U.S. Senate in 1996.
9. In print newsrooms, surveys were sent to the managing editor, political editor, city editor, chief political reporter, and a second political reporter. We also surveyed television newsrooms, contacting the news director, assignment manager, evening news producer, chief political reporter, and a second political reporter.
10. The response rate was 69.5%.

11. Newspapers were much more intent on practicing citizen-based journalism than were TV stations. Also, there was much more variation among the newspapers, with some high and some low in intent. The broadcasters were more uniformly low. For that reason, and because the TV content data take much longer to code and analyze, this report is limited to newspapers.

12. Newspapers in Minneapolis, Charlotte, Wichita, Norfolk, and the two Portlands have worked with the Project on Public Life and the Press, supported by the American Press Institute and the Kettering Foundation. Boston, Wichita, Charlotte, Raleigh, Portland (ME), Norfolk, and Boston have received support from either the Pew Charitable Trusts or the newer Pew Center for Civic Journalism.

13. Papers in Boston, Minneapolis, and the two Portlands worked in partnership with local TV stations to do citizen-based election coverage. Both Charlotte and Raleigh were part of the "Your Voice, Your Vote" partnership in North Carolina in 1996.

14. Newspapers in Charlotte, Wichita, and Columbia are part of the Knight-Ridder group, which has promoted community involvement since 1989, and the Rockland paper is owned by Gannett, whose Year 2000 program emphasizes community involvement.

15. Mean circulation in the top 10 was 215,500 compared to 264,900 for the bottom 10. Mean penetration for the top 10 was 47% compared to 38% for the bottom 10.

16. From 1–11 August our field contractor (FGI of Chapel Hill) collected 1,012 interviews in the home counties of each newspaper as listed in *Editor & Publisher.*

17. Issues were collected in each market on random days in the seven-week period before the election. A total of 2,110 election stories were identified and coded.

18. The survey, 6–17 November, recontacted a minimum of 30 people in each market and a fresh sample of 407, as a control for interviewing effects, for a total of 1,030 interviews.

19. This survey was executed in a seven-week period starting 25 November and had a response rate of 65%.

20. CBJ intent explains 34% of the variation in issue content.

21. Again, CBJ intent explains 34% of the variation in issue content.

22. We subtracted the percentage of stories with poll mentions from the percentage of stories that are mainly about issues. CBJ intent explains 53% of the variation in the combined high-issue, low-poll indicator.

23. In the straight-line model, CBJ intent as measured in June explains a statistically significant 18% of the variance in the November knowledge level ($r = .43$, $n = 20$, one-tailed $p = .03$).

24. $x^2 = 5.7$, $df = 3$, $p = .13$

25. $x^2 = 3.5$, $df = 3$, $p = .32$

26. $x^2 = 12.8$, $df = 1$, $p = .0003$

27. $x^2 = 5.0$, $df = 1$, $p = .03$

28. The vertical scale is the residual variance in media mistrust.

29. The probability of its being attributable to chance was .045, and the conventional standard is .05 (one-tailed test).

30. The one-tailed significance was .027.

31. The twenty newspapers are given equal weight in this analysis regardless of the number of staff members who responded.
32. The only apparent alternative to this hypothesis is that our content analysis was faulty. Perhaps we measured the wrong things—or measured the right things in the wrong way. In the hope of eventually finding out, we are preserving the data collected for the newspaper content analysis by converting all of the newspaper campaign stories in our sample to a machine-readable database that will open up possibilities for additional analysis.
33. Remarks at AEJMC annual meeting, Chicago, 31 July 1997.
34. Quoted in memo from Lee Hills to new employees of the *Miami Herald*, 1962. Cited from memory (first author).
35. Remarks to AEJMC, Chicago, 1 August 1997.

CHAPTER 6

Mixing Literary Journalism and Precision Journalism in the Coverage of the 1996 Presidential Election

Gerald M. Kosicki and Paul J. Lavrakas

This chapter describes a unique year-long collaboration in 1996 among a journalist, the news organization for which he worked, the *New York Times*, and two academically based public opinion researchers.[1] This effort involved a literary journalist's learning how to incorporate the types of quantitative information that comes from public opinion survey research, such as preelection polls, into his highly qualitative approach to reporting on public opinion. The project also focused on how social scientists can better serve reporters in both gathering newsworthy quantitative data and conducting sophisticated, yet news-relevant, analyses with these data. Although much has been written about the virtues of so-called precision journalism (cf. Meyer 1991), there are relatively few detailed examples of its deployment. Thus, this chapter serves to illustrate how survey research can further a reporter's news agenda in ways beyond mere reporting of frequencies and crosstabs. Furthermore, in explaining this effort, we will be discussing several important trends in journalism and political reporting, and making suggestions for the improved use of polling by the news media.

The Origin of the 1996 "An American Place" Reporting Project

In 1995, a *New York Times* reporter, Michael Winerip, became interested in doing an in-depth reporting assignment on the 1996 presidential election. His previous experience with the *Times* was primarily as a local reporter, and he had written a local column for some years. One of his professional successes had been to work on a long series of stories about the establishment of a neighborhood group home for mentally ill people in Glen Cove, New York. In the Glen Cove project, Winerip spent two years at the group home on a daily basis, with full access to staff meetings and individuals. In so doing, he became very involved with the daily lives of the people about whom he was reporting. The results of this project appeared in 1994 in a very successful book published by Pantheon Books titled *9 Highland Road*, named after the address of the group home. In this book, Winerip mentioned 150 persons and relied extensively on the techniques of literary journalism—such as quotations and personal observations to tell the background and details of an important story. It is a very up-close and personal style of reporting, and he showed himself to be a master of it.

In 1995 Winerip lobbied his editors at the *Times* for a chance to turn his literary journalism techniques to the 1996 political year. Eventually, his request was approved. The idea was that Winerip was to pick a local "bellwether" community somewhere in the United States and use that as a vantage point to report about broad political and social themes related to the 1996 election. This plan called for Winerip to move himself and his wife and four children from their Long Island home to this area and become immersed in the community for one year, from 1 January to 31 December 1996.

To pick a community, Winerip studied voting records and a variety of other data, narrowing his interests to the Midwest. In fall 1995, he talked to a number of academicians, including the two of us, about Illinois, Michigan, and Ohio. At that time Lavrakas was a professor of communication studies at Northwestern University and director of the Northwestern University Survey Lab.[2] Lavrakas was preparing to move from Northwestern University to Ohio State University and was quite interested in discussing the possibilities of Ohio for the project. Winerip eventually found Kosicki, an associate professor of journalism at Ohio State University, who has a background in both journalism and social sciences and grew up in the Northeast Ohio area, and the two talked about the goals for the kind of journalism Winerip wanted to do. They talked several times, and eventually Winerip narrowed the choices to Springfield, Dayton, or Canton, Ohio.

In November, Winerip spent a day in each city and eventually chose Canton (in Stark County) on the basis of a demographic profile for the surrounding county that closely matched the nation as a whole. The community's voting record in national elections, which was consistent with national trends, sealed his decision. Winerip arrived in Canton on 2 January 1996.

In choosing Canton for an in-depth, year-long look, Winerip was preparing to make a particular argument: Canton is a political and economic bellwether for the nation. This judgment was based in part on an analysis of thirty years of results in presidential elections in which Stark County voted as the nation every time except one, the Carter-Ford race in 1976. In addition, the Stark County area seemed to be similar to the country as a whole in general demographics, as available from the U.S. Census, and in political leanings. Although he was unaware of it, Winerip was following in the footsteps of Lazarsfeld, Berelson, and Gaudet (1944), who studied Sandusky, Ohio, in the 1940 presidential election for similar reasons, arguing that the area was a microcosm of the United States:

> The survey was done in Erie County, Ohio, located on Lake Erie
> between Cleveland and Toledo. This county was chosen because it was
> small enough to permit close supervision of the interviewers, because it
> was relatively free from sectional peculiarities, because it was not domi-
> nated by any large urban center although it did furnish an opportunity to
> compare rural political opinion with opinion in a small urban center, and
> because for every fourth year—in every presidential election in the twen-
> tieth century—it had deviated very little from the national voting trends.
> Because of the diversity of American life, there is no such thing as a "typ-
> ical American county." But it is not unlikely that Erie County was as rep-
> resentative of the northern and western sections of the country as any
> similarly small area could be. (p. 3)

From another perspective, the journalist Jonathan Schell, best known for his literary journalism efforts published in book form—*The Time of Illusion*, about the Watergate affair, and *The Fate of the Earth*, about the environmental effects of nuclear war—attempted something in journalistic terms similar to what Winerip had in mind: an in-depth study of ordinary people making sense of the political world. Schell's book on the 1984 presidential election, *History in Sherman Park*, must certainly be seen as an intellectual forerunner of Winerip's effort, for Winerip was somewhat familiar with it at the start of his project (M. Winerip, personal communication, 16 February 1996). *History in Sherman Park*, which originally appeared in the *New Yorker*, was Schell's attempt to understand the 1984 Reagan-Mondale election campaign in a detailed way, this time by study-ing a few families in Milwaukee:

> I wanted to go to some particular place in America where . . . some indi-
> vidual voters were making up their minds whom to vote for as they went
> about the business of their lives. And having put myself there, I wanted
> to look back at the campaigns and their interpreters—and to reflect on
> what was going on. I knew that on the basis of my talks with these
> people I could not make political generalizations of the kind that political
> polls allow, but I wanted to find out things that a poll could not reveal.

Instead of finding out a little about a lot of votes, I wanted to find out everything I could about a handful of votes. (Schell 1987, 3–4)

Journalistically, Canton "felt right" to Winerip. Based on his firsthand observations, he believed that for his purposes Dayton was "too large" and Springfield was "too small." Stark County felt just right to him. As he wrote in the *Times* in his first story, 13 February 1996: "Stark County is a large enough place to watch important national dramas play out and small enough to peek backstage and eyeball the players" (p. 1). In making such a judgment, Winerip was in good historical company. Other sources of inspiration to the literary journalist involved the Middletown books by Robert Staughton Lynd and Helen Merrell Lynd (1929, 1937), as well as *Hometown*, by Peter Davis (1982).

What especially attracted us to participating in Winerip's project was his willingness to supplement his traditional qualitative journalistic approaches to characterizing public opinion with quantitative information that preelection polling could yield. In agreeing to have us work with him to provide survey data on Stark County residents' opinions, Winerip knew he was taking a big risk: What if his findings and conclusions from his own news-gathering techniques as a literary journalist were not supported by the survey results?

After moving to Canton, Winerip set up a home office in his rented house and plunged into his work. He met dozens of people a day, ranging from church and school leaders to CEOs of large corporations, on the one hand, and homeless people in shelters, hangers-on at the bus station, and so on, on the other. He visited public meetings of all kinds, of labor unions, community groups, and PTAs, to develop a sense of the community. Literary journalism techniques require a great deal of impressionistic evidence, which is gathered from individual people in particular contexts; using this evidence is decidedly inductive, trying to draw larger conclusions about trends from interactions with individuals. Winerip's goal was to tell stories of national interest and importance by looking at local people and events in Stark County. This was done, whenever possible, by seeing how national political events played out in the Canton area.

The Canton Job Training Partnership: An Example of Traditional Literary Journalism

During March 1996, the Congress in Washington was fighting an epic battle over federal spending, with House Speaker Newt Gingrich and other Republican House leaders trying to cut spending on job training by 30 percent. In Canton, the local congressman, Ralph Regula, was generally credited with creating Stark Technical College and had long been a strong supporter of such technical training. Ohio Governor George Voinovich had recognized Canton's program for training young people for jobs in chicken-processing plants, and both Ohio senators, one Republican and one Democrat, had just voted to maintain current spending levels for job training, which had been advocated by the Clinton administration. Winerip interviewed Dr. John McGrath, president of Stark Technical College, as well as John Sciury, president of the Greater Canton AFL-CIO Council, and several dislocated workers who were retrained by the local Job Training Partnership in a five-month program for computerized-machine operators.

By telling the stories of the local workers, Winerip explained the value of the training partnership program and how it was preparing workers who were laid off from high-paying jobs to reenter the manufacturing workforce at rates of pay well above minimum wage. He also told the story of how Republicans such as Regula decided to break with Gingrich and the House Republicans in support of local job training programs. As Regula noted: "The press has tended to treat the House freshmen as a monolithic group, but that may get a lot less so as the election gets closer. . . . A lot of freshmen may discover that they have good Job Training Partnerships in their districts" (Winerip 1996a, 1). By using this method of storytelling, which he did many times with different issues, Winerip was able to connect national political concerns to local politics as well as explain at least in one place how local political decisions were affecting national concerns.

Describing Public Opinion in Stark County without Precision Journalism Techniques

In April 1996 Winerip set out to write about a topic that had been a major news item in North Canton for about two years—a plan by the Hoover Company, the vacuum cleaner manufacturer, to sell 241 acres in the center of town that had been owned by Hoover for more than 100 years. The plan called for Hoover to donate 70 acres to the city for Little League ball fields, and 50 acres to Walsh University, and 52 acres would be used for retail and office development. Winerip wrote that "North Canton's 15,000 residents have struggled to figure out . . . whether they could still trust Hoover" (Winerip 1996b). "It is no accident that North Canton is a Republican stronghold," he continued. "People here grew up trusting Hoover and voting Republican. If that trust was broken now, it would be bad news for the Republican vision of America" (Winerip 1996b, 1).

In this story, Winerip used several reporting techniques for dealing with public sentiment on this issue. He described "a private poll commissioned by Hoover" in 1995 that "indicated a large number of people were undecided." In this, he gave no further details about the poll or how it was conducted, but he used this as source to support a statement that "residents of this middle- to upper-middle-class suburb proceeded cautiously before challenging their biggest employer."

He also formed impressions of how people felt about the issue based on what they said at the public meetings he attended. Winerip quoted people based on individual interviews. He told a story about "families being torn" and noted that resident Judy Douglas put up a sign in her yard supporting the Hoover opponents, but her husband removed it, saying it was important to support the Hoover Company. Other expressions of public opinion were inferred from political actions taken by townspeople, such as when opponents collected 1,000 signatures on petitions forcing a citywide referendum, or when rezoning opponents put up 500-yard signs.

Supplementing and Complementing Literary Journalism with Original Survey Research

A major problem of literary journalism is to develop confidence that what one thinks one is observing based on relatively limited experience actually reflects the larger reality of public opinion, experience, and behavior. No matter how much an individual literary journalist works, there is likely to remain the nagging doubt, even in the most successful practitioners, that it is not enough. Winerip understood from the start that his impressionistic views seemed to need supplementation with more systematic, quantitative data. This opened the door to the aforementioned conversations we had with him about the value of precision journalism or "the application of social and behavioral science research methods to the practice of journalism" (Meyer 1991, 2). Winerip was also eager to attract additional resources from the *Times* in support of his project, with the idea that he could enhance his goals of receiving favorable play for his stories to the extent that the *Times* had made a significant financial investment in his year-long project.

In terms of precision journalism, we proposed doing surveys and focus groups for Winerip and the *Times* that they could use as the basis for news stories as well as general background for Winerip's benefit. This plan was unusual in that it involved the *Times* in a three-way partnership with the Northwestern University Survey Lab, the Ohio State University School of Journalism, and later the Ohio State Survey Research Unit, once Lavrakas moved to Ohio State University from Northwestern. The plan was complicated somewhat by the fact that in its history of conducting survey research, the *Times* had not, since 1975, been in a polling relationship in the United States with anyone except its longtime partner, CBS News. All this was discussed at the very highest level of the *Times*, and eventually the project was approved in early 1996. In the end, the *Times* provided approximately $20,000 to support the two surveys, an amount supplemented by discretionary research funds Lavrakas had at Northwestern University to support most of the expenses of the first survey.

To plan the first survey, Michael R. Kagay, editor of news surveys at the *Times*, agreed to visit Ohio State University to talk about the project with Winerip and us. We agreed to an overall schedule for the project, which was refined in a series of four-way conference calls. The first survey was fielded from 20 April to 5 May 1996 and consisted of sixty-eight questions to establish baseline measures for Canton and surrounding Stark County. Other goals were to assess the political landscape of the Stark County area, particularly economic perceptions and perceptions of important issues and the major party political candidates. Several questions of local interest about which Winerip wanted to write stories were also included. The questionnaire was based on typical *Times*/CBS News questions whenever possible so that the Stark data could be compared and contrasted with the nation as a whole. A total of 814 random-digit dialing (RDD) interviews with adults 18 and over were completed by the Northwestern University Survey Laboratory in Evanston, Illinois; the sample was weighted according to a number of demographic characteristics and for unequal probabilities of selection. The survey results had a margin of error of approximately plus or minus 4 percentage points.

For a typical *New York Times* poll, once the data arrive in the survey research department, the responses and percentages are typed onto a questionnaire. This makes a solid, easy-to-use record of the data. Always, if applicable, the latest data are augmented with historical data for the same questions. Kagay examines the data and any completed analyses and prepares a memorandum about the poll and its findings for the reporter's use. In this, continuing in his role as editor of news surveys, Kagay points out the key findings as seen by a survey analyst. This memorandum is then sent to the reporter who writes the actual story for the newspaper. The reporter uses this memorandum as one source of input, but he or she is free to use personal judgment, news sources, and other information in the preparation of the article. The resulting manuscript is examined by the news surveys editors for accuracy. The article is then also passed through several other layers of editors before it appears in the *Times*. As part of our collaboration with Winerip and the paper, we received confidential "embargoed" versions of these memoranda.[3]

To assist Winerip, who had not written poll stories before, Kagay prepared a seven-page "highlights memo" suggesting, from a survey research perspective, themes that might make interesting news copy. In addition, a twelve-page list of survey questions and marginals, along with most recent national benchmarks from previous *New York Times*/CBS News data, was prepared by Kagay's department for internal use by Winerip, Kagay, and others in the News Surveys unit. These materials were augmented by batches of crosstabs generated by News Surveys.

The second survey was conducted by the newly established Ohio State University survey center from 19 to 24 October 1996 and served as a "final" pre-election survey for Stark County.[4] This was also an RDD sample of Stark County, with 827 adult respondents, of whom 678 reported they were registered to vote. As was done with the April-May survey, we worked closely with Kagay and Winerip during the month before the October survey to develop the questionnaire based upon the election-related news themes that had emerged in Stark County and in the nation. Since the second survey was being conducted under tighter deadlines than those of the first survey, we worked more closely with him and the *Times* during that third week in October than had been needed previously. For example, Winerip received a set of marginals on October 22 (halfway into the field period) so that he could start preparing his story lines. He also received the names and phone numbers of survey respondents who had given permission to be called by a *Times* reporter; this allowed Winerip to get a jump start on the personal interviews he would conduct for these stories. The morning after interviewing was completed, the weighted data set was sent to the *Times* for the News Survey unit to conduct analyses for Winerip. The "results" memo that Kagay first wrote for Winerip ran to five pages and was supplemented with a two-page memo two days later. And, as discussed later, Lavrakas conducted special multivariate analyses for Winerip.

How the First Survey Was Used by Winerip

The results of the first survey documented the point that Stark County was a useful "political laboratory" to study the country as a whole as determined by the *Times*'s polling unit. As shown in Table 6.1, party identification and ideology in Stark County was similar to that of the country as a whole as determined by an April 1996 *Times*/CBS poll and the first Stark County survey. On other major demographics, Stark County also seemed quite close to the nation as a whole. Consider the case of income. In Stark County, 42 percent had family income under $30,000, and 47 percent had more than that. Nationally, the figures were 41 percent and 54 percent, respectively. Sixty-one percent of Stark County residents said religion was "extremely important" or "very important" in their lives, which compared to 55 percent nationally.

All of this is not to say that Stark County perfectly mirrored the nation. There were certain minor differences worth noting, although they were not large differences for the most part. Stark County had fewer blacks (6 percent) than

TABLE 6.1   **PARTY IDENTIFICATION AND IDEOLOGY**
IN STARK COUNTY AND THE UNITED
STATES (IN PERCENTAGES)

	STARK COUNTY	NATION
PARTY IDENTIFICATION		
Democrats	35	36
Republicans	34	31
Independents	25	28
IDEOLOGY		
Liberal	16	18
Conservative	33	31
Moderate	47	47

the nation as a whole (12 percent). Labor unions were somewhat more a part of life in Stark County than in the nation as a whole, with 27 percent of Stark County's families being labor households versus 20 percent for the nation. Stark County residents were somewhat undereducated compared to the nation as a whole, in that 35 percent of Stark County residents have been to college versus 45 percent for the nation. However, all things considered, the correspondence between the local survey and the national data was close enough to give Winerip confidence that he had not gone astray in selecting this location for his project.

Numerous informal hypotheses were built into the first survey. These were discussed between the Ohio State University researchers and Winerip and Kagay in the weekly phone conversations, as well as less formally between these occasions. For example, at the time Winerip chose Stark County, it was clear that he was interested in economic conditions and how they would play out in the political arena. These interests developed in part out of Winerip's previous reporting experiences. He quickly moved to establish relationships with the largest employers in town, Timken, Diebold, and Hoover, and these firms figured prominently in his reporting over the year.

Winerip believed that he was detecting evidence of economic insecurity in conversations around town. Thus, the first survey contained a number of items measuring this evidence in a formal way. And indeed, the first survey indicated that there was considerable economic insecurity in the area, with 18 percent being "very worried" that someone in their household would be out of work in the coming year. A substantial portion of the working households (28 percent) said someone in the house had needed to take an extra job in the past three years to make ends meet. About 19 percent reported that someone in their household had experienced a permanent job layoff in the past 5 years. This number swelled to 36 percent when the past 15 years was considered. Twenty percent of respondents who had experienced a layoff indicated that would make them more likely to vote for Democrats. Thus, the survey helped Winerip gained confidence in his own perceptions even though he did not directly use these findings in his news stories.

A major (and unanticipated) lesson we learned in working with Winerip with the first survey was the extent to which the reporter found it helpful to have names of the people polled in order to be able to call respondents as potential interviewees in researching his own reporting. Knowing the reporter would want to do this, at the end of the questionnaire we included a question asking for consent to be called by a *New York Times* reporter who might do a story about a topic related to the survey. But using the poll as a means of locating certain types of people became a major use of the polling information in its translation into literary journalism. In essence, the survey sample became a "giant Rolodex" for the journalist. He might want to do a story about Perot supporters who voted for Bush in 1992 or Republican women who favor abortion rights and support Clinton.[5]

We did another thing to help the journalist make timely use of the data— we provided Winerip a snapshot of the data about halfway through data gathering. Then Winerip and Kagay would use these data to begin formulating story ideas and making editorial choices. By reinterviewing people who were part of the first half of the data, Winerip could virtually complete a story draft by the time the full data set was ready.

Multivariate Analyses from the Second Survey

As the election was approaching, we knew from conversations with him that Winerip was interested in writing a story about people who "should be voting for Dole, but instead were going to vote for Clinton." To help Winerip locate such persons to interview in the Stark County area, Lavrakas did a discriminant analysis that used expressed vote intention in 1996 as a dichotomous dependent variable: The variable was the two-way trial heat question that asked whether the respondent would vote for Clinton or Dole. The independent variables in the analysis were a collection of demographic and past voting history variables, including gender, age, education income, union membership, 1992 reported presidential vote, party identification, and ideology. All of these variables should strongly predict voting intentions. The purpose of this analysis was to see how well the set of variables would classify the respondents into the two groups, Clinton voters or Dole voters.

Results indicated that the set of predictor variables was highly significant ($p < .00001$), predicting people's response on their reported 1996 presidential vote at an 85 percent level of accuracy as shown in Table 6.2, which is the classification output of that analysis. The 39 respondents in the upper-right cell

TABLE 6.2   PREDICTED VOTE FROM DISCRIMINANT ANALYSIS BY REPORTED VOTE INTENTION

ACTUAL REPORTED VOTE INTENTION	PREDICTED VOTE	
	Clinton	Dole
CLINTON	299	39
DOLE	40	148

Note: This analysis was conducted with the 596 respondents who said they were registered to vote and would vote for either Clinton or Dole. Seventy of these respondents were not classified in this table because of a missing value on at least one of the predictor variables.

were the "answer" to Winerip's question about the people who "should have been voting for Dole but said they were going to vote for Clinton" as derived from discriminant analyses. Winerip was given names and phone numbers of those in this group who had given their permission to be called back (about 90 percent had done so), along with basic demographic information he could use to prepare for his follow-up interviews.

Table 6.3 contains summary information about this group of respondents identified by the discriminant analysis. Fully 77 percent were Republicans, and 89 percent said they were better off or the same financially as they were in 1992. Most thought the economy was going well in the country, and nearly three quarters said they approved of the way Clinton was handling his job as president. It is interesting that 69 percent did not believe that Dole would cut taxes if elected, as he promised to do. Twenty-one percent said they were "independent," and 23 percent reported they had voted for Perot in 1992. This "logical" profile gave

TABLE 6.3   SELECT CHARACTERISTICS OF 39 SELF-REPORTED CLINTON SUPPORTERS WHO ACCORDING TO DISCRIMINANT ANALYSIS SHOULD HAVE BEEN VOTING FOR DOLE

ATTITUDE	PERCENTAGE
Approved Clinton's job as president	72
Thought the economy was now fairly or very good	72
Thought Dole's age was an obstacle to being a good president	44
Thought Dole would *not* cut taxes if he were elected	69
Thought Clinton was more honest than most in public life	15
Said they were better off or the same financially as in 1992	89
Voted for Bush in '92	74
Voted for Perot in '92	23
Said they were Republicans	77
Said they were independents	21

Winerip and us confidence that the statistical technique had found among the large pool of interviewees respondents who met Winerip's reporting needs.

"Data rich but analysis poor" is a common and legitimate complaint of the way journalists and news organizations use survey data (cf. Morin 1995). Yet in this case a complex analysis was brought to bear to answer a journalist's question in a simple, straightforward manner. It was never intended that Winerip would report the findings of this analysis, but that did not lessen the importance of it in helping him generate the news story he judged was needed. This serves as an example of one type of complex analysis tailored to answer a reporter's question and to identify key subgroups that fit into the story frames the reporter intended to pursue. It also brings considerable precision to what may appear on its face to be a relatively simple question but is, of course, anything but simple.

On Monday, 28 October 1996, the *Times* published Winerip's story, based in part on polling data, headlined "Ohio County Reluctantly Tilts toward Clinton" (p. A8). In this story, Winerip began, "In this place that votes as America does for president, Bill Clinton is winning the Battle of the Lesser Evils, stealing away support that Bob Dole must have and attracting many of the independents it takes to carry a swing county." The article contained quotations from five Stark County residents who were not public officials or local campaign officials, but survey respondents.

Other Uses of the Second Survey

Winerip used the poll results from the second survey in several other ways to support the narrative he was building for 10 months in Stark County. In his 28 October story he used the poll to note that Clinton was leading Dole and to estimate the size of his lead, 53–30, with Perot at 11 percent. Winerip compared Clinton's 23-point lead in Stark County as revealed in the *Times*/Ohio State University poll to other poll reports released about the same time by national news organizations such as the *New York Times*/CBS News national poll, showing a 22-point Clinton margin; the CNN/*USA Today*/Gallup poll, showing a 20-point Clinton margin; and the ABC News poll, showing a 15-point Clinton margin. Winerip was quick to add that "not even Democrats here expect the President to win by a 23 point margin in Stark County," but he added that the numbers are "indicative of the problems Mr. Dole is facing."

Accompanying the article was a box (see Table 6.4) containing Stark County and nationwide polling data from the *New York Times*/CBS News polls showing the close correspondence between Stark County and the nation on key variables and supporting the wisdom of Winerip's choice.

TABLE 6.4   GRAPHIC THAT ACCOMPANIED WINERIP'S 28 OCTOBER 1996 ARTICLE,
"A CLOSER LOOK: STARK COUNTY, OHIO, PARALLELS THE NATION"

	STARK COUNTY, OHIO (IN PERCENTAGES)	NATIONWIDE (IN PERCENTAGES)
VIEW OF THE ECONOMY		
Rate the national economy:		
Very good	8	6
Fairly good	66	62
Fairly bad	19	20
Very bad	5	10
Likelihood that today's youth will have a better standard of living than their parents:		
Very likely	16	11
Somewhat likely	40	41
Somewhat unlikely	28	32
Very unlikely	13	13
VIEW OF CANDIDATES		
Have a favorable view of Bill Clinton	50	49
An unfavorable opinion	31	34
Have a favorable opinion of Bob Dole	26	28
An unfavorable opinion	45	43
VIEW OF TAX CUTS		
If you had to choose, would you:		
Prefer reducing the federal budget deficit	53	51
Prefer cutting taxes	38	43
If Bob Dole is elected president:		
He will cut taxes by 15 percent	27	28
He will not	57	58

Note: Figures may not add to 100 percent because not all responses are shown. Based on a survey conducted by telephone 19–24 October of 678 registered voters in Stark County, Ohio. The poll was a collaboration of Ohio State University and the *New York Times*. National figures are from telephone surveys conducted by the *New York Times* and CBS News earlier that month.

Winerip also used other survey data in interesting ways, often just to illustrate certain points and to make a relatively complex argument about the possible impact of the final debate. In his 28 October 1996 article, he wrote that although the results were "not good for Mr. Dole, . . . the poll indicates there still is opportunity for gain by Nov. 5." This inference was supported by survey results indicating that 6 percent of respondents said they were undecided and 19 percent said they might change their minds before Election Day. Winerip noted that the poll was completed twelve days before the election, when some last-minute deciders were still not tuned into the campaign. He also wrote that 84 percent of Democrats said they were voting for Clinton and only 63 percent of Republicans were voting for Dole, concluding that "it seems likely that some of those Republicans will come home to their party before election day." He also pointed out that during the six-day period in which the poll was conducted, Dole fared more poorly on the earliest days, closest to the final presidential debate on October 16, trailing Clinton by as much as 30 points. Winerip observed that Dole did better on days toward the end of the Stark polling period, furthest from the debates, and on one day was as close as 13 percent behind. Winerip reasoned that since the 70 percent of Stark County residents polled believed President Clinton won the debates, compared to 11 percent for Dole, the more time that passed since the debates, the more the debates' negative effect on Dole would dissipate.

Lessons for Campaign Coverage from the Stark County Reporting Venture

Stark County was to be the prism through which Winerip could view the large themes of the 1996 political year but in a microcosm of the nation that could be relatively easily observed. This style of journalism has the benefit of being community based and thus context laden. Much of national election reporting purports to be about things of interest to the nation as a whole, but is in fact often very abstract. This abstractness may be one of the reasons that much national news is palatable to the national audience. This comes with a price, however, and that is its lack of immediate relevance to many people. Nobody would seriously propose covering all national politics from the vantage of one single local community. But Winerip showed clearly what an ambitious, talented, and hardworking reporter can do by immersing himself in a new community for an extended period of time.

As a supplement to ongoing, high-quality national reporting such as is common to many major newspapers, we believe that for several reasons this proved to be a most worthwhile effort for a news organization that could afford to support such an assignment.

First, the Stark County election return percentages matched the national vote pattern exactly. What might have been seen by many as "Winerip's folly" was vindicated when the area he chose ended up mirroring the national vote totals. Of course, this does not mean that other lessons he drew from Stark County fit the nation as a whole, but it did help lend credibility to the exercise.

Second, the project yielded more than forty highly readable and engaging articles over the course of the year. Many of these appeared on the front page of the *Times*, although many graced the inside "National Report" page, with a number of them running on Saturdays. It is unclear whether this was a function of the reporter's work schedule and/or a reflection of editorial judgment about the series or something else.

Third, the stories were interesting and readable because they were about people. Being hundreds of miles from the epicenters of power in Washington and New York, Winerip was free to report local reactions to events, as in the 31 May 1996 story reporting local reaction to the first Whitewater verdict. Winerip found a large group of people to react to the story, including a local television producer, Republican and Democratic barbers, the Stark County Republican Party chairman, Timken Company steelworkers, a refrigeration technician, an administrator of an environmental laboratory, and a salesman. He was also able to work in polling figures from the first Stark County poll to array these characters against a backdrop of a community-wide poll.

Whether the topic was "Is the local militiaman as dangerous as he sounds?" or the spirit of volunteerism in middle America, the stories were full of insight into the lives of ordinary people intersecting the political system in the context of their own community. For example, a 15 August 1996 story about Republican women in the wake of the Republican National Convention was able to offer insight into the political lives of women. Again, this was done against the backdrop of the first Stark County survey, which showed Clinton ahead of Dole by 52 percent to 29 percent among registered women voters. "It is not hard to find Republican and politically independent women here who have not been won over by what they have seen this week, or indeed who are angered by it," Winerip wrote about the local reaction to the Republican National Convention. This provided a setting in which to hear women, several of whom were businessowners, discussing their views on abortion and connecting this to their views of the national convention.

Fourth, most national campaign news in the nation's papers consists of the national press traipsing around to the small towns and cities that the candidates visit and filing their reports on what was said that had national significance. Winerip, stationed in Canton, had the benefit of the campaigns coming to him. His 8 September 1996 story, "2 Republicans Come to Town, One on a Mission, One More Mellow," chronicled the appearance in Canton of Republican candidate Dole and a $50-a-plate fundraiser for the local congressman, Ralph Regula, with the featured guest being former Vice President Dan Quayle. Winerip's vantage point allowed him to convey the local excitement of the event, the details of the preparation, and the behind-the-scenes stage managing. The juxtaposition of the national and local, Dole and Regula, also highlighted the differences in styles between presidential and congressional politics.[6]

Winerip wrote forty-one stories during his year in Canton, ten of which appeared on page one. He used the poll results directly or indirectly in a number of them, although no story contained poll results to the exclusion of other information. This was a very high-visibility project at the *Times*.

Lessons for Academic Researchers

First, and a fairly minor issue, the *Times* was not particularly careful about credit for the survey work, although this was not the fault of the reporter or the newspaper's own polling unit. Several times stories were edited by a general copy desk and key bits of information dropped or changed. A lesson here for other academics is not to expect too much credit for the effort you put into such ventures.

Second, how fair is the criticism of the media as "data rich, analysis poor" in this project? In part, the answer may depend on the point of view of the observer. The academic environment, given its emphasis on theory and hypothesis testing and its traditional publication outlet (peer-reviewed journals), traditionally favors a highly analytical and formal approach. Daily newspaper journalism emphasizes speed and targets large audiences generally not familiar with the rigors of scientific publication. These divergent goals lead to different priorities and at times an uneasy relationship between journalists and academics. Perhaps this anxiety is heightened when the topic involves data.

In the Stark County project, we had the rare and highly valued opportunity to observe the *Times* editorial process close up, indeed, even to participate in it to a limited extent. It was abundantly clear to us that the *Times* handles survey data in a very deliberate, careful manner and supports very well the reporters working with the data. The *Times* used the data in a great many ways and included very complex multivariate analyses in the reporting, although without sharing the burdensome jargon and details of multivariate analysis with its readers. This seems wholly appropriate and innovative, and academics and other outsiders should not underestimate the considerable effort and skill that top media organizations make and display in gathering, analyzing, and reporting data gathered through precision journalism (i.e., social science) methods.

Third, although Winerip used polling data either directly or indirectly in about two dozen stories, the data were more influential than even this suggests. Having hard data gave him confidence to try several stories that he might otherwise not have done. In fact, this may be one of the most important uses of the polling data—to inform the reporter's own mental processes by providing a reliable and objective set of benchmark data that could be referred to again and again when things became confusing. In a 1 March 1997 telephone interview several months after the project ended, Winerip reflected that "the polls were a very important part of [the series]" in that the data gave him the confidence to write about the things he thought he was seeing, as well as to see subtleties that might otherwise have gone unnoticed. "They allowed me to write with more authority," he said.

Fourth, having the names of poll respondents available and analyzed by demographic and social factors was invaluable to completing work on time, since that data enabled Winerip to contact exactly the people he needed very quickly and efficiently.

Fifth, from the academics' point of view, there was another question: Why weren't the data used more in stories, particularly the results of the second poll? Part of the answer may involve the discrepant feelings that Winerip described as the election neared and the *Times* national polls were indicating that Clinton was ahead by more than 20 points. "On a literary level, you get things that the pollsters just don't get," Winerip explained; "There was weakness in the polling too. Those numbers just didn't match what was going on." This led him to distrust the polls as the election grew closer. Winerip believed that although in the case of the second survey the horse-race aspects of the survey were the most interesting, the data were least reliable.

On a more routine level, the *Times* commonly ran tables comparing the Stark County data to the national data, examining the bellwether hypothesis on various dimensions. In making these comparisons, the *Times* also faced a dilemma, according to Kagay:

> From a news perspective, this project contained an inherent dilemma from the start. If Stark County was indeed like the nation, then any poll done there would yield findings that had already been analyzed and reported in articles based on our frequent national polls. Thus, a Stark poll story would have trouble making "news." But, if a poll in Stark County found new and different patterns, then it might make news, but it would call into question Stark County's status as a bellwether for the nation. (M. R. Kagay, personal communication, 14 July 1997)

Sixth, as indicated earlier, much of the fascination of Winerip's work resulted from the detailed picture of up-close and personal processes of nationally important events causing impact in a local community. These impacts were largely compatible with national trends, giving them additional power and interest. It was the ability of the journalist to dig out fresh impacts that made the work especially valuable.

Seventh, there is also another way to consider the matter of data analysis in journalism, as Kagay indicated in a written communication to the authors:

> Note that perhaps the most frequent types of "analysis" done by media polls is time series analysis, via frequent repetition of trend-questions over time and intense probing when interesting shifts occur. This type of analysis was precluded in the spring poll in Stark County by the lack of prior polls there, and was only minimally possible in the fall poll when

October could be compared with May ($n = 2$). But 1996 was a very static election year overall with very few shifts in key variables, so May-October trends were quite stable (boring). In some other election year (like 1988), May vs. October polls might have had *many* shifts to analyze! (M. R. Kagay, personal communication, 14 July 1997)

Conclusion: "An American Place" and the Purpose of News

Jack Fuller, the former president and publisher of the *Chicago Tribune*, in his 1996 book *News Values: Ideas for an Information Age*, provides the following definition of news: "News is a report of what a news organization has recently learned about matters of some significance or interest to the specific community that news organization serves" (p. 6). Fuller is only the latest to attempt to specify the correct balance between providing information that is necessary for the citizen to be adequately informed about the events of the day versus the need to make the news interesting and entertaining. The two goals stem from the very real need to attract large audiences and maintain respectability in democratic society. To our minds, providing a picture of reality on which the citizen can act is clearly the highest calling of the journalist. But to do so effectively, one needs to tell the news with wit, humanity, and examples to connect the news of faraway, abstract places and events with everyday life.

The *Times* invested a great deal of money and effort in Winerip's Stark County series. How successful was it?

Using literary journalism criteria, Winerip's Canton project was both informative and entertaining, providing a window on the nation's politics that fell prey to neither unflattering stereotyping of middle America nor homilies about the pastoral joys of small-town life. He was able to convey an honest view of the political year from the vantage point of a county in Ohio, providing insight into the themes with which he was able to deal over the year—Perot, the role of women, labor, business, Whitewater, and the Job Training Partnership, among others. He developed a number of stories rich in detail and full of people's personal predicaments as they were influenced by national political trends. These voices of everyday Americans certainly enriched the *Times*'s national political reporting in 1996.

The record on the precision journalism angle, on which our own scholarship is most focused, was mixed. Winerip was inexperienced in dealing with poll stories; and although proving himself quick in dealing with the marginals and their political meaning, he was not primarily interested in the systematic data analyses provided by his paper's News Surveys unit. Granted, he did not go to Canton to report about polls. But the survey data did give him the confidence to report certain things or highlight certain other things. The data added credibility to his reports. Winerip was working within a system where expensive national polls were flooding the media, however, and attracting attention to a small Stark County poll was difficult. He might have tried to compensate for this by a careful, in-depth examination of the relationships among the variables in the survey and by demonstrating by example how to make readable stories from polling data. Or lacking the skills to do this, he might have worked more closely with us to do such analyses. Instead, he seemed to become less interested in the poll when it was only a few days old, apparently believing that it had been somehow superseded by national polls showing that the race was tightening as Election Day neared.

As we looked over the entire year, we realized that the greatest single use of the polling data was a purpose quite unexpected by us. Winerip used the data frequently as an aid in finding particular types of people to interview for future stories. Although the researchers did anticipate the use of the data in this way, they underestimated how valuable this Rolodex aspect would be to the journalist. On the other hand, Winerip used the data in far more stories than is typical for most *New York Times* polls, and in this sense he probably got more out of the polling project than he might have.

Should the *Times* consider such a project in the future?

Projects such as this involve risks and benefits. They are costly. It is difficult to balance the costs with the value of the resulting literary journalism and the various insights it contained. Clearly the project added to public understanding of the political process in important ways. Projects like this probably cannot be assigned. But when a journalist is willing, enterprise reporting such as this has shown its potential to add to public understanding of national politics. We'd also suggest that if there were a next time, the social scientists involved and the reporter should spend more time together *before* the project starts to "train" the reporter on how poll data can be plumbed for more newsworthy stories than the surface marginals can tell.

Like oil and water, literary journalism and precision journalism have dramatically different antecedents and purposes, and they do not mix easily. If combined by skilled hands with other appropriate ingredients such as herbs and salt and pepper, oil and water (in the form of vinegar) are the basis for a wonderful salad dressing. Literary journalism and precision journalism are usually practiced by different people with different temperaments. In this case, a small team of people with specialized skills was assembled to assist a reporter interested in adding precision journalism to his program. Overall, we prefer to believe that the *Times* readers benefited from a tasty salad prepared by skilled hands.

Notes

1. An earlier version of this chapter was presented at the annual conference of the American Association for Public Opinion Research, Norfolk, Va., May 1997. The authors acknowledge the helpful suggestions of Michael Kagay and Michael Winerip of the *New York Times*.

2. During the project described here, Lavrakas joined the faculty at Ohio State University and became director of the new survey research center there. The second Canton survey described in this chapter was one of the first projects of this new unit.

3. *Embargo* is a journalistic term that gives a date and time for the official release of information.

4. To our knowledge, this was the only countywide preelection survey conducted in Stark County in 1996.

5. It should be noted that the *Times* routinely gathers names of respondents on every poll particularly to aid reporters who might want to recontact individuals included in the sample for additional comments.

6. One might wonder whether the decision for Dole to visit Canton was at all influenced by the reasonable assumption that it would be covered by Winerip.

CHAPTER 7

Reporters' Use of Causal Explanation in Interpreting Election Polls

Sandra L. Bauman and Paul J. Lavrakas

The media have long been interested in assessing public opinion and have been involved in its measurement and presentation since the elections of the late eighteenth century and the straw polls of the early nineteenth century (Herbst 1993, 1995; see also Cantril 1991; Crespi 1989; Gollin 1980; Lavrakas 1991; Traugott 1992). Although the conceptualization of public opinion has changed throughout its history, today public opinion is commonly thought of as the aggregation of individual opinions as measured by sample surveys (Gollin 1980; Page and Shapiro 1992).[1] And although it is recognized that polls are not the only representation of public opinion in the United States (see Herbst 1993; Peer 1994), Gollin (1980) observes that " 'Public opinion' . . . is taken by most people most of the time to mean poll findings" (p. 448). As Traugott and Means (1995) note, public opinion polls "have become a standard feature of American political reporting" (p. 194).

In modern election campaigns, public opinion polling has become an integral part of the democratic process. Candidates use poll data to decide whether or not to run, to determine which issues and positions they will stress, and to measure their images (Altschuler 1982; Roll and Cantril 1980). The media, skeptical of the selective information and survey data offered by political candidates, have responded by sponsoring their own public opinion surveys and publishing the results (cf. Cantril 1991; Gawiser and Witt 1994; Hickman 1991; Kagay 1991; Mann and Orren 1992).

Interpreting Polls

In presenting public opinion poll results to their audiences, journalists usually try to explain and interpret the results rather than merely describe them (Hickman 1991; Lewis 1991; Paletz et al. 1980). This interpretative role is not new to American journalism; historically, presenting the answers to the "why" questions has been as important as answering the more descriptive "who, what, where, and when" questions (see MacDougall 1938). Studies have shown that to a majority of journalists, the interpretative role is more dominant than that of information disseminator (Weaver and Wilhoit 1986; see also Culbertson 1983; Johnstone, Slawski, and Bowman 1976).

Some critics think that this interpretative role cannot coexist with the descriptive role under the norm of objectivity in journalism (cf. Patterson 1993). Yet when it comes to public opinion polls, explanation and interpretation are seen by many journalists as necessary and important parts of the presentation (cf. Gawiser and Witt 1994; Morin 1995). As long as the interpretations are accurately drawn from the data, many journalists are not troubled by being interpretative while also being fair and objective.

Causal Attribution in Poll Stories

One type of interpretation in poll reports is the causal explanation. This occurs when a journalist explains public opinion as the result of causal preceding conditions or as the antecedent to events or happenings. These causal explanations or attributions answer the journalists' "why" questions.[2] For example, why did voter support for a particular candidate increase or decrease since the last poll? Or why is a particular issue important to voters? Journalists can provide these causal explanations themselves, or they can include explanations from sources such as campaign spokespersons, experts, or pollsters. However, because journalists actively choose both whom to interview and which comments to include in their stories, these causal interpretations from sources are still coming from the journalist, albeit indirectly. It is these causal attributions that this chapter addresses.[3] Given the prevalence of polling in election coverage, it is important to document the extent to which journalists provide causal explanations about public opinion.

Attribution Theory and the Journalist

The theoretical underpinning for this research comes from the social psychological theory of attribution. Attribution theory posits that in order to make sense of the world and render it more controllable and predictable, people naturally make attributions as to the causes of their own and other people's behavior and events. In its broadest sense, attribution theory "is concerned with the attempts of ordinary people to understand the causes and implications of the events they witness. It deals with the 'naive psychology' of the 'man in the street' as he interprets his own behaviors and the actions of others" (Ross 1977, 174).

Research on attribution theory in interpersonal and experimental situations has been extensive. Heider (1958), considered to be the originator of formal attribution theory, suggested that similarities exist between the goals and processes of traditional scientists and those of ordinary people. A major assumption of Heider's theory is that each individual brings his or her unique perception and social experience to the causal analysis. And so, similar to Heider's naive psychologist, journalists bring to the reporting process their life experiences, their biases, their values, and their attitudes.[4] As such, journalists can be viewed as "ordinary people" who strive to understand the causes and implications of the events they witness so that they can convey them and their meaning to their expectant audiences. Thus, it follows logically that journalists consider interpretation and explanation to be very important parts of their role as information disseminators. When it comes to explaining public opinion and polling data, this role seems paramount (cf. Hickman 1991; Mitofsky 1995; Morin 1995).

Another major assumption in Heider's theory is that people inherently perceive events and behaviors as being caused. Rather than merely observing events around them, social perceivers subject their observations to a psychological analysis in an effort to understand the causes. Journalism has long been interested in answering the "why's" of the world—they are part of the five W's (who, what, where, when, and why) that make up the reporter's base of questions to answer in most news stories (cf. MacDougall 1938; Schudson 1978). Given the role and importance of the news media in mediating preelection events in this age of "the mass media election" (Patterson 1980, 1993), it seems natural that reporters would seek to answer the "why" questions in order to portray these causes and meanings of events to their audiences.

A final major assumption of Heider's theory is that causal analysis involves linking observable behaviors or events to unobservable causes. This is exactly what journalists do when they present causal attributions to explain the findings of a public opinion poll. The poll result is an observable entity—it has been measured and represents opinion within its methodological constraints (i.e., sample selection, sampling error, etc.). However, journalists can almost never directly observe *why* public opinion has changed or why it exists in the distributions it does; that is, election polls are rarely conducted with experimental designs that could begin to yield direct and valid evidence about causes and effects. When a candidate does or says something during the campaign, journalists cannot directly observe how that action affects the public's opinions. Instead, journalists rely on nonexperimental correlations in polling data and observation of change over time to infer these unobservable causes.

Two other attribution theorists, Jones and Kelley, expanded Heider's ideas in relevant ways. First, Jones and Davis (1965) introduced the idea of intentionality, saying that the perceiver of social behavior (e.g., the journalist) can infer dispositions only from actions that are intentional. In elections, the intentions of the candidates and their campaigns are often obvious: Candidates are trying to win election to office. Thus, much of what the candidates do and say can be interpreted by the journalist as attempts to win enough voter support to succeed in winning the election (cf. Patterson 1993). Jones and McGillis (1976) updated the theory to include the concept of expectancy; that is, unexpected behaviors will prompt more causal analysis by the perceiver and will yield more information in making inferences. Indeed, it makes sense that journalists will be more likely to seek out explanations for unexpected poll results in order to provide context and understanding for their readers.

Kelley (1967, 1972, 1973) broadened Heider's theory further to include covariation. With multiple sources of information, Kelley believed, causality will be assigned to factors that are perceived to covary with observed effects. This model is sometimes referred to as the ANOVA model because of its similarity to the analysis-of-variance statistical procedure: An "effect is attributed to that condition which is present when the effect is present and which is absent when the effect is absent" (Kelley 1967, 194). In evaluating and explaining public opinion, journalists appear to be doing just that. Upon seeing a change in public opinion (the effect), the journalist evaluates the possible causes that appear to have occurred since the last poll, seeing which were present and which absent. Patterson (1993) also commented on this post hoc causal analysis: "Journalists reason from effect to cause. They observe what is happening in the race and then look to the candidates for explanations" (p. 130). Media pollsters and journalists Gawiser and Witt (1994) explicitly instruct reporters to compare poll results to past polls to see what has changed over time. If the results did change significantly, journalists should determine if "anything happen[ed] between the times the polls were conducted that could explain the difference" (p. 117). In fact, Gawiser and Witt (1994) recommend journalists start with a theory when they are analyzing and interpreting poll results—even if it is proven incorrect. Therefore, journalists are likely to use their own theories in poll analysis in their efforts to explain any perceived covariation.

Heretofore, there has been limited application of attribution theory to explaining the nature of election-related reporting. Foersterling and Groeneveld (1983) compared the attributions of opposing candidates from rival political parties after an election. They found that losers were quoted as making more attributional (explanatory) statements than did election winners. They also found that causes for failure were more likely to be attributed to "unstable" and "uncontrollable" causes (e.g., candidate strategy, momentum, mistakes), whereas successes were seen as the result of "stable" and "controllable" causes (e.g., candidate positions on issues, candidate experience). They concluded that "to us, it seems that attributions that are made during a political campaign are a special case of strategic self-representation" (p. 268).[5] In other words, attributions by candidates as quoted by the media serve to boost the candidate's self-esteem and to minimize the negative and maximize the positive for the candidate.

Building on the rich history of attribution theory and the handful of real-world studies, our study applied attribution theory to the mass communication context of the newspaper election story to determine how journalists use attribution to explain preelection poll results. By documenting the extent and nature of the attributions that reporters make in explaining preelection poll results, we can begin to address the implications of this journalistic practice on the public's election-related perceptions and behaviors. It is our belief that the media have an important role to play in facilitating the public deliberation that is central to democracy. By documenting the opinions of the public as well as venturing explanations about what these opinions may portend, the media have the opportunity to both educate and serve society. However, if reporters propose interpretations (e.g., make attributions about the causes and/or effects of poll results) that are unsupported by adequate evidence, they may inadvertently harm the very processes we would hope they enhanced.

Methodology

To study the presence and type of attributional statements in election poll stories, the content of five newspapers was analyzed: the *Boston Globe,* the *Chicago Tribune,* the *Los Angeles Times,* the *New York Times,* and the *Washington Post.* The analysis included two recent presidential election years (1988, 1992), from 1 September through each year's respective Election Day. This time period was chosen because it occurs after the party conventions in which the nominees are determined and coincides with the traditional start of the general election campaign (Labor Day).

Sampling

The Lexis-Nexis database was used to search for election stories from each of the five newspapers. Articles eligible for this analysis were those (a) that were published in the front news section of the paper, (b) that were published from 1 September through Election Day of 1988 and 1992, (c) that contained at least one of the names of the presidential candidates (i.e., Bush or Dukakis in 1988; Bush,

Clinton, or Perot in 1992), and (d) that had at least one reference to a preelection poll or survey. (Thus, the intersection of these sets (a–d) represents the universe.) In all, this search yielded a universe of 2,432 stories: There were 427 from the *Boston Globe,* 454 from the *Chicago Tribune,* 608 from the *Los Angeles Times,* 445 from the *New York Times,* and 498 from the *Washington Post.* Of these, approximately 25 stories were systematically sampled from each publication and each election year (i.e., 1988, 1992), yielding a final sample size of 255. (Reliability of the coding was very high: Unit reliability was 99 percent according to Guetzkow's U, and item reliability averaged 94 percent using Coefficient Kappa.)

In addition to the content analysis, polling experts at each of the five newspapers were interviewed about their paper's use and interpretation of poll data in election stories.

The Dependent Variable: Attributional Statements

An attributional statement in this study was defined as a statement that either explains why public opinion is what it is or explains something that occurs as the result of public opinion. In these stories, public opinion was usually expressed as poll findings, candidate standings, or voter support. In general, if a statement could be put into the form of "*referent* because *explanation,*" where public opinion was either the referent (what is being explained) or the explanation (the explanation for the referent), it was considered an attributional statement. Thus there were two forms of attributional statements: one in which the public opinion expressed is the causal antecedent (e.g., Because of the latest poll result, the candidate . . .), or one in which the public opinion expressed is the causal consequence (e.g., Because of the candidate . . ., the latest poll result is XX).

The following is an example of an attributional statement in which the poll result is a referent (effect) of some explanation (cause): *Bush has gained ground significantly since the preconvention period because of a variety of economic issues, where he has benefited from improved public perception of President Reagan's record.* This attributional statement says that Bush has gained ground (candidate position) because of (a) his stand on economic issues and (b) public opinion of Reagan. In this example, the candidate's standing (as expressed by public opinion polls) is explained as a consequence or result of two preceding conditions. In contrast, the following is an example of an attributional statement in which the poll result is an explanation (cause) of some referent (effect): *The Bush campaign has experienced a recent surge in donations following his narrowing of Clinton's lead in the polls.* This statement infers that donations to Bush have increased because his support among the public has increased. That is, the rise in donations is an effect explained as a consequence of Bush's higher standing in the polls.

Findings

The content analysis of the five newspapers shows that reporters' usage of causal attributions in election poll stories is pervasive, as 85 percent of all the stories had at least one causal attribution that explained a public opinion poll result. Stories had an average of 4.5 attributional statements per story, and in those stories that had at least one attribution, the average was 5.3 statements per story. In all, 1,146 attributional statements were identified in the 255 election stories.

The Use of Causal Explanations

Causal attributions were found to be more frequent in certain types of stories: longer, in-depth stories and stories where poll findings were presented explicitly and in detail. First, longer, more in-depth stories had significantly more causal attributions ($r = .49$, $p < .001$). Of course, as the length of the story increases, the chance of an attribution statement increases, but it also was found that the ratio of the number of attributions per story to the number of words per story increased significantly as story length increased.

One would also expect that stories labeled "news analysis" would have more attributions because they would be more interpretative and in-depth than straight news stories. Although findings approach statistical significance (stories labeled "news analysis" had an average of 9.33 attributions compared with 4.38 for non-analysis stories), the difference was not significant when controlling for story length.

Prominent stories, those that appeared on page one, also had significantly more causal attributions. As shown in Table 7.1, more than twice as many causal attributions were found in page one stories than in stories that began on other pages. In addition, stories written by political writers or specialists contained significantly more attributions than those written by staff writers. Given that the science of public opinion measurement requires some detailed knowledge and expertise (Gawiser and Witt 1994; M. Kagay, personal communication, 14 March 1996), one would expect a political specialist to be better equipped to provide causal explanations of poll data than are nonspecialists. In fact, each of these newspapers has designated someone on its staff to serve as the polling director or chief analyst. These people serve as the "experts," and they are responsible for determining how the poll is interpreted (M. Goggin, personal communication, 18 March 1996; M. Kagay, personal communication, 14 March 1996; D. Lauter, personal communication, 11 March 1996; C. Madigan, personal communication, 11 March 1996; R. Morin, personal communication, 25 March 1996; S. Pinkus, personal communication, 15 March 1996).

TABLE 7.1   MEAN NUMBER OF ATTRIBUTIONS PER STORY

INDEPENDENT VARIABLE	(N = 255)	P<
Page story appeared on		
Page one	6.59	.001
Other page	3.12	
Reporter of story		
Political writer/specialist	6.61	.05
Staff writer	4.42	
Label on story		
News analysis label	9.33	.10
No label	4.38	
Type of poll story		
Poll is focus of story	6.05	.0001
Poll is supporting element	5.65	
Only vague references to poll(s)	2.72	
Number of polls mentioned		
Multiple polls	4.76	.001
Single poll	1.92	
Specificity of poll references		
Specific (numerical) references	5.77	.001
Generic references	2.97	
Subject of poll		
Horse race/presidential preference	4.67	.05
Other	3.50	
Poll sponsor/conductor		
Newspaper	8.23	.01
Other	3.98	
Expectancy		
Unexpected result	8.94	.05
Expected result	4.20	

Finally, causal attributions were found to be more frequent in stories that focused on poll findings than in stories with another primary focus. When poll results were the main focus of the article, as opposed to being used as supporting details or only as vague references, there was a significantly greater number of causal attributions. Also, causal attributions were present in greater numbers when (a) data from multiple surveys were presented; (b) specific, numeric findings were mentioned; (c) the poll was a presidential preference poll (i.e., horse-race poll); (d) the paper sponsored the poll; and (e) the results were unexpected (see Table 7.1). Stories that present information from a newspaper's own sponsored poll were expected to have more attributions for two reasons: first, because the newspapers made the financial and personnel investment in the survey and, second, because newspapers often have more in-depth and detailed data to analyze and write about. Stories with horse-race polls were expected to contain more causal attributions because presumably reporters would try to explain why candidates are doing well or doing poorly, gaining support or losing support, and so on. It appears that the more explicitly the poll is discussed in the story (such as being the focus or having numeric results), the greater the likelihood that there will be causal attributions related to public opinion. Because polling is the most common manifestation of public opinion in the United States, it makes sense that causal attributions about public opinion would increase as the data from these surveys are discussed in more detail.

The Source of Attributional Statements

Next, our analysis examined the content of attributions in election poll stories and how their characteristics vary under different contexts. As the previous results show, the journalists who wrote these stories appear to routinely utilize causal attributions in their writing and frequently include them in their interpretations of public opinion results. About half (49 percent) of the 1,146 attributions identified in this study were made by the reporting journalist. That is, the attributions were not identified as coming from any other source and therefore were in the journalist's own "voice." In addition, another 9 percent of the causal explanations were attributed to the poll itself (e.g., "according to the poll") (see Table 7.2). Obviously, a public opinion poll cannot "speak"; thus these attributions can reasonably be considered as coming directly from the journalist.

TABLE 7.2   FREQUENCIES: ATTRIBUTION-LEVEL INDEPENDENT
VARIABLES

VARIABLE	PERCENTAGE
SOURCE OF ATTRIBUTION	
Journalist	54
Candidate	28
Opposing Candidate	9
Expert	9
SUCCESS/FAILURE	
Succeeding	35
Holding	17
Failing	47
WINNER OF ELECTION	
Winner	38
Loser	62

Note: Percentages may not add up to 100% because of rounding.

According to our in-depth interviews conducted with the polling experts at each of these newspapers, their reporters should feel comfortable making interpretations in their own voices. Charles Madigan, senior writer at the *Chicago Tribune,* noted that a journalist with polling expertise is in fact the "expert": "Over the years, the emphasis has been on having the reporters use their own individual voices—or me as senior editor use my individual voice—so that I become, in essence, the specialist" (personal communication, 11 March 1996). Madigan believes that a journalist developing a voice is the direct equivalent to a television journalist's appearance: "That's what they are paying me for—my style." The *New York Times*'s Michael Kagay agreed: "As long as causal interpretation can be supported by the poll data, it can be in the journalist's voice" (personal communication, 14 March 1996; also D. Lauter, personal communication, 11 March 1996; and S. Pinkus, personal communication, 15 March 1996). Rich Morin, of the *Washington Post,* noted, "We are comfortable making our own interpretations and feel it is necessary to get reaction of others, such as strategists or pollsters for the candidates" (personal communication, 25 March 1996).

The remaining 42 percent of causal attributions about public opinion in our study represented quotations or paraphrased quotations from various other sources in the election process: the candidates, campaign spokespersons, experts, and individual citizens. Interestingly, the candidates (as quoted by the journalist) are rarely shown in the news stories as making causal attributions for themselves; rather, it is their campaign spokespersons or party representatives who do so. There are two plausible explanations for this. First, with the rigors of the campaign trail, it can be difficult for journalists to talk directly to the candidates during the campaign, so they rely instead on campaign and party spokespersons. Second, candidates may choose to remain "above the fray" to stay focused on the issues rather than become involved in making causal attributions about their current standing. Bauman and Herbst (1994) found this to be the case in their rhetorical study of candidates' reactions to polling information: "Perhaps candidates prefer not to engage in messy statistical battles, leaving this dirty work to campaign operatives. If candidates spend too much time attacking the polls and the pollsters, they will appear to be distracted from the issues and the race itself" (p. 142). Quotations from candidates (when used) and their spokespersons tended to be used as causal attributions about or for themselves (26 percent) rather than about the opposing candidate (9 percent).

Nonpartisan experts, such as academics and pollsters, were utilized less frequently by journalists as sources for the attributions in the news stories: Only 7 percent of causal attributions were attributed to these sources. Also, quotations from individual citizens or survey respondents were presented as evidence for only 1 percent of the causal explanations.

Do reporters use different sources—journalists, candidates, and opposing candidates—to make attributions in different ways? The answer appears to be yes: They use attributions in their own voices in combination with their quoted sources to attribute in a more balanced, "objective" fashion. Some attributions are positive toward the candidate(s), some negative; most attributions are purely descriptive, some prescriptive; some poll findings are attributed to candidate traits (internal causes) and some to situational (external) causes; and so forth. Attributions in the journalist's own voice tend to be less extreme (and therefore more seemingly objective) on these types of measures than are the attributions identified with candidates or their campaigns. Candidates and their campaigns are significantly more likely to make attributions in predictable, ego-defensive patterns (cf. Bauman 1996).

In addition to source differences, our study found that journalists use attributions differently under conditions of success than under conditions of failure. Overall, journalists make more attributions to explain the status of the failing or losing candidate (failing condition) than to explain that of the candidate who is winning or leading or gaining: Thus 47 percent of the causal attributions were about the failing candidate (that is the candidate who was behind), and 62 percent of the attributions were about the eventual election loser (see Table 7.2). A difference by election year was found: In 1992 there were significantly more attributions about the failing candidate than in 1988, perhaps because the incumbent, George Bush, was the loser.

These results are consistent with past research, which found that patterns of hedonic bias (where someone makes attributions in his or her own self-interest) were more apparent under the success condition than under the failure condition (e.g., Elig and Frieze 1979). Journalists appear to use their own voices to make attributions in patterns similar to the way quotations from candidates are used, but they tended to balance these attributions with more negative attributions by expert sources (see Table 7.3).

Attributional Statements in Context

A great majority (88 percent) of the causal explanations in these election news stories are not presented with explicit causal language. That is, words indicating causality, such as *because, as a result,* or *consequently,* were present only in 12 percent of the 1,146 statements. There are two possible explanations for this: First, because journalists tend to present these causal attributions in their own voices, perhaps they are more comfortable making attributions without causal language; in other words, it could be a function of the journalistic, storytelling writing style. Second, perhaps, as recommended by Gawiser and Witt (1994), journalists are actively aware

TABLE 7.3   NUMBER OF ATTRIBUTIONS BY SUCCESS STATUS AND SOURCE OF ATTRIBUTION (IN PERCENTAGES)

	SOURCE OF ATTRIBUTION			
	Journalist	Candidate	Opposing Candidate	Expert
Success/Failure				
Succeeding	43	34	49	40
Failing	57	67	52	60
n	(382)	(209)	(68)	(52)
χ^2 (3, N=711) = 6.83*				

	Journalist[a]	Candidate[a,b]	Opposing Candidate[b]	Expert
Winner of election				
Winner	41	28	49	35
Loser	60	72	51	65
n	(519)	(287)	(94)	(81)
χ^2 (3, N=981) = 18.05**				

Note: Groups are significantly different at $p < .05$ according to the Scheffé multiple comparison test. (Groups [a] and [b] are not significantly different from each other but are significantly different from group [a,b])
*$p < .10$ **$p < .001$

that correlation does not necessarily imply causation and therefore try to avoid explicit causal language. The second of these explanations seems more plausible. For example, in noting that causal conclusions are difficult in cross-sectional surveys where you usually only have measures of association, Kagay of the *New York Times* said that he recommends that his reporters "soften the language" (personal communication, 14 March 1996); and the *Washington Post's* Morin noted that he tries to "avoid explicit causal language" in the stories he writes (personal communication, 25 March 1996). Ideally, said Kagay, the journalist would want to use a panel design in order to document change in public opinion because "the pre-post design is more appropriate for making causal connections" (personal communication, 14 March 1996). Lauter and Pinkus of the *Los Angeles Times* insisted that their reporters were not allowed to make causal attributions that are not supported with evidence from the poll (D. Lauter, personal communication, 11 March 1996; S. Pinkus, personal communication, 15 March 1996).

In addition to the absence of explicit causal language, three quarters (78 percent) of the attribution statements did not refer to a specific public opinion finding. That is, some form of causal explanation was made about public opinion "generically" without specific mention of a particular poll or poll finding. This seems to indicate that the concept of public opinion is so embedded in election stories that it is not explicitly referenced. Perhaps this is another example of the reification of public opinion that Lippmann (1925) first discussed. Bauman and Herbst (1994) noted that public opinion as expressed in surveys seems to have a life of its own. Journalists refer to and campaign officials react to poll data "without ever referring to human beings: For the purposes of campaign polling, people are represented by statistics, so that is not necessary to refer to them at all" (Bauman and Herbst 1994, 138). The Bauman and Herbst (1994) study showed that there are a great number of references to public opinion (also known as voter sentiment or support, favorabilities, and approval rating) without referring to the source of this opinion—the poll.

Finally, another form of context that enhances preelection poll stories is including findings from other polls—either polls taken at another point in time or polls sponsored by other organizations (Gawiser and Witt 1994). Although some journalists may be tempted to promote their poll to the exclusion of their competitor's polls, the benefits of including other polls seem to outweigh this consideration. Nearly all (91 percent) of the stories in this analysis referenced more than one poll.[6] Gawiser and Witt (1994) believe that reporting multiple polls can enhance the credibility and validity of a single poll and thus strengthen the entire story. In addition, the presentation of multiple polls can also "provide the basis for excellent stories on change and contrast" (Gawiser and Witt 1994, 113). Indeed, this study found that stories that included multiple polls had more than twice as many attributions as stories with a single poll (see Table 7.1).

The Role of Interpretation in Preelection Poll Stories

Our research suggests that interpretation of public opinion polls is common and even expected. The role of interpretation in journalism is nothing new. In fact, MacDougall's (1938) classic journalism textbook was titled *Interpretative Reporting*. In the "note to teachers," MacDougall explains, "The trend is unmistakably in the direction of combining the function of interpreter with that of reporter" (p. v). Indeed, Weaver and Wilhoit's (1986) comprehensive study of print and broadcast journalists found that the dominant professional role of U.S. journalists today is interpretative. In election coverage in particular, Patterson (1993) has noted the shift from a mostly descriptive reporting style to one that is more interpretative. Along with the deterioration of the political parties, Patterson (1993) traces this change toward interpretation to the emergence of television and its "more aggressive style of reporting" (p. 80).

Furthermore, the journalists interviewed for this study, who also are election polling experts, thought that public opinion in particular needs to be explained and interpreted. The *Chicago Tribune*'s Madigan said that "[explanation] is what journalists are supposed to do. . . . Explanation is interpretative, but even what you choose to describe is interpretative in a way" (personal communication, 11 March 1996). Lauter, of the *Los Angeles Times,* agreed: "There is a lot of interpretation in all news stories. By definition, in presenting the data you're presenting analysis which is interpretation" (personal communication, 11 March 1996). Lauter and Goggin (of the *Boston Globe*) said their papers used graphics to present the numbers, and the goal of the story was to explain and interpret the data (D. Lauter, personal communication, 11 March 1996; M. Goggin, personal communication, 18 March 1996). Morin (1995), of the *Washington Post,* stressed that interpretation is part of the journalists' job: "Telling people who's ahead and *why* is something that's important to our readers" (emphasis added, p. 139).

One of the most interesting findings of this study, as discussed above, is that journalists tend to present their interpretations in their own voices rather than relying on other sources. Because these explanations are part of their job, the journalists interviewed did not sense any incongruence with this interpretative role and their quest to be fair and objective in their reporting. One explanation why journalists are comfortable with their dual roles of information disseminators and interpreters is that they have to be, since the press has been forced to fill the void left by party politics in the election process. Although the news media have long been charged with informing the public about campaign issues and candidate platforms, they have assumed the additional role of "election mediator" and "arbitrator of American presidential politics" since 1968, when the political parties "surrendered" their control of the nominating process (Taylor 1990, 117; see also Altschuler 1982; Mann and Orren 1992; Moore 1992; Patterson 1993). In the ensuing 30 years, public opinion polling has become more technologically and methodologically sophisticated (cf. Frankovic 1994), and the media use preelection polls as tools for more comprehensive reporting. Madigan said that his paper used "polls the same way candidates and marketers do"—to determine what is news, to direct their reporting, and to figure out how much of what people think is based on perception versus reality (personal communication, 11 March 1996). Political editor Lauter, a self-described "big believer in polls," thought that "if you're not polling, you don't know what's on people's minds. All you are getting is the conventional wisdom from inside Washington, D.C." (personal communication, 11 March 1996).

Another interesting finding is that journalists tend to interpret poll findings as the consequence rather than as the antecedent of some event(s). That is, they explain the poll findings in terms of what has happened in the campaign rather than explaining what is happening in the campaign in terms of the poll finding. In two thirds (66 percent) of the attributional statements, the poll results were the consequence rather than the antecedent (35 percent). An example:

Perot's numbers in the polls started to drop after his allegations last week-end that Republicans were planning to disrupt his daughter's wedding in August. (Mashek, *Boston Globe,* 1 November 1992)

In this example, the journalist explained Perot's descent in the polls as the result of his allegations against Bush and the Republicans. The public opinion result (i.e., support for Perot) was explained as the *consequence* of some happening (i.e., Perot's allegations).

A second example:

What matters, senior campaign officials say, is that Mr. Clinton's unex-pectedly wide strength this late in the race allows the Democrats to play a highly offensive game, spending an extraordinary amount of time in the-oretically Republican states, picking and choosing targets from New Eng-land to the Deep South. (Kelly, *New York Times,* 30 September 1992)

Here, the journalist explains Clinton's campaigning strategy in the remainder of the race as a function of his standing in the polls. The public opinion result (i.e., support for Clinton) was the *antecedent* that explains some happening (i.e., Clinton's campaign strategy). As mentioned earlier, this second type of attribution example was found to be much less common. Given that journalists appear to think that explaining public opinion (not explaining other things in terms of public opinion) is in their job description (cf. Morin 1995; and interviews for this study), it seems logical that public opinion would be utilized more as a consequence in the explanations than as the antecedent. In addition, journalists may make more attributions of public opinion as a consequence because they can do so more confidently. They can examine what intervening events occurred between polls to explain the change; whereas when the poll is the antecedent, these explanations may be seen as more speculative because the journalists are looking at an event from only one time point of a poll.

Conclusions, Implications, and Recommendations

It is clear from both the content analysis and the in-depth interviews with jour-nalists that causal attributions are routinely presented in poll stories in an effort to explain public opinion. From a journalistic standpoint, we consider this to be a positive finding, given the importance of the media in bringing the election campaign to the public and enhancing public deliberation on candidates and issues. Instead of operating strictly as information disseminators, reporters seem to be actively trying to interpret for their audiences. They are not merely presenting numerical findings from the polls; rather, they strive to put these numbers in context and to concentrate on the meaning of the findings for the public, the candidates, and the campaign itself. And this is exactly what I. A. "Bud" Lewis, former pollster of the *Los Angeles Times,* had in mind when he lamented that "there should be a greater effort to train journalists in how to find out what a poll *tells* us" (1991, 78). For Lewis, "a number should never be the lead"; rather, it is the reporter's responsibility to write about the *meaning* of the numbers (I. A. Lewis, personal communication, 21 October 1988).

However, from a social science standpoint, the presence of unsupported causal attributions can be highly disturbing. Since most surveys cannot provide true evidence of causality, mere correlational relationships may likely be misreported as causal relationships, as Noelle-Neumann (1980) and others have asserted. It seems, though, that journalists at the prestige papers in our research understand the problem of implying causality from correlational data because most of the causal attributions were made without explicit causal language. As recommended by Gawiser and Witt (1994): "Journalists should be extremely careful of any claims of causality. Most important, any story about associations must be carefully worded not to imply causality" (p. 159). Whether journalists at less prestigious papers are as careful to avoid explicit causal language is not discernible from this study. However, given that staff members at less prestigious papers are probably less experienced at writing about public opinion polls, it seems possible that their causal attributions may not be as carefully worded. In addition, tighter resources at other papers most likely limit the amount of survey research education that these newspapers can offer their staffs; most probably these newspapers do not have "on-staff experts" like those interviewed for this study. Therefore, the problem of misreporting correlational relationships as causal ones is likely to be more serious at less prestigious newspapers.

Our research also accentuates the tension between journalism and social science—between making a Type I error (a false positive) or a Type II error (a false negative). Journalists are under pressure to avoid missing a potentially important story (Type II error), whereas scientists are more concerned with not making a false assertion (Type I error). Under the strain of competition, journalists could arguably feel the pressure to make causal attributions about public opinion even when the attributions can only be considered plausible or speculative.

At the same time, there could be many other plausible or speculative attributions that are not presented in election poll stories because journalists are constrained by the institutional norms of objectivity and fairness. Just as Foersterling and Groeneveld (1983) point out that attributions made by candidates in public are probably different from those they make in private, the same could be true of journalists. In other words, when they are not "journalists" but, rather, just "ordinary people," journalists may have different causal attributions about public opinion and elections than they allow themselves (or are allowed by editors) to express in their work. Although many reporters consider interpretation and explanation important aspects of their job, they can approach explanation with an "attitude" of objectivity and a conscious effort to be fair and balanced. In addition, since the election news story is a collaborative effort of the reporter and editors, perhaps peer pressure and professionalism play a role in how attributions are made. Therefore, the number of causal attributions made by journalists in election poll stories might be significantly greater if not for the tensions of description versus explanation, private versus public attributions, and the norms of objectivity and fairness in professional journalism.

So do journalists make causal attributions as "ordinary" people do, or do they make them as do "objective" observers? The answer appears to be some of both. Journalists are expected to attribute in less-biased (i.e., not ego-defensive) ways because of the pressures of presenting the news in a fair and unbiased manner. However, in many cases journalists are not less biased than the candidates they quote in making attributions; rather, they make attributions in patterns similar to candidates (as quoted by the reporters). Thus, in this sense, they appear to be behaving like the "ordinary" people that attribution theory centers around. However, when the attributions of the journalists are combined with the attributions of their quoted expert (noncandidate) sources, the sum of attributions made appears more balanced. In other words, journalists rely on their own voices in combination with their quoted nonpartisan sources to attribute in a more "objective" fashion (Bauman 1996).

Therefore, though striving to explain and interpret public opinion polls as part of election poll stories, journalists also appear to be struggling with the institutional pressures of being objective, fair, competitive, *and* not missing a major story. Of course, journalists are operating under these tensions while trying to fulfill their many—and often competing—roles, including being the public's watchdog and the election mediator.

Several recommendations for the practice of journalism and the reporting of public opinion polls can be made from our research. First, as Patterson (1993) noted and Von Hoffman (1980) feared, the proliferation of media polls in election coverage has elevated the journalist's voice while muting other voices. Although interpretation and explanation are indeed important aspects of the journalist's job, the importance of the reaction of election participants and experts should not be lost. Two possible improvements have been suggested by other scholars. Mitofsky believes that the public would be better served if survey researchers wrote survey news reports first, since the researcher is "better equipped to explain the meaning of quantitative poll findings than [is] the typical reporter"

(Lavrakas and Traugott 1995a, 10). This shifts "the burden to the researcher for correctly presenting the most reasonable interpretation of the newsworthy findings of the survey research" (Mitofsky 1995, 73–74). The researcher's poll story should include the traditional aspects of disclosure (e.g., field dates, question wording, and margin of error) as well as a discussion of "the generalizations that can *and cannot* be made from the data" (Mitofsky 1995, 75). Then, the reporter would write the story, using the researcher's version as "a much better starting point" (Mitofsky 1995, 74). Some newspapers, including the *New York Times,* the *Washington Post,* and the *Los Angeles Times,* already make use of this approach by having their survey research experts (Kagay, Morin, and Pinkus, respectively) provide the analysis and interpretation for the reporters, and, on occasion, serve as reporters themselves.

Another approach has been suggested by Salmore (electronic message posted to Public Opinion Research group, 14 November 1995). He believes that stories that contain analysis of a survey should always be accompanied by a "news analysis" label. In other words, poll stories should never be presented as "hard news." Rather, they should be accurately labeled for what they are: news that includes interpretation by the reporter and is thus subject to the reporter's possible biases and inaccuracies in judgment. This "news analysis" approach is not utilized very frequently, as evidenced by the fact that only 2 percent of the stories in our study were labeled as such.

To our minds, either approach—relying on expert interpretation or labeling stories as analysis—would represent an improvement in reporting election polls if used consistently. A combination of the two approaches would seem ideal. The "main" poll story would be presented with ample interpretation from the survey researcher and reaction from the election participants (e.g., quotations from candidates, campaigns, or poll respondents who have agreed to be interviewed by a reporter). Then, this story could be accompanied by two or three short "analysis" news stories—each written by someone with an explicit perspective (e.g., a Democratic pollster or a Republican strategist). In this way, the public is presented with the descriptive results and the researcher's "expert" interpretation as presented by the reporter, as well as interpretations of the meaning of the results from individuals of differing political viewpoints. Obviously, given the sheer number of polls reported, this would not be a viable or practical option in all cases.

This approach would also work toward solving two other problems evidenced from this research: (a) that of the reporter's voice being present to the exclusion of the election participants' voices; and (b) that of correlational relationships likely being misreported at least to some degree as causal relationships. Journalists—and editors in particular—need to be more sensitive to these problems by encouraging reporters to seek out the interpretations and reactions of others and to continue to be careful in choosing noncausal language when describing associations. We believe it is particularly important that journalists balance the attributions they make about poll findings with attributions from other sources and be inclusive when interpreting public opinion results in these news stories.

To further address these issues, more specific standards for reporters and copy editors would be useful—similar to the National Council of Public Polls and the American Association for Public Opinion Research guidelines for reporting poll results. Such guidelines would make explicit and salient the necessary prerequisites before a relationship could be considered causal and offer examples of other more acceptable language (e.g., "one *possible* explanation" or "this *could* be the result of"). Although there are several books that guide journalists in the evaluation of polls, such as Gawiser and Witt's *A Journalist's Guide to Public Opinion Polls* (1994) and Wilhoit and Weaver's *Newsroom Guide to Polls and Surveys* (1980), these publications do not address these issues specifically or in great enough detail. Both of these books, though very helpful to journalists and contributing to the field of journalism, spend more time explaining how to evaluate the quality of a poll rather than suggesting what to do with the poll's findings after its credibility has been established.

As a methodological solution, newspapers could address the problem of misreporting causality from sample surveys by designing studies to try to more accurately document causal relationships. As the *New York Times*'s Kagay notes, panel designs are ideal for delving into causal relationships (personal communication, 14 March 1996). Furthermore, more experimental designs on question-wording and -ordering effects incorporated into surveys would provide reporters with more solid evidence to explain why opinion is what it is. If media decision makers built in a panel or an experiment when planning their election poll schedules and budgets, their reporters could address their hunches and plausible explanations through carefully crafted questions in these types of study designs.

Another implication of this research is the need for further education and practice in writing poll stories. The *New York Times*'s editor of news surveys, Kagay, notes, "There's an art to writing a poll story" (personal communication, 14 March 1996). Even though journalists at the newspapers in this analysis are likely to represent the best trained in their field, they acknowledge that writing a poll story accurately and clearly is a challenge. Journalists at papers of all sizes need to recognize this challenge and strive to be as educated and informed as possible on issues related to polling. In addition to attending conferences and relying on experts, journalists should be able to depend on journalistic think-tanks such as the Poynter Institute to provide them with the tools they need to be successful.

It should be noted that these implications and suggestions are made with the recognition of the daily challenges that journalists face. Although reporters are operating under extremely tight time frames and their poll coverage must compete with other news for space, they should continue to work with their editors to try to change this "vicious cycle of focusing on short-term demands of deadline pressures and ignoring potential long-term implications" (Lavrakas and Traugott 1995b, 260). As the *Washington Post*'s Morin acknowledges, "We are always in a state of being data-rich and analysis-poor" (personal communication, 25 March 1996; see also Morin 1995). Ideally, journalists should be given the time to conduct a proper, thorough analysis of the data and to write a careful, complete story that serves the public in the best way it can.

In conclusion, attribution theory has been a useful tool to investigate and measure causal explanations about public opinion. Since public opinion information, as measured by surveys, is so widespread in the media, especially during elections, explanation of public opinion by journalists is common and even expected. As a result, causal attributions are a significant part of election news stories and will likely continue to be prevalent in future coverage of public opinion.

Notes

1. Herbst (1993) has noted that the meaning of public opinion at any given time is largely a function of how it is measured (see also Ginsberg 1989; Price 1992). In the past twenty years public opinion has been measured most frequently by cross-sectional, sample surveys.
2. The terms *causal attribution* and *causal explanation* are used interchangeably throughout this chapter.
3. This chapter is based on Sandra L. Bauman's doctoral dissertation, which was completed in June 1996 under the direction of Professor Paul J. Lavrakas at Northwestern University. Dr. Bauman would like to thank Dr. Lavrakas, the Northwestern University Survey Laboratory, and the Graduate School of Northwestern University for the financial support received for this research.
4. Of course, journalists try to be fair and objective when reporting, but most scholars and journalists agree that it is impossible to rid themselves of their predispositions (cf. Gawiser and Witt 1994; Schudson 1978). Objectivity can be considered an ideal and is operationalized by journalists in the form of an "attitude" (Merrill and Lowenstein 1979).
5. This article was published in German. This quotation is from an English translation of the article.
6. In stories where the poll was the focus of the article, 88% had references to more than one poll. Of those stories where the poll played a supporting role, 87% had references to more than one poll. Of stories with vague, generic references (i.e., "the polls"), 95% had plural references.

PART III

Election Poll Accuracy

CHAPTER 8

Public Attention to Polls in an Election Year

Michael W. Traugott and Mee-Eun Kang

The 1996 election campaign saw more polls conducted than ever before. This was primarily a function of the growth in the number of media organizations interested in polling rather than an increase in the number of polls conducted per organization. The increased polling took place during a campaign in which the front-running incumbent president held a substantial lead throughout. The growing number of polls and the increased number of news organizations reporting their results raise questions about the impact of polls on those who are exposed to them. In this chapter, we look at the public reactions to polling and assessments of its role in a democratic society.

Public opinion researchers have focused a great deal of attention on how the public evaluates election polls, the media organizations that produce them, and the ways they are reported. This research is based upon complementary but quite different sets of theoretical assumptions. One is a normative view that citizens will be actively and knowledgeably engaged in a democracy, especially during election campaigns. Furthermore, the essence of representative government is the communication of popular preferences to elected leaders, as well as between citizens. Published polls are one way that such communication can take place.

Many mass communication theories include the widely shared assumptions that members of the public are interested in what their fellow citizens think and that many of them search for high-quality public opinion data, most commonly disseminated through the media, to satisfy themselves. This version of a "uses and gratifications" approach to the role of public opinion in a democratic society is only one of the theoretical underpinnings of contemporary research on public opinion about polls. Other competing explanations suggest that the public's limited knowledge of polling methodology either inhibits its interest in media reports of opinion or does not provide an adequate interpretive screen for filtering out the "bad" data from the "good."

These conceptual issues have been blurred since the advent of research on the public's view of polling, more than fifty years ago. Episodic data collections that often focus on only one or two key measures have limited the scope of research on these questions. What has generally been missing from past research is analysis of the relationship between the public's attention to polls and perceptions of the appropriate frequency of polling, on the one hand, and how this relates to respondents' knowledge about polling methodology and attitudes toward polls and pollsters, on the other. In this chapter, we look at data from a 1996 survey, fielded in the middle of the presidential campaign, to see how such factors relate to Americans' attention to polls and their perceptions of whether or not too many polls are conducted.

Public Attention to Polls

Even though their evidence is sporadic and episodic, public opinion researchers have been interested in how the public reacts to polls ever since the method came into widespread use.[1] Goldman (1944) conducted the first national "poll on polls" and showed that awareness was widespread and evaluations were generally positive. He reported that at least 56 percent of the respondents knew about polls at the time of his survey, and about one in four respondents followed poll results either "regularly" (9 percent) or "occasionally" (19 percent). His results also indicated that the public was generally confident that polls had a positive impact on politics. There is about a thirty-five-year gap in the time series between Goldman's study and subsequent measurements of public opinion on these issues; but questions about public attention to polls have become a regular item for measurement since then, especially in presidential election years. A review of survey databases maintained by the Roper Center and Institute for Research in the Social Sciences at the University of North Carolina provides further documentation of these measures of the public's exposure and attention to poll results. It suggests three broad trends: Attention has been increasing over time; most of the questions have been asked in presidential election years; and attention tends to be higher in such periods than at other times.

By 1985 one quarter of those surveyed indicated that they "regularly" paid attention to polls, increasing to 31 percent in 1996, more than three times the level in Goldman's survey. When the question was phrased in terms of attention to "election polls" in election-year surveys, two thirds or more of survey respondents indicated that they had seen them. In a 1988 Gallup survey, 76 percent of respondents in a national sample indicated they had "heard or read about polls that are predicting who is currently leading in the race for President," and Lavrakas and his colleagues (1991) reported that 71 percent of their national sample had a similar awareness in that campaign. Equivalent levels of attention to presidential polls were measured in a number of local surveys during this same period (see Goyder 1986 and Dran and Hildreth 1995, as examples).

There have been other measures of attention and exposure to polls, most of which have been asked only in the last twenty years. For example, a 1976 Harris survey asked respondents whether they read Gallup poll results in newspapers. Even though the focus was specifically on Gallup surveys, one in six respondents (16 percent) answered that they read poll results in newspapers "very often." Attention to polls or poll-based coverage is not equivalent to interest in such information. Although more than 70 percent of Americans were aware of poll results in election years, their interest in poll information was not necessarily as high. In Lavrakas's (1991) survey conducted in 1988, only 28 percent of the sample indicated that they were either "very interested" or "quite interested" in the results of the opinion polls conducted on the Bush-Dukakis race. Three in ten respondents (31 percent) were "not at all interested" and 41 percent were only "somewhat interested."

Research on public attention to polls has also been stimulated in part by growing acknowledgment that exposure to poll results has an impact on the audience. As with equivalent developments in the broader theoretical question of whether exposure to the mass media has any effect on the audience and the notion of "minimal effects," scholars now understand that not all the effects must be related to political campaigns and vote choice. Further, effects can occur in only theoretically relevant segments of the audience rather than among all members (Ceci and Kain 1982; Cloutier, Nadeau, and Guay 1989; Kang, Lavrakas, and Traugott 1998; Lang and Lang 1984; Lavrakas, Holley, and Miller 1991). Recent studies have now begun to focus on where and when such effects can occur, not if they can.

Public Evaluations of Polls and Pollsters

There are a variety of ways of measuring the public's evaluations of polls and pollsters, and the available data reflect differences in context and question wording about election polls and other forms of polling. One of the longest time series is anchored in an item from Goldman's first survey, a question about whether or nor public opinion polls are a "good thing or a bad thing in our country." In the 1944 measurement, a substantial minority of respondents (43 percent) indicated they were a "good thing." This finding is based upon slightly more than half of the respondents (56 percent) who indicated any familiarity with polls, as 73 percent of this subset of respondents thought polls were a "good thing." In the 1950s, about six in ten respondents responded positively in their assessments of polls. By 1985 the proportion had grown to 76 percent, and in a 1996 Gallup measurement the proportion was 87 percent. Since familiarity with polls had become almost universal by then, this trend clearly suggests more positive evaluations of polls.

There are some areas in which the use of polls raises public concern. One point on which public attitudes are more leery in an election year context is whether "horse-race" coverage in a campaign is a good or bad thing. In a 1988 poll by Gallup for the *Times Mirror,* a slight plurality of the public (45 percent to 38 percent) believed reporting who is ahead in the polls was a "bad thing" (Traugott 1991). Roper's (1986) study, based on a 1985 survey, indicated "healthy skepticism" (p. 15) in the public about the accuracy, representativeness, or influence of opinion polls, as well as about the honesty of pollsters. Schleifer (1986) analyzed the biennial Industry Image Study produced by Walker Research from 1978 to 1984 and suggested that the public does not object to surveys and polls "in principle." However, many people remain "suspicious of the industry's methods and motives" (p. 24). He concluded that though the public is supportive of the research industry in general, some of the industry's perceived practices might be eroding the public's positive feelings.

Another way researchers have asked the public to evaluate the polling industry is to have them assign a letter grade such as A, B, C, D, or F to its performance in recent elections. A search in the electronic archives of public opinion polls provides additional information on the public's evaluation of pollsters relative to other major players in election campaigns. In the 1992 and 1996 presidential elections, pollsters were graded relatively highly by the public, compared to other major players in the political arena, such as the press and campaign consultants. Whereas pollsters' ratings remained relatively steady, the latter two groups suffered a decline in their grading across this period.

Historically, there has been a positive trend since 1944 in the public's perception of the accuracy of polls. In the Goldman survey, only one out of three respondents (32 percent) considered poll results "pretty nearly right." In a 1965 Gallup survey, 45 percent of respondents believed that poll results are either "excellent" or "good." In 1975, the percentage of people who believe polls are "right most of the time" increased to 49 percent, jumped to 68 percent in 1985, and remained at 65 percent in 1996. After the 1984 election, the Gallup Organization replicated many of Goldman's items from the 1944 survey (Kohut 1986). Compared to 1944, the 1985 results suggested that a larger majority of the public who followed polls were inclined to see the polls as accurate (the difference between 57 percent and 68 percent of respondents who saw polling organizations as "right most of the time"). At the same time, there was no difference across this period in the proportion of respondents who thought that polls that did not deal with elections were "pretty nearly right" (52 percent in 1944 compared to 55 percent in 1984).

How Polls Are Reported in the Media

The two major organizations of pollsters, the American Association for Public Opinion Research (AAPOR) and the National Council of Public Polls (NCPP), have standards for the disclosure of the methodological details surrounding any particular data collection. The standards are designed to enable informed consumers to make judgments about the quality of the public opinion data being disseminated. These codes were promulgated because of a sense that pollsters should operate ethically and a belief that the public requires such details in order to make an informed judgment about the reliability and validity of data to which they are exposed. Yet one of the more interesting and conflicting set of results from survey research on polling suggests that though the public is poorly informed about the methods pollsters use, some kinds of information provided about methods positively affect public assessments of the credibility and objectivity of polls.

During the 1960s and 1970s, polls became a staple of election reporting in the media. This occurred as a function of a number of large news organizations establishing their own polling operations (Traugott 1992), as well as a growing trend for reporters from various media to incorporate in their stories polling data from any number of sources (Broh 1983). Whenever news organizations could afford their own polls, they used them (Demers and Suzzane 1987; Rippey 1980; Salwen 1985). By 1988 more than 80 percent of major circulation dailies and half of television stations either commissioned or conducted their own polls (Ladd and Benson 1992).

Across the past thirty years, there has been a continuous push by journalism educators, public opinion researchers, and the national organizations that represent public opinion researchers and pollsters to improve the quality of reporting of polls. But content analyses of how news organizations deal with the reporting of methodological details in their poll stories produces mixed results. Salwen's (1985) study of Detroit metropolitan dailies from 1968 to 1984 indicates that their level of reporting methodological details generally improved during this time. Miller and Hurd (1982) found that methodological details conforming to the AAPOR standards were more likely to be included in polls reported in presidential election years than at other times. This information was most likely to be included in articles based upon syndicated data from organizations such as Gallup and Harris than in wire service stories, local media-sponsored polls, or data from other miscellaneous sources such as data released by candidates. Miller, Merkle, and Wang (1991) performed a content analysis of poll-based coverage of the 1988 presidential campaign in three major daily papers and three weekly news magazines using a somewhat different coding scheme. They found that the nontechnical details of the polls were reported relatively frequently, but more complicated matters like sample selection, response rates, and weighting procedures were essentially absent.

The way polling methodology is reported in the media is important because most citizens receive no formal training in sampling, questionnaire design, statistical analysis, or the like. These are not topics covered in the high school curriculum, and even college students would have to search for relevant courses. Nevertheless, some research suggests that there is a relationship between the format of news stories and the inclusion of methodological details on the credibility and believability of poll results among those exposed to such content. Again, research based upon the results is decidedly mixed because differences in experimental subjects and stimulus materials, as well as differences in conceptualization, complicate evaluation of this literature. For example, Salwen (1987) conducted experiments with undergraduate students and found that the reporting of probability sampling methods was positively correlated with assessments of trustworthiness, expertise, and objectivity, even though such factors as sponsorship and source of the data were not. But Mosier and Ahlgren (1981), in a study of the effects of exposure to "precision," "pseudoprecision," and "traditional" stimulus articles with a set of 275 subjects from the Minnesota military, found no relationship between mode or style of reporting and three dimensions of credibility, measured as accuracy, trustworthiness, and believability.

One explanation for these seemingly disparate findings may be the levels of education of the subjects in the two studies, although this was not tested explicitly by Mosier and Ahlgren (1981). It is possible that education serves as a conditional variable that facilitates the processing of information about survey methods for some people, but not for others. Such a process suggests the need to include individual-level factors such as education, prior knowledge about surveys and their methodology, or even attitudes toward polls and pollsters in models for explaining citizens' attention to polls or views of their roles in contemporary democracy.

Public Knowledge of Polling Methods

News organizations have increased their reporting of some kinds of methodological information, including descriptions of the design and implementation of the sample, sample size and margin of error, dates of field work, and information about question wordings and order. But this has not increased public knowledge of how these methods work or what their impact on resulting data might be, at least in terms of measures in repeated cross-sectional surveys. The lack of results when assessing the public's knowledge about polling practices reflects a common problem in survey measurement. When asked general questions about their understanding of survey methods, about six in ten citizens say they "know how public opinion polls work." But when asked about the details of methods like sampling, their inherent belief in sampling principles, or how and why data are used, knowledge levels are quite low and indications of suspicion appear (cf. Lavrakas, Holley, and Miller 1991).

For example, when asked whether pollsters interview "typical, representative people or they get mostly unusual, nontypical, or even oddball types of people," 80 percent of respondents to a Roper survey in 1985 indicated "typical." Yet when they are asked whether "a sample of 1,500 to 2,000 people can accurately reflect the views of a nation's population," a majority (between 56 percent and 68 percent) say it cannot. In a 1995 study for the Council for Marketing and Opinion Research, O'Neill (1996) reports that the respondents were evenly divided on a statement, "I don't understand how interviewing about 500 to 1,000 people can tell how the public feels about an issue" (47 percent agreeing and 50 percent disagreeing).

A second methodological concept that is an essential part of the AAPOR and NCPP disclosure standards is the "margin of error," the imprecision of poll-based estimates that is simply a result of chance and is associated with sample size. In a 1987 Roper poll, one quarter of respondents said they found such information in a news story "useful," but 48 percent said they were not sure of the meaning of the term. Lavrakas and others (1991) asked a sample how well they understood the meaning of the "margin of error." One third of the sample (33 percent) said "completely," and 36 percent said "somewhat." However, when Lavrakas and colleagues administered an experimental test of detailed knowledge of the concept, they concluded that such knowledge was low and "many people simply 'guessed' that the hypothetical poll was not accurate enough" (p. 163). In a different form of a knowledge test in the Roper poll, only 16 percent of respondents selected one of four alternatives that correctly reflected the concept.

These findings suggest that the public's detailed knowledge of polling methods remains limited, despite an increase in the inclusion of some methodological details when polls are reported. This is not surprising, since the information news organizations report is likely to contain the less technical aspects of methodology, and this is not information ordinary citizens can be expected to learn through informal exposure. These low levels of knowledge are troubling, however, because a sound foundation of familiarity with polling concepts could be the key to the public's developing critical analytical and interpretive skills.

This review of previous literature indicates there has been a scarcity of research on the public's attitudes toward public opinion polls. Sporadic data collections on this topic have not usually gone beyond the presentation of marginals; as a result, the relationships among key concepts such as the public's attention to public opinion polls, evaluation of the frequency and accuracy of polls, and knowledge about polling methodology have not been examined thoroughly. Thus, it is the aim of this study to examine how such factors provide explanation for the public's attention to and evaluation of polls. The research reported here is based upon secondary analysis of a survey conducted in April 1996 by the Gallup Organization. It is one of the very few surveys to contain measures of a wide range of concepts associated with public knowledge and evaluations of polling. Although it was fielded in the middle of a presidential campaign, it included several general measures as well, including an assessment of nonelection polls.

The analysis proceeded in a sequence that concluded with a series of multivariate regressions. The first investigated the correlates of public attention to polls in the media, and the second to perceptions of the appropriate number of polls reported in the media. These relationships were assessed in terms of levels of socioeconomic status and other individual demographic characteristics, perceptions of the accuracy of polls, methodological knowledge, political interest, and past voting. These factors were expected to correlate positively with attention to polls. Simple demographic explanations were expected to be weak correlates, and the proportion of variance explained should have been significantly incremented by the other measures. The same procedure was followed in analyzing the correlates of perceptions of an appropriate number of polls. In addition to the previous measures, normative assessments of the role and function of polls in the American political system were added, as well as past participation in surveys and the measure of attention to polls. These factors were expected to correlate negatively with a belief that there are too many polls, and the same analytical strategy was pursued with equivalent expectations about the relative importance of attitudes in relation to respondents' personal characteristics.

Method and Measurement

This analysis is based upon a survey conducted by the Gallup Organization consisting of telephone interviews with 1,003 respondents from 25 April to 28 April 1996.[2] The survey contained ten items that are germane to the analysis of the public's attitudes toward polls. They include questions on respondents' past participation in public opinion surveys, attention to poll results, normative evaluation of polls, perceived accuracy of polls in election and nonelection contexts, knowledge of sampling concepts, and consequences of polls. In this secondary analysis, the first step was to review the basic measures that describe the public's attitudes toward public opinion polls and surveys. Next, bivariate relationships between variables were examined using cross-tabulations. Finally, hierarchical multiple linear regression models were formulated to investigate multivariate relationships. Two blocks of independent variables, reflecting demographic and attitudinal characteristics of the respondents, were entered into the model to examine their predictive power. This analysis provides only an initial perspective on these interrelationships, however, because of the correlational nature of this study; therefore, these results should be interpreted with caution in terms of causality.

The two major dependent variables for multivariate analysis were the public's attention to poll results and perceptions about the relative number of existing polls. Various independent variables were used in the analysis that reflected demographic characteristics of the respondents, attitudes about polls, and measures of political behavior. They included age, education, income, gender, and race. Respondents were also asked two questions about their perceptions of the accuracy of polls in an election or nonelection context. The questions and their response categories were not exactly parallel, so they were recoded to reflect a general perception of accuracy. The survey also asked respondents how closely they followed news about national politics and whether or not they had participated in a past public opinion survey. Respondents were also asked about their knowledge of sampling and about past voting behavior.

Finally, three questions that measured respondents' evaluations of polls were used as independent variables, one of which was presented in two alternative forms. They included attitudes about whether or not the country would be better off or worse off if leaders followed the views of the public more often, whether or not polls work for or against the best interests of the general public, and whether or not polls are a good thing or a bad thing. The details for all of these measures, including question wordings, original response categories, and recoded response categories are contained in the Technical Appendix to this chapter.

The general strategy of the analysis was to proceed in stages. After a review of the univariate results of the survey, we explored the relationship between methodological knowledge of sampling, perceived accuracy of polls, and normative evaluations of them. The previous literature, based upon both surveys and experiments, did not provide clear hypotheses for this analysis. However, we began with the expectation that methodological knowledge should be positively related to both perceptions of accuracy and normative evaluations, and this relationship should be conditional on education.

In the final stage of the analysis, multivariate models of the relationship between three sets of independent variables and attention to polls and perceptions of the number of polls were run. One set of predictors was respondents' demographic characteristics; they were used to establish a baseline measure of statistical explanation of variance in the dependent variables. Then two additional sets of variables were simultaneously introduced to determine their incremental explanatory power. In the model for attention to polls, these included attitudinal assessments and methodological knowledge of polls, as well as measures of political participation, interest, and past participation in surveys. In the model for perceptions of the appropriate number of polls, attention to polls was added as a predictor, as well as the respondents' normative assessments of polls. We expected these attitudinal and behavioral correlates to provide a significant increment to the explanatory power of simple demographic factors. With a more powerful panel design for such a survey, it should be possible to specify more complex and temporally ordered relationships between these sets of independent variables, but the cross-sectional nature of the study did not allow this.

Results

The Gallup survey shows that the American public maintains a relatively high level of awareness of polls. More than half of adults (55 percent) reported that they follow public opinion poll results either "regularly" or "occasionally" in newspapers and magazines. One out of five respondents (18 percent) reported that they had been questioned before in a public opinion survey. This is likely an overestimate of survey participation in the general population, as individuals who are disinclined generally to participate in surveys are not likely to be respondents in any particular survey.

Overall, the results also show that the public evaluates public opinion polls positively. The vast majority (87 percent) of respondents indicated that polls of the opinions of the public are a "good thing" in the country, and 68 percent of respondents believed that most opinion polls "work for the best interests" of the general public. In addition, three out of four respondents (73 percent) indicated that the nation would be "better off" if the leaders of the nation followed the views of public opinion polls more closely.

In terms of the perceived accuracy of polls, a majority of Americans showed some faith in both election and nonelection polls. About two out of three Americans say they believe in the accuracy of polls in predicting election results, and an equally large percentage said that poll returns on matters not dealing with elections are "right most of the time." However, one out of four respondents (27 percent for election polls and 23 percent for nonelection polls) believed that poll results are not accurate.

This survey confirms past research showing that the public has relatively little knowledge about one of the most important components of survey research that relates directly to its ability to represent the public's views—sampling. Two out of three respondents (68%) indicated that they do not think a sample of

1,500 or 2,000 people can accurately reflect the views of the nation's population. This result is worth noting, considering the public's positive evaluation of polls and the large proportions that believe they are generally accurate, because it raises questions about the relationship between knowledge and these two attitudes. When the relationship between perceived accuracy of public opinion polls and respondents' knowledge about the underlying concept of sampling was examined, interesting patterns emerged.

Data presented in Table 8.1 show that there is a weak relationship between these two variables, in the expected direction. Respondents who believe relatively small samples can represent the public are also more likely to believe that both election polls and nonelection polls are accurate. Yet majorities of those who believe that samples cannot represent the nation also believe polls are accurate. Education was introduced as a control variable, dividing the respondents between those with at least some college and those with less. This division was made because it is unlikely that a person would be introduced to statistics, probability theory, or research methods unless he or she had attended college. Of four possible controls on these relationships (levels of education by type of poll),

TABLE 8.1   **THE RELATIONSHIP BETWEEN KNOWLEDGE ABOUT SAMPLING AND THE PERCEIVED ACCURACY OF POLLS (IN PERCENTAGES)**

		CAN 1,500 PEOPLE REFLECT THE VIEWS OF THE NATION?	
		Not Possible	Possible
Perceived accuracy of:			
Election polls	Accurate	62	74
	Not Accurate	38	26
		($N = 726$)	($N = 275$)
		$X^2 = 12.79, p < .001$	
Nonelection polls	Accurate	60	73
	Not Accurate	40	27
		($N = 725$)	($N = 276$)
		$X^2 = 13.10, p < .001$	

Note: These data are taken from a Gallup survey conducted in April 1996. The following are the exact question wordings:

Q12. Do you think a sample of 1,500 or 2,000 people can accurately reflect the views of the nation's population, or that it is not possible with so few people?

Q10. Some polling organizations make frequent predictions of election results. What is your general impression of how well they do—do you think they are pretty nearly right most of the time, or do you think their record is not very good?

Q11. Do you think poll returns on matters not dealing with elections, but with public opinion towards such things as labor problems or international affairs, are usually pretty nearly right, or not right at all?

the only place where an effect was observed was in the perceived accuracy of non-election polls among those with at least some college education. These were the respondents who were much more likely to believe such polls were accurate.

When the relationship between perceived accuracy of public opinion polls and normative evaluation of polls was examined, the results were in the expected direction. That is, respondents who perceived public opinion polls to be accurate were more likely to have positive evaluations of polls. However, as the data in Table 8.2 show, a sizable proportion of the population evaluated public opinion polls positively even though they believe that poll results are not accurate. Because there was not much difference in the perceived accuracy of election and nonelection polls, there was no difference in these observed relationships for the two variables. Also, levels of education did not have any significant impact on the observed relationships.

TABLE 8.2   THE RELATIONSHIP BETWEEN THE PERCEIVED ACCURACY OF POLLS AND NORMATIVE EVALUATIONS OF THEM (IN PERCENTAGES)

| | PERCEIVED ACCURACY OF POLLS | | | |
| | IN ELECTIONS | | IN OTHER AREAS | |
	Accurate	Not Accurate	Accurate	Not Accurate
POLLS ARE				
Good thing	95	84	96	83
Bad thing	5	16	4	17
	$(N = 633)$	$(N = 321)$	$(N = 614)$	$(N = 339)$
	$X^2 = 29.02, p < .001$		$X^2 = 45.04, p < .001$	
THE NATION WOULD BE				
Better off	87	86	89	81
Worse off	13	14	11	19
	$(N = 598)$	$(N = 291)$	$(N = 581)$	$(N = 309)$
	$X^2 = .32, p = ns$		$X^2 = 10.51, p < .001$	
POLLS WORK				
For the public	83	62	84	61
Against the public	17	38	16	39
	$(N = 597)$	$(N = 295)$	$(N = 592)$	$(N = 301)$
	$X^2 = 49.04, p < .001$		$X^2 = 62.56, p < .001$	

Note: These data are taken from a Gallup survey conducted in April 1996. The following are the exact question wordings:

Q9: Would you say that polls of the opinion of the public are a good thing or a bad thing in our country?

Q6/7: If the leaders of our nation followed the views of *the public* (Q6) / *public opinion polls* (Q7) more closely, do you think the nation would be better off, or worse off than it is today?

Q8: Do you think most opinion polls work for or against the best interests of the general public?

A second item measured whether respondents believed the country would be better off if leaders followed "public opinion" closely. Bivariate analyses indicate that more than 60 percent of respondents believe that the country would be "better off" if leaders followed public opinion closely, even though they do not believe that 1,500 or 2,000 people can accurately reflect the nation's view. This result suggests that "views of the public" and "public opinion polls" may not reflect the same concept in the public's mind, or at least not appropriately equivalent terms in the wording of survey questions. When respondents answered that the country would be better off if leaders followed the views of the public closely, they may not necessarily have had "public opinion polls" in mind.

The strongest effect of perceived accuracy on a normative evaluation of polling had to do with perceptions of whether opinion polls work "for or against the best interests of the general public." More than three out of four respondents believed they did. But there were sharp differences in the expected direction between those who thought polls are generally accurate and those who thought otherwise. Again, these relationships were unaffected by a control on the respondents' level of education. In summary, the strongest bivariate relationship between the perceived accuracy of polls in either an election or a nonelection context was with a sense of whether they are in the public's interest. There were weaker relationships with whether they are a good or bad thing in our country or a sense the country would be better or worse off without them. Each of these relationships appeared in the expected direction, but education had virtually no impact on them.

The next step was a multivariate analysis of the relationships between a series of demographic, attitudinal, and behavioral variables and two other dependent variables: attention to polls and perceptions of the appropriate number of polls. To check the predictive power of demographic and attitudinal variables regarding the public's attention to polls and perceived number of polls, hierarchical regression analyses were conducted. They employed two separate blocks of independent variables introduced in two stages. In the first, only demographic measures were used. In the second, a combination of variables was added to the demographic variables, including perceived accuracy of polls, normative evaluation of polls, perceived consequences of polls, knowledge about polls, past participation in surveys, and voter turnout in the 1992 election.

Data are presented in Table 8.3 indicating that demographic variables alone do not explain very much about attention to polls (R^2 = .034). At the first stage, only one demographic variable, income, was a significant predictor of attention to polls; there was no relationship with education.[3] People with higher income levels were more likely to follow poll results regularly in the mass media than were people with lower incomes. However, the addition of the block of attitudinal and behavioral variables provided a significant increment to the explained variance

TABLE 8.3 HIERARCHICAL REGRESSION: DEMOGRAPHIC AND ATTITUDINAL PREDICTORS OF ATTENTION TO PUBLIC OPINION POLLS

PREDICTORS	MULTIPLE REGRESSION COEFFICIENTS (DEPENDENT VARIABLE = ATTENTION TO PUBLIC OPINION POLLS)		
	REGRESSION 1	REGRESSION 2	REGRESSION 3[a]
Age	.002	.000	.000
	(.001)	(.001)	(.001)
Education	.001	.018	.009
	(.008)	(.020)	(.018)
Gender	.066	−.043	−.011
	(.055)	(.062)	(.056)
Income	.085*	.046*	.046*
	(.015)	(.019)	(.018)
Race	−.087	−.067	−.052
	(.079)	(.087)	(.079)
Accuracy of polls in elections (1 = accurate)		.016	
		(.070)	
Accuracy of nonelection polls (1 = accurate)		.100	
		(.071)	
Number of polls (3 = too many)		−.136*	−.130*
		(.047)	(.041)
Attention to national politics (3 = close attention)		.304*	.304*
		(.040)	(.036)
Survey participation experience (1 = former respondent)		.138*	.165*
		(.079)	(.072)
Sampling knowledge (1 = knowledgeable)		−.047	
		(.066)	
Voted in 1992 (1 = voter)		.044	
		(.072)	
N	1053	739	874
R^2	.034	.131	.121

*$p < .05$

[a]Regression 3 is a rerun of Regression 2, leaving out attitudinal and behavioral variables that did not achieve statistical significance. The result indicates that there were no significant changes in the amount of explained variance or individual coefficients for the independent variables. In each equation, the coefficients are unstandardized; their standard errors are included in parentheses below them.

in the attention to polls (R^2 = .131). These results indicate that Americans who follow news about national politics closely are also most likely to follow public opinion poll results regularly, as are past survey participants. In contrast, those who think there are too many polls are less likely to follow public opinion poll results regularly than those who think there are not enough polls. Neither methodological knowledge, perceptions of accuracy, nor recent voting behavior was a significant predictor of attention to polls in the media.

A second regression analysis investigated the correlates of perceptions about the frequency of reported polls.[4] At the first stage, data in Table 8.4 indicate that respondents who are older white males with more education are more likely to believe that there are too many polls in this country.[5] As in the case of attention to polls, demographics account for only a small amount of variance in this measure (R^2 = .066). The results presented in Table 8.4 again show that attitudinal variables added a significant increment to the predicted variance, increasing the R^2 to .183. Two out of the three normative evaluations of polls are strongly related to perceptions about the number of existing polls, although perceived accuracy again is not. As expected, those who think the country would be "better off" if leaders followed public opinion polls more closely tend to believe that more public opinion polls need to be conducted, and those who evaluate polls as a "good thing" also appear to think that more polls could be conducted.

An interesting pattern emerged, however, when exposure to national politics and attention to public opinion polls were considered. On the one hand, those who voted in 1992 and who claim to follow news about national politics regularly are more likely to believe that there are too many polls. On the other hand, people who report greater attention to public opinion poll results in the mass media tend to think that there are not enough polls in the country. Does past exposure to polls, in the context of recent past political activity or attention to a recent campaign, temper attitudes about appropriate levels of polling? Was this just a function of an experience in 1992, or is the phenomenon more general? These are important questions that need further research with appropriate data.

Conclusions

The results presented here raise many interesting questions about issues that require further research even as they clarify some relationships between the characteristics of the public and their interest in poll results. The analysis suggests that attitudinal and behavioral explanations of the public's reaction to polls and their expectations about the roles of polls are more important than simple demographic explanations. Experienced social scientists and scholars of American political behavior will not be surprised by this conclusion.

The literature review and the secondary analysis of the 1996 Gallup survey suggest that public confidence in polls is and remains high. The public is attentive to polls, especially in election years, even without a strong a priori interest in them. This part of the analysis suggests that the public is receptive to polls reported in the news but may not be actively interested in searching out such

TABLE 8.4 HIERARCHICAL REGRESSION: DEMOGRAPHIC AND ATTITUDINAL
PREDICTORS OF PERCEIVED NUMBER OF PUBLIC OPINION POLLS

	MULTIPLE REGRESSION COEFFICIENTS (DEPENDENT VARIABLE = ARE THERE TOO MANY POLLS?)		
PREDICTORS	REGRESSION 1	REGRESSION 2	REGRESSION 3[a]
Age	.008*	.006*	.005*
	(.001)	(.001)	(.001)
Education	.033*	.009	.018
	(.014)	(.016)	(.014)
Gender	.140*	.095*	.114*
	(.045)	(.050)	(.045)
Income	−.017	−.014	−.015
	(−.017)	(.016)	(.015)
Race	.125*	.143*	.131*
	(.064)	(.072)	(.065)
Accuracy of election polls (1 = accurate)		−.059 (.058)	
Accuracy of nonelection polls (1 = accurate)		−.071 (.060)	
Attention to poll (3 = close attention)		−.053* (.030)	−.082* (.027)
Polls for the public (1 = for the public)		−.097 (.070)	
Polls as good thing (1 = good thing)		−.433* (.101)	−.571* (.084)
Attention to national politics (2 = close attention)		.074* (.033)	.086* (.030)
Survey participation experience (1 = former respondent)		−.035 (.065)	
Sampling knowledge (1 = knowledgeable)		−.020 (.054)	
Voted in 1992 (1 = voter)		.168* (.058)	.181* (.054)
Leaders using polls (1 = country better off if leaders follow polls closely)		−.193* (.074)	−.237* (.067)
N	893	647	780
R²	.066	.183	.181

*p < .05

[a]Regression 3 is a rerun of Regression 2, leaving out attitudinal and behavioral variables that did not achieve statistical significance. The result indicates that there were no significant changes in the amount of explained variance or individual coefficients for the independent variables. In each equation, the coefficients are unstandardized; their standard errors are included in parentheses below them.

information. This seems to be as true for nonelection year polls as it is for election year polls. The nature of this relationship deserves further investigation, specifically so we can better understand the temporal order in the process. What kinds of audience members actively search for poll results because they are interested in what their fellow citizens think? And what kinds of citizens become interested in public policies because of chance exposure to news reports that contain information about what their fellow citizens think?

Generally, regardless of their low levels of knowledge about polling procedures or their perceptions about the accuracy of polls, the public approves of polls. The most interesting finding is the lack of a relationship between knowledge of polling procedures (which is very low among the public), perceptions of the accuracy of polls, and the positive evaluations they generally receive. This analysis and the results from several past studies suggest that these public judgments or evaluations are not well grounded in knowledge. This is significant in two regards: In the first place, the finding raises a question of whether or not the public values polls for some reason other than the quality of the information they contain. Conceivably these positive evaluations are a function of subscribing to a basic tenet of democratic theory that elected officials should be paying attention to the wishes of their constituents. This is quite a different basis for positive evaluations than having a well-grounded understanding of polling methods or believing that the media's reporting of polls would be "good" for public consumption only when important policy issues are being debated.

Furthermore, these results raise an interesting question about the AAPOR and NCPP standards for disclosure of polling methodology when results are reported publicly. One assumption underlying the standards is the expectation that consumers of polling information have the necessary knowledge base to make informed judgments about whether a particular poll reported in the media is reliable and valid. The lack of a strong and consistent effect of education suggests that this assumption is probably unwarranted and never likely to be reflected in a well-informed public in the real world.

Does this mean that the AAPOR and NCPP standards are meaningless or without merit? The answer is "of course not." But perhaps their educational efforts should be more vigorously directed to elite constituencies such as journalists, who are the conduits for the flow of so much public opinion data in the United States. If the public has neither the knowledge of polling methods nor the inclination to assemble sufficient information to make critical judgments about the quality of polling data reported in news stories, renewed effort should be devoted to screening "bad" data out of the news stream. The best way to do this is to deal more directly with journalists (both editors and reporters), who are the most likely to come in contact with data at the source.

Notes

1. Goyder (1986) most recently highlighted the "epistemological limitation" of using the survey method to measure public reactions to surveys. One part of the problem lies in response rates, where people who are not favorably predisposed to the survey process have already eliminated themselves from the data collection by refusing to participate. Dran and Hildreth (1995) point out a second issue, namely, that the pleasant experience of being interviewed may bias the respondent toward giving positive evaluations of the method. We acknowledge these problems and their potential influence on the results presented here.
2. We are grateful to David Moore of the Gallup Organization, who provided us with a copy of the data and documentation. The design of the survey is described in the *Gallup Poll Monthly* (May 1996).
3. The lack of a relationship between education and exposure to poll results was unexpected, so a check was made to see whether this might be attributable to the coding of the variable. Each of the three regression equations was rerun using a dichotomous measure of education (college educated or not) and a trichotomous measure (eight grades or less, nine to twelve grades, some college or more). The variable achieved statistical significance only in the base equation when only demographic measures were used. It had no statistically significant contribution when the attitudinal and behavioral variables were added to the equation. This contributed to our view that education does not play a role in explaining citizens' attention to public opinion polls in any meaningful way, but this is a relationship that requires additional study if we are to understand it fully.
4. Each of these dependent variables was entered as an independent variable in the prediction of the other, and each was a statistically significant correlate. This is an instance in which, conceptually, temporal ordering would be a critical matter for understanding the nature of causality. This is an analysis that would be worthwhile but must await other longitudinal data.
5. Again the relationship of education to the dependent variable was evaluated as a function of the way the independent variable was coded. When just demographic variables were used as predictors, education was a significant predictor of perceptions of the appropriate number of polls in two out of three instances when it was dichotomized and measured in years of education. When the attitudinal variables were added to the equations, then, education was a statistically significant predictor of perceptions of the number of polls for only one of six alternative equations.

APPENDIX 8.A

Technical Appendix

This appendix contains a description of the measures used in the analysis.

Dependent Variables

The two major dependent variables for multivariate analysis were the public's attention to poll results and perceptions about the relative number of existing polls.

Attention to poll results

In the Gallup survey, respondents were asked whether they "follow the results of any public opinion poll regularly in any newspaper or magazine." Response categories were recoded so that the higher value corresponds to greater attention (2 = yes, regularly; 1 = yes, occasionally; 0 = no).

Appropriate number of polls

Respondents were also asked whether "there are too many public opinion polls in this country, not enough public opinion polls, or is the number of public opinion polls about right the way it is?" This variable was recoded so that a higher value corresponds to concern about the prevalence of polls (3 = too many, 2 = about right, 1 = not enough).

Independent Variables

A variety of independent variables were used in the analysis that reflected demographic characteristics of the respondents, their attitudes about polls, and measures of their political behavior.

Demographics

Standard demographic variables such as age, education, income, gender, and race provide the background information about respondents. For analysis, gender and race were recoded into dummy variables that had values of 1 and 0 (0 = female, 1 = male; 0 = nonwhite, 1 = white). Age was measured at the ratio level in terms of number of years. Education was recorded from a question asking the respondent for the last grade completed in school. Income was measured as an ordinal variable in terms of bracketed categories.

Perceived accuracy of polls

Respondents were asked two questions about their perceptions of the accuracy of polls in an election or nonelection context. The questions and their response categories were not exactly parallel, so they were recoded to reflect a general perception of accuracy; and "don't know" responses were coded as the equivalent of an "inaccurate" response. In the election context, respondents were asked the following: "Some polling organizations make frequent predictions of election results. What is your general impression of how well they do—do you think they are pretty nearly right most of the time, or do you think their record is not very good?" (0 = not accurate, 1 = accurate). In the nonelection context, they were asked the following question: "Do you think poll returns on matters not dealing with elections, but with public opinion towards such things as labor problems or international affairs, are usually pretty nearly right, or not right at all?" (0 = not accurate, 1 = accurate).

Exposure to national politics

The survey also asked respondents how closely they followed news about national politics. Response categories were recoded so that the higher value would correspond with closer attention (3 = very closely, 2 = somewhat closely, 1 = not too closely, 0 = not closely at all).

Past participation in surveys

Past participation in public opinion surveys was measured using dichotomous response categories (1 = yes, 0 = no).

Knowledge of sampling

Respondents were asked whether "a sample of 1,500 or 2,000 people can accurately reflect the views of the nation's population, or whether it is not possible with so few people." Responses were coded dichotomously (1 = can accurately reflect the views, 0 = not possible/don't know).

Voter turnout in the 1992 election

Voter turnout was recoded into a dummy variable, and "don't know," "refused," and "not ascertained" responses were recoded as nonparticipation.

Normative evaluations of polls

Four questions measured respondents' evaluations of polls and were used as independent variables:

Q6/7: "If the leaders of our nation followed the views of *the public/public opinion polls* more closely, do you think the nation would be better off, or worse off than it is today?" Q6 and Q7 were split-sample items testing for question-wording effects. Even though these wording differences may reflect different conceptualizations of "public opinion," the bivariate analysis did not show significant marginal differences between the two versions of the questions. Therefore, they were combined to construct a single variable that had two response categories (1 = better off, 0 = worse off).

Q8: "Do you think most opinion polls work for or against the best interests of the general public?" (1 = for, 0 = against).

Q9: "Would you say that polls of the opinion of the public are a good thing or a bad thing in our country?" (1 = good thing, 0 = bad thing).

CHAPTER 9

Who Will Vote? Ascertaining Likelihood to Vote and Modeling a Probable Electorate in Preelection Polls

Robert P. Daves

The 1996 postelection analysis of the polls and their accuracy had several major threads. One thread was an exercise in polemic excess, a criticism of the polls for being less accurate than they were in the 1948 fiasco. This chapter addresses another thread, which developed a bit later. It is a more reasoned examination of one aspect of the key, below-decks machinery crucial to preelection polling—modeling the population of voters. Not every eligible citizen who can vote will, and public opinion researchers for decades have been tinkering with ways to fine-tune their sampling to best infer their sample statistics from the population of people who vote on Election Day.

This chapter reviews the techniques researchers use to ascertain respondents' likelihood of voting and considers how the data are used in estimating candidate support in preelection polls. It also examines how several of the major polls model a probable electorate.

What Went Right?

William Jefferson Clinton's trouncing of Senator Robert Dole in 1996 was barely a week old when some scholars tried to claim in the heat of a postelection snit that the polls had performed even worse than they had in the 1948 election, when some polls foreshadowed a Truman loss and a Dewey win. But that criticism is not justified in the 1996 election. On the average, the polls did a little better than average. Table 9.1, based on a table originally found in the *New York Times* after the 1996 election (Kagay 1996), shows that in terms of average error for the Clinton lead, the polls were well within the margin of sampling error compared with the election outcome. That is especially true if one exempts the final CBS News poll from that comparison.

The National Council of Public Polls (NCPP), an industry watchdog that sometimes serves as a "quick response" organization to alert the public to polling charlatans and other issues about polls, was quick to counter the postelection criticism. It concluded that "the average error in 1996 was well within the margin expected from sample surveys of these sizes" and, moreover, that "average error in 1996 was low relative to historical experience" (NCP 1997, 1). Warren Mitofsky, who examined national, state, and exit polls after the 1996 election, came to the same conclusion (Mitofsky 1998).

TABLE 9.1   TREATMENT OF LIKELIHOOD TO VOTE BY VARIOUS NATIONAL POLLS PRIOR TO THE 1996 ELECTION

POLL	DATE TAKEN	CLINTON LEAD	SAMPLE SIZE	ELECTORAL MODEL	TURNOUT ESTIMATE
ABC News	2–3 November	12	703	Likely voters	— [a]
CNN/*USA Today*/ Gallup					
No. 1	3–4 November	13	1,641	Probable voters	58
No. 2	3–4 November	8	1,448	Index cutoff	51
Harris	1–3 November	12	1,339	Likely voters	62
NBC/*Wall Street Journal*	2–3 November	12	1,020	Registered voters	—[b]
NY Times/CBS News					
NYT	30 October– 2 November	16	1,513	Probable electorate	60
CBS	30 October– 2 November	18	1,513	Probable electorate	60
Pew Research Center	31 October– 3 November	13	1,211	Index cutoff	50
Reuters/Zogby	1–3 November	7	1,200	Likely voters	—[b]
Actual election results/turnout		8			49

[a]Not able to ascertain from the polling organization.
[b]The polling organization didn't ascertain turnout.

Source: Kagay (1996); various polling organizations.

If Not Accuracy, What Did Go Wrong?

Since the 1996 election, many have criticized various polls for their methodologies. One of those discussions took place in Norfolk, Virginia, at the 1997
conference of the American Association for Public Opinion Research (AAPOR).
Public opinion scholars and research practitioners dissected one research effort
in particular, the tracking polls John Zogby conducted for Reuters. Zogby's
methodology came under scrutiny not so much for its accuracy—Gallup and
others have been as accurate in the past and were certainly well within expected
margins this year—but for its nonprobability method of ascertaining a likely
electorate. More about that later.

First, it is important to understand how public opinion researchers who conduct preelection polls try to model the electorate's attitudes, opinions, and beliefs,
and, ultimately, whom it will cast its collective force behind on Election Day. In
a presidential or any other highly visible election, public opinion researchers can
pay a severe penalty for doing a poor job estimating turnout—that is, for poorly
discerning in their polls who is most likely to vote. Perry's (1960) work represented
a major development in the sophistication of turnout prediction. Recognizing
that superior sampling techniques may not eliminate all sources of poll error,
Perry pointed out that even a sample completely representative of a given population it may still produce biased estimates if it is not also representative of voting
participation. Furthermore, he noted that the risk of error resulting from differential turnout increased as turnout decreased (Perry 1973).

Scholars from Perry (1960) to Freedman and Goldstein (1996) have demonstrated that different screens used to determine the likelihood of respondents'
actually voting can produce different samples—different "electorates"—and vary
from the actual presidential vote.

In lower-turnout elections, when it is tougher to determine who is going to
vote and who is not, there is even greater potential for error in estimating candidate support in a trial heat question or vote in a referendum. In low-turnout
races such as primaries, mayoral elections, and bond referenda, the penalty can
be even more severe for miscalculating who will or will not vote or for incor-
rectly modeling a probable electorate. Many pollsters who do work in such elections believe that people who really care about the issues at question and those
who may not care as much about the issue but want to be "good citizens" are
the ones who turn out to vote. And finding them in a random-digit dialing
(RDD) telephone poll can be difficult, costly, and time consuming.

Preelection polls that do not mirror election outcomes—or a candidate's
perception of reality prior to the election—often face "the screen wasn't tight
enough" criticism or some such comment hinting that the poll's respondents

were not of the same ilk as the real electorate. After his win, a 1990 Minnesota gubernatorial primary candidate observed after the polls showed him far behind that there was nothing wrong with the polls except a lack of tight-enough screens. It turned out that the real reason the polls differed from the election outcome was that the polls were taken well in advance of the election—several weeks—for that acid-test measure of accuracy to be made. But the candidate made a common mistake, blaming the difference on poor measurement of likely voters.

Defining Turnout

Ostensibly, the trick for researchers is to identify a population—likely voters, the "electorate," or whatever—and then measure it. Even such methodologically demanding organizations as the U.S. Bureau of the Census and the Center for the Study of the American Electorate (CSAE) find estimating turnout a daunting task, and they have done so for years. From time to time researchers quibble over their definitions of a *voting age population* (VAP) (cf. Bruce 1997 and Gans 1997), lamenting along the way that turnout continues to drop. Turnout is usually expressed as a percentage of the VAP, but determining what constitutes the VAP is a tough job. A simplistic definition of VAP is the number of people old enough to vote in the next election.

Many exceptions nibble away at this definition, and the CSAE takes into account naturalization rates, age-eligible citizens residing outside the country, the census undercount, aliens, and convicted felons who are not permitted to vote, among other factors. Those who are mentally incompetent, those in group quarters such as nonresident students in dorms, those in nursing homes, or nonresident soldiers in barracks, who may or may not be included, are tough to measure—and to poll.

There also are situations that make the VAP larger than it should be in some states. In one California congressional district, a nine-term incumbent Republican claimed that he lost the close 1996 election to a novice Democrat because noncitizens voted in the election. California Secretary of State Bill Jones reported that more than 5,000 noncitizens were registered to vote, but it was unclear how many had actually voted in that 1996 congressional election (Levin 1997).

Few would disagree with Peter Bruce (1997) when he expressed hope that discussions of measurement methodologies will lead to enhancement of public awareness of the turnout problem. That hopefulness does not mitigate the fact that it is a tough task for all organizations to sort out just exactly what the VAP is and whom it includes, and it is an even tougher task for preelection pollsters to sample that population.

Divining Likely Voters: Measuring Turnout

So how do pollsters—in the 1996 elections and others—determine who is likely to vote and who isn't? On the surface, it appears an easy task: Ask a respondent if he or she will vote in the election, and if the answer is no, then politely end the interview. Thank you for your help; goodbye.

But as with most survey research issues, it is not that simple. For one thing, in most states one has to be registered to vote. (An exception is North Dakota, where a voter can just show up with an accepted form of ID and cast a ballot.) Most states require registering ahead of time. (There are even more exceptions to this observation: In Minnesota, for example, one can register on Election Day—and many do. In the 1992 election, about one of every six voters registered on Election Day, a proportion duplicated in 1998 when Jesse Ventura captured the governor's seat; in 1996, Election Day registration totaled 15 percent.) So using only registration status as a screen would potentially have serious problems, particularly late in the election cycle when many states have closed their books.

For another thing, people may not or cannot abide by their answers to a pollster's question about intention to vote. They get sick. They get hit by a truck. They go out of town and do not vote by absentee ballot. They get tied up at work and forget to vote. They get lazy. Despite good intentions—and a "definitely will vote" answer to a screening question about the likelihood of voting—some respondents say "yes" but never show up at the polls. (A related but separate problem is the growing number of those who vote by absentee ballot, particularly in states such as Oregon, Washington, and Texas. Consequently, using only one question to divine likelihood to vote is likely to result in measurement error.

Scholars have come up with several taxonomies to classify the methods by which election researchers deal with likelihood to vote. (Crespi 1988 and Freedman and Goldstein 1996 have good discussions of likely voter methods.) Essentially, there are five ways to ascertain likelihood to vote in a preelection poll:

1. Use one or more questions as a screen.
2. Use the answers to a series of questions to compute a "turnout score" on a likely voter index, then analyze responses only from those who meet certain criteria for turnout.
3. Weight for likelihood of voting, that is, assigning case weights for differing probabilities of voting.
4. Do some combination of 2 and 3.
5. Use no screening or weighting technique, that is, do unweighted polling of the entire voting age population.

One can—and should—ignore the last option. Of course, all the national polls that publish final estimates use widely varying methods of treating likelihood to vote (see Table 9.2). Before discussing those methods, it is useful to define some terms.

When a *screening* method is used, one can divide respondents into likely voters and unlikely voters. Usually unlikely voters are screened out of the sample and do not complete the interview. When a *weighting* method is used, one could call respondents likely voters, but it is best to call the sample a model of a *probable electorate*. In George Orwell's *Animal Farm*, some of the piggy population reasoned that all pigs were equal, but that some pigs were more equal than other pigs. In a similar vein, when weighting is used to model a probable electorate, all voters are "likely" voters, but some are more likely to vote than others.

As Traugott and Lavrakas (1999) observe in their election polling primer, there is no standard, generally accepted method of dealing with likely voters in a preelection poll, and some methods work better than others. Let us examine some of these common methods (and one uncommon one), as well as some of the polls that used them in the recent presidential elections.

The Screen

The screen is perhaps the easiest and least expensive method of determining who is likely to vote. It involves asking one or more questions, and if the answer to any one indicates a likelihood of not voting, the interview is terminated. Favorites are registration status and self-professed probability of voting. In the 1992 election, for example, the *Washington Post* poll queried only respondents who were registered and said they would definitely vote. In 1988 the *Post* had an additional screen: how closely respondents followed the election (Daves and Warden 1995). There are many merits to the screening approach: it is less expensive than other approaches because unlikely voters do not go through the whole interview; it is easy to explain to reporters, readers, and viewers; and it yields an "absolute" data set, one that is a hard-and-fast definition of a sample of a population—likely voters.

But the screen has its drawbacks, too. Some potential voters may be screened out and not counted, particularly those who live in states that have Election Day registration. A large drawback is the method's diminished ability to analyze varying turnout scenarios. A simple screen cannot answer very well questions such as, "What would the election look like if there's a higher-than-average turnout?" or "What would the election look like if there's a lower-than-average turnout?" The screen is also problematic if the wrong questions are used. One polling company, for example, rather than determining a self-professed probability of voting, asks respondents if they "usually vote" in whichever election they are measuring.

TABLE 9.2   QUESTIONS POLLSTERS USE TO HELP ASCERTAIN LIKELIHOOD TO VOTE

Researchers use various questions to measure likelihood to vote, or to ascertain a probable electorate. Here are examples from past elections, both state and national, primary and general.

REGISTRATION
"Are you registered to vote?" (*Washington Post*)
"Are you registered to vote in the precinct or township where you live?" (Minnesota Poll)

INTEREST AND KNOWLEDGE
"Generally speaking, how much interest would you say you have in the upcoming [September primary/November general] election, a great deal, a fair amount, only a little, or no interest at all?" (Minnesota Poll)

"How closely are you following the 1988 presidential race: very closely, somewhat closely, not too closely, or not closely at all?" (*Washington Post*)

SELF-PROFESSED PROBABILITY
Primary election
"Some people vote in a party's primary election in September, and others wait until the candidates have been decided, then vote in the November election. How about you? Would you say you definitely will vote, probably will, probably won't, or definitely won't vote in the primary election and just wait until the November general election?" (Minnesota Poll)

General election
"How likely is it that you will vote in the election [in November/next Tuesday]? Would you say you definitely will vote, probably will vote, probably won't vote, or definitely won't vote? (Minnesota Poll)

"Some people have busier schedules than others. Because of this, some people who plan to vote can't always get around to it on election day. With your own personal daily schedule in mind, I'd like you to rate the chances that you will vote in the 1992 presidential election next November: Are you certain to vote, will you probably vote, are the chances about 50–50, or don't you think you will vote in that election?" (*Washington Post*)

"People tell us that there are things that come up on the last minute that sometimes keep them from getting to the polls on election day. How much of a chance is there that things will come up to keep you from voting on election day, a fair chance, some chance, hardly any chance, or no chance at all?" (Minnesota Poll)

PAST VOTING BEHAVIOR
"Did you vote in the general election in November when George Bush, Bill Clinton, and Ross Perot were running for president, or did something come up that kept you from getting to the polls that day?" (Minnesota Poll)

"A lot of people weren't able to vote in the _____ election last _____, even though they had wanted to. How about you? Did things come up that kept you from voting, or did you vote last _____ ." (Buckeye State Poll)

10-POINT SCALES FOR INTENTION TO VOTE
"For this question, please use a scale from zero to ten, where zero means there is no chance you will vote in the election and ten means you are completely certain you will vote. Using this scale, how likely is it that you will vote in the _____ election?" (Buckeye State Poll)

TABLE 9.2 (CONTINUED)

"At election time, sometimes things come up that keep a person from voting. I'd like you to imagine a scale that runs from zero to ten. If I asked you how likely you are to vote next Tuesday, and you thought there was no chance of you voting, you would answer zero. If you were certain you would vote, you would answer ten. If you weren't sure, you would choose another number as close to zero or ten as you think it should be. Now using this scale, how likely are you to vote in Tuesday's election?" (Minnesota Poll)

INFORMATION ABOUT THE ELECTION
"Generally speaking, how much information have you received about _____? Would you say quite a bit of information, a fair amount of information, not much information, or hardly any information?" (Buckeye State Poll)

ATTENTION PAID TO THE ELECTION
"Overall, how much attention have you paid so far to discussions and news coverage of _____? Would you say a great deal of attention, some attention, not much attention or no attention at all?" (Buckeye State Poll)

This line of inquiry opens the door to social response bias and likely results in a sample that has a too liberal definition of likely voters.

Irving Crespi, a senior public opinion researcher with decades of polling experience, surveyed a number of other pollsters in the 1980s to compare their methods with their accuracy in forecasting elections. He concluded that using several likely voter-screening questions produces more accurate results than using only one question (Crespi 1988). Pollsters use many different kinds of questions that they believe useful in divining likelihood to vote, including ones that measure "affect," or involvement and interest in the election, and knowledge about the election.

The screen appears to be the method most frequently used by pollsters to deal with likely voters. In the 1996 election, John Zogby's poll for the Reuters news agency was one of the most accurate. Zogby's exact methods have been documented elsewhere (cf. Zogby 1996), but he screens out those who are not registered to vote, those who say they are not likely to vote, and those who did not vote in the last election.

The "Cutoff" Index

Researchers employing the cutoff index use a series of questions that are correlated with likelihood to vote to create an index based on the responses to the questions. Lower index scores mean lower likelihood of voting—not registered, low interest in the election, and so on—and higher scores mean higher likelihood of voting—being registered and having a great deal of interest in the election, for example. This is a simple but ingenious method pioneered by researchers at the Gallup Organization to yield a sample of likely voters in a pre-election poll (cf. Perry 1960).

Here's how a cutoff index might work. Let's say that there is a 7-point index that ranges from 0 (least likely to vote) to 6 (most likely to vote). Then researchers can just go from the top down to analyze the answers of the most likely to vote, whether they be only 5s, 6s, and 7s, or whether they be 3s through 7s. The proportion of those likely to vote to the total sample would be the turnout ratio.

The cutoff index has several advantages over screening for likely voters. First, it gives the public opinion analyst the ability to analyze the effect different turnout scenarios might have on the trial heat measure, assuming the trial heat questions are asked of all respondents. Second, by not "throwing away" any respondents, it enables postelection verification of respondent voting behavior, thus allowing analysts to reconcile respondent behavior after the election with what was said before the election. This is important in fine-tuning the model from election to election and in testing how well the model works in different types of elections.

But using a cutoff index can be more costly than screening. Typically one uses more questions to build an index than to build a screen, so the process takes more interviewing time, which is costly. Using an index can also cost more because one must ask all respondents all the questions, including trial heat and demographics, as well as index component questions and any others the researcher wants to ask. Further, as in screening, trimming the sample size can make for a larger margin of sampling error. If one wants to maintain the same margin of sampling error, one just interviews more respondents—but this also drives up the cost.

Another problem with the cutoff index is that it assumes one knows the turnout ratio ahead of time, which is almost never the case. Gallup, however, attempts to ascertain an estimate of turnout and then tailors its index to get as close to that turnout estimate as possible. In 1996, Gallup used two questions, interest in the election and self-professed probability of voting, to estimate a turnout. Lydia Saad, managing editor of the Gallup poll, said Gallup's projections indicated a 48 to 53 percent turnout, but the Gallup team had the most confidence in the formula that yielded a 51 percent estimate. After that, they used several questions to construct a cutoff index. "We went with the model that had questions that were comparable to 1980, because it was the most similar election, we believed," explained Saad (personal communication, 12 February 1999).

There were seven of those questions, and Gallup scored respondents zero through 7, based on their answers: A "vote" answer was scored 1 and a "not vote" answer was scored 0. The seven questions indicated the following:

1. Amount of thought given to the election
2. Voting frequency
3. Intent to vote
4. Certainty to vote
5. Knowing where to vote
6. Having ever voted there
7. Having voted in the last election

Gallup then took all 7s, which yielded too small a turnout. To bring the sample size up to the estimated turnout ratio, Gallup had to find additional respondents in the data set to include as likely voters. These they identified by including those who scored 6 points in the sample, but counting each of them as only a third of a response (a weight factor of 0.33). This yielded a new sample size that was close to the 51 percent turnout they had estimated. But this procedure was used only for the final estimate. Before that—during the whole campaign—Gallup used the "probable electorate" method.

The Gallup Organization, which polled for *USA Today* and CNN, switched at the end from the probable voter definition it had used throughout the fall campaign to a stricter definition of likely voters and then released the results of both methods. Gallup researcher David Moore said the stricter definition produced the more correct result: "48 percent for Mr. Clinton and 40 percent for Mr. Dole" (Kagay 1996).

Modeling a Probable Electorate: Weighting for Likelihood to Vote

In many ways the "probable electorate" method is similar to the cutoff index method. Researchers use a number of questions correlated with voting and construct an index on which each respondent has a score. If an interval- or ratio-level of measurement is employed, those lower on the index would be less likely to vote, whereas those higher on the index would be more likely to vote, just as in the cutoff method. Instead of using the index to trim "unlikely" voters from the sample, though, researchers assign case weights to each respondent based on their score on the index. Those having the highest scores receive the heaviest weights, those with lower scores the smaller weights.

The *New York Times/*CBS News poll uses this method of ascertaining a "probable electorate," as does the *Minneapolis Star Tribune*'s Minnesota poll (in general elections). (See Chapter 2 in this book for a discussion of the *Times*'s poll performance in the 1996 election.)

This method usually yields a weighted sample size smaller than the original sample size because weighting methods almost always assign weights smaller than one, even to the most "likely" respondents. (The argument here is that almost no one is 100 percent certain to vote: One might, perhaps, be hit by a truck on the way to the polling booth, even after making a perfect "likely voter" score on the index.) By dividing the weighted sample size by the original sample size, one can estimate the turnout ratio.

Investigating this approach, Traugott and Tucker (1984) identified variables that had a strong relationship with turnout, a process that resulted in the use of three dichotomized variables (voter registration, past voting behavior, and interest in the election) to estimate the likelihood that respondents would vote. They recognized that some respondents who have a high probability of voting will, in fact, not vote, whereas others who appear unlikely to vote do actually go on to cast a ballot. They used logit regression to develop maximum likelihood probabilities of voting for each respondent. These probabilities then served as weights, producing a probable electorate comprising differential contributions from all respondents.

The model Traugott and Tucker used to develop their weighted probabilities, however, used validated voting as its dependent variable. Thus, before the probability weights could be developed, the actual behavior itself had to be known. They suggested that weights be recalculated for each election and noted that the weights could not be generalized from one context to another. Consequently, despite the elegance of this approach, it cannot be used to predict turnout for an election (unless, despite warnings, the weights calculated for a previous election are used). Petrocik (1991) suggested some improvements to Traugott and Tucker's model, but these did not address the problem of logic described earlier. Instead, he noted that Traugott and Tucker's model employed variables likely to be affected by social desirability error; and to counter this problem he advocated the inclusion of variables related to nonvoting. Although the variables he explored did reduce the error associated with Traugott and Tucker's estimates, Petrocik's work also relied on prior knowledge of respondents' voting behavior. He tested his model on News Election Service (NES) data for the 1980 Carter-Reagan election and reported doing a better job at predicting Reagan's win. He cautioned, however, that this turnout model might not be effective in nonpresidential elections.

This method has a number of benefits, and like all methods it contains built-in assumptions. It assumes, of course, that some proportion of the voting age population will vote. It also assumes that people who say they will vote are more likely to vote than those who say they will not vote, just as those who are registered to vote are, in general, more likely to vote than those who are not registered. But the weighting model recognizes that although some people are quite unlikely to vote—they are not registered, they have little interest in the election, and they have said they would only "probably" vote, for example—it is not a sure thing that they *will not* cast a ballot. A neighbor could pressure them into walking to the polls and voting, despite their not intending to. Or a dynamic candidate might garner support in the latter stages of a race, creating a bandwagon effect. At the other end of the spectrum, a prospective voter could, for example, have an accident late in the day on the way to vote and thus not be able to cast a ballot. Consequently, the weighting model uses all the qualified interviews, unlike the other methods, which eventually screen some respondents out.[1]

The Deluxe Combos

Another method of handling likely voters in a preelection poll is to use a combination of the other methods. This effectively means screening out those judged to be solid "nonvoters" and assigning some fractional likelihood of voting to the remaining "voters" by weighting their responses.

Freedman and Goldstein (1996) advocate this method. They found by analyzing the 1988 National Election Study that about eight in ten interviewees who said they would not vote did not, in fact, cast a ballot. The message: Believe respondents, they advise, when they tell you they are not going to vote and exclude them from your sample. Thus the first step involves identifying nonvoters and not interviewing them.

The second step involves identifying "misreporters," those who say they will vote, but don't cast a ballot. Freedman and Goldstein use a series of seven demographic questions, plus strength of partisanship and frequency of church attendance, to model a likely electorate by assigning an estimated probability of voting to every respondent. The turnout estimate, which includes a zero probability for those who were screened out originally, is the mean of all the respondents' probabilities. (It is the author's experience that this can work well in low-turnout elections, such as primaries; he has not tried the model in general elections.)

The 1996 Presidential Election

The 1996 presidential election had a far smaller turnout than earlier similar elections and a smaller turnout than many public opinion researchers estimated. Whereas some models showed that turnout would approach the 60 percent levels in recent presidential elections—and 70 percent in high-turnout states such as Minnesota—the actual national turnout was estimated at closer to 49 percent of the VAP, the lowest since the 1924 election (Ladd 1996b).

Scholars and pundits have cited a number of reasons for the lower turnout: a good economy, lack of choice of candidates, negative campaign advertising, and perhaps the polls themselves. Those who suggest that the economy had a great deal to do with the turnout say that when voters are fat and happy, as in good economic times, fewer voters show up at the polls with the goal of throwing the bums out. Keeter (1997), for example, noted that "good economic conditions, or at least the perceptions of them, can make voters overlook other flaws an incumbent president might have."

A perennial claim is that the poor quality of the current crop of candidates keeps voters at home, but that excuse trips too lightly off the tongue of the politically alienated to ring true when the Republicans have the experience and seniority of a Bob Dole for a candidate and the Democrats have a relatively popular incumbent president as the candidate.

Germond and Witcover (1996) suggest that, it was instead, negative advertising. Quoting Curtis B. Gans, of the Committee of the Study of the American Electorate, they suggest that despite the "motor-voter" law, which provided easy opportunity to register, the mudslinging of negative advertising caused voters to "simply wash their hands of the whole business" and stay at home on Election Day. The Minnesota poll found that there might be a kernel of truth to that, at least at the state level. A poll in the 1996 U.S. Senate race between Senator Paul Wellstone and challenger Rudy Boschwitz, whom Wellstone beat in 1990, found that mudslinging was negatively affecting Boschwitz's chances of recapturing his old seat, and it may have been alienating voters.

But at least two prominent public opinion researchers, Everett Carll Ladd of the Roper Center and Burns Roper Jr. believe that the polls themselves helped lower turnout in 1996. "It is likely that pollsters and reporters dampened voters' interest, and hence participation, by announcing that the presidential contest was really no contest at all," Ladd (1996a) said in a *Wall Street Journal* article critical of the way the polls were used by the media in 1996. And in a free-wheeling discussion at a public opinion conference in May 1997, Roper expressed similar sentiments. Scholars who study preelection polls' effects on turnout have found bandwagon *and* underdog effects. One study found both effects appearing in the same election (Lavrakas, Holley, and Miller 1991). Thus, it is almost certain that polls have some effect on turnout; but further research is needed to understand the extent, direction, and dynamics of the effect and whether there is more effect in some types of elections than in others.

Some researchers suggest that there are "litmus test" issues in a significant portion of the population (Tompson and Lavrakas 1997) that affect turnout. These issues are hot buttons for some voters, and if a candidate disagrees with the voter, then those issues—abortion rights, taxes, and gun control are good examples—can serve to foster turnout. In Minnesota, between one quarter and two fifths of the population indicate on various Minnesota polls that there is a single issue that would cause them to vote against a candidate if that candidate's position disagreed with theirs on the issue. Thus, the absence of these litmus test issues could have fostered a malaise among voters and driven down turnout.

One criticism of the polls that always comes up is response rates, which seem to drop election-by-election. If one cannot interview a representative sample of respondents, it is argued, then it will be difficult to ascertain a data set that mirrors the electorate, at best getting the trial heat numbers wrong, and at worse doing a poor job of predicting turnout. Columnist Arianna Huffington made the news in 1998, criticizing national polling with this argument:

> The key to polling's accuracy is the principle of "equal probability of selection." But if larger and larger numbers among those randomly selected refuse to participate, this principle no longer applies. (Huffington 1998, 1)

Although nonresponse is an increasing problem for those who conduct sample surveys, Huffington attempted to tar all pollsters by employing a common rhetorical device—making a sweeping generalization by oversimplifying a complex problem. Increasingly, the methodological mavens who study polling techniques are learning that nonresponse may not have the detrimental effect on data quality that was once thought (see Chapter 10 in this book). Certainly it is not the all-or-nothing effect that Huffington espoused.

However, even such respected researchers as Humphrey Taylor, chairperson and CEO of the Louis Harris Organization, believe that nonresponse error has the potential for seriously affecting preelection polling results. His post hoc analysis of the public polls' performance in the election suggested that four sources of forecasting error were at work in the 1996 polls, including "differential nonresponse" (Taylor 1997).

Other researchers have found that nonresponse is less of a problem. Bolstein (1991a, 1991b) concluded from examining a preelection poll of 608 registered voters in 1988 that "(a) there is no significant difference between the percentage of voters among respondents and interview refusals; (b) these two groups combined have a significantly higher percentage of voters than the call-rule-exhausted group; and (c) the interview refusal and call-rule-exhausted groups combined have a significantly higher percentage of voters than the unavailable group" (1991a, 649). This suggests that refusals are not the problem in predicting turnout, but not interviewing the correct proportion of hard-to-reach respondents may be. There is a growing body of evidence that suggests that nonresponse may not be as big a contributor to total survey error in many surveys of the public as once thought. A 1997 study by the Pew Center for Civic Journalism comparing findings from commonplace survey research techniques with those from more rigorous techniques concluded that nonresponse error was slight in most variables. Similarly, Voter News Surveys (VNS) methodologists Murray Edelman and Dan Merkle found that "contrary to conventional wisdom, there is no relationship between a precinct's response rate in the 1996 VNS exit poll and the precinct's signed error (i.e., the bias measure) or the precinct's absolute error" (see Chapter 3 in this book). These findings suggest that when error occurs in a preelection poll, explanations other than nonresponse bias may be more valid. Understanding the reason for a lower turnout can help pollsters understand how to discern who is likely to vote and who is not, or it can enable them to model the probable electorate more accurately. To better understand how an election can affect a model or likely voter screen, it is important to examine the inner workings of each of the examples given. Individual polls used different approaches to ascertaining likely voters, or to modeling the electorate, in the 1996 presidential election.

The Minnesota poll used a method similar to that of the *New York Times*/CBS News poll—the "probable electorate" method. Both the state polls' and the national polls' methods overestimated turnout, both by about 10 to 11 points. Kagay concluded after the election that his poll's probable electorate method needed fine-tuning, rather than throwing the methodological baby out with the quantitative bath water.

Kagay (1996) said that though 1996 was expected to have a lower turnout, it was far lower than expected. He said the probable electorate's turnout ratio "usually runs a bit high—5 to 6 points above what happens to be the case" in usual election. He indicated that in previous years it made little difference. The voting intentions of the probable electorates and the improbable electorates were virtually the same. In 1996 it was different. His postelection analysis of the poll found that the more stringent the definition of "probable electorate," the smaller the Clinton margin. Turnout in 1996 fell substantially, but not equally in both political parties. David W. Moore, then managing editor of the Gallup poll, said, "In 1996 the likely voters were significantly more Republican. Voters who turned out were disproportionately more likely to be Republican. In other recent presidential elections, there was no difference" (Moore 1996, 7). A Gallup poll taken just before the election suggested that "if all registered voters had turned out for the elections and the undecideds had divided their vote similar to the way in which the undecideds did among the likely voters, Clinton would have had a 16-point margin over Dole and would have won a majority of the popular vote.

But there were some things about the 1996 election that were not new. The 1980 election was one that found a number of final polls being conducted a week or two away from the election. Those that failed to conduct weekend interviewing just prior to the election missed a shift toward Ronald Reagan and away from Jimmy Carter. There was a similar effect in 1996. Keeter (1997, 129) found that polls conducted closer to the election were more accurate: "The relationship between the error and the timing of the poll is almost linear."

Reporting Polling Methods: The Toughest Task?

It is apparent that determining a model of the electorate's support in preelection polls is no small task, given the difficulty of reaching respondents, having to poll close to the election, and having to choose correctly the best method of ascertaining an individual respondent's likelihood to vote. That is the pollster's view.

From a reporter's view, it is just as difficult to take the fruits of the researcher's labor and to turn them into graphics and news articles that are complete, accurate, balanced, and fair—to the candidates, to the readers, and to the research itself.

As more news organizations—especially newspapers—opt for shorter stories, it is increasingly difficult to explain a poll's findings. Many news organizations with their own polling units publish explanations in a "poll box" or methodology sidebar to give some hint at how the pollster divined likelihood to vote. This is not enough, the methodological mavens say. In newsrooms, editors tell reporters they have only so many inches of space, or seconds of airtime; so write it short, they say.

This puts pressure on news organizations to give enough space or time to tell readers and viewers about how a poll was conducted so that they have enough information to judge the quality of the work. So what should be included?

The AAPOR has published standards of disclosure to which its members have agreed to abide.[2] They include definitions of the population under study and how the researcher drew the sample and selected respondents. That is a very tall order for a poll story that might be limited to 15 column inches in the newspaper, or 30 seconds of broadcast airtime. With this in mind, how can one expect journalists to explain weighting to model a probable electorate, or using an index cutoff method to interview only the likeliest voters?

The simple journalistic answer is that one cannot. Methodologists will not be happy with that answer because they want to know more about how the research was conducted than the journalist has space or time for. But there is another problem on the journalism side—making the poll story interesting and readable for the mass audiences, not just the "polity wonks." "You can't write [complex methodological descriptions] in a story if you want people—average human beings—to read past that paragraph," according to Bob von Sternberg, a *Minneapolis Star Tribune* national correspondent (personal communication, 26 February 1999).

Consequently, I think that reporters are justified in describing respondents as "likely voters" and leaving it at that, assuming that the poll is based on some reasonable method of modeling the electorate or screening for likelihood to vote.

Looking at Future Elections

The nation's pollsters—at both the state level and the national level—appear to know how to measure candidate support accurately. They command the ability in a large-turnout election to ascertain the Election Day vote accurately if they adhere to several principles:

- Poll close to the election
- Allocate undecided voters properly
- Use a method of ascertaining a likely electorate

Notice the phrase "a likely electorate." Despite their inability to predict turnout levels as well as they predicted the popular vote, the polling organizations that polled closest to the election were quite close to actual vote.

One recommendation is to pay more attention to the "type" of election—history provides us a lot of comparisons—and use a turnout model that might be best for that type of election. Elections in which the economy is strong and people are lackadaisical about voting might be different from elections during a recession. Both could have different dynamics than when a military conflict is occurring, and citizens might feel the need to band together in national solidarity.

A second recommendation is to explore new methods. Hauck and Daves (1997) reported the results of a 1996 test in Minnesota using the *Juster scale*, a zero to 10 scale mainly used in marketing research, in which the respondent provides researchers a self-described probability of behaving a certain way—purchasing a washing machine, for example. Researchers have compared the Juster scale with intention scales and have found it consistently provided more accurate estimates of respondents' purchase behavior. Given this, it is logical to consider whether the scale might also provide more accurate predictions of other behaviors typically measured using intentions. In principle, there seems no reason why a scale used to predict behavior in one context could not also predict behavior in another. Because the problems experienced in eliciting turnout intentions are analogous to those experienced by researchers eliciting buying intentions, it seems logical to surmise that the substitution of subjective probabilities for voting intentions could produce more accurate estimates.

Unfortunately, Hauck and Daves found that the Juster scale overestimated turnout, as did the probable electorate method. The study highlighted the difficulty of predicting voter turnout. The authors intend to validate respondents' voting to further explore ways of ascertaining a probable electorate or screening for likely voters. But other researchers have found the Juster scale useful. Lavrakas, Mockabee, Monson, and Tompson (1997) used the scale as an index component to estimate more accurately turnout in three statewide ballot referenda.

Finally, those who do preelection polling must keep the necessary records and maintain the data files that would allow them to fine-tune the way they ascertain likelihood to vote or estimate a probable electorate. Peter D. Hart Research did the NBC News/ *Wall Street Journal* polling in the 1996 election. In its final poll for NBC and the *Journal,* Hart used only voter registration as a screen (T. Ross, personal communication, 24 October 1997). That poll showed a Clinton-Dole split of 49 to 37 percent (see Table 9.1). The researchers later pared the sample of registered voters to include only those who voted in 1992 (or who were 18 to 24 years old), to 89 percent of the original sample. The Clinton-Dole support closed by a percentage point to more closely mirror the actual 8-point split in the election.

Although the NBC/ *Wall Street Journal* poll was able to do post hoc analysis, it could not fully research the effect of including a more sophisticated "likely voter" screen in its postelection analysis because it had not kept track of unregistered voters' opinions nor had it asked more sophisticated screening questions.

If they have the financial wherewithal, researchers should design their polls well enough so that they later can verify whether respondents—whether screened in as likely voters or excluded from the analysis as unlikely voters—actually voted or not. That way, they can do a postelection analysis that can help them further fine-tune their method of ascertaining a probable electorate and reduce one of the potential sources of error from future preelection polls. In Table 9.1, we saw that not all polls estimate turnout or even have the data to do the estimation. Such recordkeeping is crucial so that they—or scholars who work with their data later—can verify who voted and who did not and use the appropriate statistical techniques to continue to refine methods of ascertaining turnout, measuring probable electorates, and screening for likely voters.

Notes

1. In a weighting model, it is possible that a respondent's case weight may drop to zero and thus exclude him or her from the sample. This would have the same effect as screening out and might defeat the purpose of the model if the researcher assumes that everyone in the VAP has a nonzero probability of voting.

2. For more about AAPOR, including its standards of disclosure for public polls, see http://www.aapor.org on the Internet.

CHAPTER 10

Improving Election Forecasting: Allocation of Undecided Respondents, Identification of Likely Voters, and Response Order Effects

Penny S. Visser, Jon A. Krosnick, Jesse F. Marquette, and Michael F. Curtin

Everything's fine in Pollsville these days. Yes, we had a rocky start in the early days when the polls predicted that Landon would defeat Roosevelt in the election for U.S. president. And yes, we made a little mistake in 1948 when we predicted that Dewey would defeat Truman by 5 percentage points, when in fact Truman won by 5 percentage points instead. But we've solved those problems now. It all came down to bad sampling in those days, and we know how to sample now.

This is what we hear from many quarters these days. On 15 December 1996, for example, Michael Kagay (1996) proclaimed in the *New York Times* that the average error of the seven national polls conducted the weekend before the 1996 presidential election was a mere 2 percentage points. And in a press release issued on 13 February 1997, the National Council on Public Polls (NCPP) announced that the average error of the nine "major" polls done in 1996 forecasting that election was even smaller: 1.7 percentage points. That press release included Figure 10.1, illustrating that forecast errors made by the major polls were not so terrific in the 1930s but have been consistently within sampling error in recent years. And it is not just on this side of the Atlantic— the final NOP poll predicted that Labour would win 47 percent of votes in races for the British House of Commons in 1997, and the party in fact won 44.4

percent, resulting in forecast error of just over 2 percentage points. Everything's *fine* in Pollsville—really!

Well, maybe not. On 22 November 1996, Everett Carll Ladd published an article in the *Chronicle of Higher Education* entitled "The Election Polls: An American Waterloo." In it, he began:

> Election polling had a terrible year in 1996. Indeed, its overall perfor-
> mance was so flawed that the entire enterprise should be reviewed by a
> blue-ribbon panel of experts—from academe, commercial polling firms,
> and the news media—who should recommend ways to improve the accu-
> racy of polling. (p. A52)

Ladd is a distinguished professor of political science at the University of Connecticut and director of the Roper Center for Public Opinion Research, certainly not someone biased against survey research or disposed to be overly critical of it. And Ladd was not alone. In the *New York Times* magazine of 15 December 1996, for example, editor Max Frankel said that "in 1996, the opinion polls were disturbingly wide of the mark" (p. 34). This sentiment was echoed by *New York Times* editorialist William Safire a year later: On 7 December 1997, he cited the "grievously misleading" preelection polls of 1996 as evidence that the U.S. Census Bureau should not look to sampling as a means of generating accurate estimates of the population.

One source of concern that Ladd, Frankel, and Safire all mentioned was that the final CBS/*New York Times* poll forecast a Clinton victory over Bob Dole of 18 percentage points, whereas the actual margin of victory was only 8

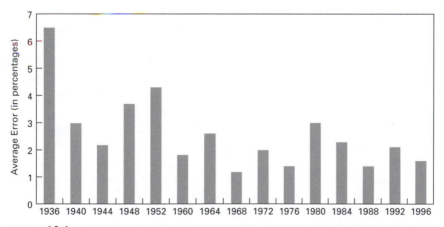

FIGURE 10.1   AVERAGE ERROR IN PRESIDENTIAL ELECTION FORECASTING POLLS

percentage points. Other concerns included the fact that in Britain the polls predicted a Labour victory in 1992, whereas the Conservatives actually won (Jowell et al. 1993). And of course there was the well-publicized 1989 race for governor of Virginia: The polls all predicted that Douglas Wilder would win by a margin of between 4 and 11 percentage points, whereas his actual victory margin was less than 1 percentage point.

How could there be so much error in these cases, when Kagay (1996) and the NCPP say there is almost no error in predictions? One answer involves the selection of polls to describe. Kagay and NCPP described the accuracy of only some polls. Yet more comprehensive analyses of poll accuracy have revealed quite a bit more error. For example, Crespi (1988) found the average error of 430 pre-election polls to be 5.7 percentage points. More recently, Gelman and King (1993) reported an average error of 4.5 percentage points in forecasts of presidential races from 1984 through 1992.

These figures, all about 5 percentage points, are *average* errors in the predictions of each candidate's vote share. That means that on average in two-candidate races, one candidate's vote share will be overestimated by 5 percentage points, and the other candidate's share will be underestimated by 5 percentage points. This exaggeration of the difference between the two candidates of 10 percentage points on average is exactly the CBS/*New York Times* overestimation of Bill Clinton's victory margin in 1996. Thus, the poll's "mistake" was not an outlier but, rather, an *average* amount of error. Furthermore, in about half of races, according to Crespi's (1988) and Gelman and King's (1993) analyses, error will be *larger* than 5 percentage points.

Some observers will tell you that these errors are random and are well within sampling error. In fact, though, it appears that the errors in forecasts are systematically biased in one direction. Critics have at times charged that the polls overestimate the popularity of Democratic Party candidates, and some evidence might appear to be consistent with this. For example, all but one of the "major" polls discussed in the NCPP press release overestimated Bill Clinton's victory margin in 1996. And in 1992, all six of the "major" polls examined by the NCPP also overpredicted Clinton's victory margin. But in 1988, four of the five NCPP "major" polls overestimated George Bush's victory, and in 1972, all three "major" polls overpredicted Richard Nixon's victory margin. Instead of a bias in favor of Democratic candidates, then, these results suggest that the bias may be in favor of the leading candidate, no matter what his or her party affiliation. Although this pattern did not hold for all elections in the NCPP analysis, it did hold for many of them. Thus, it appears that the winner's margin of error is typically overpredicted (see also Gruca 1994; Panagakis 1989; Wright 1990, 1992, 1993).

So all is *not* well in Pollsville after all. In fact, we can do better, and we should do better. But how? What can be done to improve a method that has been so carefully fine-tuned over a period of decades? One answer to this question, we argue, lies in a little-recognized phenomenon that has been happening quietly in Columbus, Ohio, for nearly two decades.

The *Columbus Dispatch* Mail Surveys

As we reported in 1996 (Visser et al. 1996), the *Columbus Dispatch* mail surveys have been strikingly accurate in forecasting election outcomes since 1980, with an average error of only 1.6 percentage points. They have been substantially more accurate than telephone polls forecasting the same races conducted by the University of Akron (average error = 5.4 percentage points), the University of Cincinnati (average error = 4.9 percentage points), and the Gallup Organization (average error = 5.2 percentage points), each of which has average error rates comparable to the those reported by Crespi (1988) and Gelman and King (1993).

Interestingly, the *Dispatch*'s unusual accuracy is not a new phenomenon, as documented in Claude Robinson's (1932) book *Straw Votes*. Robinson reviewed the methods and findings of preelection polls attempting to forecast U.S. elections during the first three decades of the twentieth century. The *Columbus Dispatch* newspaper was polling back then, and with unusual accuracy for the time. Whereas some polls made predictions with average errors as large as 20 percentage points, the average error of the *Dispatch* forecasts was 7 percentage points (pp. 68–69). Only the *Chicago Tribune* performed better, with an average error of 6 percentage points. Sampling and questioning methods have changed quite a bit over the century, but the unusual accuracy of the *Dispatch* polls has not.

In our 1996 report, we detailed not only the superior accuracy of the *Dispatch* polls in the 1980s and 1990s but also their invulnerability to usual sources of error in preelection surveys. Telephone survey forecasts are less accurate when a race has received little publicity, when a lot of voters who go to the polls abstain in that race rather than voting in it, when the race is listed low on the ballot, and when voter turnout is lower (Crespi 1988).

Furthermore, we explored a number of possible explanations for the mail polls' accuracy. We found no evidence that weighting of the *Dispatch* samples improved accuracy or that interviewer effects compromised the accuracy of the telephone polls. We did identify four partial explanations, however:

1. The mail surveys have typically involved samples of about 1,600 respondents, in contrast to samples of 500 to 900 for the telephone polls. Error was reduced by almost half a percentage point on average by the increased sample size.

2. The mail survey procedure recruited samples of respondents that more closely resembled the actual voting population, perhaps because the act of completing a self-administered questionnaire is in many ways comparable to the act of voting.

3. The mail surveys did not offer respondents an opportunity to say they had not decided how they would vote in a race, whereas the telephone surveys invited and routinely received many such responses from people. Having to allocate those "undecided" voters introduced error into the telephone polls.

4. The mail surveys simply asked people for whom they will vote in each race, whereas the telephone surveys used a variety of other question wordings (e.g., "Which candidate would you like to see win?") and preceded the vote choice questions with other questions on related topics. By mirroring the Election Day ballot precisely, the mail surveys avoided error attributable to question wording and question order effects (for other evidence of such question order effects, see also Hoek and Gendall 1997; Kagay 1992, 101).

This Chapter

Inspired partly by Crespi (1988), our goal in this chapter is to take a comprehensive and systematic approach to testing various hypotheses about the errors in election forecasts. We report results from our ongoing investigation of the differences between mail and telephone survey methods. In particular, we address a series of new questions:

1. In our 1996 report, we focused only on statewide elections in Ohio. What about the accuracy of mail survey forecasts of the outcomes of referenda and local races? Did the mail surveys forecast these outcomes better than telephone surveys?

2. How do various methods of allocating undecided respondents in the telephone surveys compare in terms of effectiveness? Can we identify an optimal method?

3. How do various methods of screening out telephone respondents who are unlikely to vote compare in terms of effectiveness?

4. Even if the mail and telephone surveys differ in accuracy, do they track similar trends in candidate support over time?

5. Does the order in which candidates' names are presented to respondents affect answers?

We also expanded the scope of our investigation of mail and telephone survey accuracy by looking not just at the forecasts generated immediately before the elections, but at those generated weeks and months beforehand as well. In conducting the research to be described, we tested various hypotheses about the conditions under which forecasts are more and less accurate, in order to develop techniques for improving forecast accuracy, and we ended up with many intriguing results.

In the end, however, the implications of this work are much broader. Elections offer a unique opportunity for assessing the validity of survey data because each Election Day provides a benchmark of truth against which to measure forecast accuracy. Such benchmarks are difficult if not impossible to obtain in many areas of social science research, and when they are obtained, there is sometimes error in their measurement. But we can have strong confidence in the benchmark used here, so we can have confidence in the implications of our findings as well. As a result, the findings we report here shed new light on methods by which the precision of all survey data can be enhanced.

Mail Survey Accuracy in New Contests

Table 10.1 displays the accuracy of the mail survey forecasts for the statewide candidate races that we already examined (in column 1, with the addition of a new figure for the 1996 U.S. presidential race), plus forecasts for new contests that occurred before June 1997: local candidate races (in column 2), statewide referenda (in column 3), and local referenda (in column 4). At the bottom of each column is the average error for races in the column. As is apparent, the statewide candidate races (average error = 1.5 percentage points) were predicted more accurately than were the other contests. The average error for the local candidate races was 2.7 percentage points, as compared to 5.8 percentage points for the statewide referenda and 3.9 percentage points for the local referenda. Some of the errors for referenda were quite substantial, peaking at 12.8 percentage points. We do not yet have evidence to explain why the mail poll forecasts are not as good in these cases, and we look forward to future research exploring this puzzle.

The University of Akron did not conduct surveys on the local candidate races and referenda addressed by the *Dispatch* polls. However, both outfits conducted surveys forecasting some of the same statewide referenda. As Table 10.2 shows, the average error for *Dispatch* forecasts of these referenda was 5.4 percentage points, compared to 7.2 percentage points for the telephone surveys. Thus, it appears that although referenda were more difficult to forecast than candidate races using either method, the mail surveys still outperformed the telephone surveys when doing so. However, in one of the six referenda examined

TABLE 10.1 ACCURACY OF THE FINAL *COLUMBUS DISPATCH* FORECASTS (IN PERCENTAGE POINTS)

YEAR	STATEWIDE CANDIDATE RACES		LOCAL CANDIDATE RACES		STATEWIDE REFERENDA		LOCAL REFERENDA	
	Race	Average Error	Race	Average Error	Issue	Average Error	Issue	Average Error
1980	President	1.4						
1982	Governor	0.6						
	Attorney General	1.1						
	Auditor	0.8						
	Treasurer	0.8						
	Secretary of State	4.0						
	U.S. Senate	0.7						
1984	President	0.7						
1986	Governor	0.5						
	Attorney General	1.2						
	Auditor	1.3						
	Treasurer	1.4						
	Secretary of State	0.5						
	U.S. Senate	3.2						
1988	President	0.7						
	U.S. Senate	0.5						
1989					Gambling	0.7	Amendment	0.6
					Housing	3.4	COTA tax	2.9
					Tax increase	6.4	Park District	4.4
							Children's Services	8.3
1990	Governor	0.2						
	Attorney General	4.5						
	Auditor	3.7						
	Treasurer	1.6						
	Secretary of State	0.9						

Year								
1991			Mayor	4.7				
			City Council	0.8				
1992	President	1.5			Convention	11.2	Amendment	7.3
					Federal term limits	9.4	Levy	3.2
					State term limits	7.3	City Charter 1	6.1
					State term limits	6.6	City Charter 2	1.5
					Safety warnings	8.6		
1993			City Clerk	1.9				
			City Council	1.5				
			City Attorney	4.7				
1994	Governor	0.6			Death penalty appeals	3.8		
	Attorney General	2.6			Victim rights	8.1		
	Auditor	0.5			Tuition credits	6.8		
	Treasurer	1.5			Soft drink tax	12.8		
	Secretary of State	0.9						
	U.S. Senate	1.8						
1995					Amendment 1	0.9		
					Amendment 2	4.1		
					COTA tax	2.7		
					Mental health tax	4.8		
					Gambling	0.2		
1996	President	2.7					Arena tax	0.9
1997								
Average		1.5		2.7		5.8		3.9

TABLE 10.2   COMPARING THE *COLUMBUS DISPATCH* AND UNIVERSITY OF AKRON
FORECAST ACCURACY ON REFERENDA (IN PERCENTAGES)

YEAR	STATEWIDE REFERENDA	*DISPATCH* AVERAGE ERROR	AKRON AVERAGE ERROR
1990	Gambling	1.6	1.6[a]
1994	Death penalty appeals	3.8	8.3[b]
	Victim rights	8.1	0.9[b]
	Tuition credits	6.8	10.7[b]
	Soft drink tax	12.8	17.2[b]
1996	Gambling	0.2	4.5[a]
Average		5.4	7.2

[a]Using data from respondents who were very or somewhat interested in the election and definitely intended to vote; dropping undecided

[b]Using data from all respondents; dropping undecided

(Victim rights, in 1994), the telephone survey was much more accurate than the mail poll, so the superiority of the mail polls is not universal.

An examination of the direction of the forecast errors uncovers the expected overprediction of the winner's share of the vote. In the thirty-three statewide forecasts of candidate races by the telephone polls, 73 percent overpredicted the winner's share of the vote, and only 27 percent did not. Across the thirty-three races, the margin of victory was overpredicted by 2.65 percentage points. In the six statewide forecasts of referenda by the telephone polls, 67 percent overpredicted the winner's share of the vote, and only 33 percent did not. Across the six referenda, the margin of victory was overpredicted by 1.97 percentage points. Thus, these surveys manifest the same systematic error as national surveys.

The same bias was apparent in the mail surveys, but more weakly in the candidate races. In the thirty-three *Dispatch* forecasts of candidate races, the winner's share of the vote was overpredicted in 64 percent of the cases and was not overpredicted in 36 percent of the cases. On average across the thirty-three races, the margin of victory was overpredicted by 0.67 percentage points. In the twenty-five mail survey forecasts of referenda, the margin of victory was overpredicted in 76 percent of the cases and was not overpredicted in only 24 percent of the cases. On average across twenty-five referenda, the margin of victory was overpredicted by 2.8 percentage points.

Allocating Undecided Respondents

Can the accuracy of the telephone forecasts be improved? As mentioned earlier, our 1996 investigation revealed that one source of inaccuracy in these forecasts involved allocation of respondents who said they had not yet decided how to vote in a particular contest. Whereas the final mail surveys did not solicit "undecided" responses, and respondents volunteered them extremely rarely, the telephone surveys have routinely gotten relatively large numbers of such responses, even less than a week before Election Day. As Table 10.3 shows, the University of Akron telephone surveys have found proportions of "undecideds" ranging from 3.2 percent to 73.4 percent, averaging 19.9 percent in the early September surveys, 36.9 percent in the late September surveys, and 19.0 percent in the early October surveys.

Various methods have been used to handle these "undecided" responses (e.g., Crespi 1988; Daves and Warden 1995; Fenwick et al. 1982), based upon different presumptions about the meanings of these responses. One possibility is

TABLE 10.3   PERCENTAGE OF UNDECIDED RESPONDENTS IN THE UNIVERSITY OF AKRON SURVEYS (IN PERCENTAGES)

YEAR	RACE	EARLY SEPTEMBER		LATE SEPTEMBER		EARLY OCTOBER	
		Percent of Undecided	Percent Who Lean toward One Candidate	Percent of Undecided	Percent Who Lean toward One Candidate	Percent of Undecided	Percent Who Lean toward One Candidate
1988	President	18.1	10.9	20.9	11.3	13.1	6.5
	U.S. Senate	17.4	8.2	17.3	7.3	13.0	6.2
1990	Governor			37.4	27.1	30.0	19.7
	Attorney General			61.2		37.7	
	Auditor			44.8		38.2	
	Treasurer			73.4		47.7	
	Secretary of State			38.9		19.5	
	Gambling amendment			27.5		9.0	
1992	President	24.2	13.5	27.7	18.4	18.2	13.0
1994	Governor			38.5	11.5	13.9	7.7
	Attorney General			33.0	9.2	12.9	5.4
	Auditor			40.5	8.7	16.9	5.6
	Secretary of State			32.5	9.8	13.7	5.4
	U.S. Senate			31.4	9.8	11.6	6.1
	Issue 1			40.2		8.5	
	Issue 2			28.2		3.2	
	Issue 3			57.8		14.9	
	Issue 4			40.8		3.8	
1996	President					30.2	17.2
	Gambling amendment					23.2	
Average		19.9	10.9	36.9	12.6	19.0	9.3

that people who say they are undecided do in fact have no real candidate preference in a race. Therefore, if these individuals were pressed to express a candidate preference, any answer they would give would be a meaningless nonattitude (Converse 1964) and would only reduce forecast accuracy. Based upon this logic, respondents should be encouraged to say they are undecided, and people who give such responses should be presumed not to vote in a race.

However, many of the people who claim to be undecided may in fact have real preferences but may be reluctant to report them. For example, some might not want to do the cognitive work required to think about and choose between candidates, and opting for the "don't know" option is a way to avoid that work (Krosnick 1991). Alternatively, some people might have very little information with which to justify their preferences, so they might lack confidence to feel comfortable expressing them. Other people might be reluctant to express their preferences because of "spiral of silence" processes (Noelle-Neumann 1984); that is, they may believe that their candidate preferences are not shared by most other people, either as the result of conversations with others or by learning about opinion poll results through the news media. Admitting their preferences would identify these people as being out of step with the majority of voters, so they may claim not to favor any candidate. Consistent with this last possibility is evidence that the number of people claiming to be undecided drops significantly when survey respondents can "vote" in a secret "ballot box" instead of telling an interviewer how they will vote, and the apparent popularity of "losing" candidates increases on secret ballots (Perry 1979).

In all these cases, encouraging individuals to express their opinions might yield valid data that would increase forecast accuracy. One way to do so in telephone surveys involves asking respondents who initially say they are undecided whether they lean toward one of the candidates in a race. For most races, the University of Akron did exactly this. As Table 10.3 shows, sizable proportions of people indicated leaning, ranging from 5.4 percent to 27.1 percent. If we examine the races where surveying was done in both early and late September (the 1988 and 1992 races), there is no clear decline in "undecided" responses (averaging 19.9 percent and 22.0 percent in early and late September, respectively), but these responses were notably less common in early October than in late September for races where polling was done at both times (averaging 36.9 percent and 18.1 percent in late September and early October, respectively). If people had insight into their final decisions, making use of these reports might increase the accuracy of forecasts. Table 10.4 reports all possible tests of this hypothesis with the available Akron data from three waves of surveying, in early September, early October, and late October.

When undecided people who declined to indicate a leaning were dropped altogether, taking people's reports of leaning seriously consistently increased forecast

TABLE 10.4 IMPACT OF ALLOCATION STRATEGIES ON FORECAST ERROR IN THE UNIVERSITY OF AKRON SURVEYS ON CANDIDATE RACES (IN PERCENTAGE POINTS)

	EARLY SEPTEMBER				EARLY OCTOBER				LATE OCTOBER			
	UNDECIDED DROPPED		UNDECIDED ALLOCATED EQUALLY		UNDECIDED DROPPED		UNDECIDED ALLOCATED EQUALLY		UNDECIDED DROPPED		UNDECIDED ALLOCATED EQUALLY	
	Leaners Dropped	Leaners to Candidate	Leaners Allocated Equally	Leaners to Candidate	Leaners Dropped	Leaners to Candidate	Leaners Allocated Equally	Leaners to Candidate	Leaners Dropped	Leaners to Candidate	Leaners Allocated Equally	Leaners to Candidate
1988												
President	3.1	3.2	3.6	3.3	1.3	0.8	0.4	0.5	4.3	3.5	3.1	2.9
U.S. Senate	5.6	5.2	3.4	4.1	7.1	1.9	4.7	4.3	5.1	4.5	3.6	3.7
1990												
Governor					7.6	3.1	2.4	1.2	1.5	0.6	0.7	1.1
1992												
President					5.4	7.6	4.5	6.2	2.9	1.1	1.0	1.5
1996												
President									6.0	5.6	4.3	4.0
Average	4.4	4.2	3.5	3.7	5.4	3.4	3.0	3.1	4.0	3.1	2.5	2.6

accuracy. The first two columns of Table 10.4 show that for the two races forecast with early September data, the average error was 4.4 percentage points when the leaning "undecideds" were dropped from forecasts and 4.2 percentage points when the leaning "undecideds" were allocated to the candidates. The same average figures for the early October forecasts were 5.4 and 3.4 percentage points, respectively, again suggesting a gain in accuracy when allocating leaning "undecideds" to the candidates (see columns 5 and 6). Finally, the same pattern is apparent in the late October surveys, with an average error of 4 percentage points when leaning "undecideds" were dropped and 3.1 percentage points when they were allocated to the candidates (see columns 9 and 10). This improvement in accuracy is consistent with the claims that some people who initially say they are undecided do indeed have real preferences and that the people who say they don't lean also don't vote.

Another possible strategy is based upon a different sort of speculation about the behavior of nonleaning undecided respondents. These individuals may be drawn to their precincts in order to cast votes in other races, about which they do have strong preferences. Finding themselves there, they may feel the obligation to vote in all the other races on the ballot and may do so essentially randomly (e.g., Converse 1964). Consequently, we might see an improvement in forecast accuracy if we were to allocate the nonleaning undecided respondents equally to the various candidates instead of dropping them (e.g., Crespi 1988, 22).

To test this idea, we can first compare column 2 of Table 10.4 to column 4, where the nonleaning undecided respondents were allocated equally to the candidates. In fact, this did improve accuracy, as the average error for column 2 is larger (4.2 percentage points) than the average error for column 4 (3.7 percentage points). Similar comparisons for the October surveys reveal the same gain in accuracy: 3.4 versus 3.1 percentage points for early October, and 3.1 versus 2.6 percentage points for late October. All this is consistent with the claims that people's answers to questions about leaning are valid and that people who say they are undecided and don't lean vote randomly.

Before concluding this exercise, we explored one other possibility: that all undecided respondents, those who said they leaned toward a candidate and those who said they did not lean, might vote randomly and should therefore be allocated equally among the candidates. To our surprise, this approach yielded the most accurate forecasts of all (see Table 10.4). The average in column 3 (3.5 percentage points) is the lowest of the early September columns. Likewise, the average error in column 7 (3.0 percentage points) is the lowest of the early October columns. And the average error in column 11 (2.5 percentage points) is the lowest of the late October columns.

We were able to test this approach more thoroughly by including races that were omitted from Table 10.4 because undecided respondents had not been asked whether they leaned, or because they were given the option of saying they would not vote in the race. The larger set of races shown in Table 10.5 again offers strong support for random allocation of all undecided respondents. The average errors for columns 2, 4, and 6, where such allocation was done (4.7, 4.2, and 3.1 percentage points, respectively), were smaller than the average errors for columns 1, 3, and 5, where the undecided respondents were dropped altogether (5.3, 7.5, and 5.9 percentage points, respectively). Averaging across all the columns, the average error when undecided respondents were dropped was 6.2 percentage points compared to 4.0 percentage points when the undecided respondents were allocated equally to the candidates.

Indeed, this method even appeared to improve the accuracy of forecasts of referenda. As Table 10.6 shows, the average error of forecasts dropping the undecided respondents was 4.6 percentage points compared to 2.6 percentage points when half of the undecided respondents were presumed to vote yes and the other half were presumed to vote no. Because so few referenda could be examined here, additional studies of this sort are clearly needed before we can have strong

TABLE 10.5   IMPACT OF ALLOCATION STRATEGIES ON FORECAST ACCURACY
IN THE UNIVERSITY OF AKRON SURVEYS ON CANDIDATE RACES
(IN PERCENTAGE POINTS)

	EARLY SEPTEMBER		EARLY OCTOBER		LATE OCTOBER	
	DROP UNDECIDED	ALLOCATE EQUALLY	DROP UNDECIDED	ALLOCATE EQUALLY	DROP UNDECIDED	ALLOCATE EQUALLY
1988						
President	3.1	3.6	1.3	0.4	4.3	3.1
U.S. Senate	5.6	3.4	7.1	4.7	5.1	3.6
1990						
Governor			7.6	2.4	1.5	0.7
Attorney General			9.7	3.7	7.5	4.7
Auditor			19.8	9.7	15.5	8.5
Secretary of State			2.6	2.8	1.2	1.6
Treasurer			6.1	5.3	8.8	0.1
1992						
President	7.2	7.2	5.4	4.5	2.9	1.0
1996						
President					6.0	4.3
Average	5.3	4.7	7.5	4.2	5.9	3.1

TABLE 10.6 IMPACT OF ALLOCATION STRATEGIES ON FORECAST ACCURACY IN THE UNIVERSITY OF AKRON SURVEYS ON REFERENDA (IN PERCENTAGE POINTS)

	EARLY OCTOBER		LATE OCTOBER	
	Undecided Dropped	Undecided Allocated Equally	Undecided Dropped	Undecided Allocated Equally
1990 STATE POLL				
Gambling amendment	0.3	3.1	0.9	0.3
1996 STATE POLL				
Gambling amendment			12.6	4.3
Average	0.3	3.1	6.8	2.3

confidence in this pattern; but the pattern is certainly consistent with the evidence regarding candidate races.

It is tempting to infer from this that people who said they leaned toward one candidate or another did not really do so, voting randomly instead. However, there is another possible explanation for these results. It may be that people who leaned toward one candidate did, more often than not, vote for that candidate. But because of spiral of silence pressures, some of the respondents who claimed to be nonleaning undecideds or who claimed to support the most popular candidate might in fact have voted for an unpopular candidate. Correcting for this bias can be accomplished by mixing in some 50/50 forecasts along with all the other survey data, and this is what our last allocation strategy did. Although this may be the best approach to forecasting, its success does not necessarily mean that people who claimed to lean toward one candidate in fact voted randomly.

In 1994, the Akron surveys offered respondents the option to say they would not vote in each particular race, and the proportions of people saying so ranged from 10 percent to 28 percent (see Table 10.7). These respondents were asked whether they leaned toward one candidate or another, and relatively small but nontrivial numbers said they did. Therefore, although it might be best to presume that these respondents will indeed skip the race, it might be preferable to incorporate answers to the leaning question in forecasts if they have some validity and if those respondents might in fact vote. We decided to test the impact of such a move, and Table 10.8 displays the results of these tests. Specifically, we tried allocating leaners to candidates, dropping leaners, dropping nonleaning undecideds and people who said they would skip the race, and allocating equally the nonleaning undecideds and people who said they would skip the race.

The implication of these tests is apparent in the lower-right-hand corner of

TABLE 10.7   PROPORTION OF RESPONDENTS IN THE UNIVERSITY OF AKRON
SURVEYS WHO SAID THEY WOULD SKIP EACH RACE (IN PERCENTAGES)

		LATE SEPTEMBER		EARLY OCTOBER	
YEAR	RACE	Total Number of "Skip Race"	Number of "Skip Race" Who Lean toward One Candidate	Total Number of "Skip Race"	Number of "Skip Race" Who Lean toward One Candidate
1994	Governor			14	5
	Attorney General	18		14	3
	Auditor	26		28	4
	Secretary of State	19		23	4
	U.S. Senate			10	2

the table, where the smallest average error appears. This was obtained by allocating all people who said they leaned toward a candidate to that candidate and allocating equally all respondents who were nonleaning undecideds or were nonleaning people who said they would not vote in the race. This reinforces the notion that answers to leaning questions do have some validity, so people who say "don't know," "undecided," or "skip the race" should be pressed to express candidate preferences. The worst inaccuracy of all in Table 10.8 occurred when all people who said "undecided" or "skip the race" were dropped entirely from the predictions, which is the approach taken these days by many survey research groups.

Adding Random Responses to the Mail Survey Forecasts

Although the mail surveys conducted just before Election Day did not offer respondents an explicit option to say they were "undecided," the earlier mail surveys did, and some respondents regularly expressed indecision (see Table 10.9). If we focus just on those races where polling was done at all four time points (the 1990 races for governor, attorney general, secretary of state, and the gambling amendment referendum), it is clear that "undecided" rates were highest in January (averaging 18.2 percent, 12.0 percent, 12.3 percent, and 10.2 percent for January, June, September, and October, respectively). When examining all races where polling was done in June, September, and October, we noted that "undecided" responses declined from June (14.2 percent) and September (14.4 percent) to October (12.4 percent). When examining all races where polling was done in September and October, we noted that "undecided" responses were more common in September than in October (averaging 15.9 percent and 12.8 percent, respectively). Thus, there appears to be a decline in indecision over the

TABLE 10.8 IMPACT OF ALLOCATION STRATEGIES ON FORECAST ACCURACY IN THE 1994 UNIVERSITY OF AKRON SURVEYS ON CANDIDATE RACES (IN PERCENTAGE POINTS)

| | DROP NONLEANING "SKIP THE RACE" | | | | | | ALLOCATE NONLEANING "SKIP THE RACE" EQUALLY | | | | | |
| | DROP NONLEANING UNDECIDED | | | ALLOCATE NONLEANING UNDECIDED EQUALLY | | | DROP NONLEANING UNDECIDED | | | ALLOCATE NONLEANING UNDECIDED EQUALLY | | |
RACE	Drop All Leaners	Undecided Leaners to Cand.	Undecided and "Skip" Leaners to Cand.	Allocate Leaners Equally	Undecided Leaners to Cand.	Undecided and "Skip" Leaners to Cand.	Drop All Leaners	Undecided Leaners to Cand.	Undecided and "Skip" Leaners to Cand.	Allocate Leaners Equally	Undecided Leaners to Cand.	Undecided and "Skip" Leaners to Cand.
Governor	7.4	6.8	6.1	4.7	4.9	4.7	4.8	4.6	5.0	5.0	4.6	3.9
Attorney General	8.4	8.3	7.2	7.3	7.4	6.5	7.2	7.2	6.5	6.5	6.5	6.0
Auditor	14.4	14.2	13.5	12.9	12.9	12.5	12.3	12.2	12.1	11.7	11.6	11.5
Secretary of State	8.5	8.4	7.2	4.4	4.7	3.9	2.3	2.3	2.3	.0	.2	.3
U.S. Senate	1.8	1.8	2.0	1.4	1.1	1.4	1.3	1.4	1.4	2.7	2.3	2.4
Average	8.1	7.9	7.2	6.1	6.2	5.8	5.6	5.5	5.5	5.2	5.0	4.8

course of the election campaigns. The proportion of undecideds was often large, reaching a maximum of 50.3 percent, so handling of these responses can, in principle, have a substantial impact on forecast accuracy.

As Table 10.10 displays, the accuracy of forecasts was indeed improved when undecided respondents were allocated equally to the candidates. Specifically, the average error across all surveys was 3.9 percentage points when the undecided responses were allocated equally to the candidates, compared to 4.6 percentage points when the undecided responses were dropped instead of being allocated. This gain in accuracy was also apparent for the referenda shown in Table 10.11.

TABLE 10.9   **UNDECIDED RESPONDENTS IN THE *COLUMBUS DISPATCH* SURVEYS (IN PERCENTAGE POINTS)**

YEAR	RACE	JANUARY	JUNE	EARLY SEPTEMBER	EARLY OCTOBER
1988	President			9.0	
	U.S. Senate			8.0	
1990	Governor	15.3	8.4	7.4	6.9
	Attorney General	28.6	16.4	18.3	16.8
	Auditor		14.1	13.9	12.0
	Treasurer		23.2	23.6	21.4
	Secretary of State	17.5	10.6	11.0	9.1
	Gambling amendment	11.2	12.7	12.4	8.0
	Housing amendment				23.5
	Tax amendment				7.7
1991	Mayor			22.4	16.3
1992	President			8.8	
	Issue 1			10.6	
	Issue 2			7.5	
	Issue 3			8.0	
	Issue 4			8.0	
	Issue 5			13.1	
1993	City Clerk			50.3	
	City Attorney			39.8	
	Amendment			16.9	
	Levy			13.2	
1994	Governor			11.6	7.7
	Attorney General			17.8	12.0
	Auditor			26.2	20.2
	Treasurer			27.0	22.1
	Secretary of State			14.1	12.3
	U.S. Senate			8.6	5.6
	Issue 1				19.8
	Issue 2				5.3
	Issue 3				26.6
	Issue 4				4.2
1996	Gambling amendment			8.6	8.2
Average		18.2	14.2	16.0	13.3

TABLE 10.10   IMPACT OF ALLOCATION STRATEGIES ON *COLUMBUS DISPATCH* FORECAST ACCURACY FOR CANDIDATE RACES (IN PERCENTAGE POINTS)

	JANUARY		MAY		EARLY SEPTEMBER		EARLY OCTOBER	
	Drop Undecided	Allocate Equally	Drop Undecided	Allocate Equally	Drop Undecided	Allocate Equally	Drop Undecided	Allocate Equally
1988 STATE POLL								
President					2.8	3.0	3.2	3.5
U.S. Senate					1.5	2.0	2.1	1.5
1990 STATE POLL								
Governor	0.9	0.2	3.8	3.0	4.0	3.3	1.4	0.9
Attorney General	10.9	7.8	1.3	1.0	10.3	8.3	5.7	4.8
Auditor			13.2	10.9	4.0	3.1	6.5	5.3
Secretary of State	4.3	4.1	3.3	3.3	0.8	1.0	0.4	0.7
Treasurer			2.4	4.1	1.9	3.7	3.5	4.8
1991 CITY POLL								
Mayor					6.4	4.5	5.0	3.9
City Council								
1992 STATE POLL								
President					10.3	8.7		
1993 CITY POLL								
Clerk					10.9	8.9		
Attorney					9.5	2.1		
City Council								
1994 STATE POLL								
Governor					8.5	8.0	0.8	1.8
Attorney General					1.9	1.8	2.7	0.5
Auditor					0.3	2.5	1.1	0.9
Secretary of State					6.6	3.6	5.2	2.7
Treasurer					1.4	5.1	1.1	3.7
U.S. Senate					5.7	4.2	5.6	4.5
Average	5.4	4.0	4.8	4.5	5.1	4.3	3.2	2.8

The average error when undecided respondents were dropped was 9.1 percentage points, compared to 8.7 percentage points when half the undecided respondents were presumed to vote yes and the other half were presumed to vote no.

We went one step further, testing whether the final mail survey forecasts could be improved by adding more random responses. As Table 10.12 shows, the average discrepancy between the actual election outcome and an even distribu-

TABLE 10.11   **IMPACT OF ALLOCATION STRATEGIES ON *COLUMBUS DISPATCH* FORECAST ACCURACY FOR REFERENDA (IN PERCENTAGE POINTS)**

	JANUARY		MAY		EARLY SEPTEMBER		EARLY OCTOBER	
	Drop Undecided	Allocate Equally	Drop Undecided	Allocate Equally	Drop Undecided	Allocate Equally	Drop Undecided	Allocate Equally
1990 STATE POLL								
Gambling amendment	3.4	4.4	9.6	9.9	15.6	15.1	2.3	3.1
Housing							3.8	2.3
Tax							7.7	4.0
1992 STATE POLL								
Issue 1					22.3	18.7		
Issue 2					11.8	9.7		
Issue 3					10.6	8.3		
Issue 4					10.4	8.1		
Issue 5					58.1	54.0		
1993 CITY POLL								
Amendment					12.9	8.4		
Levy					1.3	0.7		
1994 STATE POLL								
Issue 1							6.9	3.3
Issue 2							9.4	7.1
Issue 3							0.8	4.7
Issue 4							17.5	17.1
1996 STATE POLL								
Gambling amendment					5.0	5.6	6.1	6.6
Average	3.4	4.4	9.6	9.9	16.4	14.3	6.8	6.0

tion of votes for all candidates was 11.3 percentage points, whereas the average discrepancy between the final *Dispatch* forecasts of these elections and an even distribution of votes was 12.0 percentage points. Thus, the *Dispatch* forecasts were farther from evenly distributed than were the actual election outcomes, which is consistent with our earlier demonstration that the forecast errors over-predicted the winner's share of the votes more often than not. Therefore, adding a bit more random responses to the *Dispatch* data would enhance the accuracy of the final forecasts further. As the last column of Table 10.12 shows, this strategy would have increased forecast accuracy for 76 percent of the candidate races and decreased accuracy for only 24 percent of them.

To assess how much more randomness would be optimal, we executed an

TABLE 10.12   IMPACT OF ADDING 50/50 RESPONSES ON *COLUMBUS DISPATCH*
FORECAST ACCURACY IN THE STATEWIDE CANDIDATE RACES
(IN PERCENTAGE POINTS)

YEAR	RACE	AVERAGE DISCREPANCY BETWEEN ACTUAL ELECTION RESULTS AND AN EVEN DISTRIBUTION OF VOTES	AVERAGE DISCREPANCY BETWEEN DISPATCH POLL RESULTS AND AN EVEN DISTRIBUTION	ACCURACY IMPROVED BY ADDING 50/50 RESPONSES?
1980	President	17.7	16.1	no
1982	Governor	10.0	11.5	yes
	Attorney General	20.6	20.9	yes
	Auditor	2.2	3.0	yes
	Treasurer	18.2	18.9	yes
	Secretary of State	19.3	19.6	yes
	U.S. Senate	23.9	24.0	yes
1984	President	9.4	10.0	yes
1986	Governor	10.6	10.1	no
	Attorney General	9.8	11.0	yes
	Auditor	16.5	17.8	yes
	Treasurer	4.9	6.3	yes
	Secretary of State	9.7	10.2	yes
	U.S. Senate	12.5	9.3	no
1988	President	5.5	4.9	no
	U.S. Senate	7.0	7.8	yes
1990	Governor	5.7	5.9	yes
	Attorney General	0.0	4.5	yes
	Auditor	2.8	6.5	yes
	Treasurer	9.5	11.1	yes
	Secretary of State	3.0	3.9	yes
1992	President	7.9	9.4	yes
1994	Governor	25.6	26.2	yes
	Attorney General	1.4	1.2	no
	Auditor	8.5	9.0	yes
	Treasurer	19.6	19.2	no
	Secretary of State	14.8	15.7	yes
	U.S. Senate	17.3	17.0	no
1996	President	14.8	17.4	yes
	Average	11.3	12.0	

iterative procedure using the twenty statewide and local candidate races gauged by final *Dispatch* surveys between 1988 and 1996. The average error in forecasts of these races was 1.75 percentage points. In the first step of iteration, we added 1 percentage point to the distribution of votes predicted for each candidate and then repercentaged to obtain a new set of forecasts. This yielded an average error of 1.67 percentage points. Then, we added another percentage point to the number of votes predicted for each candidate and repercentaged. This yielded an average error of 1.65 percentage points. When we went another step and added an additional percentage point to each candidate's share, the average error rose to 1.7 percentage points. Thus, the optimal amount of additional random voting to add was between 2 percent and 3 percent.

This improvement in accuracy could occur for a number of possible reasons. First, a few people who do ultimately vote randomly may not respond to the *Dispatch* surveys. Alternatively, a few *Dispatch* respondents may be reluctant to admit supporting unpopular candidates and instead claim to support more popular ones. Because the *Dispatch* survey is so clearly confidential and anonymous, we suspect the former of these two possible explanations is more likely than the latter.

Eliminating Respondents Unlikely to Vote

One reason for concern about telephone survey forecasts of election outcomes is the fact that some adults who are interviewed will not in fact vote. Therefore, researchers must identify and eliminate these respondents from forecasts. Various approaches to this task have been taken (see Crespi 1988, 79; Freedman and Goldstein 1996; Petrocik 1991; Traugott and Tucker 1984; Voss, Gelman, and King 1995), and the University of Akron's approach has involved three filters: reported registration status, reported likelihood of voting, and reported interest in the election. Specifically, forecasts have been based upon only those respondents who said they were registered to vote, said they would definitely vote in the election, and said they were very interested or somewhat interested in the election.

It certainly seems wise to ignore data from telephone survey respondents who are unlikely to vote. But it is not obvious that basing the filtering process on self-reports is best. Surveys typically generate rates of predicted turnout that significantly exceed actual rates (Clausen 1968; Traugott and Katosh 1979). In the case of the 1996 University of Akron survey, the proportion of respondents who reported being registered to vote matched the actual proportion quite well (83 percent of respondents said they were registered to vote, whereas the actual proportion of Ohio adults registered to vote that year was 82 percent). Self-reported intention to vote, however, vastly overestimated actual turnout. Fully 97.6 percent of respondents who said they were registered said they would definitely (85.5 percent) or probably (12.1 percent) vote in the election, whereas in fact 68 percent of registered Ohio adults actually participated in the 1996 election.

In order to present themselves to interviewers as responsible citizens, people may be biased toward overreporting likely turnout. Yet these reports may have been quite accurate, and the overestimation of turnout rates may have occurred because members of the survey sample who were not interviewed were especially unlikely to vote (Clausen 1968). Had these latter individuals been interviewed, the total sample's turnout estimates may have been quite a bit more accurate. Therefore, eliminating some telephone survey respondents may actually have reduced forecast accuracy instead of improving it. We set out to test this possibility.

In nearly all University of Akron surveys, respondents who said they were not registered to vote were not asked their candidate preferences at all. But in 1996 all respondents were asked about their preferences. As Table 10.13 shows, forecasts from all respondents yielded an average error of 4.6 percentage points, compared to 2.8 percentage points when respondents who said they were not registered to vote were dropped. Although this test is based only upon a single race, this result does suggest that accuracy can be improved by focusing only on respondents who said they were registered.

Using the final telephone surveys, we next explored whether further elimination of respondents improved accuracy. Specifically, in Table 10.14, we compared the accuracy of forecasts from all respondents who said they were registered (in columns 1–4) to those from respondents who said they were registered, would definitely vote, and were very or somewhat interested in the election (in columns 5–8). This latter group represented 76 percent of all telephone survey respondents in 1996, a much greater percentage than the 56 percent of Ohio adult residents who voted that year. We also examined forecasts from a more restricted set of respondents: those who said they were registered, would definitely vote, and were very interested in the election (in columns 9–12). This group represented merely 35 percent of all telephone survey respondents in 1996, a much smaller proportion than the 56 percent of adults who voted that year. Thus, we tightened up the interest filter well beyond what the University of Akron has typically done and well beyond what would be representative of the state.

If we focus on the third column in each set of four (which our earlier analyses suggested optimized accuracy by allocating all undecided respondents equally among the candidates), we see a clear improvement in forecast accuracy by using a tighter "likely voter" filter. The average error for all respondents who said they

TABLE 10.13   IMPACT OF VOTER REGISTRATION SCREEN ON UNIVERSITY OF AKRON FORECAST ACCURACY (IN PERCENTAGE POINTS)

CANDIDATES	ALL RESPONDENTS	REGISTERED TO VOTE	ACTUAL RESULTS
Clinton	49.7	49.0	47.4
Dole	34.9	37.2	41.0
Perot	15.3	13.8	10.7
Average	4.6	2.8	

Note: Undecided respondents have been allocated equally to the candidates.

TABLE 10.14 IMPACT OF "LIKELY VOTER" SCREENS AND ALLOCATION STRATEGIES ON FORECAST ACCURACY IN THE UNIVERSITY OF AKRON CANDIDATE RACES (IN PERCENTAGE POINTS)

| | REGISTERED | | | | REGISTERED, DEFINITELY WILL VOTE, VERY OR SOMEWHAT INTERESTED | | | | REGISTERED, DEFINITELY WILL VOTE, VERY INTERESTED | | | |
| | UNDECIDED DROPPED | | UNDECIDED ALLOCATED EQUALLY | | UNDECIDED DROPPED | | UNDECIDED ALLOCATED EQUALLY | | UNDECIDED DROPPED | | UNDECIDED ALLOCATED EQUALLY | |
	Leaners Dropped	Leaners to Candidate	Leaners Allocated Equally	Leaners to Candidate	Leaners Dropped	Leaners to Candidate	Leaners Allocated Equally	Leaners to Candidate	Leaners Dropped	Leaners to Candidate	Leaners Allocated Equally	Leaners to Candidate
1988 STATE POLL												
President	4.3	3.5	3.1	2.9	3.3	2.8	2.3	2.7	3.8	3.7	3.2	3.4
U.S. Senate	5.1	4.5	3.6	3.7	2.7	1.8	1.6	1.3	1.5	0.5	0.4	0.1
1990 STATE POLL												
Governor	1.5	0.6	0.7	1.1	0.6	0.7	0.8	1.2	1.5	1.8	2.1	2.1
1992 STATE POLL												
President	2.9	1.1	1.0	1.5	5.2	2.3	1.0	1.9	2.5	1.6	1.3	1.3
1996 STATE POLL												
President	6.0	5.6	4.3	4.0	2.2	4.6	2.0	3.0	0.6	2.8	0.6	2.8
Average	4.0	3.1	2.5	2.7	2.8	2.4	1.5	2.0	2.0	2.1	1.5	1.9

were registered was 2.5 percentage points (column 3), compared to 1.5 percentage points for people who said they were registered, would definitely vote, and were very or somewhat interested (column 7), and 1.5 percentage points for people who said they were registered, would definitely vote, and were very interested (column 11). As we saw earlier, it is apparent throughout Table 10.14 that allocating all undecided respondents equally to the candidates improves accuracy over the other three methods for handling the undecideds.

Therefore, Table 10.15 uses this optimal allocation method and expands the pool of races to include ones where undecided respondents were not asked whether they leaned toward a candidate. Here, it is even clearer that the tightest filtering works best. When undecided respondents were allocated equally to the candidates (shown in columns 2, 4, and 6), average error was 3.1 percentage points for all registered voters; 2.8 percentage points for people who said they were registered, would definitely vote, and were very or somewhat interested in the election; and

TABLE 10.15 **IMPACT OF "LIKELY VOTER" SCREENS AND ALLOCATION STRATEGIES ON FORECAST ACCURACY IN THE UNIVERSITY OF AKRON CANDIDATE RACES (IN PERCENTAGE POINTS)**

	REGISTERED		REGISTERED, DEFINITELY WILL VOTE, VERY OR SOMEWHAT INTERESTED		REGISTERED, DEFINITELY WILL VOTE, VERY INTERESTED	
	Undecided Dropped	Undecided Allocated Equally	Undecided Dropped	Undecided Allocated Equally	Undecided Dropped	Undecided Allocated Equally
1988 STATE POLL						
President	4.3	3.1	3.3	2.3	3.8	3.2
U.S. Senate	5.1	3.6	2.7	1.6	1.5	0.4
1990 STATE POLL						
Governor	1.5	0.7	0.6	0.8	1.5	2.1
Attorney General	7.5	4.7	7.9	5.2	2.9	2.1
Auditor	15.5	8.5	14.5	8.6	11.0	7.1
Secretary of State	12.0	1.6	2.6	2.7	2.0	2.1
Treasurer	8.8	0.1	8.5	1.0	5.9	0.7
1992 STATE POLL						
President	2.9	1.0	5.2	1.0	2.5	1.3
1996 STATE POLL						
President	6.0	4.3	2.2	2.0	0.6	0.6
Average	5.9	3.1	5.3	2.8	3.5	2.2

TABLE 10.16   IMPACT OF "LIKELY VOTER" SCREENS AND ALLOCATION STRATEGIES ON FORECAST ACCURACY IN THE UNIVERSITY OF AKRON REFERENDA (IN PERCENTAGE POINTS)

	REGISTERED		REGISTERED, DEFINITELY WILL VOTE, VERY OR SOMEWHAT INTERESTED		REGISTERED, DEFINITELY WILL VOTE, VERY INTERESTED	
	Undecided Dropped	Undecided Allocated Equally	Undecided Dropped	Undecided Allocated Equally	Undecided Dropped	Undecided Allocated Equally
1990 STATE POLL						
Gambling amendment	0.9	0.3	1.6	0.5	1.6	0.7
1996 STATE POLL						
Gambling amendment	12.6	12.4	11.5	11.5	4.5	4.5
Average	6.8	6.4	6.6	6.0	3.1	2.6

2.2 percentage points for people who said they were registered, would definitely vote, and were very interested. Allocating the undecided voters equally to the candidates again clearly improved prediction accuracy over dropping them.

The same improvement in accuracy with tighter filtering is apparent in Table 10.16, which displays results for the referenda. When undecided respondents were allocated equally between yes and no votes, average error was 6.4 percentage points for people who said they were registered; 6.0 percentage points for people who said they were registered, would definitely vote, and were very or somewhat interested in the election; and 2.6 percentage points for people who said they were registered, would definitely vote, and were very interested in the election. Therefore, it seems that the University of Akron forecasts would have been more accurate if a tighter "likely voter" screen had been used.

Trends over Time

Forecast error declines as the months of an election campaign pass. Table 10.17 focuses on races that were forecast in all waves and shows that average error was largest using the first survey's data and progressively smaller in later months. In the *Columbus Dispatch* surveys, average error in early September was 3.8 percentage points, compared to 2.3 percentage points in early October and 1.5 percentage points in late October. In the telephone surveys, average error was 4.7 percentage points in early September, 3.2 percentage points in early October, and 2.6 percentage points in late October.[1] These results replicate the findings of

TABLE 10.17 *COLUMBUS DISPATCH* **AND UNIVERSITY OF AKRON FORECAST ERROR (IN PERCENTAGE POINTS)**

	COLUMBUS DISPATCH			UNIVERSITY OF AKRON		
	Early September	Early October	Late October	Early September	Early October	Late October
1988						
President	3.0	3.5	0.6	3.6	0.4	3.1
U.S. Senate	2.0	1.5	0.5	3.4	4.7	3.6
1990						
Governor	3.3	0.9	0.2			
Attorney General	8.3	4.8	4.5			
Secretary of State	1.0	0.7	0.9			
1991						
Mayor	4.5	3.9	4.7			
1992						
President				7.2	4.5	1.0
1994						
Governor	8.0	1.8	0.6			
Attorney General	1.8	0.5	2.6			
Auditor	2.5	0.9	0.5			
Secretary of State	3.6	2.7	0.9			
U.S. Senate	4.2	4.5	0.6			
Average	3.8	2.3	1.5	4.7	3.2	2.6

Campbell and Wink (1990) and Crespi (1988), who also showed that forecasts become more accurate as the date of the survey approaches Election Day.

This trend in accuracy could have occurred simply because people's senses of their candidate preferences were fuzzy early in a campaign. Those preferences may not have truly changed in a systematic way over a campaign, but people may have gotten better at reporting those preferences precisely. If so, the greater error in early waves would presumably be random. At the same time, the trend in accuracy may have occurred because people's candidate preferences genuinely changed during the course of the campaign. That is, campaign events may have led people to shift their loyalties in one direction or the other. It is therefore of interest to see whether the two survey methods tracked comparable trends in preferences over time. If the shifts paralleled each other, that would suggest that real change occurred. But if the shifts were largely independent of each other, that would suggest random error, perhaps attributable to vague internal cues.

To explore this, we assessed the measured changes in candidate preferences between early September and late October, and they appear in Table 10.18. These percentages are changes in the predicted proportion of votes for the Republican candidate.[2] A positive percentage means the candidate gained predicted votes between early September and late October. A negative number means the candidate lost predicted votes between early September and late October.

Although some of these trends are quite small, others are relatively large and could make the difference in whether a candidate is predicted to win or lose. Interestingly, the telephone surveys tracked larger changes (average absolute value = 4.3 percentage points) than the mail surveys (average absolute value = 2.9 percentage points). This may reflect greater measurement error in the telephone surveys, but it may also reflect a greater ability of the telephone surveys to detect real trends.

The correlation between columns 1 and 2 of Table 10.18 is only .33, suggesting that the changes documented by the two methods are quite different from one another. That is, the two columns of numbers share only about 10 percent of their variance. For the majority of the races (nine of fourteen), the two surveys tracked trends in the same direction, whereas for the other five races, the two surveys tracked trends in opposite directions. But in some cases where the two surveys agreed on the direction of a trend (governor in 1990 and attorney general in 1994), the Akron surveys showed a relatively large trend whereas the mail surveys showed essentially no trend at all. So it is difficult to view the "correspondence"

TABLE 10.18   TRENDS IN SUPPORT FOR THE REPUBLICAN CANDIDATE FROM EARLY SEPTEMBER TO LATE OCTOBER (IN PERCENTAGE POINTS)

		TREND	
YEAR	RACE	University of Akron	*Columbus Dispatch*
1988	President	6.6	2.4
	U.S. Senate	0.2	1.5
1990	Governor	−3.1	−0.7
	Attorney General	1.0	−0.3
	Auditor	1.2	1.6
	Treasurer	−5.4	−6.4
	Secretary of State	1.2	1.6
1992	U.S. Senate	13.3	1.4
1994	Governor	12.7	6.3
	Attorney General	−2.2	−0.8
	Auditor	−1.0	3.0
	Treasurer	−3.5	5.7
	Secretary of State	6.0	−2.7
	U.S. Senate	2.5	−5.8
Average Absolute Value		4.3	2.9

in these cases as especially meaningful. We are therefore inclined to view these results as suggesting surprisingly little agreement between the two survey methods in terms of trends.

Although this could mean that one of the survey methods is more accurate at tracking trends than the other, there is no way to test this possibility because there is no "gold standard" with which to know what real trends in candidate popularity occurred for these races. But because the early September mail surveys forecast the final election outcomes more accurately than the telephone surveys, the mail surveys evidence indicating relatively little change in candidate popularity over time may be most on target, and the changes documented by the telephone surveys may be mostly the result of random error.

Response Order Effects

The University of Akron telephone surveys have routinely rotated the order of candidate names across respondents. Krosnick's (1991) theory of satisficing anticipates an effect of name order on responses. Specifically, when response alternatives are read aloud to respondents, as they were in these surveys, recency effects are expected, advantaging names presented last in a list. To test this prediction, we analyzed data from telephone surveys asking about the two-candidate races listed in Table 10.19. The proportions of people saying they were undecided were not significantly different in the groups of people who received different name orders, so these respondents were dropped from these analyses. As the third column of numbers in Table 10.19 shows, each candidate received more support when listed last than when listed first, by an average of 3.1 percentage points. A meta-analysis of these tests revealed that this recency effect was statistically reliable ($d = .08$, $z = 3.06$, $p < .003$).

This finding has at least two practical implications. Ohio rotates candidate name order in elections, thereby eliminating any impact of name order on election outcomes. Therefore, it has been wise for the University of Akron to rotate name order to eliminate any order-induced bias in forecasts. But many states do not rotate candidate name order (e.g., Nevada, Illinois, Georgia, Massachusetts, and Colorado). Instead, for example, an incumbent running for reelection is always listed first in Massachusetts. In New Hampshire, the candidate of the party that won the last election for an office is listed first; and in Georgia, Connecticut, and Maryland, the first candidate listed on the ballot for each office is that of the party that won the most recent election for governor of the state. In states such as these, one might imagine, forecasting surveys should present the candidate names in the same order as they will appear on the ballot, so as to have the same order effect present in the survey as will appear in the election.

TABLE 10.19   IMPACT OF CANDIDATE NAME ORDER ON UNIVERSITY OF AKRON ELECTION FORECASTS

| | | CANDIDATE NAME ORDER | | | | |
YEAR	RACE	Democratic Candidate First	Republican Candidate First	Difference	X^2	p
1986	Governor					
	Democratic Candidate	61.3%	63.7%			
	Republican Candidate	38.7%	36.3%	2.4	0.22	0.64
	N	199	168			
	U.S. Senate					
	Democratic Candidate	70.9%	73.7%			
	Republican Candidate	29.1%	26.3%	2.8	0.35	0.55
	N	206	167			
1988	President					
	Democratic Candidate	38.0%	42.8%			
	Republican Candidate	62.0%	57.2%	4.8	2.36	0.12
	N	465	511			
	U.S. Senate					
	Democratic Candidate	60.5%	64.0%			
	Republican Candidate	39.5%	36.0%	3.5	1.29	0.26
	N	461	516			
1990	Governor					
	Democratic Candidate	42.5%	43.1%			
	Republican Candidate	57.5%	56.9%	0.6	0.02	0.89
	N	275	276			
1992	U.S. Senate					
	Democratic Candidate	51.4%	56.0%			
	Republican Candidate	48.6%	44.0%	4.6	7.77	0.01
	N	439	420			
Average				3.1		

However, recent research by Miller and Krosnick (1998) suggests that this may be unwise if the preelection surveys are done by telephone. Krosnick's (1991) theory of response order effects anticipates primacy effects (advantaging candidates presented first) when a list of alternatives is presented visually, as are candidate names on election ballots and voting machines. Indeed, Miller and Krosnick (1998) found that in the 1992 Ohio elections, reliable name order effects appeared in 48 percent of 118 races. These significant name order effects nearly always advantaged the candidate listed first on the ballot, who gained an average of 2.5 percent more votes. Such primacy effects were largest in races where candidate party affiliation was not listed on the ballot, in races that had been minimally publicized, and when no incumbent was running for reelection.

Therefore, in states that do not rotate candidate name order across precincts on Election Day, telephone surveys may find it more difficult than mail surveys to forecast outcomes. Because the mail surveys present the names visually, the primacy effects that appear on Election Day should appear in the preelection surveys as well. But telephone surveys can only (1) generate results containing recency effects, or (2) counterbalance name order across respondents to generate results unbiased by order. Both of these would be less than optimal. Therefore, the best approach might be to rotate name order in the telephone surveys, estimate the size of the recency effect for each race, and use those effect sizes to introduce primacy advantages of the same magnitudes into the forecasts.[3] We look forward to future research exploring the effectiveness of this approach.

One final step we took in this investigation was to explore whether the *Dispatch* surveys overstated support for candidates listed first, which would follow from Krosnick's (1991) response order theory, given that names were presented visually. Candidate names in these surveys were presented to respondents only in alphabetical order. Therefore, their forecasts might have systematically overpredicted the vote share of the alphabetically first candidate, because primacy effects present in the survey are canceled out of the real election outcome by the name rotation across precincts.

To test this, we assessed the directions of the forecast errors made by the final mail surveys. As the first column of Table 10.20 shows, the first-listed candidate was sometimes predicted to receive more votes than he or she actually received (indicated by positive numbers) and was sometimes predicted to receive fewer votes than he or she actually received (indicated by negative numbers). The primacy effect prediction anticipates mostly positive numbers in this column, but this is not the case. Only 38 percent of the errors listed are positive, compared to 59 percent that are negative. Further, although the primacy hypothesis anticipates mostly negative errors for the candidate listed last, only 46 percent of the numbers in the second column of Table 10.20 are negative, and 49 percent are positive. Thus, there is clearly no indication that errors were in line with primacy effects, and indeed, there is a trend toward recency effects.

According to the evidence reported by Miller and Krosnick (1998), response order effects would not be expected in most of these races because partisan affiliations of the candidates were listed on the questionnaires. Specifically, only four of the races in Table 10.20 were nonpartisan: the race for chief justice and the two races for justice in 1986, and the city attorney race in 1993. Averaging across these four races, there was no greater error for candidates listed first alphabetically (mean forecast error for the candidate listed first = −.10). This is certainly a surprise and may suggest that no steps need to be taken to correct for primacy bias in the mail survey forecasts.

TABLE 10.20   DIRECTION OF *COLUMBUS DISPATCH* FORECAST ERROR FOR CANDIDATES LISTED FIRST AND LAST (IN PERCENTAGE POINTS)

YEAR	RACE	FORECAST ERROR FOR CANDIDATE LISTED FIRST	FORECAST ERROR FOR CANDIDATE LISTED LAST
1980	President	2.1	−5.5
1982	Governor	−1.0	0.0
	Attorney General	1.7	−0.5
	Auditor	−0.8	0.8
	Treasurer	−0.9	−0.1
	U.S. Senate	−0.1	−1.1
	Secretary of State	−0.6	−0.4
1984	President	−0.1	1.1
1986	Governor	−0.5	0.5
	Attorney General	1.2	−1.2
	Auditor	1.3	−1.3
	Secretary of State	0.5	−0.5
	Treasurer	−1.4	1.4
	U.S. Senate	3.2	−3.2
	Chief Justice	0.4	−0.4
	Justice	−0.6	0.6
	Justice	4.5	−4.5
1988	President	−0.1	1.0
	U.S. Senate	−0.5	0.5
1990	Governor	−0.2	0.2
	Attorney General	−4.5	4.5
	Auditor	3.7	−3.7
	Treasurer	−1.6	1.6
	Secretary of State	−1.6	1.6
1991	Mayor	−4.7	4.7
	City Council	−1.0	0.7
1992	President	1.4	−2.2
1993	City Clerk	−1.9	1.9
	City Council	−1.3	−0.2
	City Attorney	−4.7	4.7
1994	Governor	0.0	0.9
	Attorney General	2.6	−2.6
	Auditor	0.5	−0.5
	Treasurer	1.7	−2.2
	Secretary of State	−0.9	0.9
	U.S. Senate	0.3	0.6
1996	President	−0.1	0.0

Discussion

Our findings can be summarized as follows. First, mail surveys have been more accurate than telephone surveys in forecasting the outcomes of all sorts of contests, although local candidate races and referenda are more difficult than statewide candidate races for both methods to predict. Both methods manifested a bias toward overpredicting the winner's margin of victory, although the mail surveys manifested this less than the telephone surveys did.

One way to overcome this bias is to allocate undecided respondents randomly to the various candidates or referendum response options. Although taking seriously undecided respondents' reports of which candidate they lean toward does increase accuracy, it can be increased even more if these respondents are assumed to vote randomly. In fact, adding 2 percent random responses to each candidate's predicted take in the mail surveys also improved their accuracy by reducing the predicted margin of victory of the winner.

Thus, in contrast to the implication of Converse's (1964) observation that random responses plague surveys and introduce error, we found here that forecast accuracy could actually be increased by adding *more* random responses. Further, our experimental evidence that the handling of "undecided" responses influences accuracy challenges correlational evidence suggesting that "undecided" responses do not influence accuracy (Lau 1994). Our evidence might also appear at first to contradict Daves and Warden's (1995) conclusion that equal accuracy is obtained regardless of whether one drops undecideds or apportions them equally. In fact, a close look at their results reveals a pattern in line with ours: Dropping the undecideds yielded an average error of 2.33 percentage points across seven polls in their Table 7.1, compared to average error of 2.01 percentage points when undecideds were allocated equally. Our finding in this regard is in line with similar evidence reported by Erikson and Sigelman (1995) showing that allocating undecided voters equally improves the accuracy of forecasts of congressional elections.

It is interesting to note that results from 1997 preelection surveys in Amsterdam, Holland, further reinforce our conclusions (Neijens et al. 1997). In March 1997 the city of Amsterdam held a referendum regarding the building of a new housing project. Polling was done each day from 25 February through 18 March, the day before the election. The first day's data included 45 percent of respondents against the referendum, 30 percent in favor, and 25 percent saying they were undecided. If the latter respondents are simply dropped, the predicted final vote is 60 percent against and 40 percent in favor. If instead the "undecided" respondents are divided equally, the predicted final vote is 58 percent against and 42 percent in favor, precisely the actual election outcome.

As we have suggested, there are at least two possible reasons that allocating undecided voters equally to the candidates improved forecast accuracy. It may be that a small proportion of voters enter the voting booth without a clear preference for one candidate over another in some races. Instead of refraining from casting a vote in these races, they may randomly select a candidate from the list presented to them. Thus, allocating undecided respondents equally to the candidates may capture the randomness with which some voters make their vote choices on Election Day, thereby improving forecast accuracy.

Alternatively, the observed improvement in forecast accuracy may be attributable simply to the fact that dividing undecided voters equally among the candidates was the allocation strategy that gave the greatest advantage to the underdog. That is, preelection surveys may systematically underestimate the support for the candidate perceived to be behind (because of the spiral of silence), and any allocation strategy that gives more of the undecided voters to the trailing candidate may improve accuracy.

Our results in this regard challenge Crespi's (1988) recommendation to drop undecided respondents when calculating election forecast on the assumption that people without a candidate preference will not participate in the election. Our findings suggest, instead, that dropping undecided respondents is the least effective of all the allocation strategies we examined.

It is important to note that our tests of the various allocation and likely voter selection strategies were conducted using unweighted data from the *Dispatch* and Akron surveys. The decision to do so was based on a few considerations. First, preelection survey nonresponse appears to be highest among people least likely to vote (Greenwald et al. 1988). Underrepresentation of members of some social or demographic groups in survey samples is therefore likely to help, rather than hurt, forecast accuracy. Weighting data would therefore counteract this tendency for nonvoters to also be nonresponders. Furthermore, weighting more heavily the responses from members of underrepresented groups is based on the tenuous assumption that members of the group who did not participate in the survey will vote identically to members of the group who did participate in the survey. For both of these reasons, weighting preelection survey data to reflect the demographic composition of the population seems likely to detract from, rather than enhance, the degree to which the survey sample accurately represents the subset of the population that will participate in the election.

Many survey organizations do routinely weight their data to match the demographic characteristics of the entire population, and it is not clear that the optimal allocation and selection strategies that we identified here would be as effective at improving forecast accuracy with weighted data. It seems quite likely, in fact, that the optimal allocation and selection strategies may be quite different for weighted and unweighted data. We therefore caution investigators not to presume that the techniques we developed will work equally well with weighted data, and we encourage experimentation with unweighted data.

Our results have implications for how to make a decision that questionnaire designers routinely confront: whether to offer respondents an explicit "don't know" response option in attitude and belief questions. Many studies document that offering a "don't know" option reduces the likelihood that respondents will offer substantive answers to such questions (e.g., Bishop, Tuchfarber, and Oldendick 1986; Schuman and Presser 1981). Some observers have presumed this to be evidence of improved data quality because people without real opinions are thought to be admitting this, rather than concocting meaningless answers because they feel pressure to appear opinionated.

In contrast, Krosnick's (1991) theory of satisficing suggests instead that these "don't know" filters may do more damage than good by discouraging people with real opinions from reporting them. According to this perspective, some respondents employ low-effort response strategies to avoid the cognitive effort required to provide optimal responses. One such low-effort strategy is choosing the "don't know" response option when it is offered. If this option is not offered, respondents may instead choose to expend the effort needed to generate a valid substantive response. Consequently, data quality would not be compromised by omitting a "don't know" response option. Indeed, a number of previous investigations have supported this notion (e.g., Gilljam and Granberg 1993; Krosnick and Berent 1993; McClendon and Alwin 1993).

Our results can be viewed as consistent with this latter line of thinking. We found that a substantial proportion of respondents claimed to be undecided in the University of Akron surveys, which explicitly offered this as a response option. However, when probed, many of these respondents said that they did lean toward one candidate. When these responses were treated as valid preferences, forecast accuracy was improved. Thus, encouraging respondents to generate substantive responses by eliminating the "undecided" response option led to the collection of data that improved survey quality, a conclusion in line with Crespi's (1988) on this point.

We also found that filtering out respondents who are unlikely to vote (based upon their self-reports of registration status, likelihood of voting, and interest in the campaign) improves forecast accuracy. Surprisingly, though, very strong filtering worked better than weaker filtering. In fact, our evidence indicated that the telephone survey forecasts were most accurate when they were based on data from about only one third of the respondents. Across the nine statewide candidate races from 1988 through 1996, the tight "likely voter" selection screen and the allocation strategies that we devised generated election forecasts with an average error of 2.2 percentage points (see Table 10.15).

This finding is really quite remarkable. On the basis of sampling error alone, we would have expected an average error of 5.04 percentage points for estimates based on samples of these sizes. Therefore, the selection and allocation strategies outlined here consistently produced telephone survey forecasts that contained less than half the inaccuracy that would be expected simply on the basis of sampling error. Of course, other sources of error (e.g., mistakes by respondents and interviewers) are likely to have created imprecision as well, making this small error appear to be even more remarkable.

These results suggest that part of the reason the University of Akron's preelection surveys were less accurate than the *Dispatch* mail surveys has been that the telephone surveys employed relatively weak "likely voter" screens. Our evidence that these forecasts were most accurate when only about one third of respondents contributed data is consistent with the fact that *Dispatch* forecasts have also been based upon very small proportions of potential respondents.

In his examination of the features associated with election forecast accuracy, Crespi (1988) found that survey organizations that relied on a single question about voting intention to identify likely voters generated less accurate election forecasts than did organizations that used several questions. This is consistent with our finding with the University of Akron data that more stringent "likely voter" screens based on more questions yielded more accurate forecasts than did less stringent screens based on fewer questions.

However, our findings in this regard contradict another of Crespi's (1988) recommendations. He suggested that the identification of likely voters should be based in part on estimated turnout for a given election, which provides researchers with a rough guide for approximating the proportion of a survey sample that should be considered likely voters. Our evidence suggests that the most accurate forecasts are generated from much smaller proportions of the sample than would be expected on the basis of turnout rates. Projected turnout, therefore, appears not to be particularly useful for calibrating the stringency of a survey organization's "likely voter" screen.

The two survey methods paint only weakly correlated portraits of change in candidate popularity over the course of campaigns, and the telephone surveys registered larger changes than did the mail surveys. Based upon the limited information available on this matter, we are inclined to believe that the mail surveys are probably more accurate in tracking trends and that real trends are probably quite small in most elections. This conclusion is consistent with Gelman and King's (1993) argument that much of the variation over time in telephone survey forecasts is unrelated to actual election outcomes.

Finally, we found that telephone surveys are likely to be biased by recency effects, which can be eliminated by rotating candidate name order. However, primacy effects are likely to appear in some races in states that do not rotate candidate name order on Election Day, which poses a challenge for telephone surveys. We look forward to the testing and development of techniques to manage this problem.

We look forward, as well, to replications of the findings reported here with data from other states and from the nation as a whole. Most of the conclusions reached here were supported by data from several election years and in many cases across the two survey modes, strengthening our confidence in the generalizability of the observed results. But stronger tests of generalizability require data collected from other populations by other survey organizations.

Conclusions

Screening and allocation are currently done differently by different survey organizations, and relatively little collective wisdom in published research has established an empirically validated set of guidelines that have been shown to be optimal. We hope that the approach taken in this chapter will be paralleled by the future work of more researchers systematically exploring the impact of specific survey procedures, subjecting common intuitions and conventional wisdom to rigorous empirical scrutiny and contributing to the establishment of a proven set of professional standards for survey research.

Such systematic explorations may well affirm many of the intuitions that underlie current survey practices. However, empirical scrutiny may also call into question elements of conventional wisdom. The tests we have reported in this chapter shed new light on procedures for optimizing the accuracy of preelection surveys, and future research taking a similar approach will undoubtedly do the same. We look forward to such research, and to the systematic development of empirically validated guidelines for conducting quality survey research.

Notes

The authors thank Quin Monson for his help. This chapter was prepared partly while the second author was a Fellow at the Center for Advanced Study in the Behavioral Sciences. Support was provided by grants SBR-9503822 and SBR-9022192 from the National Science Foundation. The authors wish to thank Michael Tichy and Robert Hudson for their help in preparing the manuscript. Correspondence regarding this chapter should be addressed to Penny S. Visser or Jon A. Krosnick, Department of Psychology, Ohio State University, 1885 Neil Avenue, Columbus, Ohio 43210 (e-mail: visser.102@osu.edu or krosnick@osu.edu).

1. These percentages are based upon the most accurate allocation and screening methods (*Dispatch*: allocating undecideds equally; Akron: allocating undecideds and race-skippers equally and including only people who were registered, said they would definitely vote, and said they were very interested in the election).
2. These percentages are again based upon the most accurate allocation and screening methods (*Dispatch*: allocating undecideds equally; Akron: allocating undecideds and race-skippers equally and including only people who were registered, said they would definitely vote, and said they were very interested in the election).
3. Although it is not necessarily the case that primacy and recency effects will be of the same magnitude, this approach provides at least a starting point for addressing the problem of opposing order effects for visual versus oral presentation of response options.

PART IV

Controversial Issues in Election Polling

CHAPTER 11

Deliberative Polling in the 1996 Elections

Vincent Price

At the core of much democratic theory is a conception of the public as a deliberative body. Public opinion, according to its "classical" formulation, emerges out of widespread popular discussion and debate (Price 1992). This debate is ideally free flowing, uncensored, open to all citizens on equal terms, and well informed (Habermas 1982, 1989).

Many who study public opinion have argued, however, that the American public falls a good deal short of being a truly deliberative body. The typical American, it seems, bears little resemblance to the ideal democratic citizen. The latter, as depicted in various wishful accounts, confronts public issues with care and zeal, actively debates the merits of competing policies, grapples with their collective consequences, and expresses informed opinions in the common interest. In contrast, the typical American, as rendered in various portraits drawn from survey research over the past fifty years, appears uninvolved with many public issues, engages infrequently in political discussion, has little appetite for news about public affairs, and displays surprisingly weak knowledge of even the most prominent issues of the day (Delli-Carpini and Keeter 1996; Luskin 1987; Neuman 1986). The opinions citizens offer to pollsters are often merely top-of-the-head judgments, grounded neither in much public debate nor in much private contemplation (see, e.g., Kinder and Sears 1985; Lane and Sears 1964; Luskin 1987). In light of such findings, it is not surprising that questions are often raised about the extent to which conventional opinion polls adequately reflect true public judgment (e.g., Boyte 1995; Salmon and Glasser 1995; Yankelovich 1991).

The 1996 U.S. presidential election brought to Americans a new kind of opinion poll—the "deliberative poll"—one designed to measure not simply top-of-the-head opinions but fully informed, thoughtful opinions forged in the heat of careful public debate. At a cost approaching $4 million, a probability sample of 459 American citizens was assembled at the University of Texas at Austin at the onset of the primary season. Over several days (and after reading through extensive briefing materials dealing with the American family, foreign affairs, and the economy), participants met in discussion groups, prepared questions for presidential candidates, met with candidates to raise their concerns, and then registered their opinions on a wide variety of issues. The event, dubbed the National Issues Convention (NIC) by its designer, political scientist James Fishkin of the University of Texas, was aired nationally on public television, received fairly prominent attention in the news media, and stimulated extensive methodological and philosophical debates within the academic and commercial polling communities. It also stimulated other deliberative projects of similar design, including the statewide Minnesota Citizens' Issue Conference undertaken by the *Minnesota Star Tribune* and KCTA-TV several months later, in May 1996.

This chapter reviews deliberative polling in the 1996 elections, focusing on the National Issues Convention. To set the stage, I examine some of the concerns about contemporary public opinion and opinion polling that motivated the development of the deliberative poll. I next review its implementation in advance of the 1996 presidential primaries, noting points of controversy that surrounded its design and results. In closing, the chapter looks at prospects for the future of deliberative polling and takes critical stock of the costs and benefits of the technique.

Polls, the News, and the Ailing Body Politic

In 1925 prominent journalist Walter Lippmann flatly termed the American public a "phantom." Partly this was so, he argued, because of dependence upon the commercial news media for public debate. Rather than offering a full account of complex public affairs, the news tended toward partial, simplistic, and sensationalistic treatments (Lippmann 1922, 1925). Even if the news media could offer some semblance of truth, suggested Lippmann, most citizens would hardly take notice. Rather than actively participating in political life, most Americans were merely spectators, and only half-attentive ones at that. "The private citizen today," he wrote, "has come to feel rather like a deaf spectator in the back row, who ought to keep his mind on the mystery off there, but cannot quite manage to keep awake" (1925, 13). Democratic theory simply asked too much of ordinary people, who had neither the time nor the inclination to devote much energy to public affairs. In place of rationally considered opinions, most people could offer only shallow, prejudicial reactions based on fragmentary news reports and misunderstandings.

Survey evidence gathered since Lippmann wrote his pessimistic account does seem to support the view that many people lack basic knowledge of public affairs and often express opinions that are poorly informed and unorganized (e.g., Bishop et al. 1980; Luskin 1987, 1998; Neuman 1986). Subsequent appraisals of the news media have similarly echoed and extended many of Lippmann's concerns about the fitness of the press as carriers of public debate. Campaign news, for example, tends toward minimal "sound bites" and horse-race coverage, emphasizing the tactical and strategic aspects of political gamesmanship over substantive, often complex issues (Bennett 1996; Hallin 1992; Patterson 1993). The prominence of opinion polling in contemporary American society, although viewed by some as a triumph of popular democracy, appears to other critics as an "echo chamber," in which sound bites and catch phrases projected by the media are simply reflected back through opinion polls by a relatively ignorant public (Fishkin 1991, 1995; Luskin, Fishkin, and Jowell 1997; Salmon and Glasser 1995).

The potential gap between deliberative, informed public opinion and what standard opinion polls measure has long been a concern of social scientists (e.g., Blumer 1948). In the past decade, however, these concerns have taken on a new urgency. Deliberative polls, along with "educational" polls and variants of focused group discussions, have been advanced recently as supplements (and in some cases alternatives) to conventional mass opinion surveys and polls. These efforts are intended to remedy perceived problems of superficiality in mass opinion, help address deficiencies in media performance, or both. Some researchers have proposed modified survey procedures that provide information to respondents about the issues on which they are questioned—varying in scope from brief interviewer explanations to more elaborate briefing materials—in an attempt to assess "informed" public opinion rather than more superficial responses (e.g., Kay et al. 1994; Neijens 1987; Neijens, Ridder, and Saris 1992). Others, like the planners of the deliberative poll, have developed more radical departures from standard survey practice, attempting to gather a statistical "microcosm of society" that could take the time to do what most people do not: engage in informed debate and reach cogent opinions on important matters of the day (Fishkin 1991).

These research trends have developed alongside a growing fascination with what has become known as "civic journalism" or "public journalism" (e.g., Charity 1995; Rosen 1991; Rosen and Merritt 1994), a reform movement in the press community aimed at modifying reporting behavior in ways that might foster more popular engagement and political participation. Advocates of public journalism often criticize the objective stance of the journalist as a disinterested and impartial observer, arguing that this perspective has led to an unhealthy insulation of reporters and editors from the readers and viewers they should serve. The problem, according to proponents of public journalism, is that the news too often follows journalists' and politicians' agendas rather than the public agenda. Symptomatic of the problem are most opinion polls, which typically reflect the concerns and interests of media researchers rather than respondents, pushing "people into corners where an opinion is demanded rather than freely given" (Fouhy 1996, 52). Polls have come under harsh criticism from a variety of quarters. They are seen as manufacturing or "seducing" public opinion (Salmon and Glasser 1995), as substituting for public engagement, or even as contributing in various ways to the demise of public debate and the collapse of the discursive public sphere (Herbst 1993).

A Proposal for Treatment: The Deliberative Poll

In 1988 political scientist James Fishkin proposed a novel technique for bridging the gap between informed, deliberative opinion and the superficiality of mass opinion. Writing in the *Atlantic Monthly,* he took account of various problems in the presidential nomination and campaign process. The growth of mass primary campaigns, though helping to break elite control over candidate selection in "smoke-filled rooms," had unfortunately emptied the nomination process of any true deliberation. Although mass primaries did offer greater political equality, mass opinion was largely uninformed by any careful political discussion and debate. Returning control of the nomination process to party elites might restore active deliberation, but at the expense of broad representation and equality. How might we manage a truly deliberative process that ensured political equality? Fishkin's solution was a national caucus among a representative sample of 1,500 American citizens. Selected participants would travel to a single site to hear from all candidates in their chosen party, engage in discussions with other citizens, and then select at-large delegates to the parties' national conventions.

The idea of a national caucus was further elaborated and generalized in Fishkin's subsequent book, *Democracy and Deliberation* (1991). His plan was to alter the presidential selection process with a new, deliberative forum of citizens who would represent the entire population. Fishkin proposed that the national caucus—which he now termed a "deliberative poll"—should be a high-profile media event. It would be able to harness television as a constructive rather than a corrosive force, establishing campaign momentum as a positive rather than a negative phenomenon for strong but underfinanced candidates in the primary season. It would "pass on the full range of serious candidates before they dropped out from lack of funding" (Ladd et al. 1992, 31). As the 1992 election neared, Fishkin garnered support for his idea among influential members of the news media, and plans began to be formulated for a deliberative poll to be held early in the nominating season.

According to Fishkin, "An ordinary poll models what the electorate thinks, given how little it knows. A deliberative opinion poll models what the electorate *would* think if, hypothetically, it could be immersed in intense deliberative processes" (1991, 81; italics in original). The basic design was to select a national, random sample of the voting age population and transport them as "delegates" to a single site for several days of debate and deliberation. The delegates would debate issues with political leaders and each other before being polled on their preferences.

The plan was intended "to adapt the deliberative possibilities of small-scale politics to the problem of selecting candidates and launching issues in a large-scale nation state" (Fishkin 1991, 8). The exercise would combine the thoughtfulness and depth of face-to-face politics with the representative character of a national event. Fishkin modeled his general design on the ancient, Athenian practice of constituting juries of about 500 citizens, by lottery, to judge accusations against political leaders. Such citizen juries enjoyed great power in Athens, even in certain cases the right to review and overturn decisions of the Athenian Assembly (Fishkin 1991).

As conceived by Fishkin, then, the deliberative poll would create a face-to-face, open, communicative forum that is fully representative of the population at large. It aimed to increase the quality of mass participation in politics by offering citizens a chance to inform themselves on the issues before issuing their opinions. Importantly, it also aimed to increase the *force* of mass participation by creating a televised media "event" that would allow ordinary citizens to penetrate the "hocus pocus" and "amplification" of press-mediated political debate and engage directly with their leaders (Fishkin 1991, 8). Properly managed, the deliberation would be a fair and honest two-way exchange between political representatives and their constituents. It would be no less than a new social institution, offering "direct democracy among a group of politically equal participants who, as a statistical microcosm of the society, represent or stand in for the deliberations of the whole" (Fishkin 1991, 93).

The deliberative poll was thus a "complex, multi-faceted event" (Luskin, Fishkin, and Jowell 1997). It was intended to be, simultaneously, (1) an innovative way of assessing and communicating public preferences, (2) a public-interest television program with its own educational value, and (3) a social-scientific quasi experiment that could shed light on political behavior and democratic theory (Fishkin and Luskin 1998).

Thus the deliberative poll was conceived of as a new tool for popular decision making, intended to inject fully informed public choice directly into the political process. It is interesting to note that although its formulators were apparently unaware of the connection, the deliberative poll was quite similar in spirit—

if not in particulars of method—a European effort undertaken some twenty years earlier, known as the "planning cell" and designed to engage ordinary citizens in careful, educated, face-to-face debate over complex public issues (Dienel 1978). As we later discuss, the similarities between these two independent efforts have grown even stronger in recent years as the deliberative poll has evolved from a program intended for nationwide application into a procedure for dealing with regional and local issues, particularly those involving technical policy matters such as regulation of public utilities.

Development and Early Implementations

Fishkin's attempt to launch a deliberative poll in advance of the 1992 presidential primaries ultimately failed for lack of funding. But the idea took hold, both in the United States and abroad, particularly in England, where the first deliberative poll was carried out in April 1994. The event was produced by Granada Television (which had throughout the 1980s conducted similar exercises in connection with its *Granada 500* programs) and the *Independent*. It was broadcast nationally by Channel 4 in May (Fishkin 1994).

A national probability sample of 1,174 citizens was drawn by the Social and Community Planning Research (SCPR), and of these, 869 (74 percent) were interviewed on the question, "Rising crime: What can we do about it?" Each respondent was invited to attend an all-expense-paid, two-day meeting in Manchester, England, including a tour of the Granada Television studios and a stipend of £50. After numerous recruitment efforts, 302 (35 percent of survey respondents, about 26 percent of the total sample) chose to attend. They received carefully balanced briefing materials, participated in small-group discussion about crime and crime prevention, and addressed questions to competing experts and politicians. At the end of the session, they were again polled on their views. The proceedings were videotaped, edited, and broadcast two weeks later.

The deliberations in Manchester appeared to have contributed to several major shifts of opinion, including an increase in the sense that prisons were a limited tool in fighting crime, a greater sensitivity to criminal defendants' procedural rights, and a move toward greater valuation of ameliorating the social causes of crime such as absentee parents, weakened emphasis on discipline, and violence on television (Luskin, Fishkin, and Jowell 1997). These outcomes, together with findings that the eventual sample of conference attendees looked by all accounts to be an excellent representation of the full sample, led to a positive enough evaluation by the sponsors that a second exercise was held in June 1995, this time dealing with Britain's role in the European Union.

The 1996 National Issues Convention

Following the two British deliberative polls and a second book elaborating the concept (*The Voice of the People*, published in 1995), Fishkin was able to assemble almost $4 million to fund a deliberative poll in connection with the 1996 presidential elections. The National Issues Convention (NIC) was held at the University of Texas at Austin, where Fishkin serves on the faculty, in January 1996. The event was supported by the Public Broadcasting System (PBS), the University of Texas, the Presidential Libraries, and a number of other public and private sponsors, including Freddie Mac, Southwestern Bell, the Annie E. Casey Foundation, and American Airlines. As with the British effort, the NIC was developed purposely as a media event, was well publicized by its organizers, and ultimately produced over five hours of television coverage aired nationally on PBS.

As it gathered supporters and financial backing, the concept of the deliberative poll also collected a good deal of criticism from academic survey specialists and commercial opinion researchers. Essays critical of the idea were published as plans were being discussed originally in 1992, and controversy over the merits of Fishkin's plan built to a peak during the 1996 campaign. Much of the debate appeared in *Public Perspective*, a publication of the Roper Center for Public Opinion Research. The criticism followed several basic lines. First, some writers objected that reference to the Fishkin exercise as a "poll" was actually a misnomer (Mitofsky 1996; Traugott 1992; Worchester 1993). Noting that it was creating conditions that were not at all like naturally occurring conditions and creating rather than simply assessing opinions, several critics suggested the deliberative poll was better termed a national "caucus" (Traugott 1992) or a "deliberative forum" (Worchester 1993). Concerns were expressed about the difficulties in obtaining a representative sample, control of the discussion agenda and selection of materials, and the lack of a true experimental control group against which changes of opinion apparently stimulated by the convention could be compared (Mitofsky 1996; Tringali 1996). Other critics charged that to the extent the convention *did* induce effects, it would be very difficult to know whether these were the genuine product of deliberation or merely a manifestation of participants' self-conscious participation in an experiment (what has become known as the "Hawthorne effect," after the name of a Bell System plant that was the site of experiments in management and employee behavior in the 1920s) (Adair 1996; Ladd 1996). The very fact of deliberation gave rise to another set of concerns: How would group dynamics, implicating phenomena like leadership, reticence, loquacity, and normative pressures, alter the outcomes (e.g., Tindale 1996; Traugott 1992)? Numerous critics found the exercise potentially illuminating but expressed serious reservations about the cost of the endeavor, echoing concerns that had been voiced earlier about the high cost of the British deliberative polls (Worchester 1993). As a high-profile media event, some argued, the deliberative poll would ultimately be shaped by the media and by political handlers into just another opportunity for spin (Traugott 1992).

Behind many of the specific criticisms were broader concerns about what was not merely a different kind of poll but, in fact, a rather sweeping democratic reform (e.g., Ladd et al. 1992). Writers were uncomfortable with Fishkin's main goal: to create a "superior form of democracy" (Fishkin 1992, 29). He was quite committed to the idea that the deliberative poll, in allowing a representative sample of citizens to become well informed about the issues and candidates, would issue a more compelling set of public preferences. The deliberative poll would thus have a "moral force" or "recommending force." As Fishkin put it,

> I think that there's a serious conceptual problem in thinking that the only form of democracy that appeals to the American public is something more direct and majoritarian. I hold a different model of democracy— and I'm proposing a demonstration of it. . . . I'm trying to get political equality and deliberation at the same time." (Ladd et al. 1992, 33)

By claiming that the deliberative poll would give a different and superior rendering of public opinion, one that would have greater moral force and deserved to be taken more seriously than the often superficial data gathered by conventional polls, Fishkin had launched a controversial experiment in democratic decision making, and a challenge to conventional opinion polling.

By the time of its implementation, the focus of the deliberative poll had shifted somewhat from the candidate selection process to an attempt to identify key issues in the presidential campaign. This was so in part because organizers of the convention believed that candidate preferences would receive too much attention in the news media and in part because of the difficulty of knowing, as far in advance as was necessary for design of the initial survey interview, which main Republican candidates would emerge (Merkle, 1996). Another reason for deflection of interest away from candidate selection onto major issues was that attempts to involve President Clinton and all the major Republican candidates were only partially successful. President Clinton declined, although Vice President Gore attended in person. Four Republican candidates participated, three (Lamar Alexander, Phil Gramm, and Steve Forbes) by satellite and one (Richard Lugar) in person. Unfortunately, front runner Bob Dole declined, as did Pat Buchanan.

Issues for discussion at the convention were selected by Public Agenda (a nonpartisan, public interest group), in consultation with participants in the National Issues Forums of the Kettering Foundation. The aim was to select issues that would prove to be important in the campaign. Three topics were selected, and each became the focus of a nonpartisan briefing packet sent to delegates in advance of the convention: (1) "Mission Uncertain: Reassessing America's Global Role," (2) "Pocketbook Pressures: What Should Be Done about Them?" and (3) "The Troubled American Family: Which Way Out of the Storm?" These advance materials were reviewed by a bipartisan blue-ribbon committee chaired by former members of Congress.

The goal was to bring 600 delegates, fully representative of adult American citizens, to Austin for the convention. To select delegates for the convention, the National Opinion Research Center (NORC) at the University of Chicago drew a national probability sample of 1,278 persons of age 18 or older who were eligible to vote and were English-speaking. Personal interviews were conducted with 914 (72 percent) of these people in late November and early December 1995. The interview was intended not only to recruit participants to the NIC, but also to gather basic demographic information and baseline (preconvention) measures of opinions, knowledge, political interest, and media use. Because delegates would eventually complete a self-administered questionnaire booklet immediately following the convention, the initial interview included a self-administered questionnaire of eighty-four questions, most of them about opinions bearing on the three broad issue areas that would be the focus of the convention.

All survey respondents were invited to serve as delegates to the Austin convention. Participants' transportation and housing expenses were paid, and they received a $300 honorarium and $25 toward the cost of telephoning their families during the convention. The NORC staff assisted in arranging child care and in securing time off from work if necessary; and in cases of financial hardship, additional funding was provided. In the end, 459 delegates (50 percent of those interviewed and invited, 36 percent of the total sample) attended the event.

Upon arriving in Austin, delegates were randomly assigned to one of thirty small groups. On the first day of the program, they spent a total of nine hours discussing the issues within their groups—three hours per each issue area—guided by moderators supplied by the National Issues Forums. Each group prepared three questions to ask presidential candidates. Over the following two days, delegates met as a single body with issue experts, the Republican candidates (three via satellite), and the vice president. On the final day, they met again in their smaller groups to discuss candidates and the issues. Before leaving, delegates individually completed a questionnaire booklet with eighty-four items repeated from the initial survey.

The basic design of the NIC survey was undertaken by another blue-ribbon panel, this time of respected academic and commercial researchers. As a control, 300 initial survey respondents who declined to participate, or who had agreed to participate but could not for some reason attend, were randomly sampled, and

176 (58 percent) of these citizens were reinterviewed by telephone. A separate random-digit-dialing sample of 431 people was also later contacted and interviewed by telephone using the same postconvention questionnaire.

Evaluating the NIC

As noted earlier, the National Issues Convention was intended to be an innovative way of assessing and communicating public preferences. It also attempted to be a public-interest television program with its own educational value and a social-scientific quasi experiment that would shed light on political behavior (Fishkin and Luskin 1998). How well did it meet these objectives?

The most thorough review of the NIC to date is that of Merkle (1996). After a careful examination of the sampling methods and results, he reports that the sample did indeed closely match the population on many variables but diverged among a few potentially important characteristics. Attendees of the National Issues Convention were less likely to be older (with only 11 percent age 60 or older, compared to 21 percent nationally) and more likely to be better educated (with 28 percent college graduates, compared to 21 percent nationally). Politically active people were more likely to accept the offer to attend the convention. Among those accepting the invitation, 70 percent reported talking about politics at least once a week; only 49 percent of those declining the invitation reported the same frequency of political discussion. Participants also reported significantly higher income, more time watching and reading the news, and a higher likelihood of having voted in the past presidential election than did nonparticipants (Fishkin and Luskin 1998). As Merkle (1996) notes, the representativeness of the National Issues Convention, albeit fairly good in consideration of the difficulties involved in recruitment, was nonetheless a bit wider of the mark than were earlier British deliberative polls—despite what appears to have been a superior response rate in the U.S. project.

Most of the attention given to the results of the convention focused, understandably, on aggregate opinion changes measured by the before- and after-convention surveys. The general question had to do with whether or not the results of the deliberative poll would suggest conclusions about American public opinion that differed from those drawn on the basis of conventional opinion polls (Merkle 1996). Several changes did receive attention in the news following the event. Among the largest were a decrease in favorable ratings of a flat tax (which fell from 44 percent to 30 percent), an increase in support for turning the safety net for low-income Americans over to the states (which rose from 56 percent to 66 percent), and an increase in the percentage of respondents who favored military cooperation with other countries to address global trouble spots (up to 38 percent from 21 percent). The basic outcome, however, according to Merkle (1996, 611), was that despite some changes, "in the end the recommending force of the NIC was very similar to what the preconvention survey (i.e., the traditional poll) measured." Of the more than eighty opinion questions repeated after the convention, only twenty showed statistically significant changes. Among those items that did change, only seven showed a change in the direction of majority opinion (Kohut 1996). The general conclusion of most critics was that the event produced a surprisingly small amount of change, given its intensity as a political stimulus, and if anything underscored the robustness of popular opinion as measured in conventional surveys and polls (Kohut 1996; Mitofsky 1996).

This view has been challenged by Fishkin and his colleagues (e.g., Fishkin and Luskin 1998), who argue that the amount of aggregate change observed was considerable, in light of what might have been expected.[1] Substantially more change occurred at the individual than at the aggregate level. Across sixty-six opinion items focusing in the three general issue areas, the average proportion of participants who gave a different answer on the second survey was about 4 out of 10 (Kenneth Raskinski of the National Opinion Research Center, cited in Merkle 1996; see also Fishkin and Luskin 1998). Fishkin and Luskin (1998) found that although complete changes of side on the issues were less common, they were still substantial—with the proportion of respondents changing sides completely running between 1 in 10 and 3 in 10. The researchers did not account for how much of this gross change may be attributable merely to chance, but they argue that it can be interpreted as motivated by gains in knowledge. Seven of the eleven knowledge questions included on the survey showed significant increases, with an average gain of just above 11 percent.

Was the opinion rendered by participants in the convention of higher quality? Answers to this question are unfortunately difficult to determine. In comments made to an Internet discussion group focused on public opinion polling, researcher Philip Meyer (1996) suggested that the focus on directional changes of opinion was perhaps misguided, and that it would be more important to discern whether, after participating in the event, people's opinions were any more internally consistent, more connected to one another, and less labile. To date, however, analyses have not been conducted to address such quality issues; in any event, opinion quality criteria were not elaborated in advance of the exercise (Price and Neijens 1997). Consequently, few relevant measures are available for examination.

Did the NIC outcomes amount to a "recommending force"? Although debates about how much change was actually stimulated by the convention will in all likelihood continue, there is little argument about the event's influence on the nominating process or the presidential campaign that followed. Its impact appeared minimal. The convention received a fair amount of media coverage, most of it casting the event in a favorable light. However, television ratings for the program were lower than were those for the 1992 primary debates, and over-all the results appeared to register little influence on the course of the nomina-tion campaigns (Merkle 1996).

The full value of the NIC as a social-scientific quasi experiment that might illuminate American political behavior or the workings of democracy has yet to be demonstrated, although Fishkin and Luskin (1998) have recently begun to explore the data more systematically. Unfortunately, data from the project (now a few years old) have still not been released for public analysis. Given the design of the study, however, some questions—for example, about possible experimenter demand or the role of group dynamics—will be very difficult to address (Merkle 1996). Price and Niejens (1998) have argued that we must at present, accept the unsatisfying conclusion that we cannot be certain just how to interpret data from such deliberative exercises. This is so, they submit, because of failures to iden-tify specific objectives for assessing experimental success, lack of any acknowl-edged measures of opinion quality, and use of a complex experimental "stimulus" that confounds many potentially influential variables.

Other Uses of Deliberative Polling in 1996

The National Issues Convention, with its attendant publicity and controversy, stimulated several other experiments of similar design and intention. Most notably, the *Minneapolis Star Tribune* and KTCA-TV conducted a statewide deliberative poll in May. The Citizens' Issues Conference (CIC) was carried out as part of the Minnesota Citizens' Forum, a joint public journalism project of the newspaper and national public television affiliate station (Daves 1997). In general outline, the project mirrored the NIC. The *Star Tribune* Minnesota poll conducted an initial telephone survey of 1,699 adults in late March and April. Respondents were asked to participate in a two-day conference to be held at a hotel in a Minneapolis suburb and offered a $50 to $100 travel stipend plus lodg-ing at the conference hotel. Although the aim was to bring 400 people to the conference, in the end 214 chose to attend. Participants read briefing booklets that contained balanced, factual information about topics such as health care, education, poverty, race and opportunity, the American family, the economy, America's global role, and the federal deficit—ten topics in all—that had been chosen by Public Agenda (the same nonpartisan, public interest group that had collaborated in design of materials for the NIC). After small-group meetings and discussions, conference participants gathered in a large-group session to rate the importance of the ten issue areas.

Despite a good deal of individual-level shifts of opinion, the aggregate distributions of opinion changed little in response to the Minnesota CIC deliberations. Daves (1997), echoing Kohut (1996), interpreted the results as largely confirming the robustness of conventional polling. Yet, according to Daves (1998), aside from any recommending force a deliberative poll may or may not have, it has very useful applications in public journalism. Indeed, the news organizations that conducted the Minnesota Citizens' Issues Conference had precisely these applications in mind when planning the project. First, it provided them with a readily available pool of knowledgeable people to interview. The group discussions offered useful material to reporters and helped inject into their reporting a wider range of voices. Second, in the Minnesota case the initial event was followed up with discussions that were periodically repeated in Citizens' Forum groups, allowing reporters to continue to draw observations from the deliberative process. The general goal of these exercises—in keeping with the aims of civic journalism—was to better determine citizens' values and priorities and to encourage greater community involvement in politics. On the basis of his experience with the Minnesota project, Daves (1998, 26) concludes that "deliberative polling—*per se*—is not an efficient use of limited resources for most news organizations that don't have partners with deep pockets. . . . But its methods— random selection to bring citizens together, presentation of unbiased materials, etc.—are valuable."

Subsequent Uses of Deliberative Polling

Channel 4 in Britain has continued to conduct deliberative polls for national broadcast, including one on the general election in 1997. In the United States, in contrast, many of the applications since 1996 have been local, involving public utilities in Texas, which are required to incorporate public participation in formulating "Integrated Resource Plans" pertaining to their service territories (Fishkin and Luskin 1998). The utilities must allocate resources in various alternatives: new fossil fuel plants, renewable energy sources like wind and solar power, energy conservation programs, and purchasing power from outside sources. Fishkin and Luskin (forthcoming) report that a series of deliberative polls on electric utilities has been conducted over the past several years, with a consistent pattern of results. When asked to choose a first-choice energy option from among four alternatives (fossil fuels, renewables, conservation, or outside sources), those who participate in deliberative forums tend to become less supportive of renewable energy sources as their first choice, while increasing in support for conservation. Overall, participants express a desire for a mix of energy sources and are willing, after deliberation, to pay at least $1 more per month for renewable energy.

The application of deliberative polling to such technical issues—about which the public is generally very poorly informed—highlights its remarkable similarity to another, much earlier deliberative program for citizen involvement that was developed and implemented in Germany (Price and Neijens 1998). The planning cell (*Planungszelle*) is a technique devised over twenty years ago by Peter Dienel (1978). It shares with the deliberative poll many common objectives and methodological features. As with the deliberative poll, the technique aimed at increasing the possibilities for popular participation in decision making. More specifically, it sought to improve the accuracy and efficiency of societal decision making on complex technological issues.

In general design, the planning cell is quite similar to the deliberative poll. A group of citizens are selected at random, given paid leave from work, and engaged in collaborative, face-to-face planning sessions with other citizens with the assistance of technical advisers (Dienel 1978; Renn et al. 1984). Unlike the deliberative poll, however, planning cells are usually limited in size (roughly twenty-five persons per cell). Rather than being focused around a single, full-sample meeting for the purposes of broadcast to a mass audience, planning cells are intended to be replicated a number of times, in a number of locales, in order to increase their validity and legitimacy.

The planning cell procedure is highly standardized in order to guarantee replicability and comparability of results (see Price and Neijens 1998, for a review of the methods). As implemented in a study of public energy supply systems in Germany (Dienel 1989; Renn et al. 1984), the planning cell programs involved alternating periods of information provision, discussions, small-group working sessions, and survey evaluations. To prevent the emergence of group hierarchies, membership in small-group sessions is rotated from session to session (Dienel 1989). Dienel (1989) reports that the technique has been employed in dealing with a wide range of problems—city planning, highway routing, planning of recreation areas, choosing local energy sources and siting of waste disposal facilities, implementation of new information technologies—at the national and regional levels. Research on the planning cell has been relatively extensive, although its similarities to the deliberative poll have not to date been widely recognized.

Prospects for the Future

The National Issues Convention turned out to be, in many ways, a more important event for public opinion research than for the public at large or for the political process. It clearly fell short of the critical electoral intervention that Fishkin originally envisioned in 1988. Nevertheless, the NIC and other deliberative polls have proved to be thought-provoking experiments in democratic procedure and will in all likelihood continue to influence opinion researchers for years to come.

The Center for Deliberative Polling has now been established at the University of Texas at Austin, with Fishkin serving as director. National deliberative polls continue to be conducted in Britain under the sponsorship of Channel 4's *Power and the People* series (Luskin, Fishkin, and Jowell 1997). It was unclear whether it would prove possible, in light of the NIC experience, to gather comparably large amounts of funding and logistical support to mount a similarly large-scale, national event in the United States in the year 2000. However, it is quite possible that deliberative polling could become more common in regional rather than national settings. Fishkin and Luskin (1998) report that deliberative polls on electric utilities continue to be carried out in Texas, where the Public Utilities Commission now requires that public participation in resource planning must be statistically representative of customers, include accurate and balanced information representing competing points of view, and involve a two-way dialogue. Such activities, more or less along the lines of the earlier German planning cell, seem to hold out the prospect of more direct impact on policymaking. Integrated resource plans developed in response to deliberative polls have incorporated public preferences for investments in conservation, renewable energy, and subsidies for low-income customers (Fishkin and Luskin 1998).

Deliberative programs roughly similar to Fishkin's have also been planned for local elections, where they may prove more practical than in national applications. For example, the *Philadelphia Inquirer* undertook a year-long program of deliberative meetings—dubbed "Citizens' Voices '99"—with the hope of shaping the 1999 Philadelphia mayoral election. Citizens participating in this project would, designers hoped, attend a variety of deliberative meetings and candidate forums over the course of many months leading up to primary and general elections. Plans called for close to thirty neighborhood-based forums in the early winter (each with 15 to 30 participants), followed a month later by four, larger issue-framing meetings, then a series of expert lectures, an issues convention involving all participants (along the lines of the NIC), and finally a televised candidate debate before all participants in advance of the spring primary election. This cycle of deliberative events would subsequently be repeated, with the same panel of citizen participants, during the general campaign in the late summer and fall.

What, then, of possible applications of deliberative techniques in the 2000 presidential campaign? Trends suggested that deliberative citizens' forums of a variety of shapes and sizes were likely to be held during the campaign, although these might well be regional and local rather than national in nature. There were clear indications that such events were more likely to be intended as adjuncts to public journalism or civic journalism (along the lines of the Minnesota Citizens'

Issues Conference or Philadelphia's "Citizens' Voices '99"), rather than more fundamental attempts to reform campaigns or the candidate-selection process. Indeed, one foreseeable avenue for development would consist of moving toward smaller-scale, community-based deliberative exercises, in which citizens attempt to articulate the relevance of national political debates and policy issues for their own cities and regions. Such events would be of natural interest to media organizations—newspapers in particular—concerned about appealing to localized interests and appetites.

Should this indeed be the line of development, experiences to date suggest that a number of considerations be borne clearly in mind. First, due caution should be exercised in using data from such exercises as a substitute for scientific opinion polls. The sample of participants in citizens' forums may often diverge considerably from a probability sample of the general population. Given the substantial cost of gathering probability samples on site for deliberations, it is quite likely that media-sponsored forums will not begin to approach the NIC or British deliberative polls in terms of statistical representation of populations. For instance, the *Philadelphia Inquirer*'s 1999 mayoral campaign program of deliberations employed a volunteer sample of participants (although, for research purposes, a probability-based sample of participants recruited by the Annenberg Public Policy Center at the University of Pennsylvania was also incorporated into the project). Even when attempting probability samples, low response rates for deliberative polls, as with any opinion poll, may severely undercut their potential "recommending force."

We should also not accept without evidence that these deliberative efforts actually produce beneficial effects on the conduct of campaigns by politicians, the conduct of media organizations, or the quality of opinions held by the communities in question. As with any research technique, deliberative polls have both costs and benefits, which vary depending upon the purpose to which the technique is applied. Among the clear benefits is that the procedure reaffirms our basic, democratic investment in open deliberation as an avenue toward sound collective decision making and—given rigorous sampling procedures—may do so with groups that may be generally representative of the population whose interests are at stake. To date, participants give their experiences in deliberative polls very high marks and express both enthusiasm and gratitude for the opportunity to exercise their civic responsibilities in this fashion (Daves 1998; Smith 1996). Yet it remains quite unclear whether or not viewers of a televised deliberation or readers of news coverage stemming from a deliberative poll experience any increased sense of efficacy or interest in engaging with the political process. Nor is it clear whether these events in any way modify the behavior of candidates or their campaigns. Although the intention may be to hold politicians' "feet to the fire," that is, to make them more accountable to public interests and desires, we have to date no clear evidence that such intentions materialize.

This state of events suggests one important recommendation bearing on deliberative polls conducted in future elections. We would do well to incorporate into deliberative polls more refined and theoretically driven programs of evaluation research. To date, despite claims that these deliberative techniques result in superior opinions, little empirical evidence has actually been presented to that effect. Measures of opinion are, in certain instances, different after participants have engaged in deliberation. But are these changed opinions of any higher *quality*? Price and Niejens (1997) note that

> little is to be gained by arguing that certain combinations of decision-making methods or polling technologies are simply, of themselves, intrinsically better. First, one must articulate a theory that a particular aspect of method . . . will produce improvements in some particular aspect of quality. (p. 355)

They argue that careful experimentation and empirical analysis may eventually help resolve debates over the putative value of deliberation in improving the quality of opinion, but "this hope will only be realized . . . once specific qualities of alternative decision-making techniques have been clearly identified and examined in relation to clearly defined and measured qualities in opinion processes or outcomes" (p. 355). In fact, other programs of research aimed at measuring informed public opinion, such as the Choice Questionnaire developed by survey researcher Willem Sarris in the Netherlands, have been more direct in empirically specifying and testing improvements in opinion quality (Neijens 1987; Price and Niejens 1998). Absent more convincing demonstrations of quality, the changes produced by deliberative polls will remain difficult to interpret. Given that they result from such a large and complex combination of interventions, none of which has yet been clearly associated with opinion quality, such induced changes will remain politically and scientifically ambiguous.

Data from deliberative polls, if gathered in a careful and rigorous fashion, could take us further in explaining the opinion formation process, the role of group dynamics in opinion change, the relationship of knowledge and opinion, and other central theoretical questions in the field of opinion research. As with so many putative benefits of deliberative polls, these research utilities are as yet unrealized. Whether they are worth the considerable financial costs associated with conducting deliberative polls is also open to question. "We are only beginning," write Fishkin and Luskin (1998), to explore the possibilities for informed statistical microcosms to be heard in the public dialogue and the policy process. Our hope is that in an age of pseudo-public voices, of spin doctors, attack ads, self-selected polls and staged town meetings, the Deliberative Poll can provide a useful insight into public opinion and a useful input into public decision making. (p. 33)

The aims are noble, and the experience of 1996 represented an admirable effort to achieve them. But the utility of these techniques is presently unknown. Certainly, well past the year 2000, they will remain matters for careful and informed deliberation.

Note

1. Fishkin and Luskin (1998) report that 5 of 10 opinion items concerning the family exhibited significant change, along with 7 of 16 foreign policy questions and 13 of 23 economic items. Significant change is also reported on 4 of 10 empirical premises (for example, whether or not the average worker receives fair pay or whether improving the economy helps American families).

CHAPTER 12

Push Polls as Negative Persuasive Strategies

Michael W. Traugott and Mee-Eun Kang

Push polling is a relatively new kind of campaign technique designed to move the support of voters away from one candidate and toward another. It has been adopted by candidates, political parties supporting a candidate, and organized interest groups supporting a candidate or an issue. Initially developed and employed with some success in presidential campaigns, especially in the 1996 primaries and general elections, it has increasingly been used in contests for smaller constituencies and for many different contests, including referenda and initiatives. The technique has raised alarms among advocates of good government and fair campaign practices as well as in the polling and survey research industry. Push polls simulate an interview on the telephone, but they often do not involve data collection or analysis. As a result, they have been labeled "pseudo polls" (Traugott and Lavrakas 1999). The form of questioning can offend people who are subjected to it, and the fear of the polling business is that the technique will contribute further to already declining response rates and public trust in polls.

Many state legislatures have responded to the rise of push polling by drafting legislation to outlaw it, and a similar bill was introduced in the U.S. House of Representatives in 1997. Such legislation has proved problematic because many of these laws fly in the face of protected forms of political speech under the First Amendment to the U.S. Constitution. The key issue for legislators is defining an unacceptable practice with sufficient precision that the proposed "illegal" behavior does not include protected speech. In this chapter, we review the rise of push polling, paying attention to the distinctions between "negative persuasion telephoning" and strategic polling designed to assess the potential effectiveness of alternative campaign themes. We employ a systematic search of reported occurrences of push polls in the past few election cycles in order to develop a conceptual framework that describes who is using them and under what electoral circumstances. We then review current attempts at the development of legislation to regulate the technique, with an emphasis on the level of specificity and targeting of unethical practices.

Definition of the Term

The term *push poll* generally refers to a survey in which questions are asked to "push" voters away from the opposition candidate toward the candidate who sponsored the poll (Traugott and Lavrakas 1999, 165). According to Sabato and Simpson (1996a), a push poll is essentially political advertising masquerading in the guise of legitimate scientific research, and it spreads lies, rumors, and innuendo about candidates. It represents a form of political telemarketing by which one candidate is promoted by means of the dissemination of negative information about another. Sabato and Simpson (1996b, 27) distinguish among the following three types of polling that attempt to change the opinion of the voters: (1) "opposition research" efforts to learn about opponents' records and discover what might reduce public support for them; (2) "agenda-driven surveys" intended to produce favorable results for the client-candidate so that favorable "horse-race" polls can be reported in the mass media; and (3) "negative persuasive" or "advocacy" phoning, which is not really a poll at all but a form of targeted voter contact and canvassing.

Sabato and Simpson (1996a) provide the following two examples of negative persuasion phoning scripts used in the 1994 election that do *not* simulate polls:

Script 1
Hello, this is [interviewer's name] calling on behalf of the Florida Association of Senior Citizens. We are calling to let you know that [Republican nominee for governor] Jeb Bush is no friend of seniors. Bush's running mate has advocated the abolition of Social Security and called Medicare a welfare program that should be cut. We just can't trust Jeb Bush and [lieutenant governor nominee] Tom Feeney. Thank you and have a good day/evening.

Script 2
Hello, my name is [interviewer's name] calling from the Citizens for Tax Fairness. I'm calling to remind you that unlike thousands of your fellow citizens, Jeb Bush failed to pay local and state taxes, and he has profited at the taxpayers' expense from business deals involving failed savings and

loan properties. Mr. Bush doesn't play by the same rules like the rest of us and we want to make sure you are aware of this before you cast your vote on Thursday. Thank you and have a good day/evening.

(Sabato and Simpson 1996a, 257–58)

Our concern is with the form of negative persuasive phoning that *does* simulate polling. The distinction between legitimate surveys that collect data for strategic purposes and push polls whose purpose is to move voters from one candidate to another is an important one. In the first case, the polls involve probability samples of registered or likely voters, and data are actually collected, analyzed, and used to develop a strategy. In the second, the telemarketing firm contacts as many people as possible (within budget), and they are usually targeted in terms of some common characteristics rather than sampled. There is often no data collection at all; even if data are collected, they are never analyzed to produce any change in the candidate's behavior, policy positions, or strategy.

Political consultants and telemarketers who engage in push polling adopt the guise of survey research because it facilitates entree to a voter. During a campaign, citizens are more sensitized and attuned to politics than they are at other times. They are often interested in giving their views about candidates and issues that are in the news. At the same time, some citizens may be reluctant to listen to partisan political messages, especially those that are negative in tone. People doing push polls take advantage of these predispositions to contact potential voters to try to shift their candidate preferences. It is this very technique of approach and deception that concerns legitimate pollsters about the potential effect of such methods on response rates and trust in the profession and the methodology.

So the definition of the term *push poll* should be clarified to distinguish between a deceptive practice and a legitimate political survey testing campaign themes. Push polls are a misleading strategy designed to persuade voters not to vote for certain candidates by providing negative information about them. In contrast, legitimate political surveys serve as appropriate strategic devices that often test negative themes in order to evaluate which ones would work effectively in the campaign. In this case, questions used in a poll are a valid survey research method to measure voters' attitudes about events that have not yet occurred or about political statements that have not yet been made. The mass media often use the term *push poll* to describe any survey that includes negative information about a candidate, and such undifferentiated use of the term could make legitimate political surveys appear illegitimate.

According to a report prepared by the staff of the Committee on Election Reform in the Florida House of Representatives (1997), the key concept for distinguishing between push polls and legitimate political surveys testing campaign themes is the "intention" of the survey sponsor. If the intent of the survey sponsor is to "sway" voters from other candidates, the survey could be considered a push poll. If the intent is to test possible campaign themes, including negative ones, then the survey could be categorized as a legitimate political survey. Therefore, legitimate public opinion polling is "essentially an information gathering prelude to guiding campaign decisions," whereas push polling "serves to implement previously established plans, goals, or strategies" (Florida House of Representatives 1997). However, determining the survey sponsor's intention is not an easy task in any context.

Some Objective Measures to Distinguish Negative Persuasion and Strategic Polls

One way to assess intent would be to interview the sponsor of a political poll; but that is often impossible during a campaign, if ever. Some measures, however, could be used to distinguish push polls and legitimate opinion surveys. They include sample size, length of survey, target population, identification of the survey organization, negative message content, collection and analysis of data, and the like.

Sabato and Simpson (1996a) suggest the following characteristics of surveys as indications of push polling: a specific target population, brevity of the message, negativity in statements, and the use of controversial issues in statements. When the survey process is simulated for the purpose of moving opinions or preferences, the questionnaire contains certain characteristics that often signal this purpose. One is that the candidate preference or "trial heat" question is usually asked more than once. In addition to an initial version at or near the beginning of the poll, the question is typically asked again at the end, after the negative persuasive messages. The second characteristic is a series of leading or potentially biased questions in between the two trial heat questions whose purpose is clearly to shift preferences. This is indicated by the fact that most or all of the intervening questions cast one of the candidates in a consistently negative light.

Generally, an interviewer from a legitimate survey research firm will provide the name of his or her employer and even a way to contact the organization or a supervisor there if asked. This information is made available to indicate legitimacy in order to encourage participation. People working on push polls tend not to provide any name of a sponsor, and the names of their organizations are often created for the specific purpose at hand. In lieu of a probability sample with a targeted size associated with a desired level of precision, push polls contact as many voters as possible, usually targeted on the basis of some particular demographic characteristics. Another distinctive feature of the push poll is that the phone call is short, usually no more than a few minutes, so that more voters can be contacted. Since push polls are designed solely with a persuasive purpose in mind, data from these surveys are seldom collected, analyzed, or reported. Push polls usually omit key questions about demographics or party affiliations. In addition, push polls often provide false or misleading information to elicit specific responses from a respondent against a candidate. Thus, push polls as negative persuasion phone calls are not entitled to the term *poll* in any form. Whereas none of these characteristics alone might be conclusive, in combination they are generally indicative of push polling.

The Case of Dole and Forbes Early in the 1996 Prenomination Race

One of the most prominent cases of the use of push polls in the 1996 election was reported in the primaries contested by Bob Dole and Steve Forbes, Republican presidential candidates. Push polls involving these two candidates were some of the first to raise public and professional concerns about the use of simulated surveys as negative persuasion devices. During the primaries, a number of news reports documented the Dole campaign's use of push polls in Iowa and New Hampshire, following complaints by the Forbes campaign. Survey organizations, using contrived names like "National Market Research" and "Iowa's Farm Families," called voters and asked questions about Forbes's alleged positions.

In the questionnaire or "script" for these conversations, obtained by the Associated Press, questions were asked about whether the respondents would be more likely or less likely to vote for Forbes if they knew "Steven Forbes supported President Clinton's policy allowing gays to serve in the military" and "Steve Forbes is pro-choice and supports abortion for almost any reason during the first three months of pregnancy." Dole initially denied that his campaign used push polls, but journalists uncovered expenditure records on file at the Federal Election Commission indicating that the Dole campaign hired Campaign Tel Ltd., a firm well known for push polling.

The *Wall Street Journal* (Simpson 1996) also reported the details of Dole's use of Campaign Tel Ltd. and printed excerpts from scripts that company "interviewers" used to attack Forbes. The telephone script, according to notes taken by a campaign employee while making calls, read as follows:

My name is _____ and I'm calling with a special message from Iowa's Farm Families. Iowa's Farm Bureau has adopted a resolution that opposes the flat tax like the one offered by candidate Steve Forbes. Under the Forbes flat tax, Iowa's farmers would pay an average of $5,000 more in taxes.

One employee estimated that the office completed between 10,000 and 30,000 anti-Forbes calls to farmers. There were also Campaign Tel scripts containing negative information about Senator Phil Gramm and Lamar Alexander, although fewer calls were targeted at them.

However, Steve Forbes, who had accused Bob Dole of conducting push polls against him, was reported to have used a similar strategy. According to a report by the *Hotline* (12 February 1996), a memo to Forbes from his pollster shows that the Forbes campaign used "similar tactics." One Forbes push poll, cited in the memo and obtained by the Associated Press, asked, "What do you like the least about Bob Dole?" The Associated Press reported the contents of the poll conducted by Forbes, which listed a series of Dole positions and asked whether knowing that information made voters more likely or less likely to vote for Dole. The Forbes polls asked, for example, "if voters were more likely or less likely to vote for Dole if they knew he voted to spend $6.4 million to build a ski resort in Idaho or $18 million to build a subway for Senators to shuttle from their offices to the Capitol." Forbes argued that his campaign just explored potential Dole weaknesses to test the themes to be used in the campaign. However, there is no indication of whether data were actually collected and analyzed in this case.

Examples of Strategic Polling prior to a Campaign

An appreciation of the utility and power of strategic polling will make it easier to understand the power of push polls. Sabato and Simpson (1996a) documented an example of a strategic poll questionnaire produced in January 1994 for Representative Leslie Byrne (Democrat of Virginia). The questionnaire was written by the Democratic firm of Cooper & Secrest, although interviewers were instructed to say they were calling from "Virginia Public Opinion, the national public opinion research firm." The purpose of the survey was to test potentially positive and negative aspects of Byrne's record; but only negative aspects of her likely opponent, Thomas Davis (Republican), were assessed. In the questionnaire, the interviewer listed "several arguments some people have made as to why Leslie Byrne *should not* be reelected as Congresswoman." For each statement, respondents were asked whether they thought the statement was "a *very persuasive reason not* to reelect her, an *only somewhat persuasive reason not* to reelect her, or a *not at all persuasive reason.*" Some of the statements given to the respondents include the following:

- Leslie Byrne voted in favor of the Clinton budget plan, which includes $241 billion in new taxes.

- Although she campaigned against government waste, Leslie Byrne refused to kill several unnecessary congressional subcommittees.
- Leslie Byrne voted against the North American Free Trade Agreement, a treaty which would reduce tariffs and other trade barriers with other North American countries.
- Leslie Byrne supports allowing homosexuals in the military.
- Even though the government runs a $400 billion deficit, Leslie Byrne supported using taxpayer money for artists, including some artists who produce art many consider obscene. (Sabato and Simpson 1996a, 249–50)

Then the respondents were asked about the persuasiveness of reasons to reelect her. These included such statements as the following:

- Leslie Byrne voted for the 5-day waiting period for the purchase of handguns and cosponsored a bill to eliminate the sale and possession of assault rifles.
- To protect Northern Virginia taxpayers, Leslie Byrne has fought against DC Statehood.
- Leslie Byrne has more legislation she sponsored pending than any other member of Congress. (Sabato and Simpson 1996a, 250–51)

In the next section of the questionnaire, statements were made about her likely Republican opponent, Thomas Davis, chairperson of the Fairfax County Board of Supervisors. Respondents were asked whether they thought each statement was "a *very persuasive reason not* to elect Tom Davis, an *only somewhat persuasive reason not* to elect him, or a *not at all persuasive reason.*"

- Less than a week after being sworn in as Chairman of the Board of Supervisors, Tom Davis proposed three separate tax increases and since then has supported or proposed at least eight tax or fee increases in Fairfax County.
- Fairfax voters now pay more in real estate taxes than when Tom Davis took over as Chairman of the Board of Supervisors.
- After accepting thousands of dollars in campaign contributions from millionaire Herbert Haft, Tom Davis orchestrated a meeting between Haft and zoning officials to help Haft get around the usual local zoning application process.

- As a member of the Board of Supervisors, Tom Davis supported the building of the Fairfax Government Center, the so-called Taj Mahal which has cost the County millions of dollars in waste and cost overruns. (Sabato and Simpson 1996a, 252–53)

This was clearly a survey designed to test strategic alternatives and potentials—for the public's evaluation of the sponsoring candidate as well as of the opponent. Certain elements look like a push poll, but there were data collected for analysis that helped to shape campaign themes.

In the Byrne case, data were not provided to illustrate the impact of the questioning technique. However, another incident of strategic polling in a nonelectoral context does provide such data. This poll involved the tobacco industry and Texas State Attorney General Dan Morales. The case in Texas provides an unusual opportunity to examine an actual questionnaire used to assess the potential effects of various campaign themes as an example of the general form and content, as well as to assess how much difference the technique can make in candidate support. Attorney General Dan Morales sued the tobacco industry for $4 billion to cover smoking-related Medicaid costs. In response to Morales's lawsuit, the four largest tobacco companies commissioned a poll concerning the lawsuit Morales had filed. This push poll was conducted by Public Opinion Strategies, an Alexandria-based Republican polling firm, among 800 registered voters and an oversample of 135 citizens in East Texas, from 20 January to 25 January 1996.

The tobacco companies actually presented the results to Morales, presumably as a way of indicating how effective a negative campaign organized against him might be. This survey provides an example of how the technique works and the potential impact of a negative strategy. It is unusual because data were collected to demonstrate to the intended victim how much trouble could be caused in his reelection campaign. By that route, the details eventually became public. The entire questionnaire used by the tobacco industry and the marginal results for each question were made public on the Web by *Mother Jones* magazine (http://www.mojones.com).

In the interview, general questions about respondents' opinions on various issues were asked first. Then came job approval questions involving prominent political figures such as George W. Bush (governor), Bob Bullock (lieutenant governor), and Dan Morales (attorney general), as well as questions about whether each of them should be reelected. In the next section, the respondents were read fourteen negative statements as "some reasons people are giving to vote *against* Dan Morales for Attorney General." The respondents were provided with an unbalanced set of response alternatives (Traugott and Lavrakas 1999, 167) about whether "each statement makes you [respondent] much more likely to vote against Dan Morales, somewhat more likely to vote against Dan Morales, or if it makes no difference at all."

Some of the fourteen statements given to the respondents regarding Dan Morales included the following:

- Morales's political campaign purchased two tickets to a fund-raiser for Louis Farrakahn's Nation of Islam organization.
- Juvenile crime has increased by one third in Texas since Morales became attorney general.
- Conservative political groups rate Morales as a liberal Democrat.
- As attorney general, Morales has made consumer issues a higher priority than fighting violent crime.
- Morales has said that young gang members don't need harsh treatment and prison, but that they need nice recreational facilities, drug counseling, and summer jobs.
- Victims Rights activists say Morales sold out crime victims when he settled a prisoner's lawsuit without even taking the case to court.
- Morales asked for $75,000 in campaign contributions from casino gambling interests shortly before issuing a ruling on whether or not to allow gambling in Texas.
- Morales regularly flies for free in private planes provided by some of the country's richest personal injury lawyers.
- Some of Morales' biggest campaign contributors are wealthy personal injury lawyers. Morales has taken over $340,000 in political campaign contributions from them.
- Morales has been criticized by Democrats and Republicans alike for mismanagement and failing to represent state agencies effectively.

After they were read these statements, respondents were again asked whether or not they thought Morales should be reelected. The differences in percentage clearly show the effects of the negative statements. Before listening to the statements, 42 percent of those polled said Morales should be reelected, and 27 percent said he should not. However, after they were read the statements, only 21 percent said he should be reelected and 58 percent said he should not. The poll shows a significant drop in public support (21 percentage points in those saying Morales should be reelected) after respondents were given negative information about the attorney general. This is a substantial political impact in any kind of campaign.

The Response from Professional Organizations of Pollsters

Responding to the proliferation of push polls and concerned about their threat to the credibility of legitimate polls, professional pollsters issued a rare collective disavowal of the practice in 1996. Professional organizations such as the American Association of Political Consultants (AAPC), the American Association for Public Opinion Research (AAPOR), and the National Council on Public Polls (NCPP) issued separate statements condemning the conduct of push polls in election campaigns.

The AAPC, an organization of campaign specialists, issued a statement declaring that the organization condemned advocacy phone calling that does the following: (1) masquerades as survey research, (2) fails to identify the sponsor of the call clearly and accurately, or (3) presents false or misleading information to the voter. The AAPC urged political candidates to pledge to abstain from push polling.

The AAPOR also adopted a statement regarding push polls at its January 1996 council meeting. The AAPOR statement defines push polls as a "telemarketing technique in which telephone calls are used to canvass potential voters, feeding them false or misleading 'information' about a candidate under the pretense of taking a poll to see how this 'information' affects voter preference." The association declared that push polls violate its code of ethics by "intentionally lying to or misleading respondents, and they corrupt the electoral process by disseminating false and misleading attacks on candidates." It also expressed concerns that push polls may damage the reputation of legitimate polling, thereby discouraging the public from participating in authentic survey research. The association urged the survey research community to respond promptly when push polling is used and called for the respondents' cooperation in identifying push polls.

The NCPP also took a stand against push polls by issuing a press release condemning the use of push polls by presidential candidates in the primaries and caucuses. During the 1996 general election campaign, the NCPP sent letters to Bill Clinton and Bob Dole asking them to refrain from push polling.

Push Poll Cases in the 1996 Elections

Sabato and Simpson (1996b) reported that there were over three dozen cases of push polls during the 1994 federal election cycle. In an attempt to conduct a systematic investigation of the use of push polls in the 1996 elections, an electronic search was conducted using Lexis-Nexis to collect information about reported incidents.[1] Major newspapers were searched with the key word "push poll!" to include phrases like "push poll," "push polls," and "push polling." A total of ninety news stories were retrieved, including push poll incidents in both election and nonelection contexts, at both the state level and the national level.

Push Polls in Different Electoral Contexts

The citizens and candidates in Florida experienced a proliferation of push polls during the 1996 election campaign involving several congressional districts. In June, during the Democratic primaries, the *Tampa Tribune* (Edwards 1996a) reported that the campaign of a former mayor, Sandy Freedman (Democrat), was the source of a push poll attacking Jim Davis (Democrat), an opponent. Voters were asked whether they would agree that "Jim Davis is a lightweight because he listens to what people say and does what people tell him." Another report in the *Tampa Tribune* (Edwards 1996b) indicated that Phyllis Busansky (Democrat) employed push polls making unfavorable statements to move voters away from the other three Democrats, Jim Davis, Pat Frank, and Sandy Freedman. The *Tampa Tribune* (Edwards 1996c; Ruth 1996) reported that push polls were conducted suggesting that state representative Jim Davis was "soft on child abuse, anti-family values, a tool of big business interests and opposed senior citizens."

Personal issues were also used to make negative statements about candidates in push polls during the general election campaign. A push poll was conducted in Florida House District 43 asking voters if they would be less likely to vote for Nancy Argenziano (Republican) if they knew she had had plastic surgery (Morgan 1996b). In a Florida Senate district, voters were asked if they would be more or less likely to vote for Jack Latvala (Republican) if they knew he had failed to pay child support (Morgan 1996a). In another House race, push polls were conducted to suggest that "Bob Stein (Democrat) favors late-term abortions, has several blemishes on his employment record with the school district, and . . . feels the state's school system is satisfactory the way it is" (Nurse 1996).

In Georgia, the *Atlanta Journal and Constitution* (Mantius 1996) reported that callers from outside Georgia asked people questions implying that Tommy Chambless (Democrat), a candidate in a House race, was soft on crime. The newspaper also reported that Cliff Oxford (Democrat), in the Sixth Congressional District, was attacked in a push poll asking voters whether they would vote for him if they knew he had cheated on his taxes (Manuel 1996).

In Texas, the National Republican Congressional Committee was reported to have commissioned a push poll to support the incumbent U.S. representative Greg Laughlin (Republican). According to reports in *USA Today* (Moore 1996) and the *New York Times* (Clymer 1996), Laughlin was rewarded for switching parties with a seat on the House Ways and Means Committee. His campaign also received a direct payment of $10,000 from the National Republican Congressional Committee.

Push Polling by Interest Groups

A different case of push polling in a campaign for a state legislative seat occurred in Wisconsin, involving state representative Michael Huebsch (Republican) and the Wisconsin Education Association Council (WEAC). The *Milwaukee Journal Sentinel* (Walter 1996) reported that the WEAC had called about 300 households asking whether the respondents knew that Huebsch "sided with insurance companies and against families" by voting against a bill that would require insurance companies to pay for at least forty-eight hours of hospital care for new mothers. The respondents were also asked how concerned they would be if they knew that "Huebsch voted to give corporate buyers of luxury sky boxes at the new Brewers stadium an exemption from the sales tax but didn't exempt any of the regular seats from sales tax." A recorded tape of the call indicated that a number of distorted claims were made about the voting record of Representative Huebsch. Even though the WEAC claimed that they were conducting a purely legitimate poll to obtain information, the survey questions indicate that this is a case of negative persuasion telephoning.

In another campaign, the *Philadelphia Inquirer* published a story (Downs 1998) about how Planned Parenthood employed push polling as part of its efforts to unseat Congressman Jon Fox (Republican). According to the news report, a question was first asked about whether the respondent favored legalized abortion. The respondent was then asked, "Are you aware that Jon Fox would vote to make abortion illegal?" Even though Planned Parenthood said the poll was a legitimate effort to "motivate, educate and excite the pro-choice majority in the 13th Congressional District," Jon Fox called it a "push poll" presenting him negatively on his views about abortion. A Planned Parenthood spokesperson said data were being collected for analysis for public release, but the newspaper never reported a subsequent press conference.

A Contextual Framework for Thinking about Push Polls

Push polls are a serious threat to the polling industry because they create negative impressions among citizens about the polling business and the experience of being interviewed. This, in turn, can lead to reduced response rates and declining trust in polls. Push polls are as close as we get in the American political system to an unfair campaign practice because they can hurt candidates against whom they are aimed by the nature of their appeals and because they often go undetected. The insidious aspect of push polls is that they generally occur below the radar of most observers, especially journalists who cover campaigns. There are a limited number of ways to try to eliminate the practice, and they all depend upon a clear understanding of how push polls function and where they are likely to be used.

The preceding analysis of journalistic reports of push polls that appeared in major newspapers since 1996 supplements the examples cited by Sabato and Simpson (1996a) and suggests a systematic way of thinking about where and how push polls are likely to occur. This framework will help to identify the campaign locus of potential push polls and their sponsorship. As such, it is an alert to journalists and editorial writers about where to look for push polls and how to describe them to readers and viewers and explain how the procedure affects the political system and the trust citizens have in it.

Essentially, there are four dimensions that define the context for push polls: (1) the nature of partisanship, (2) the type of contest, (3) the geographical scope of the campaign, and (4) the type of push poll sponsor. The nature of partisanship is simply dichotomous and can be thought of as partisan or nonpartisan. The type of contest generally follows the three main branches of government—legislative, executive, or judicial—although the nonpartisan dimension can also include referenda, initiatives, and tax or bond issues. The geographical scope of the campaign can be local (any substate constituency), statewide, or national. And the nature of the sponsor can reflect an opponent from the same party in a primary or from the opposition party in a general election; the opposition party itself in a general election (a candidate's party does not usually take a position or use push polling in its own primary); or an outside interest group not necessarily affiliated with a political party.

The full range of these alternatives is depicted conceptually in Table 12.1, with an appropriate indication of the cells that represent null sets. The attributes of the contest predict the nature of sponsors in a conceptually straightforward way—and not vice versa. As a result, there is some predictive value in the framework, as it indicates where certain types and sponsorship of push polls are likely to occur. For example, candidates in either primaries or general elections do not exert effort or expend resources on push polls regarding initiatives or referenda. However, the framework does not give any guidance about the expected frequency of occurrence of push polls. Yet there should be more push polls at the local level, especially in partisan contests, because this is the most frequent kind of election in the United States. At the same time, campaign budgets for

TABLE 12.1   A CONCEPTUAL FRAMEWORK FOR THE USE OF PUSH POLLS
IN DIFFERENT KINDS OF CAMPAIGNS

LEVEL OF PARTISANSHIP/ GEOGRAPHICAL SCOPE/ TYPE OF CONTEST	PUSH POLL SPONSOR			
	Primary Opponent	General Election Opponent	General Election Opposition Party	Other Interest Group
PARTISAN				
LOCAL: Legislative Contest				
(Local council or board)	X	X	X	X
Executive Contest				
(Mayor, local executive)	X	X	X	X
Judicial Contest	X	X	X	X
STATE: Legislative Contest				
(State House or Senate)	X	X	X	X
Executive Contest				
(Governor)	X	X	X	X
Judicial Contest	X	X	X	X
NATIONAL: Legislative Contest				
(U.S. House or Senate)	X	X	X	X
Executive Contest				
(President)	X	X	X	X
NONPARTISAN				
LOCAL: Elective Nonpartisan Office				
Referendum, Initiative,				X
Tax or Bond Issue				X
STATE: Elective Nonpartisan Office				
Referendum, Initiative,				X
Tax or Bond Issue				X

these contests are the lowest. It is in the contests for statewide and national offices where funds are most likely to be available for this purpose.

Possible Remedies to Reduce the Use of Push Polls

The rise of push polling has produced a need for remedies to deal with a socially and politically undesirable campaign technique. These remedies fall into three different areas: legislative efforts to prohibit push polls, a renewed call for a journalistic focus on disclosure standards when reporting poll results, and increasing the public's awareness of and willingness to report push polls. Most legislative efforts face strong legal challenges resulting in a number of limitations on the form the laws can take. Therefore, increasing the media's focus on disclosure and the public's active participation in reporting push polls needs to receive greater emphasis.

Legislative Efforts

Several states have attempted to impose legislative controls on push polling, but controls have been difficult to implement because political speech is protected by the First Amendment. There are concerns that laws prohibiting push polls might restrict freedom of speech more generally. State laws requiring an identification disclaimer on surveys, for example, have been construed by some as an inhibition of free expression. In addition, there is a problem of enforcement. Even though objective measures exist to identify push polls, it is still difficult to determine the survey sponsor's intent—a key factor in distinguishing between push polling and legitimate surveys testing campaign themes. Furthermore, it is questionable whether a state law prohibiting push polling would be enforceable, since calls can be made from another state.

Legislative efforts have been made in several states to prohibit the conduct of push polling. West Virginia is the only state that specifically restricts push polling. The West Virginia law prohibits the use of any poll that is "deceptively designed or intentionally conducted in a manner calculated to advocate the election or defeat of any candidate or group of candidates or calculated to influence any person or persons so polled to vote for or against any candidate or group of candidates" [W.Va. Code sec. 3–8–9 (10)]. This law limits the use of public opinion polls to the "gathering, collection, collation and evaluation of information reflecting public opinion, needs and preferences as to any candidate, group of candidates, party issue or issues."

A common requirement in other states regarding surveys is the identification of the survey sponsor. The state of Wisconsin requires all pollsters conducting telephone surveys to identify their sponsors if respondents ask for that information [Wis. Stat. Sec. 11.30(5)]. Legislative efforts were made in 1995 and 1996 (A.B. 90 & S.B. 549, respectively) to change existing law to require pollsters to identify the survey sponsor, regardless of whether or not the respondent requests the information. However, this legislation failed to pass the House.

In New Hampshire, the state House passed a bill (H.B. 443) on 15 January 1998, and the bill passed the state Senate on 12 March 1998 that defines "push-polling" as "(a) calling voters on behalf of, in support of, or in opposition to, any candidate for public office by telephone; and (b) asking questions related to opposing candidates for public office which state, imply, or convey information about the candidates' character, status, or political stance or record" (RSA 664:2, XVII). Under this law, "any person who engages in push-polling, as defined in RSA 664:2, XVII, shall inform any person contacted that the telephone call is being made on behalf of, in support of, or in opposition to a particular candidate for public office, identify that candidate by name, and provide a telephone number from where the push-polling is conducted." The bill as amended can be found on the Web at (http://webster.state.nh.us/gencourt/rereferred/hb0443.html). Considering the significant role New Hampshire plays in the presidential nomination process, this state's laws regarding push polls are crucial.

Florida law now requires all written and broadcast "political advertisements" to carry a sponsorship disclaimer [Sec. 106.143(1), F.S., 1995]. However, the definition of "political advertisement" excludes telephone solicitations and telephone polls [Sec. 106.011(17), F.S., 1995]. As a result, telephone solicitations or telephone polls including push polls are not restricted completely. Several bills addressing telephone solicitation and polling failed to pass the 1996 Florida legislature (Florida House of Representatives). The Senate bill (S.B. 964), which failed in the House, required a sponsorship disclaimer on all political telephone solicitations and polls.

At the national level, the "Push Poll Disclaimer Act" (H.R. 248) was introduced in the U.S. House of Representatives in January 1997 to require people conducting polls by telephone during campaigns for election for federal office to disclose certain information. In detail,

> Any person who conducts a poll by telephone to interview individuals on opinions relating to any election for Federal office shall disclose to each respondent to the poll the following information: (1) The person's identity, (2) The identity of the person sponsoring the poll or paying the expenses associated with the poll, (3) If during the course of the interview the person provides to the respondent any information relating to a candidate for the election, the source of the information (or, if there is no source, a statement to that effect). (H.R. 248)

A Renewed Journalistic Focus

The AAPOR and NCPP have standards of disclosure for survey results that require reporting relevant details about the methodology of surveys, including samples used in the survey and question wordings. In *Best Practices for Survey and Public Opinion Research,* AAPOR (1997) states that

> Good professional practice imposes an obligation upon all survey and
> public opinion researchers to include, in any report of research results, or
> to make available when that report is released, certain minimal essential
> information about how the research was conducted—to ensure that con-
> sumers of survey results have an adequate basis for judging the reliability
> and validity of the results reported. (p. 8)

Good practice in survey research involves describing how the research was done
in sufficient detail and making data available for independent examination so that
a knowledgeable consumer can make an independent assessment of data quality. One problem is that push polls are usually conducted under the radar screen
of most election observers. Since it is often the case that no data are collected
for analysis because the goal of the effort is to move voters one at a time, it is
difficult to apply the disclosure standards to push polls.

As a consequence, the best way to educate the public is through increased
coverage of the technique as it is uncovered in campaigns. Journalists should
write more about its use when discovered, including interviews with candidates
or consultants who employ it. In addition, negative attention to push polling and
its social and political consequences should extend to editorial writers and columnists who can educate the public to its problems and consequences by writing
about the harmful effects.

Increased Public Participation in Disclosure

Perhaps the best way to identify instances of push polling comes from opponents who make a claim of being attacked or from citizens who complain
about calls they receive containing negative persuasion attempts through push
polls. When such persons suspect that push polls are being used in a campaign, they should report this fact to journalists immediately. When news
organizations receive complaints about push polls from opponents or citizens,
they need to run stories on them. This alerts the public to the fact that the
technique is being used by an interested party in a campaign (disclosure) as
well as sensitizes citizens to the prospect of receiving such a call themselves
(inoculation).

The public's cooperation is crucial in identifying and stopping push polls.
Because of the absence of a written record of questionnaires from such telephone
"interviews," it is difficult to discover push polls even if they are conducted.
Thus, greater public awareness of the push poll technique is a key factor in producing reports of the use of push polls and dissuading candidates and interest
groups from using them.

Conclusion

Push polling—negative persuasion phoning disguised as legitimate survey research—is a new form of campaigning that is opposed by good government groups, professional organizations interested in polling and survey research, and lawmakers at the state and local levels. Each of these groups has an interest in curtailing or eliminating the practice because of the cynicism it breeds about the political process and about polling in general. This technique can reduce levels of political trust and confidence, turnout, and response rates in legitimate surveys. That is why the AAPC, AAPOR, and NCPP have all issued statements decrying the use of push polls.

State legislatures and the U.S. Congress have attempted to design legislation to outlaw the practice, but they have met with opposition from supporters of unrestricted political speech. This opposition does not arise from support for push polling; rather, it reflects a basic concern about implementing limits on any form of political speech or designing laws that might also restrict legitimate political speech in an effort to restrict negative campaign techniques. There is a need to refine proposed legislative remedies so that they narrowly target inappropriate campaign behavior without constraining unpopular but legitimate forms of political speech.

The analysis presented here has tightened the description of what a push poll is, distinguishing it clearly from other forms of political polling for strategic purposes. In addition, the typology of push polls developed here should provide some guidance about where and how push polls are likely to occur, with reference to four specific dimensions that describe the various contexts where they have recently been used. Ultimately, the reduction and elimination of push polls will depend upon political parties, candidates, and special interest groups disavowing their use. The most efficacious way to do this is to have instances of push polling reported by citizens to news organizations, who will in turn widely disseminate reports of their use by specific candidates in particular campaigns. Public disclosure of the use of push polls through news media and good government groups will be the most effective deterrent to their increased adoption by more and more campaigns. Steve Forbes would be unlikely to use push polls in his run for the presidency in 2000 because of the negative press coverage he received in 1996. This can be a lesson to other candidates as well.

Note

1. The media, and political reporters in particular, play a critical role in identifying push polls. The technique itself is highly targeted and eschews the mass media to avoid detection. Citizens or candidates who contact journalists are the main source of disclosure.

Appendix 12.A

Legislation

FULL TEXT OF BILLS

105TH CONGRESS; 1ST SESSION
IN THE HOUSE OF REPRESENTATIVES
AS INTRODUCED IN THE HOUSE

H.R. 248

1997 H.R. 248; 105 H.R. 248

Retrieve Bill Tracking Report

SYNOPSIS:
A BILL To amend the Federal Election Campaign Act of 1971 to require the disclosure of certain information by persons conducting polls by telephone during campaigns for election for Federal office.

DATE OF INTRODUCTION: JANUARY 9, 1997

DATE OF VERSION: JANUARY 21, 1997—VERSION: 1

SPONSOR(S):
Mr. PITTS INTRODUCED THE FOLLOWING BILL; WHICH WAS
        REFERRED TO THE COMMITTEE ON HOUSE OVERSIGHT

TEXT:
* Be it enacted by the Senate and House of Representatives of the United*
States of America in Congress assembled,
SECTION 1. SHORT TITLE.
    This Act may be cited as the "Push Poll Disclaimer Act".
SEC. 2. DISCLOSURE OF INFORMATION BY PERSONS
CONDUCTING POLLS DURING FEDERAL ELECTION CAMPAIGNS.
    (a) IN GENERAL—TITLE III OF THE FEDERAL ELECTION
CAMPAIGN ACT OF 1971 (2 U.S.C. 431 ET SEQ.) IS AMENDED
BY ADDING AT THE END THE FOLLOWING NEW SECTION:
    "DISCLOSURE OF INFORMATION BY PERSONS CONDUCTING
POLLS BY TELEPHONE

"SEC. 323. Any person who conducts a poll by telephone or electronic means to interview individuals on opinions relating to any election for Federal office shall disclose to each respondent to the poll the following information:

"(1) The person's identity.

"(2) The identity of the person sponsoring the poll or paying the expenses associated with the poll.

"(3) If during the course of the interview the person provides to the respondent any information relating to a candidate for the election, the source of the information (or, if there is no source, a statement to that effect)".

(b) EFFECTIVE DATE.—THE AMENDMENT MADE BY SUBSECTION (A) SHALL APPLY WITH RESPECT TO ELECTIONS OCCURRING AFTER THE DATE OF THE ENACTMENT OF THIS ACT.

CHAPTER 13

Politics, Polls, and Poltergeists: A Critical View of the 1996 Election

Leo Bogart

In the presidential election campaign of 1996, surveys made more news than anything that Clinton and Dole had to say. Only 37 percent of evening network newscast stories addressed policy issues, while 53 percent dealt with the "horse race" of rival personalities as tracked by the polls (John and Mary R. Markle Foundation 1996). How well did the polls do? Can they do better? And can they be better reported?

To some degree, the problem of forecasting elections is unique. But the difficulty of the task reflects a more fundamental fragility in the survey research on which society has become increasingly dependent.

Were the Polls Right or Wrong?

The news media often misrepresent or misinterpret polls either because they take them too literally or because, at the other extreme, they underestimate their technical complexity. It is important to remember that (1) projections from election surveys are uncertain because many people change their minds and some who say they will vote do not, (2) all surveys are subject to errors that go beyond the laws of chance, and (3) survey statistics arise from a series of professional judgments—just because they come out of a computer does not make them right.

Table 13.1 shows the final numbers released by eight national election surveys in 1996. All predicted a Clinton victory, by margins that ranged between 7 and 18 percentage points on the eve of the election. (That "spread" reflected the candidates' individual showings and is not meaningful in itself.) Had the election been close, the disparate results could easily have produced different forecasts of who would win. All but one of the major polls underestimated the Dole vote by

TABLE **13.1** ACTUAL VOTE AND FINAL POLLING FORECASTS (IN PERCENTAGES)

	CLINTON	DOLE	PEROT	OTHER	UNDECIDED[a]
Actual Vote	49.2	40.8	8.5	1.6	
Gallup/CNN/*USA Today*	48	40	6		6
Adjusted[b]	52	41	7		
Harris	51	39	9	1	
CBS[c]	53	35	9	2	
New York Times[c]	50	34	8		7
ABC	51	39	7	2	
NBC/*Wall Street Journal*	49	37	8		5
Pew	49	36	8		7
Zogby/Reuters	44	37	7		12
Adjusted[b]	49	41	8	2	
Hotline/Battleground	45	38	8	2	9

[a]Some surveys lumped the undecided with supporters of minor party candidates.

[b]Gallup and Zogby released two sets of figures, in the second case allocating the undecided (and for Gallup, tightening the criteria for likely voters). The *Washington Post* did not report final results, and the *Los Angeles Times* did not poll in the last week before the election.

[c]CBS and the *New York Times* worked from the same data.

an average of 4 percentage points. To understand why, we must consider the difficulties faced by all surveys and by those of election surveys in particular.

Did something go wrong, and if so, can or should it be fixed? Soon after the election, on the op-ed page of the *Wall Street Journal*, Everett Carll Ladd, who directs the Roper Center, a polling archive at the University of Connecticut, called 1996 "the pollsters' Waterloo" and urged that a commission of experts review their failings (Ladd 1996). Ladd linked the polls' underestimate of Dole's strength to a persistent overstatement of the Democratic vote in recent elections. His starting assumption was that polls do influence election outcomes. "It is likely," he wrote, "that pollsters and reporters dampened voters' interest, and hence participation, by announcing that the presidential contest was really no contest at all" (p. A24).

Ladd's criticisms met with indignant rejoinders, and even threats of future noncooperation, from a number of leading polling organizations that provide the Roper Center with their survey data, an important historical and scholarly resource. Ladd subsequently retracted his earlier statement with regret and said that the polls' "final estimates in 1996 were generally good ones" (Ladd 1997, A24). He added, "American survey companies have set a proud example for the rest of the world in sharing with all comers both their data and how they collect it." In this case, as so often, the initial attack drew far more media attention than the subsequent apology. Although Ladd admits he went overboard in his conclusions, the data he cited still require explanation and the questions he raised are bound to surface again in the future.

Humphrey Taylor (1997), the chairman of the Harris poll, asserts that "the notion that we screwed up is totally wrong." The average 1996 election poll was off by 1.7 points, compared with 2.19 for all the presidential elections since 1952, according to an analysis by Nick Panagakis of Market Shares Corporation, an Illinois research firm (Panagakis 1997). Frank Newport, the Gallup poll's editor-in-chief, points out that the average final estimates by eight polling organizations for the three candidates were "within the typical 3% [he means percentage points] margin of error . . . and two . . . are within less than one point of the actual results" (Newport 1997, 50). Take care, though. The "average error" was reduced by the comparatively small range of estimates for Perot's small share of the vote.

Larry Hugick of Princeton Survey Research Associates stresses that the Clinton and Perot percentages were almost identical to the actual vote (Roper Center Symposium 1997). But those, again, are the averages. Although all the polls used very similar procedures, the range for Clinton was between 45 percent and 53 percent; and for Perot, between 7 percent and 9 percent. The Dole figures varied between 35 percent and 41 percent. (Dole's actual share was 41 percent; Clinton had 49 percent and Perot 8 percent.)

The differences merely echoed the polls' record during the course of the race, in which they showed inexplicable variations and fluctuations. Toward the end of June a Yankelovich Partners CNN/*Time* poll was showing a Clinton lead of 6 points at the same time that an ABC/*Washington Post* poll showed a 20-point advantage. Gallup's daily tracking poll gave Clinton a 9-point lead over Dole on Saturday, 28 September; by Tuesday, 1 October, this had increased to 25 points. Gallup's Newport (1997) observes that "changes in preferences are what a campaign is all about." He ascribes Dole's initial good showing to an effective television commercial mocking Clinton's youthful experiment with marijuana and Clinton's weekend jump to a Middle East summit meeting at the White House. However, such a relatively low-interest event does not satisfactorily explain so big a swing.

The inconsistencies among polls are not unique to the United States. Shortly before the British election of 1 May 1997, the *Guardian*'s ICM poll showed Labour with a 5-percentage-point lead, while the *Daily Telegraph*'s Gallup poll had it ahead by 21 points.

Polling's Traumas and Triumphs

In early postwar election polling, the field was dominated by firms run by the "founding fathers"—George Gallup, Elmo Roper, and Archibald Crossley. Newspapers were the main clients. Then as now, research firms polled public opinion without profit, and often at a loss, as a form of promotion to attract commercial business. More recently, media organizations have taken over polls' sponsorship and even technical management.

Election polling is not easily differentiated from other ongoing public opinion surveys. Opinions about the 1996 presidential race were being introduced into polls long before the primaries, along with a variety of other subjects. (In 1995, ten of CBS's thirty-five surveys had questions on the O. J. Simpson trial.) As the campaign proceeded, different kinds of people were queried. As a typical example, the Harris poll began its early preelection surveys by reporting the opinions of the general public; it then switched its base to registered voters in the summer. In September and October it moved on to those who said they were "absolutely" or "very likely" to vote. Finally, it went to the 50 percent of the original sample who were "absolutely" certain to vote and who (if eligible by age) said they had voted in the last election.

Local Polls

The same research apparatus called into play in presidential politics is also at work at the state level, in congressional districts, and in very big cities. The quality of the state and local polls varies widely. The polls use different questions to define likely voters, different sampling procedures, and different quality controls. Some are year-round operations; others are activated only for election campaigns. Many work on shoestring budgets. "Some of them are awful, but nonetheless they have excellent predictive value," says research consultant Warren Mitofsky, who once directed polling at CBS. "Their overall performance in each state was better than the national polls." More than 400 statewide election surveys were published in 1996 by some 35 to 40 local organizations. A Maryland firm, Mason-Dixon Research, conducted polls in all fifty states for newspapers and television station clients. Polls once run by specialists on major newspapers are with few exceptions now farmed out to independent research organizations.

Exit Polls

On election night, as always, the television networks vied to be first on the air to announce who won. "We need to have some tool to bring the public into the broadcast," says ABC's Jeff Alderman. "There are plenty of other means of doing it beyond polling, but there's certainly no better way."

Prognostications on election night began at CBS in 1956. In 1960 MIT's Ithiel de Sola Pool fed early returns into a computer model built on a database that incorporated precinct-by-precinct figures from previous elections. In 1964 the networks got together to set up the News Election Service to gather and count actual voting results. By the end of the decade, they had shifted to exit polls—polls conducted outside polling places, with questionnaires filled out by people who had just voted.

Exit polls gather considerable information besides the choice of candidate and serve an invaluable diagnostic function by comparing the characteristics and opinions of different voter groups. Today they are conducted by the Voter News Service (VNS), a consortium of ABC, CBS, NBC, Fox, CNN, and the Associated Press, which also sells its data to 150 other news media. The VNS represents a 1993 merger of News Election Service and Voter Research and Surveys, set up in 1990 to do exit polling. In 1996 VNS conducted 71,000 interviews in the primaries and 150,000 in the general election, with 2,000 to 6,000 per state. The results are computer-aided projections incorporating factors besides the exit polls: the preelection polls, actual vote returns in sample precincts, county returns, and the historical data. Interpreting all this is an art, not a science. In 1994 ABC decided to do its own on-air interpretations of the exit poll results. The other networks felt disadvantaged and have since hired their own experts.

VNS's record is excellent, but not impeccable. Like preelection polls, it relies on a sample—of polling points and voters who fill out different questionnaire forms. In 1992, when the Perot voters may have been more ornery types, suspicious of questioners, VNS overstated the Democratic vote. No such error was made in 1994, and the national results in 1996 were off by only 1 percentage point. But VNS went wrong in forecasting the outcome of the Senate race in New Hampshire, and years later it was still trying to figure out how that happened.

The Influence of Polls

Publication of polls stopped one week before the French election of 1997. France is only one of many countries that bar election surveys after a cutoff date because of fears about their effects on the actual vote (Foundation for Information 1997). In the United States, restricting or banning polls is not an option, though 68 percent of the public told a First Amendment Center poll in 1968 that TV should not be allowed "to project winners of elections early." As Humphrey Taylor puts it, "Like any other media organization, our job is to publish and be damned."

Did some pro-Dole people not bother to vote because the preelection polls showed such a big lead for Clinton? It is just as reasonable to suppose that many Clinton supporters did not vote because they thought his victory was a sure thing.

Was that expectation fed by greater visibility for polls in 1996, compared with previous elections? Twice as many polls were released as in 1992 simply because a number of organizations were doing continuous tracking. The results were released daily, usually averaged over three days early in the race and two later, with the first day's numbers dropped as new interviews were added. These daily reports did not heighten public awareness, though. In November, 59 percent of the voters reported they had seen or heard preelection poll results—less than the 77 percent who said this in 1992.

Anxious questions have long been raised about the effects of exit polls on turnout in western states where many people had not yet voted before they were told the outcome. Close local races may be influenced when voters stay home. Murray Edelman, VNS's editorial director, says, "No one would disagree that early projections affected one person on the West Coast. The real question is, how many were affected?" No one can really say. California pollster Mervin Field comments, "In the last election the turnout in California was running 1 to 2 percent behind 1992 for hours before there could have been any interference. One or two percent of those who didn't vote said it was because they had heard the results." He admits that "there's no conclusive evidence either way. But if people think they're being disenfranchised, why do it?"

Picking the Winners

Election polls are judged by tougher standards than those applied to other surveys. Corporations that conduct market research to measure brand share take the numbers very, very seriously and treat them as though they could literally be translated into dollars and cents; but usually they have no way of determining if those numbers are wrong. There can be only one winner in an election race, and political polls are judged by their accuracy in forecasting who that winner will be. Yet elections can be won by the narrowest margin of the popular vote, as in 1960, and the peculiar institution of the electoral college makes projections of the national popular vote nothing more than a preliminary indicator of the outcome state by state.

Who Will Vote?

Pollsters are not only expected to deliver precise estimates of the public's choices; they must base those estimates on the choices of those individuals who are really going to cast a ballot. This is daunting indeed in the case of primary elections to fill local offices, when only a small fraction of the electorate may turn out. Turnout is affected by the weather and by public interest in concurring local or statewide contests. It makes a very big difference in some presidential election years, but not in others. Primary election turnout dropped to 48 percent in the relatively boring contest of 1996, even though this was the first since passage of the Motor Voter Act, which made registration to vote easier.

Calculations of turnout are based on the number of valid ballots cast in relation to the voting age population, though this includes millions of aliens, recent movers, and felons who cannot be counted exactly. (There were 17 million of these disenfranchised adults in 1996, according to the Center for the Study of the American Electorate 1997.) Some states allow registration at voting time. An unknown number of enthusiasts register in more than one precinct. Between 70 percent and 80 percent of election poll respondents claim to be registered, but not all of them are. Many registered voters do not vote, and there is no easy way of determining who will. The University of Michigan Survey Research Center, which conducted election polls between 1964 and 1988, found that 90 percent of registered voters did vote, but nobody really knows how many eligible people are actually registered. In the 1987 Chicago mayoralty primary race, 29 percent of those who said they were registered voters did not have their names on the rolls.

Needless to say, people who take the trouble to vote are not a general cross-section of the public. Even the exit poll respondents are not a random sampling of voters. VNS's questionnaires were completed by 55 percent of the voters at the selected precincts. About one fourth of the remainder were "misses"—people not interviewed because interviewers were busy with other respondents when they walked by. The rest did not want to cooperate. While 43 percent of VNS's respondents were college graduates (compared to 20 percent in the U.S. Census), only 6 percent (compared to another 20 percent of the population) had failed to complete high school. People under 25 were 9 percent of the voters, though they are 13 percent of the population over 18. Since voters are not a random cut of the nation's adults, their choice of candidates may be different from that of a general sampling.

Why was Dole's vote underestimated? Was there a last-minute shift to Dole that the polls missed by stopping too soon? Gallup continued to interview through the evening before Election Day and as a result showed an increasing Republican choice. The last survey conducted by CBS and the *New York Times* was Wednesday through Saturday before the election, with over half the interviews done by Thursday. "Clinton was so far ahead we didn't feel we had to do any last-minute polling," says CBS's Kathleen Frankovic.

In fact, Perot was the main beneficiary of late choices in an election in which many of the undecided were evidently dissatisfied with both major contenders. Of all the Perot voters, 43 percent made up their minds in the last week, compared with 16 percent of Clinton voters and 18 percent of Dole voters.

Did the polls underestimate the Dole vote because Republicans distrust the "liberal" media and see polls as their instrument? Experienced practitioners see no substance to this charge. Refusals were a bigger problem in the 1997 election in Britain, where newspapers are correctly perceived as mainly Conservative and where the polls mistakenly forecast a Labour victory in 1992.

The most likely explanation is that Dole's better-educated, higher-income Republican supporters were more likely to vote than Democrats were. The social differences that explain variations in turnout are also reflected in political choices, and not just in this election. Polls reveal what a cross-section of the public thinks, but underprivileged people simply do not exercise their franchise as predictably as those with greater advantages, who tend to vote Republican.

Why Surveys Are Not Perfect

The Margin of Error

The problems of political pollsters are to a large degree those faced by all surveys. Today most survey findings are published with a brief accompanying statement about their margin of error, commonly given as plus or minus 3 percentage points when the response is evenly divided in a sample of 1,000. (An important qualifier is that there is 1 chance in 20 that the error is greater.) The margin becomes smaller as the sample increases and as the response moves farther from an even division.

In reporting research, news media sometimes choose to ignore this warning, just as a habitual smoker is blind to the surgeon general's message on the cigarette pack. Reuters, in reporting its election poll by John Zogby, commented on differences of less than a percentage point. (Zogby reported figures to a decimal place "only because it sets us apart" [Roper Center Symposium 1997].)

Error does not mean a "mistake." It is a statistical term, based on pure mathematical probability, which assumes that the sample is perfectly representative and the survey process itself completely unflawed. In practice this never happens.

Budgets set limits on sample size and on the time-consuming procedures required to make samples properly representative of their parent populations. There are innumerable lapses between plans and execution. Consider just the matter of rapport between interviewer and respondent, essential to get honest answers. Rapport affects even telephone polling, where the interviewer's race can be inferred only from speech patterns. (Cotter, Cohen, and Coulter 1982; Finkel, Guterbock, and Borg 1991). When opposing candidates are of different races, the forecast may be affected. In the New York 1988 presidential primary, for example, 57 percent of black respondents interviewed by blacks said they had voted for Jesse Jackson; just 39 percent gave this answer when interviewed by whites (Edelman and Mitofsky 1989).

Poorly paid interviewers are sometimes unintelligible in their frenzy to get the call over with. Even in the most professionally run enterprises, interviewers may be inadequately selected or instructed; questionnaires may be improperly constructed; mistakes can occur as respondents' answers are encoded and processed into statistics. Most important, the public has become steadily less cooperative as telephone interviewing is increasingly identified with the annoying intrusion of telemarketing.

The Poltergeist Factor

Accidental and inexplicable occurrences can affect the top-line survey findings that find their way into the headlines. This is most visible in media research. Not long ago one of the two leading measurement services said *Reader's Digest* had 40 million readers per issue; the other said 50 million. For buyers and sellers of advertising, this is no trivial matter. Such incongruities are commonplace, even in successive reports from the same research firm.

The imprecision of survey projections results from the fact that research is a complex human enterprise that involves many different steps, some mechanical, some judgmental. In more than 7,000 verification checks of market research interviews by the Advertising Research Foundation, only 63 percent were found to have met specifications without error (Lipstein 1975). There is no reason to assume that political surveys have a better record.

But definable errors cannot account for all the surprises that confront both those who do polls and those who use them or follow them. There always appears to be a residue of anomalies and inconsistencies. Obviously, poltergeists are at work here—the same malevolent imps that perpetually louse up nice smooth trends on product consumption, brand share, and media audiences. Election polls present them with a tempting target.

Changes in Methods

In the history of survey research, two signal events have forced dramatic reassessment of prevailing methods: the elections of 1936 and 1948. Gallup's 1936 poll, along with Roper's and Crossley's, established the supremacy of sample surveys on the political and marketing scene. Their polls were based on modest-sized samples compared to that of the *Literary Digest*, which received 2.2 million mailed-in ballots from overwhelmingly Republican-leaning respondents. Mail questionnaires draw responses from a self-selected portion of the public to whom they are addressed.

In 1948, after Gallup and his fellow pollsters forecast a Dewey victory, their debacle hastened the wholesale adoption of probability sampling. With this procedure, the locations of interviews, households, and respondents were all selected in a predesignated and random way. This was considered much more scientific than the quota method, which rested on the judgment of interviewers who presumably picked respondents to accord with their own conservative proclivities. At a time when polls were conducted in person door to door, interviewers tended to avoid neighborhoods and people who were not "nice."

Most survey data collection in the United States today is neither by mail nor by the personal interviews that the U.S. Census Bureau has traditionally used to complete its decennial exercise. Since the mid-1970s, under the pressure of rising costs, most opinion and market surveys have been done much more cheaply by telephone, an instrument considered a necessity of life even for people on public assistance.

But though telephone service may be almost universal, directory listing is not. Thirty-seven percent of all residential phones have unlisted numbers. This includes 55 percent of black and 58 percent of Hispanic households. To make sure that unlisted phones are included in their samples, most research organizations use variations of a method called random-digit dialing, starting with the area codes and prefixes for what are believed to be mainly residential exchanges in designated localities.

A strict two-step probability sampling procedure, in which the chance pick of a household is the first step, requires a listing of every person 18 or over in the household and then a random selection of one to be interviewed. But asking up front for a list of household members can invoke suspicion and reduce cooperation. There is no absolutely sure way of eliminating nonresidential phones and unassigned or nonworking numbers. Thus it is difficult to say exactly what proportion of the households in the planned sample correspond to the phones that are answered (even by a machine).

All the national polling organizations conduct election interviews by phone, and there is no indication that differences of methodology bring some closer to the mark than others. Most call back repeatedly when they do not make contact. In 1996 Gallup did up to five call-backs; the joint CBS/*New York Times* poll did up to four. Both selected respondents randomly from a full roster of household members. The Harris and Pew Center polls asked first for the youngest voting age male, since these are the most difficult to reach. Pew then asked for the oldest woman. CBS and the *Times* got through to 90 percent of the numbers and completed interviews with a randomly picked respondent in half the cases. In one fourth to one third of households, an initial refusal could be converted into an interview, and the hard-to-get people were "not essentially different," according to CBS's Frankovic. The average refusal and noncompletion rate among those contacted by the Harris polls in 1996 was 60 percent. But this does not include every household in the predesignated sample, some of whom cannot be reached even after a number of tries, and pollsters facing cruel deadlines typically must halt their attempts within a short period of time.

ABC did not use call-backs. Instead it moved on to a new phone number. "Call-backs beyond the same evening are a waste of time and money," says polling director Alderman. About 20 percent of each night's sample were at phone numbers that did not answer the phone the night before. (But Alderman acknowledges that more Democrats turn up on the weekend—not because of their politics, but because of their social characteristics.) Zogby, who polled for Reuters (and previously for Rupert Murdoch's Fox News and *New York Post*), sampled only listed telephone numbers, since he believes random-digit dialing "is more likely to cause caller fatigue, which can lead to frustration and greater inaccuracy." Most pollsters would raise their eyebrows at this notion, as well as at Zogby's practice of interviewing during daylight hours on the rationale that the polls are open all day (Roper Center Symposium 1997).

Who Isn't Polled?

Martin Frankel, a distinguished sampling statistician, thinks that most surveys are based on between 10 percent and 20 percent of the people who should have been picked by pure chance. In an era when people are continually solicited with unwanted sales calls at odd hours, that is what researchers have to live with.

In 1995 a group of major research firms collaborated in a study of telephone survey methodology (Council for Marketing and Opinion Research 1995). Among contacted respondents, the cooperation rate in a fairly brief interview was 26 percent, but that is 26 percent of an unknown base of predesignated respondents in a true probability sample. The real base is unknown because each of the nine commercial market research organizations that participated in the project used its usual methodology. Not-at-homes, answering machines, and hang-ups reduced the figure substantially as a percentage of the original universe.

The rate at which interviews are successfully completed depends on their length, the public's interest in the subject matter, and the nature of the population being questioned. In a one-minute interview, one research company, Statistical Research, Inc., has someone in 85 percent of contacted households tell them whether or not a television set is on. By spending enough money, the level of cooperation can be raised. First-rate research companies, working with knowledgeable clients who have deep pockets and are willing to pay the cost of persistent call-backs, can obtain interviews from half or more of the people they want to contact. Using personal interviews, the National Opinion Research Center at the University of Chicago can achieve a completion rate of 75 percent, though it averages 60 percent. But clients for commercial research are typically unwilling to undertake that extra expense. After all, the pressure to cut costs— and time—drove them to telephone interviews in the first place.

There has been a steady drop both in the ability of telephone surveys to make contact with designated households and respondents and in the rate of cooperation required to complete interviews—which have gotten longer and longer. This makes survey results more uncertain and should cause concern, caution, and above all humility in reporting the results.

Pollsters generally accept the notion that people who cannot be reached differ from those who can, in ways that may be reflected in their opinions, including their political choices. This is also true of people who are reached but who refuse to go through a whole interview. There have been more such people with each passing year.

Consider how those who are interviewed differ in terms of educational attainment, a good index of social position. The Census of 1990 found that 42 percent of American adults had attended college (however briefly), and a personal interview poll by the Roper Organization six years later came up with a roughly similar percentage—44 percent. At the same time, the Gallup Organization and the ABC/*Washington Post* and CBS/*New York Times* polls, all with telephone surveys on the same subject (use of new media), came up with college-educated proportions of 59 percent, 53 percent, and 57 percent respectively. (Among Gallup's final sample of likely voters, 64 percent were college-educated; so were 60 percent of ABC's.) Such discrepancies do not present an insurmountable obstacle because all research organizations adjust the raw interview data to bring them into balance with the whole population to which they will be projected and thus to make them more accurate.

Weighting the Results

No one in polling today can say, "I talked to *x* people, and this is what they said." Whether or not they use the random-digit-dialing method, all the election polls—using their own special formulas—weight results to conform to the characteristics of the universe, as described by the census.

The trouble is that 1990 Census figures, even though updated by annual surveys, share the affliction of all those who seek to extract information from an ever more recalcitrant public. Only 63 percent of U.S. households sent back the initial census long-form questionnaire in 1990. In north central Brooklyn, only 38 percent of the forms were sent in. (The Census Bureau works diligently, and at great expense, to make up for the deficiencies of this initial effort, with repeated personal visits. Census methodology became a hot political issue in 1998, with the Republican majority in Congress opposing a plan proposed by the National Academy of Sciences to introduce sampling methods to supplement the actual canvassing. The aim of improving accuracy and reducing the undercount might produce changes in the apportionment of seats in the House of Representatives.)

Weighting survey results to match the census data in effect reintroduces the fundamental technique of the now-discredited quota sampling method—at a high-tech level. No matter how much researchers try to correct their raw data to conform to the demographic profile of the parent population, it is not all that easy to ascertain the psychological attributes of the many people with whom interviews are never completed. The personality quirks that differentiate the growing number who cannot be found or who just don't want to be bothered are bound to be reflected in the top-line findings of studies on every subject from aardvarks to zygotes, and especially on politics.

In the early days of postwar election forecasting, a retreaded journalist named Samuel Lubell roamed the country talking to everyone he encountered. He was scoffed at for failing to follow any particular plan for sampling or even for questioning his respondents, but he made some uncannily accurate predictions. Some pollsters still use curiously personal ways of adjusting their data to conform with their hunches. This starts with the respondents who cannot answer questions because they "don't know," are reluctant to answer, or haven't made up their minds.

The Undecided

One unresolved technical question pollsters face is how to dispose of the people who claim to be registered voters and who intend to vote, but who have still not made their pick at the time they are interviewed. This can be a substantial proportion when a race is in its early stages. By the time of the final preelection surveys in 1996, this number was between 3 percent and 12 percent—a large enough proportion to make a difference in some elections. (The percentage varied in different polls, depending on how much the questions forced an expression of preference. Some polls included the supporters of minor party candidates in this category; others showed them separately.)

Should these people be included in the final count, and if so, should their votes be allocated in the same proportions as those of the rest of the voting public? The survey organizations followed differing procedures. In the Harris poll, Clinton's lead shrank as the undecided were "squeezed" to express a preference for a candidate. No one method of allocating the undecided is effective over all election races, each with its own dynamics. "There is no principle for doing it," says Mitofsky.

Adjustments and Judgments

VNS's Edelman points out that by asking the undecided which way they are leaning, and then assuming that they will all follow that forced inclination, "you're already making an allocation." How far should pollsters' subjective judgments go in manipulating the data?

Studies of how voters make their choices have long shown that those who stray from their original political orientations tend to gravitate back as they approach the moment of truth. Irving Crespi, a long-time Gallup executive, says that it was obvious by midsummer that potential Republican defectors would be returning to the fold, and that a low turnout would help Dole: "The processes were well-known, and the pollsters should have taken them into account when they reported their findings." This seems to suggest that pollsters should either adjust their data or warn that they should not be accepted unquestioningly. Similarly, Princeton Research Associates' Hugick argues that "poll results in incumbent races should not be taken at face value." If they cannot be taken at face value, should they be reported, or should the numbers be altered?

Nick Panagakis (1997), after examining thirty-six presidential polls as well as hundreds of state and local races, concludes that undecided voters generally go from challengers to the incumbent because "it is easier to decide whether or not to vote for an incumbent than it is to decide about a relatively unknown challenger" (p. 21). Presumably the devil you do not know has an edge over the devil you do. Dole, however, was hardly unknown, as Clinton had been in 1992.

Zogby's Reuters poll showed Clinton's lead narrowing from 7 to 4 points as the campaign wound down, and forecast Clinton's 8-point lead exactly in an adjusted set of numbers that he released along with the original figures from his final poll. Was there a magic touch in the way he "massaged" the data? At a 1997 symposium, "Controversies in Preelection Polling," Zogby remarked:

To determine how to adjust our sample to reflect a fair representation of Democrats, Republicans and independents, we take a close look at exit polls [presumably from previous elections], party registration figures, and a compilation of polls to get a sense of how many Democrats, Republicans and independents exist. . . . I feel that it is reasonable to assume that, despite the lack of enthusiasm for their presidential candidate, there are still approximately the same number of Republicans out there as Democrats. . . . Essentially, we bumped both parties down a little and slightly increased the numbers of independents so that our weighted samples reflected about 34 percent each for the two parties . . . and 32 percent independents.

Does Weighting by Party Preference Make Sense?

The procedure has long been used by some private pollsters who want to develop campaign strategy by talking to a batch of voters for or against their own candidate, pollsters who are not shooting for an exact forecast that will be published with their names attached to it. But party preference has no independent reality that warrants its use to jiggle the numbers. CNN's Keating Holland comments, "Fill a questionnaire with items on the environment, poor children, and seniors on limited incomes, and you're bound to get a higher number of Democrats than if the identical sample were asked questions on welfare cheats, flag-burners, and the death penalty." The important thing to remember is that in the search for accuracy, the numbers were being jiggled by subjective criteria.

Hidden Polls

Of the approximately $200 million spent on election polls in 1996, only a fraction went for the public surveys made to be published or broadcast. Many more confidential polls were done privately to test the waters, appraise candidates' chances, and assess the strengths and weaknesses of reputations and policies. They were not merely a source of political intelligence; when favorable findings were leaked to the press, they were actively used as a campaign tool.

Candidates' staffs scrutinize the run-of-the-mill studies that survey public opinion on all the innumerable political and social questions that may be up for comment and discussion. In planning strategy, political consultants apply the full panoply of advertising research techniques—"concept testing" to gauge the appeal of various campaign themes; evaluations of candidates' appearance, demeanor, dress, and speaking style; and "segmentation" studies that classify probable voters into different demographic or psychological categories and relate these to ideological outlooks and voting inclinations. There is heavy use of so-called focus groups, a market research technique useful in eliciting creative ideas for survey questionnaires or even for advertising campaigns but useless as a basis for generalization. Dubious methods can lead to inane conclusions, like political consultant Dick Morris's directive that Clinton should vacation at Jackson Hole to get votes from camping enthusiasts among "swing" voters (Morris 1997).

Increasingly the line has been blurred between the pollster's role as a gatherer of objective information and the new role as political consultant. A similar transition often occurs in the business world, where successful researchers are usually those who can draw actionable recommendations from data to guide advertising and marketing strategy.

The research organizations that conduct public polls are generally different from those that work for candidates and parties. There are some exceptions and ambiguities in this area. Jimmy Carter's pollster, Patrick Caddell, and Ronald Reagan's, Richard Wirthlin, capitalized on the cachet they acquired through their political associations to establish successful companies that also do market and opinion research. Apart from its published surveys, Mason-Dixon Research has an affiliate that polls for political candidates. Louis Harris was campaign manager for Franklin D. Roosevelt Jr.'s unsuccessful 1962 race for New York's governorship, and his firm (whose reports are now carried by more than 100 newspapers) once did both public and private polling. (It still conducts private polling outside the United States.)

Robert Teeter, who became George Bush's campaign manager in 1992, and Peter Hart, a Democratic Party pollster, teamed up to do public polling for NBC and the *Wall Street Journal*, although Hart retains an interest in an affiliated company that does private polls. Democratic pollster Celinda Lake and counterpart Republican Ed Goeas poll for Hotline, a political newsletter, and for *US News*. In these arrangements, the theory seems to be that the two partners neutralize each other's biases.

Push Polls

Increasingly, telephone canvassing on behalf of candidates has taken on the guise of opinion surveys, thereby making life more difficult for honest pollsters who are seeking the truth, not making a sale. "Push polls," intended to sway rather than measure opinion, evolved out of legitimate research designed to gauge reactions to candidates' views, both real and hypothetical. Now the intention is to create an "interview effect" by asking tendentious questions such as "Would you still vote for candidate X if you knew that he was once arrested on a morals charge?" Most of this is done by telemarketing firms, rather than by research companies.

Illinois pollster Richard Day observes:

> The political process is an advocacy process. For those people in the middle of it, push polls are seen in a very different light than they are by the research professionals. In the real life and death struggle of win or lose, no holds are barred. Everyone thinks that everyone else is doing it. It's on the increase as it goes further down the line to the state representative level. It's a difficult genie to put back in the bottle.

In 1996 the Dole campaign used push polls against Forbes before the Iowa caucuses. Afterward the National Council on Public Polls asked the candidates to desist in the future. Clinton and Perot agreed; Dole never responded, but his campaign did not use push polls after the conventions. Push polls are likely to appear again in state and local races.

The Outlook

The major public polling organizations use slightly different methods, but they openly and fully describe what they do and are constantly reviewing and improving their procedures. They are all doing as well as they know how—within the budgets they have to work with. Since they feel comfortable with their performance in 1996, they are not going to conduct future election polls very differently. Judging from past experience, those polls should be reasonably—not perfectly—correct. Even if all the pollsters had failed to predict Clinton's victory in 1996, they would have been back in business the next day because there is no alternative to what they do. Not only politics but also the business world would grind to a halt without them.

For better or for worse, polls are now an integral part of the American electoral process. The media rely on them to make news; politicians lean on their guidance. Their real value is not in forecasting but in showing the dynamics of an ever-changing public opinion. News media can make much better use of this analytical function if they pay more attention to the issues under debate and less to the transient popularity of different candidates.

The variety of competing public polls may appear to be a source of confusion, but it is a cause for rejoicing, not dismay. The very fact that polls are not unanimous presents a constant reminder of their inherent uncertainties, which journalists and the public alike seem reluctant to accept. Integrity and professional competence cannot ensure total accuracy in an enterprise that entails lots of gut judgment and thrives on dumb luck.

The polls of which one should be most wary are the ones that are never published, the research that is done by and for political consultants. The biggest operators in this domain are outside the reach of the research profession, and they are not committed to the standards and codes of its associations. They do not follow the fundamental rule of explaining to all comers exactly what they do. With sometimes skimpy evidence and shabby inferences, they cultivate the notion that politicians should cater to the superficial vagaries of public opinion rather than lead it by the strength of their convictions. Journalists and the public should pay less attention to the inexact art of election forecasting and more to the sinister implications of political marketing.

Conclusion

CHAPTER 14

Election Polling in the Twenty-first Century: Challenges and Opportunities

Paul J. Lavrakas and Michael W. Traugott

Elections polls have been conducted in one form or another for nearly two centuries, going back to the "straw polls" of the early 1800s in the United States (cf. Frankovic 1998, 1999a; Herbst 1995). Since those early days, there has been a tremendous change in the methods used to gather survey data, and the ability to analyze quickly the massive amounts of data these polls generate has changed even more (Frankovic 1994). Nowadays the largest of these data collection and analysis efforts are the one-day exit poll marathons conducted by the Voter News Service (VNS) on Election Day each November in the United States (cf. Mitofsky and Edelman 1995). For example, on 3 November 1998, VNS gathered and processed several million pieces of data from more than 100,000 randomly sampled respondents and then began reporting the results of its analyses in the early evening hours. And in 2000, there will an even greater effort to meet the additional challenge of measuring the presidential contest for each state's electoral votes. In 1998, the Harris-Black Organization became the first to mount a major effort to conduct large-scale "on-line" election polling via the Internet, and the number of such "interviews" will sky rocket as well in 2000.

Along with changes in the methods of data collection and analysis have come changes in the way the statistical findings from poll data are used by the news media and by other important actors on the American political scene. In the 1990s the sheer amount of information routinely disseminated from election polls and other political surveys mushroomed from previous decades (cf. Lavrakas and Bauman 1995). Of greater importance, the prominence of this information in framing news coverage about politics, politicians, and elections has increased greatly since the mid-1970s, when the *New York Times* and CBS News began their now legendary media-polling partnership. During the 1996 presidential campaign, the preelection polls in the months up to the election indicated a certain victory for President Clinton. This expectation influenced myriad news decisions about how to cover the Clinton, Dole, and Perot campaigns, the result of which led many Republicans to cry foul. In fact, some partisan election-polling critics even suggested that the news media's overreliance on "faulty" polls assured Clinton of the 1996 victory, in part by depressing turnout among Dole supporters (cf. Ladd 1996).

In 1998 and early 1999, the findings of public polls, showing consistent majority public support for keeping President Clinton in office, played a singular role in protecting him from removal by the Republican congressional majority (cf. Schneider 1999). In this case, conservatives again cried foul and mounted concerted efforts to discredit the polls by arguing they were based on invalid methods (e.g., Huffington 1998). These claims of a liberal, Democratic bias in the 1998 polls were quieted only by what turned out to be a clear underestimate of how well the Democrat candidates for Congress would do in the 1998 off-year election.

For more than ten years, we, the editors of this book, have been working together to address the broad issue of the role of election polling in our democracy. During this time we have witnessed not only a continued growth in the use of polls and a parallel increase in the criticism directed toward this growth but also history-making examples of the *power of poll-based news*. For example, there are few political analysts who think that the public polls of 1998 and early 1999, which showed mostly strong and consistent approval of Bill Clinton's handling of his presidential duties, did not play a central role in thwarting Republican efforts to remove him from office (cf. Schneider 1999).

We also have witnessed an increased reliance on election polls by politicians to stimulate and maintain financial support for their campaigns (cf. Mutz 1995) and to help refine their own policy positions (cf. Morris 1997; Stephanopoulos 1999). Recent movies, such as *An American President*, *Primary Colors*, and *Wag the Dog*, drive home the latter point by showing how this has come to be accepted (and probably even expected) as common practice among elected officials.

As we approach the twenty-first century, we find ourselves at a time when various forms of political polls are being used more and are having greater effects than ever in history. As a result, it has never been more important to American democracy that

- Pollsters gather and report accurate data and do so ethically
- Journalists know how to use poll-based information accurately and in ways that enhance and expand their news judgments

- News organizations report poll-based information in nonsuperficial, yet timely, ways
- The public and so-called experts alike become more discerning consumers of the poll-based information to which they are exposed

We believe it is a crucial time for election polling, and many others in the polling enterprise share this view. As *Washington Post* pollster Richard Morin recently warned, "Polling has never been so risky—or so in demand" (Morin 1999).

The Need for Better Election Polls

Because of their power to affect varied political issues and outcomes through their influence on the judgments of citizens, journalists, and politicians alike, the credibility of public election polls will most certainly be attacked in the coming years (cf. Newport 1999). These attacks will most often come from organized interests that support a particular policy area and/or have a particular partisan bent, and the attacks are likely to grow in frequency and in strength. To withstand these attacks, pollsters (including those involved in the business and study of public opinion, as well as those responsible for particular survey data collection efforts) and those who fund these polls must build their own capacity to respond quickly and adequately. Pollsters also must both conduct better polls and anticipate the types of criticism likely to be directed at them in the design and implementation of their polls.

In the past few years some significant and embarrassing moments have been visited upon prominent public pollsters. An important one was the final performance of some of the major preelection polls in predicting the margin of Bill Clinton's 1996 victory over Bob Dole and Ross Perot. Several of the most prominent polls (e.g., the *New York Times*/CBS News poll; see Chapters 2 and 13) overestimated Clinton's victory margin, and none beat the prediction of the relatively unknown Zogby firm that polled for the Reuters news agency and used a nontraditional and irreproducible methodology. Immediately following the 1996 election, Everett Ladd, of the Roper Center at the University of Connecticut, had an op-ed essay published in the politically conservative *Wall Street Journal* that lambasted the media's use of "biased" preelection polls to assure a Clinton (i.e., liberal) victory (Ladd 1996). Ladd called for a major investigation of what he claimed was an unacceptable lack of accuracy in the 1996 preelection polls.

A second embarrassing moment was less public and occurred in late summer 1998. This was the very slow response of many major media pollsters to a request from ultraconservative columnist Arianna Huffington for information about the response rates for their polls. In an effort to undermine the credibility of the public polls at that time—ones that were showing strong and consistent majority approval of Bill Clinton's job as president—conservative interests began to raise questions about the methodology of the polls in an effort to discredit them as flawed and thus biased. One focus of the attack was the wording of the overall presidential "approval" question these polls asked. Another focus of the attack was on the "low" response rates achieved by most public media polls. Whether or not these polls' response rates were associated with nonresponse error is not the issue raised in the present context—nor, by the way, was that an issue Huffington appeared to appreciate or care about. Rather, the issue is why it took so long for the pollsters whom Huffington contacted to make a public statement about their polls' response rates. The message seemed clear: The pollsters were embarrassed that their response rates were as low as they were (well under 50 percent) and preferred not to make this information public.

Furthermore, as part of this mounting conservative attack on election polls and other political polls, many other less public but nonetheless well-known news sources have begun to spread a "crisis in poll credibility" message. In early 1999, for example, a popular political news service told its readers that "more people refuse to respond [to polls]—40 percent to 60 percent of those who are asked. That's a dirty little secret in the business and may be skewing results. Also, self-selected respondents aren't typical of the general public" (*Kiplinger Washington Letter* 1999, 1).

These are just a few examples of recent and important criticisms leveled at public polls and their credibility—criticisms that received quite of bit of attention. Coupled with these direct public attacks are findings from a recent national study of Americans' views of public opinion polls, conducted at the University of Michigan and funded by the Pew Charitable Trusts, on which we have worked. As part of this study, a national random-digit dialing (RDD) survey of 1,001 adults conducted in 1998 found that many Americans question the credibility of the poll findings to which they are exposed in the news media. Nearly half of the public (45 percent) said they thought that "we have too many public opinion polls in this country," and only one in four Americans thought that "public opinion polls are [typically] right in reporting how people feel about issues" (24 percent said "most of the time" and 1 percent said "all the time"). More than one third (37 percent) agreed that "polls do more harm than good in our society," and 29 percent thought that the record of polls was "not very good" in accurately predicting election outcomes. Furthermore, only 15 percent of Americans believed that "a sample of 1,500 or 2,000 people can accurately reflect the views of the nation's population." Across the board, Americans with the least trust in the accuracy of public polls were those who had less education and who did not identify with (or lean toward) either the Democratic Party or the Republican Party. Similarly, a 1999 Gallup poll found that "the [American] public's view of polling and more specifically, of pre-election polling is less than overwhelmingly positive" (Newport 1999).

Thus, it is reasonable to conclude that the polling industry and the media that depend on pollsters for important news do not enjoy a high level of trust among the American public vis-à-vis the accuracy of poll findings. However, the lack of an outcry of distrust from the general public in 1998 and early 1999 regarding poll findings that a clear majority supported Bill Clinton's remaining in office as president suggests that the majority of Americans believed these results accurate, not because the public judged them to be methodologically sound, but mostly because they coincided with their own personal opinions. Likewise, many Republicans and conservatives thought these same polls to be wholly inaccurate, reflecting their own preferences about what should happen to Clinton. This in itself supports another important finding from the Michigan-Pew project—that many citizens attribute relatively greater credibility to poll results when those results coincide with their own personal opinions and beliefs, and this occurs regardless of how those polls are conducted (Presser et al. 1998). All in all, this is a very weak branch upon which the credibility of public polls too often rests.

The simultaneous challenges that pollsters face are the need to conduct public polls with the best possible methods, on a timely basis, and to raise the credibility accorded well-conducted public polls. From our own recent research we see that one critical test of meeting this challenge will be future levels of credibility assigned to public polls by those whose own opinions differ from the majority opinion documented in those polls. Another important test will be the level of respect expert survey methodologists hold for public polls—especially experts who are independent from the media and the companies that produce and report public polls.

The second of these "tests" will be easier to assess because experts in survey methods can readily and directly judge the "quality" of a poll if they know about the methods used to conduct it. Convincing impartial experts of a poll's credibility, however, by no means assures that members of the public without this expertise will agree. Many factors contribute to the formulation of public perceptions of the accuracy of opinion polls. But it is a safe assumption that if public polls do not use credible methods to gather their data or are challenged for not doing so without an adequate response, they quickly will lose all standing for accuracy and thereby undermine their own potential value to serve our democracy. If polls are well planned and well conducted, attacks on their credibility can be countered and perhaps defeated by appealing to the quality of the methods by which the polls were conducted. If the methods themselves are questionable, the public polls and their pollsters and sponsors are left in a weakened and defensive position to weather attacks on their credibility.

The foundation of the credibility of the polls is the manner and methods by which they are conducted. When we say we need "better" election polls in the twenty-first century, what we mean is that we need to know more about how various changes in the scientific design of these polls affects their outcomes (cf. Crespi 1988). For example, if adding one more day to the field period of a two-day preelection poll does not increase its accuracy by a meaningful amount, then it is incumbent on those who commission and use the poll's findings to know this and to proactively report this to experts and to the public. If increasing the response rate of a preelection survey, say from 30 percent to 50 percent, does not appreciably change the accuracy of the poll's election outcome predictions, this too should be known and publicized. If conducting interviews both on the telephone and by means of the Internet does not lead to less accuracy than using the telephone alone, then this too should be known and publicized. (This is just a partial list of areas in which more research about poll accuracy is needed.)

The message here is that those organizations and professionals who conduct election polls, and those who use their results, must always strive to know the most cost-effective and beneficial ways to gather information that is accurate enough for the purposes for which it will be used (cf. Frankovic 1999b). Then they should fight for the resources needed to attain this goal. Unfortunately, the choice of methods used nowadays to conduct most preelections polls that are meant for public dissemination is too often linked primarily to news deadlines rather than to confident knowledge that the chosen methods are adequate to the task of producing accurate findings. When pollsters become more certain of the research-based adequacy of their methods—rather than trusting practices simply because they worked in the past—and routinely engage in efforts to improve and/or adapt their methods to the changing political scene (see Chapters 2 and 3), then future problems with election polling accuracy are less likely to occur.

As documented in Chapters 9 and 10, there are no industrywide standardized methods for selecting respondents for preelection polls using screens for likely voters, for allocating undecided voters, or even for the wording of trial heat (horse-race) questions, despite more than three quarters of a century of systematic election polling. Although the goal is not necessarily the development of a *single* standard, these are among the many areas of serious research pollsters need to engage in more to increase the likely accuracy of their future polls. Other areas that affect poll accuracy and need more attention include (1) the length and timing (days or week, time of day) of preelection field periods, (2) response rates and the nature of nonresponse error in election surveys, (3) the effects of post-stratification weighting, and (4) mode effects.

Until pollsters know much more about *when* and *why* their polls are *accurate* and *when* and *why* their polls are *inaccurate*, they and their sponsors risk making crucial mistakes in future elections. Some suggest that such potential disasters could occur as early as the 2000 election campaign because of the likely volatility of the public's primary candidate preferences and the possible complacency that some pollsters may be experiencing from their relatively "easy" successes in measuring the public's very stable political opinions in 1998 on Clinton-Lewinsky issues (Morin 1999).

Granted, the risk of a major polling debacle is of relatively low probability, but the consequences of such blunders can be terrible for the credibility of election polling—indeed, for all polling because election polls and preelection estimates of outcomes are the "standard" by which the entire effort is typically evaluated. One major setback—such as a series of clearly inaccurate election polls that somehow are conclusively linked to an otherwise unwarranted political outcome—could lead the entire opinion polling enterprise into a downward spiral of rapidly dwindling credibility. This unlikely but disastrous course could be stemmed if the major public pollsters worked to guard against its occurrence by taking a more proactive stance both in improving their methods and in routinely disseminating information about the accuracy of their polls. Otherwise, we suspect, such a disaster and its resultant fallout are just waiting to happen.

As a solution, we believe that the major news organizations that conduct and sponsor elections polls, the major professional organizations whose members conduct and use these polls, and major foundations with concerns about enhancing democratic processes should collaborate on a *significant initiative* to identify "best practices" for the methods used in public election polls. The participants should include

- Newspapers such as the *Los Angeles Times*, the *New York Times*, the *Wall Street Journal*, *USA Today*, and the *Washington Post*
- National television networks (ABC, CBS, CNN, FOX, and NBC)
- Major companies that conduct election polls for public dissemination, including the Gallup Organization, Harris-Black, and others
- The American Association for Public Opinion Research (AAPOR), the American Marketing Association (AMA), the American Association of Political Consultants (AAPC), the American Statistical Association (ASA), the National Council of Public Polls (NCPP), and the Council of American Survey Research Organizations (CASRO)

Failure to acknowledge this need and to do something *serious and significant* about it is a simple recipe for disaster in the twenty-first century. If it is not the responsibility of these organizations to do this in the U.S. democracy, then whose is it?

The goal of this effort would be to raise the credibility of election polls and other public polls by assuring that their methods are the best possible, given the resources that can and should be committed by their sponsors. These devices to gather information from a representative cross-section of the public have too great a potential for furthering democratic principles and practices to be allowed to be threatened by inadequate attention to their methods (cf. Cantril 1991; Crespi 1989; Gallup and Rae 1940; Lavrakas and Traugott 1995; Mann and Orren 1992; Traugott and Lavrakas 1999). In the twenty-first century, with new lifestyles and technologies likely to further insulate individual citizens from face-to-face contact with the larger polity, other new technologies also will provide the opportunity to gather information about public attitudes and intentions more rapidly and more accurately than ever before. If this is the result, then the potential to feed accurate information about the political and policy preferences of Americans into the public news stream can enhance democratic deliberations regardless of what forms those deliberations may take in the future.

This will not happen just because these new technologies exist, however. It will happen only if those involved in the election-polling enterprise band together, individual and corporate competition notwithstanding, and work to achieve a heightened level of credibility for the industry that benefits all.

Another challenge this group must address is the threat to the credibility of their product from unethical polls and other pseudo polls that became too commonplace in the 1990s (cf. Traugott and Lavrakas 1999). These "surveys" take many guises, but they share a basic characteristic in that they masquerade as legitimate polls when they are not. In the case of unethical "push polls" (see Chapter 12), no legitimate surveys are being conducted, although the polls are represented as such to "respondents." Thus innocent people who agree to cooperate with the "interviewer" are being duped. Furthermore, these push polls employ blatantly unfair business practices in which no legitimate political consultant should engage and no ethical politician should sponsor. Other pseudo polls may not be direct and unfair business practices per se, but they are nonetheless deceptive in that they trick "respondents" into thinking they are participating in a real survey. These include efforts to raise funds (FRUGing), sell products or memberships (SUGing), and any of a variety of so-called call-in polls. All pseudo polls harm the credibility of the legitimate polling enterprise since the public too often cannot differentiate one from the other. Coupled with the effects of the explosion of telemarketing ventures in the 1990s that routinely hound people with sales calls, the public's tolerance for these intrusions on their privacy has reached its limit, as testified by the growing appeal of various telecommunications "blocking" services that create barriers to unsolicited calls, faxes, or e-mail messages.

To counter the problems that pseudo polls cause legitimate polls, a concerted effort must be made by the "pro-polling" consortium whose creation we recommend. This effort must teach the public what constitutes a legitimate survey and why it is valuable to participate in these polls, as distinct from what constitutes a pseudo poll and why the public should or should not want to participate in such exercises. If, for example, the consortium could agree on the basic information all legitimate polls should use to inform their respondents—and we do not believe that this would be all that difficult—then a public service advertising campaign could be mounted to teach the public how to be more discriminating in their decisions to participate (or not) when they are "sampled" (cf. Traugott and Lavrakas 1999).

In sum, we believe that a major initiative must be mounted in a proactive fashion first to shore up and then to raise the credibility of election polls and other public polls. Of course, the call for this effort is not new. Yet past efforts have been woefully inadequate to the task, as evidenced by the defensive position pollsters often find themselves in and by the relatively lower than desirable level of trust the public has in polls. To succeed, this effort would require a well-funded, multiyear commitment. Further, we do not believe this effort will succeed unless it includes the meaningful participation and support of major news organizations, polling firms, professional organizations that address polling methods and issues, and foundations and agencies concerned with nurturing and promoting democratic practices.

The Need for Better Use of Poll-Based Information by Journalists

In addition to improving the quality of election polls and their public credibility, there is a need for more reporters, editors, and producers to become more sophisticated and selective users of the information these polls generate. Journalists need to recognize the effects this information often has on their own news judgments, as well as the effects it has on their readers and viewers. And we do not mean to suggest that all these potential effects are negative—in fact, many are positive (cf. Lavrakas 1999).

Although no definitive studies have been conducted, we believe that the accumulation of recent evidence gives little reason to doubt the great power that pre-primary and preelection polls have on journalists (cf. Morin 1999). Most certainly, the aspect of election polls that has the strongest effects on journalists is trial heat (so-called horse-race) polling that emphasizes which candidate is ahead and which is behind. This poll-based information affects myriad decisions the media make in allocating resources and news coverage to specific candidates because trial heat measures are interpreted by journalists as a direct reflection of a candidate's viability. Before and during primary election season, these numbers are inextricably linked to success in fundraising or lack thereof (cf. Burke 1999). A successful candidate must build and sustain momentum by showing that he or she can raise funds and stands well in the polls. These two indicators of viability go hand in hand and build upon each other (cf. Mutz 1995). A third key measure of candidate viability is the extent and quality of news coverage the candidate receives. Would-be candidates who cannot demonstrate success in the polls, in raising funds, or eventually in securing delegates are perceived by the news media as lacking viability, and they tend to receive less coverage as a result. In exceptional cases, when candidates exceed poll expectations and as a result receive a boost in coverage, such news itself helps candidates with low poll numbers and low funding start momentum for building their viability.

We believe that journalists who cover elections and politics should routinely engage in serious *self-evaluation* to review the extent to which their own news organization's coverage of different candidates might too closely follow a knee-jerk reaction to the candidate's perceived viability. For a democracy to work at its normative best, a candidate's policy positions, past record and experience, and character should drive important news decisions about coverage of the candidate or the important issues in the campaign—at a minimum they should be central factors.

Take as an example a relatively little known and underfunded candidate of good character who proposes a new long-term vision for shoring up Social Security, one that is both innovative and sound. Also imagine that this vision will take several decades to achieve and thus will not provide any immediate political payoffs for current elected officials who might support the plan. If a pre-primary poll showed this candidate as relatively unknown among the voting public and thus not faring well when pitted against a well-known but "status quo" incumbent, a typical scenario would be that the new candidate would appear to journalists as having little chance of winning and therefore would receive diminished news coverage. But what if the polls on this race focused more on the public's opinions of the policy stances of the candidates rather than on trial heat measures? In fact, imagine that public opinion on the different policy stances was measured in a way that did not directly tie a specific candidate to a specific policy stance. Using this information, news coverage of the primary campaign might focus on comparing and contrasting the candidates' different policy stances and showing which policy positions were supported by which segments of the voting public. The polling that would support such coverage might also uncover any "litmus test" issues that would, by themselves, determine how a citizen would vote (cf. Tompson and Lavrakas 1997, 1998). This scenario would be one in which early trial heat measures would not drive news decisions about levels of coverage each candidate received. This might in turn provide the public better choices at election time by allowing candidates with good ideas a longer "incubation" period to develop their support.

This is just one example of how the news media might better use election polls to cover campaigns. We have written previously that a serious problem with the media's use of polling information—the "data" these polls produce—is that the media are often ill-equipped to mine the data for the "right" story (cf. Lavrakas and Traugott 1995; Traugott and Means 1995). That is, when it comes to polling, most news organizations remain "data rich but analysis poor" to an extreme (Morin 1995, 124). Most news organizations do not have staff who know how to quickly search and extract meaning from polling data other than what readily appears on the surface (in simple frequencies or bivariate crosstabs), and they also believe they do not have the time required to conduct in-depth analyses (cf. Frankovic 1999b).

We do not agree that deadlines force news staffs to conduct only superficial analyses of poll results, because not all analyses have to be conducted under deadline pressures. In fact, an exceptional example of a news organization making sophisticated, yet timely, use of election-related polling data was a 18 September 1998 article by Richard Berke and Allison Mitchell that ran on the front page of the *New York Times*. This article was based upon and reported multivariate analyses to show the likely consequences of various "voter turn-out scenarios" on the outcome of the November 1998 congressional elections. By plumbing the data with multivariate analyses, the *Times* research staff provided its reporters with key insights into what might happen in the 1998 elections if historical voting patterns were repeated. By reporting this story, the *Times* provided the nation with information about what looked likely to happen in the November 1998 election unless traditional past voting patterns in off-year elections changed. We use this example to call attention to the need for the media that sponsor election polls to plan their questionnaires with a more creative mindset and to formulate an a priori strategy about how they will use the resulting data both to help make behind-the-scenes news decisions and to provide actual content in their entire campaign coverage (see Chapter 2).

Achieving the goal of improved poll-based reporting in the twenty-first century will directly benefit the goal of raising the credibility of public polls. Now is an opportune time for media executives to resist doing business as usual by allowing competitive dynamics to completely dictate their news agenda (cf. Lavrakas and Traugott 1995). Many news organizations, especially daily newspapers, are extremely profitable businesses. In the striving to eke out "just 1 percentage point more" profit, year after year, as many news CEOs appear to do, short-term gains are being traded for the long-term health of the news business. Election coverage and polling are a relatively small but nonetheless important part of most news organizations' scope of work. Obviously, the need to increase the quality of polling and its use in news making is part of the larger need for news organizations to recognize that the quality of their news product does matter to their long-term profitability. We think that news organizations will benefit their product as well as their profitability by taking a serious and proactive stance toward improving their use of election polling in the twenty-first century. In doing so, they will also be aiding the democracy that they mean to serve and that supports their existence.

The Need for More Discerning Poll Consumers

In addition to the need for better election polling and for better use of election polling by the news media, there is also a need for the public and elites alike to expect more from election polling news. For these expectations to be realized, citizens and elites must become more discriminating poll consumers. The marketplace of news in a democracy works like any other marketplace: News organizations are the suppliers, and readers, listeners, and viewers the consumers. Through myriad forms of feedback to news organizations, the consumers of their current products affect the nature of their future products. Unresponsive news organizations will lose audience members.

Thus there is a need for at least a significant portion of the public—significant in size and/or in influence—to become better educated in interpreting election polls, knowing what to expect from quality polls, and understanding how well (i.e., accurately and fairly) polling information is employed by the media. To the extent that citizens understand what factors contribute to quality polls and quality polling news, they will recognize when quality is missing. This will also contribute to recognition of those instances in which poorly executed polls have been conducted and poor reporting of poll information has occurred.

Three segments of society must help to educate the public and raise the ability of at least some significant proportion to be better consumers of polls and poll-based news. First, the media themselves can and must play a central role in raising public appreciation for qualitative differences between good polls and bad polls, and it is clearly in the media's self-interest to do so. This group includes columnists and editorial writers as well as those who conduct and report upon polls. Second, academics, especially those in journalism, communication, and political science as well as those who study survey methods, can play a special role in evaluating public polling and exposing their students to information about how polls should be used to cover elections and further democratic deliberations. Slowly, the number of students who learn these lessons will grow. Finally, society's "everyday" opinion leaders—people who influence their relatives, friends, neighbors, and coworkers—who have enough knowledge about polling must make the effort to point out ignorance about polling when they see it and try to educate their fellow citizens who have less understanding about polling.

Conclusion

When election polls are accurate—which is very often the case—and news organizations take full advantage of the information the polls provide—which is too often not the case—democracy is the winner. In the best instances, election polls are used by the news media to help them make important and prodemocratic news decisions about how the campaign should be covered. In these cases, the polls are used to make news that helps the public think carefully about their election choices. If polls are ever to reach the potential that we believe they have in aiding democratic deliberations in the United States, these efforts must be increased. If they are not, we expect that controversy surrounding the use of election polls by the news media will continue to become more politicized in the early twenty-first century. This will in turn likely further erode confidence in the polls and in the news stories that report poll results. If that happens, pollsters, the media, and democracy will all be the losers.

References

Adair, J. G. 1996. The Hawthorne effect is a common artifact in social research. *Public Perspective* 7, no.1:14–16.

Altschuler, B. E. 1982. *Keeping a finger on the public pulse: Private polling and presidential elections.* Westport, Conn.: Greenwood Press.

American Association for Public Opinion Research (AAPOR). 1997. *Best practices for survey and public opinion research and survey practices AAPOR condemns.* Ann Arbor: University of Michigan Press.

Baden, P. L. 1996. Wellstone pulls ahead of Boschwitz: Results suggest Republicans' negative ads are backfiring. *Minneapolis Star Tribune,* 15 October, p. A1.

Bailey, R. W. 1998. *Out and voting: The gay, lesbian and bisexual vote in congressional House elections.* Washington, D.C.: The Policy Institute, National Gay and Lesbian Task Force.

Balz, D. 1994. GOP "Contract" pledges 10 tough acts to follow. *Washington Post,* 20 November, p. A1.

Barlow, Y. 1994. Term-limit proposals gain support; Initiatives are on ballots in 8 states. *Dallas Morning News,* 23 October, p. 8A.

Barone, M., and G. Ujifusa. 1997. *The almanac of American politics 1998.* Washington, D.C.: National Journal.

Batten, J. K. 1989. We're in this together. Newspapers, community and leadership: A symposium on editorial pages. Miami: Knight-Ridder.

Bauman, S. L. 1996. Causal attribution in election news stories: How journalists explain public opinion polls. Unpublished doctoral dissertation, Northwestern University.

————, and S. Herbst. 1994. Managing perceptions of public opinion: Candidates' and journalists' reactions to the 1992 polls. *Political Communication* 11:133–43.

Bennett, W. L. 1996. *News: The politics of iIllusion.* 3d ed. New York: Longman.

Best, K. 1994. 350 GOP House hopefuls sign "Contract" with voters. *St. Louis Post-Dispatch,* 28 September, p. 1A.

Biemer, P. P., R. M. Groves, L. E. Lyberg, N. A. Mathiowetz, and S. Sudman, eds. 1991. *Measurement errors in surveys.* New York: John Wiley.

Bishop, G. F., R. W. Oldendick, A. J. Tuchfarber, and S. E. Bennett. 1980. Pseudo-opinions on public affairs. *Public Opinion Quarterly* 44:198–209.

————, A. J. Tuchfarber, and R. W. Oldendick. 1986. Opinions on fictitious issues: The pressure to answer survey questions. *Public Opinion Quarterly* 50: 240–50.

Blomquist, D., and C. Zukin. 1997. Does public journalism work? The "Campaign Central" experience. Washington, D.C.: Pew Center for Civic Journalism; Hackensack, N.J.: *Record,* May.

Blumer, H. 1948. Public opinion and public opinion polling. *American Sociological Review* 13, no. 5:542–49.

Bolstein, R. 1991a. Comparison of the likelihood to vote among pre-election poll respondents and nonrespondents. *Public Opinion Quarterly* 55:648–50.

———. 1991b. Predicting the likelihood to vote in pre-election polls. *Statistician* 40:277–83.

Boorstin, D. J. 1964. *The image: A guide to pseudo-events in America.* New York: Harper & Row.

Bowman, K. H., and C. E. Ladd. 1994. Clinton and the economy. *The Public Perspective* 5, no. 6:112.

Boyte, H. C. 1995. Public opinion as public judgment. Pp. 417–34 in *Public opinion and the communication of consent.* Edited by T. L. Glasser and C. T. Salmon. New York: Guilford.

Broder, D. 1997. A new assignment for the press. Enterprise Lecture Series No. 26. Riverside: University of California Press.

Broh, A. 1983. Polls, pols, and parties. *Journal of Politics* 45:732–44.

Bruce, P. 1997. How the experts got voter turnout wrong last year. *Public Perspective* 8, no. 6:9–43, 49.

Bryce, J. 1891. *The American commonwealth.* London: Macmillan and Company.

Campbell, J. E. 1993. *The presidential pulse of congressional elections.* Lexington: University of Kentucky Press.

———, and K. A. Wink. 1990. Trial-heat forecasts of the presidential vote. *American Politics Quarterly* 18:251–69.

Cantril, A. H. 1991. *The opinion connection: Polling, politics and the press.* Washington, D.C.: Congressional Quarterly Press.

Ceci, S., and E. Kain. 1982. Jumping on the bandwagon with the underdog: The impact of attitude polls on polling behavior. *Public Opinion Quarterly* 46:228–42.

Charity, A. 1995. *Doing public journalism.* New York: Guilford Press.

Clausen, A. 1968. Response validity: Vote report. *Public Opinion Quarterly* 32: 588–606.

Cloutier, E., R. Nadeau, and J. Guay. 1989. Bandwagoning and underdogging on North American free trade: A quasi-experimental panel study of opinion. *International Journal of Public Opinion Research* 1:206–20.

Clymer, A. 1996. Phony polls that sling mud raise questions over ethics. *New York Times,* 20 May.

Cohen, J. 1988. *Statistical power for the behavioral sciences.* 2d ed. Hillsdale, N.J.: Lawrence Erlbaum.

Committee for the Study of the American Electorate. 1997. *1996 election report.* Washington, D.C.: Author.

Converse, P. E. 1964. The nature of belief systems in mass publics. In *Ideology and discontent.* Edited by D. E. Apter. New York: Free Press.

Cook, C. 1994. National overview. *Cook Political Report,* 19 August, p. 1.

Cotter, P., J. Cohen, and P. B. Coulter. 1982. Race-of-interviewer effects in telephone interviews. *Public Opinion Quarterly* 46:278–84.

Council for Marketing and Opinion Research. 1995. *The respondent cooperation and industry image survey.* New York: Author.

Crespi, I. 1988. *Pre-election polling: Sources of accuracy and error.* New York: Russell Sage Foundation.

———. 1989. *Public opinion, polls and democracy.* Boulder, Colo.: Westview Press.

Culbertson, H. M. 1983. Three perspectives on American journalism. *Journalism Monographs* 83.

Daves, R. P. 1997. Adapting deliberative polling to public journalism. Paper presented to the 52nd annual meeting of the American Association for Public Opinion Research, Norfolk, Va., May.

———. 1998. Deliberative polling—fitting the tool to the job. Unpublished manuscript.

———, and S. P. Warden. 1995. Methods of allocating undecided respondents to candidate choices in pre-election polls. Pp. 101–19 in *Presidential polls and the news media.* Edited by P. J. Lavrakas, M. W. Traugott, and P. V. Miller. Boulder, Colo.: Westview Press.

Davis, J. S., and T. W. Smith. 1992. *The NORC General Social Survey: A user's guide.* Newbury Park, Calif.: Sage Publications.

Davis, P. 1982. *Hometown.* New York: Simon & Schuster.

Delli-Carpini, M. X., and S. Keeter. 1996. *What Americans know about politics and why it matters.* New Haven, Conn.: Yale University Press.

Demers, D., and N. Suzzane. 1987. *Precision journalism: A practical guide.* Newbury Park, Calif: SagePublications.

Dienel, P. C. 1978. *Die planungszelle: Eine Alternative zur Establishment-Demokratie. Der Bürger plant seine Umwelt.* Opladen: Westdeutscher Verlag.

———. 1989. Contributing to social decision methodology: Citizen reports on technological problems. Pp. 133–51 in *Social decision making for technological problems.* Edited by C. Vlek and G. Cvetkovich. Dordrecht: Kulwer Academic Publishers.

Downs, J. 1998. For up in arms over phone survey. *Philadelphia Inquirer,* 12 July.

Dran, E., and A. Hildreth. 1995. What the public thinks about how we know what it is thinking. *International Journal of Public Opinion Research* 7: 128–44.

Drinkard, J. 1994. Republican Contract with the voters: Tax cuts, term limits, balanced budget. Associated Press wire service story, 27 September, 1:35 P.M.

Duncan, P. D. 1995. Fine print in the "Contract" was hidden. *The Commercial Appeal,* 3 December, p. 6B.

Edelman, M., and W. J. Mitofsky. 1989. *The effect of the interviewer's race in political surveys with multiracial candidates.* Paris: International Statistical Institute.

Edwards, B. 1996a. Phone "poll" tactic upsets candidates; slanted questions critical of rivals. *Tampa Tribune,* 17 June.

———. 1996b. Candidate issues challenge; Phyllis Busandsky's foes agree in principle, but see no need to sign her clean campaign pledge. *Tampa Tribune,* 26 June.

———. 1996c. Freedman tests negatives in poll. *Tampa Tribune,* 20 September.

Elig, T. W., and I. H. Frieze. 1979. Measuring causal attributions for success and failure. *Journal of Personality and Social Psychology* 37:621–34.

Erikson, R. S., and L. Sigelman. 1995. Poll-based forecasts of midterm congressional election outcomes: Do the pollsters get it right? *Public Opinion Quarterly* 59:589–605.

Fenwick, I., F. Wiseman, J. F. Becker, and J. R. Heiman. 1982. Classifying undecided voters in pre-election polls. *Public Opinion Quarterly* 46:383–91.

Finkel, S. E., T. M. Guterbock, and M. J. Borg. 1991. Race-of-interviewer effects in
a preelection poll: Virginia 1989. *Public Opinion Quarterly* 55:313–30.

Fishkin, J. S. 1988. The case for a national caucus: Taking democracy seriously.
Atlantic Monthly, August, 16–18.

———. 1991. *Democracy and deliberation: New directions for democratic reform*. New
Haven, Conn.: Yale University Press.

———. 1992. A response to Traugott. *Public Perspective* 3, no. 3:29–30.

———. 1994. Britain experiments with the deliberative poll. *Public Perspective* 5,
no. 4:27–29.

———. 1995. *The voice of the people: Public opinion and democracy*. New Haven,
Conn.: Yale University Press.

———, and R. C. Luskin. forthcoming. *Bringing deliberation to the democratic dialogue: The NIC and beyond*.

Florida House of Representatives. 1997. Push polling: The art of political persuasion.
A report prepared by the staff of the Committee on Election Reform, Representative Lisa Carlton, Chair.

Foersterling, F., and A. Groeneveld. 1983. Ursachzuschreibungen für ein Wahlergeb-
nis: Eine Überprüfung von Hypothesen der Attributionstheorie in einer Feld-
studie anhand die niedersachsischen Kommunalwahl [Attributions for election
results: A study of attributional hypothesis in a field study of Lower Saxony
community elections]. *Zeitschrift für Sozialpsychologie* 14:262–69.

Fouhy, E. 1996. Civic journalism and the polls. *Public Perspective* 7, no. 3:51–53.

Foundation for Information. 1997. *The freedom to publish public opinion polls: Report
on a worldwide study*. Amsterdam: Author.

Frankel, M. 1996. Margins of error. *New York Times*, 15 December, pp. 34–36.

Frankovic, K. A. 1994. News media polling in a changing technological environment. In 12th Annual Van Zelst Lecture in Communication. Evanston, Ill.:
Northwestern University.

———.1998. Public opinion and polling. Pp. 150–70 in *The politics of news: The
news of politics*. Eited by D. Gaber, D. McQuall, and P. Norris. Washington,
D.C.: Congressional Quarterly Press.

———.1999a. Public opinion polling: The U.S. experience. ESOMAR Conference,
Santiago, Chile, April.

———. 1999b. Election polling under stress: Media adaptations to survey research
methodology. *Election polling: 1999 Nebraska Symposium on Survey Research*.
Lincoln: University of Nebraska Press and the Gallup Organization.

Freedman, P., and K. Goldstein. 1996. Estimating turnout in preelection polls.
Public Opinion Quarterly 60, no. 4:574–87.

Freeman, H. 1953. A note on the prediction of who votes. *Public Opinion Quarterly*
17:288–92.

Gallup Poll Monthly. 1996. Design of the sample. May, p. 52.

Gallup, G. 1972. *The sophisticated poll watcher's guide*. Princeton, N.J.: Princeton
Opinion Press.

———, and S. F. Rae. 1940. T*he pulse of democracy: The public opinion poll and how
it works*. New York: Simon & Schuster.

Gans, C. 1997. It's Bruce who got the turnout story wrong. *Public Perspective* 8, no. 6:44–48.

Gawiser, S. R., and G. E. Witt. 1994. *A journalist's guide to public opinion polls.* Westport, Conn.: Praeger.

Gelman, A., and G. King. 1993. Why are American presidential election campaign polls so variable when votes are so predictable? *British Journal of Political Science* 23:409–51.

Germond, J. W., and J. Witcover. 1996. Why Americans don't go to the polls. *National Journal,* 23 November, p. 2562.

Gilljam, M., and D. Granberg. 1993. Should we take don't know for an answer? *Public Opinion Quarterly* 57:348–57.

Ginsberg, B. 1989. How polling transforms public opinion. Pp. 271–93 in *Manipulating public opinion: Essays on public opinion as a dependent variable.* Edited by M. Margolis and G. A. Mauser. Pacific Grove, Calif.: Brooks/Cole.

Glynn, C. J., S. Herbst, G. J. O'Keefe, and R. Y. Shapiro. 1999. *Public opinion.* Boulder, Colo.: Westview Press.

Goldman, E. 1944. Poll on the polls. *Public Opinion Quarterly* 8:461–67.

Gollin, A. E. 1980. Exploring the liaison between polling and the press. *Public Opinion Quarterly* 44:445–61.

Goyder, J. 1986. Surveys on surveys: Limitations and potentialities. *Public Opinion Quarterly* 50:27–41.

Greenwald, A. G., M. Vande Kamp, M. R. Klinger, and K. L. Kerr. 1988. A contactability bias in surveys of voter turnout. Unpublished manuscript. Seattle: University of Washington.

Greve, F. 1995a. "Contract" poll was flawed, pollster says. Knight-Ridder Service, 10 November.

———. 1995b. The birth of Republican fine print: America sees Contract's big picture. Knight-Ridder Service, 26 February.

Groves, R. M. 1989. *Survey errors and survey costs.* New York: John Wiley.

———, and M. P. Coupero. 1998. *Nonresponse in household interview surveys.* New York: John Wiley.

Gruca, T. S. 1994. The polling business: Expecting the unexpected: The problem of undecided voters. *Public Perspective* 5:24.

Habermas, J. 1982. A reply to my critics. Pp. 218–83 in *Habermas: Critical debates.* Edited by J.B. Thompson and D. Held. Cambridge, Mass.: MIT Press.

———. 1985. *The theory of communicative action: Reason and the rationalization of society.* Vol. 1. Boston: Beacon Press.

———. 1989. *The structural transformation of the public sphere: An inquiry into a category of bourgeois society.* Translated by T. Burger. Cambridge, Mass.: MIT Press. (Original work published 1962.)

Hallin, D. C. 1992. Sound bit news: Television coverage of elections, 1968–1988. *Journal of Communication,* 42:5–24.

Hauck, J., and R. Daves. 1997. Turnout predictions: A comparison of methodologies. Norfolk, Va.: American Association for Public Opinion.

Heider, F. 1958. *The psychology of interpersonal relations.* New York: John Wiley.

Herbst, S. 1993. *Numbered voices: How opinion polling has shaped American Politics.* Chicago: University of Chicago Press.

————. 1993. The meaning of public opinion: Citizens' construction of political reality. *Media, Culture and Society* 15:437–54.

————. 1995. Election polling in historical perspective. Pp. 23–34 in *Presidential polls and the news media,* Edited by P. J. Lavrakas, M. K. Traugott, and P. V. Miller. Boulder, Colo.: Westview Press.

Hickman, H. 1991. Public polls and election participants. Pp. 100-33 in *Polling and presidential election coverage.* Edited by P. J. Lavrakas and J. K. Holley. Newbury Park, Calif.: Sage Publications.

Hoek, J., and P. Gendall. 1997. Factors affecting political poll accuracy: An analysis of undecided respondents. *Marketing Bulletin* 8:1–14.

Huffington, A. 1998. Investigating the pollsters. 12 October. Internet: http://www.ariannaonline.com/columns/files/101298.html.

————. 1998. Margin of arrogance is huge for pollsters. *Chicago Sun-Times,* 14 October.

John and Mary R. Markle Foundation. 1996. Presidential election watch. New York: Press release of 12 November.

Johnstone, J. W. C., E. J. Slawski, and W. W. Bowman.1976. *The news people: A sociological portrait of American journalists and their work.* Urbana: University of Illinois Press.

Jones, E. E., and D. McGillis. 1986. Correspondent inferences and the attribution cube: A comparative reappraisal. Pp. 389–420 in *New directions in attribution research.* Edited by J. H. Harvey, W. Ickes, and R. F. Kidd. Vol. 1. Hillsdale, N.J.: Lawrence Erlbaum.

————, and K. E. Davis. 1965. From acts to dispositions: The attribution process in person perception. Pp. 219–66 in *Advances in experimental social psychology.* Edited by L. Berkowitz. Vol. 2. New York: Academic Press.

Jowell, R., B. Hedges, P. Lynn, G. Farrant, and A. Heath. 1993. The 1992 British election: The failure of the polls. *Public Opinion Quarterly* 57:238–63.

Kagay, M. R. 1991. The use of public opinion polls by the *New York Times*: Some examples from the 1988 presidential election. Pp. 19–56 in *Polling and presidential election coverage.* Edited by P. J. Lavrakas and J. K. Holley. Newbury Park, Calif.: Sage Publications..

————. 1992. Variability without fault: Why even well-designed polls can disagree. Pp. 95–124 in *Media polls in American politics.* Edited by T. E. Mann and G. R. Orren. Washington, D.C.: Brookings Institution.

————. 1996. Experts say refinements are needed in the polls. *New York Times,* 15 December, p. A34.

Kang, M., P. Lavrakas, and M. Traugott. 1998. Contingent conditions for the influence of preelection polls on voting intentions: The role of individuals' motivation and ability. Paper presented at the annual conference of the Midwest Association for Public Opinion Research, Chicago, November.

Kay, A. F., H. Henderson, F. Steeper, and C. Lake. 1994. *Interviews with the public guide us . . . on the road to consensus.* St. Augustine, Fla.: Americans Talk Issues Foundation.

Keeter, S. 1997. Public opinion and the election. In *The election of 1996.* Edited by G. M. Pomper. Chatham, N.J.: Chatham House.

Kelley, H. H. 1967. Attribution theory in social psychology. Pp. 192–240 in *Nebraska Symposium on Motivation*. Edited by D. Levine. Lincoln: University of Nebraska Press.

———. 1972. Attribution in social interaction. Pp. 1–26 in *Attribution: Perceiving the causes of behavior.* Edited by E. E. Jones, D. E. Kanouse, H. H. Kelley, R. E. Nisbett, S. Valins, and B. Weiner. Morristown, N.J.: General Learning Press.

———. 1973. The processes of causal attribution. *American Psychologist* 28, no. 2:107–28.

Kelley, M. 1992. Political memo: Those chicken Georges and what they mean. *New York Times*, 30 September, p. 21.

Kinder, D. R., and D. O. Sears. 1985. Public opinion and political action. In *Handbook of social psychology.* Edited by G. Lindzey and E. Aronson. Vol. 2. New York: Random House.

Kohut, A. 1986. Rating the polls: The views of media elites and the general public. *Public Opinion Quarterly* 50:1–9.

———. 1996. The big poll that didn't. *Poll Watch* 4:2–3.

Krosnick, J. A. 1991. Response strategies for coping with the cognitive demands of attitude measures in surveys. *Applied Cognitive Psychology* 5:213–36.

———, and D. F. Alwin. 1987. An evaluation of a cognitive theory of response-order effects in survey measurement. *Public Opinion Quarterly*, 51, no. 2:201–19.

———, and M. K. Berent. 1993. Comparisons of party identification and policy preferences: The impact of survey question format. *American Journal of Political Science* 37:941–64.

Ladd, C. E. 1996. Magic town: Jimmy Stewart demonstrates the "Hawthorne Effect." *Public Perspective* 7, no. 3:16–17.

———, and J. Benson. 1992. The growth of news polls in American politics. Pp. 19–31 in *Media polls in American politics.* Edited by T. E. Mann and G. R. Orren. Washington, D.C.: Brookings Institution.

Ladd, E. S. 1996. The election polls: An American Waterloo. *Chronicle of Higher Education*, 22 November, p. A52.

———.1996a. The pollsters' Waterloo. *Wall Street Journal*, 19 November, op-ed.

———. 1996b. The turnout muddle. P. 34 in *America at the polls: 1996.* Storrs, Conn.: Roper Center for Public Opinion Research.

———. 1997. Assessing the polls' performance in the 1996 election. *Public Perspective* 8:149.

———, J. Fishkin, M. Traugott, and R, Morin. 1992. A roundtable discussion with J. Fishkin, M. Traugott, and R. Morin. *Public Perspective* 3, no. 3:31–34.

Lampert, S., and A. Tziner. 1985. A predictive study of voting behavior using Lampert's Pollimeter. *Social Behavior and Personality* 13:1–9.

Lane, R. E., and D. O. Sears. 1964. *Public opinion.* Englewood Cliffs, N.J.: Prentice Hall.

Lang, K., and G. Lang.1984. The impact of polls on public opinion. *Annals of the American Academy of Political and Social Science* 472:129–42.

Lau, R. R. 1994. An analysis of the accuracy of "trial heat" polls during the 1992 presidential election. *Public Opinion Quarterly* 58:2–20.

Lavrakas, P. J. 1991. Introduction. Pp. 9–18 in *Polling and presidential election coverage.* Edited by P. J. Lavrakas and J. K. Holley. Newbury Park, Calif.: Sage.

————. 1993. *Telephone survey methods: Sampling, selection, and supervision.* New-bury Park, Calif.: Sage Publications.

————. 1999. The effects of election polls on elites and the public. *Election polling: 1999 Nebraska Symposium on Survey Research.* Lincoln: University of Nebraska Press and the Gallup Organization.

————, and S. L. Bauman. 1995. Newspaper use of presidential pre-election polls: 1980–1992. Pp. 35–50 in *Presidential election polls and the news media.* Edited by P. J. Lavrakas, M. K. Traugott, and P. V. Miller. Boulder, Colo.: Westview Press.

————, and J. K. Holley. 1991. *Polling and presidential election coverage.* Newbury Park, Calif.: Sage Publications.

————, J. K. Holley, and P. V. Miller. 1991. Public reactions to polling news during the 1988 presidential election campaign. Pp. 151–83 in *Polling and presidential election coverage.* Edited by P. J. Lavrakas and J. K. Holley. Newbury Park, Calif.: Sage Publications.

————, S. Mockabee, Q. Monson, and T. Thompson. 1997. Predicting voter turnout and vote outcome in ballot elections: The results of four pre-election surveys. Paper presented at the 53rd annual conference of the American Associa-tion for Public Opinion Research, St.Louis, Mo., May.

————, and M. W. Traugott. 1995a. News media's use of presidential polling in the 1990s: An introduction and overview. Pp. 3–22 in *Presidential polls and the news media.* Edited by P. J. Lavrakas, M. W. Traugott, and P. V. Miller. Boulder, Colo.: Westview Press.

————, and M. W. Traugott. 1995b. The media's use of election polls: A synthesis and recommendations for 1996 and beyond. Pp. 257–66 in *Presidential polls and the news media.* Edited by P. J. Lavrakas, M. W. Traugott, and P. V. Miller. Boulder, Colo.: Westview Press.

————, M. W. Traugott, and P. V. Miller. 1995. *Presidential polls and the news media.* Boulder, Colo.: Westview Press.

Lazarsfeld, P., B. Berelson, and H. Gaudet. 1944. *The people's choice: How the voter makes up his mind in a presidential campaign.* New York: Columbia University Press.

Levin, D. 1997. Top state official: Many of election's voters not citizens. *Inland (Calif.) Daily Bulletin,* 14 October, p. A3.

Lewis, I. A. 1991. Media polls, the *Los Angeles Times* poll, and the 1988 presidential election. Pp. 57–82 in *Polling and presidential election coverage.* Edited by P. J. Lavrakas and J. K. Holley. Newbury Park, Calif.: Sage.

Lippmann, W. 1922. *Public opinion.* New York: Harcourt Brace.

————. 1925. *The phantom public.* New York: Harcourt Brace.

Lipstein, B. 1975. In defense of small samples. *Journal of Advertising Research,* 15:33.

Lowery, S. A., and M. L. DeFleur. 1995. *Milestones in mass communication research.* 3d ed. White Plains, N.Y.: Longman.

Luntz, F. L. 1994. GOP aims its "Contract" at alienated voter. *Wall Street Journal,* 27 September, p. 16A.

Luskin, R. C. 1987. Measuring political sophistication. *American Journal of Political Science* 31:856–99.

Luskin, R. E. forthcoming. From denial to extenuation (and finally beyond): Political sophistication and citizen performance. In *Thinking about political psychology.* Edited by J. H. Kuklinski. New York: Cambridge University Press.

————, J. S. Fishkin, and R. Jowell. 1997. Considered opinions: Deliberative polling in the U.K. Unpublished manuscript.

Lynd, R. S., and H. M. Lynd. 1929. *Middletown: A study in American culture.* New York: Harcourt Brace.

————, and H. M. Lynd. 1937. *Middletown in transition: A study in cultural conflicts.* New York: Harcourt Brace and World.

MacDougall, C. 1938. *Interpretative reporting.* New York: Macmillan.

Mahek, J. 1992. Perot reaches out for first-time voters. *Boston Globe*, 1 November, p. 23.

Mann, T. E., and G. R. Orren. 1992. *Media polls in American politics.* Washington, D.C.: Brookings Institution.

————, and G. R. Orren. 1992. To poll or not to poll and other questions. Pp. 1–18 in *Media polls in American politics.* Edited by T. E. Mann and G. R. Orren. Washington, D.C.: Brookings Institution.

Mantius, P. 1996. Election '96: Georgia; GOP makes more inroads in legislature. *Atlanta Journal and Constitution*, 7 November.

Manuel, M. 1996. Venomless campaign draws little attention. *Atlanta Journal and Constitution*, 27 June.

McClendon, M. J., and D. F. Alwin. 1993. No-opinion filters and attitude measurement reliability. *Sociological Methods and Research* 21:438–64.

McGuire, M., L. Stilborne, M. McAdams, and L. Hyatt. 1997. *The Internet handbook for writers, researchers, and journalists.* New York: Guilford Press.

Merkle, D. M. 1996. Polls-review: The National Issues Convention Deliberative Poll. *Public Opinion Quarterly* 60:588–619.

————, M. Edelman, K. Dykeman, and C. Brogan. 1998. An experimental study of ways to increase exit poll response rates and reduce survey error. Paper presented at the 53rd annual conference of the American Association for Public Opinion Research, St. Louis, Mo., 14–17 May.

Merrill, J. C., and R. L. Lowenstein. 1979. *Media, messages, and men: New perspectives in communication.* 2d ed. New York: Longman.

Merritt, W. D. 1995. *Public life and the press: Why telling the news is not enough.* Hillsdale, N.J.: Lawrence Erlbaum.

————. 1998. *Public journalism and public life.* 2d ed. Mahwah, N.J.: Lawrence Erlbaum.

Meyer, P. 1989. Precision journalism and the 1988 elections. *International Journal of Public Opinion Research* 1, no. 3:195–205.

————. 1991. How to do an election. Pp. 214–35 in *The new precision journalism.* Bloomington and Indianapolis: Indiana University Press.

————. 1991. *The new precision journalism.* Bloomington: Indiana University Press.

————. 1996. Re: National Issues Convention polls. Comments posted to AAPORNET@usc.edu, 4 February.

————, and D. Potter. 1997. The effect of pre-election polls on issue knowledge in the U.S. presidential election of 1996. Prepared for the annual Conference of the World Association for Public Opinion Research, Edinburgh, September.

Miller, E. D. 1994. *The Charlotte Project: Helping citizens take back democracy.* St. Petersburg: Poynter Institute for Media Studies.

Miller, J. M., and J. A. Krosnick. 1998. The impact of candidate name order on election outcomes. *Public Opinion Quarterly* 62:291–330.

Miller, M. 1952. The Waukegan Study of voter turnout prediction. *Public Opinion Quarterly* 37:99–109.

———, and R. Hurd. 1982. Conformity to AAPOR standards in newspaper reporting of public opinion polls. *Public Opinion Quarterly* 46:243–49.

———, D. Merkle, and P. Wang. 1991. Journalism with footnotes: Reporting the "technical details" of polls. Pp. 200–214 in *Polling and presidential election coverage.* Edited by P. Lavrakas and J. Holley. Newbury Park, Calif.: Sage Publications.

Mitofsky, W. J. 1981. The 1980 pre-election polls: A review of disparate methods and results. Pp. 47–52 inAmerican Statistical Association Proceedings of the Section on Survey Research.

———. 1995. How pollsters and reporters can do a better job informing the public: A challenge for campaign '96. Pp. 69–79 in *Presidential polls and the news media.* Edited by P. J. Lavrakas, M. W. Traugott, and P. V. Miller. Boulder, Colo.: Westview Press.

———. 1996. The emperor has no clothes. *Public Perspective,* 7, no. 3:17–19.

———. 1998. Was 1996 a worse year for polls than 1948? *Public Opinion Quarterly* 62:230–49.

———, and M. Edelman. 1995. A review of the 1992 VRS exit polls. Pp. 81–100 in *Presidential polls and the news media.* Edited by P. J. Lavrakas, M. W. Traugott, and P. V. Miller. Boulder, Colo.: Westview Press.

Moore, D. W. 1992. *The superpollsters: How they measure and manipulate public opinion in America.* New York: Four Walls Eight Windows.

———. 1996. Low turnout helped GOP. *Polling Report,* 12, no. 22:7.

Moore, M. 1996. Switch to Republican Party will be put to test in Texas. *USA Today,* 2 April.

Morgan, L. 1996a. Latvala tries to head off attack. *St. Petersburg Times,* 1 November.

———. 1996b. State races riddled with cheap shots. *St. Petersburg Times,* 5 November.

Morin, R. 1995. The 1992 election and the polls: Neither politics nor polling as usual. Pp. 123–42 in *Presidential polls and the news media.* Edited by P. J. Lavrakas, M. W. Traugott, and P. V. Miller. Boulder, Colo.: Westview Press.

———. 1997. A pollster's peers cry foul: GOP strategist Luntz is accused of unprofessionalism in his "Contract with America" surveys. *Washington Post National Weekly Edition,* 28 April, p. 35.

———. 1999. What Monica taught me about polling in the 2000 presidential election. *Election polling: 1999 Nebraska Symposium on Survey Research.* Lincoln: University of Nebraska Press and the Gallup Organization.

Morris, R. S. 1997. *Behind the Oval Office: Winning the presidency in the nineties.* Thorndike, Maine: Thorndike Press.

Mosier, N., and A. Ahlgren. 1981. Credibility of precision journalism. *Journalism Quarterly* 58:375–81.

Mutz, D. C. 1995. Media, momentum, and money: Horse race spin in the 1988 Republican primaries. Pp. 229–54 in *Presidential election polls and the news media.* Edited by P. J. Lavrakas, M. K. Traugott, and P. V. Miller. Boulder, Colo.: Westview Press.

National Council on Public Polls (NCPP). 1997. Polling council analysis concludes criticisms of 1996 presidential polls accuracy are unfounded. Press release dated 13 February.

Neijens, P. 1987. *The choice questionnaire. Design and evaluation of an instrument for collecting informed opinions of a population.* Amsterdam: Free University Press.

———, F. Molenaar, W. E. Saris, and J. Slot. 1997. Information, media, and public opinion: A referendum case. Paper presented at the annual meeting of the World Association for Public Opinion Research, Edinburgh, Scotland.

———, J. A. de Ridder, and W. E. Saris. 1992. An instrument for collecting informed opinions. *Quality and Quantity* 26:245–58.

Neuman, W. R. 1986. *The paradox of mass politics: Knowledge and opinion in the American electorate.* Cambridge, Mass.: Harvard University Press.

Newport, F. 1997. The pre-election polls performed well in '96. *Public Perspective* 8:1, 50–51.

———. 1999. Common objections to horse race polling. *Election polling: 1999 Nebraska Symposium on Survey Research.* Lincoln: University of Nebraska Press and the Gallup Organization.

Noelle-Neumann, E. 1980. The public opinion research correspondent. *Public Opinion Quarterly* 44:585–97.

———. 1984. *The spiral of silence.* Chicago: University of Chicago Press.

Nurse, D. 1996. Candidate claims poll is derogatory. *Tampa Tribune,* 12 October.

O'Neill, H. 1996. Respondent cooperation and industry image survey. A report by the Council for Marketing and Opinion Research.

Oliver, J. E. 1996. Who votes at home? The influence of state law and party activity on absentee voting and overall turnout. *American Journal of Political Science,* 40:498–513.

Page, B. I., and R. Y. Shapiro. 1992. *The rational public: Fifty years of trends in Americans' policy preferences.* Chicago: University of Chicago Press.

Paletz, D. L., J. Y. Short, H. Baker, B. C. Campbell, R. J. Cooper, and R. M. Oeslander. 1980. Polls in the media: Content, credibility, and consequences. *Public Opinion Quarterly* 44:495–513.

Panagakis, N. 1989. The incumbent rule. *Polling Report* 5:1–3.

———. 1997. Undecideds generally go to the challenger. *Public Perspective* 8:1, 21–24.

Pateman, C. 1970. *Participation and democratic theory.* London: Cambridge University Press.

Patterson, T. E. 1980. *The mass media election: How Americans choose their president.* New York: Praeger.

———. 1993. *Out of order.* New York: Knopf.

Peer, L. 1994. Communicating the meaning of public opinion: A comparison of American and Israeli newspapers. Unpublished doctoral dissertation, Northwestern University.

Perloff, R. M. 1998. *Political communication: Politics, press, and public in America.* Mahwah, N.J.: Lawrence Erlbaum Associates.

Perry, P. 1960. Election survey procedures of the Gallup poll. *Public Opinion Quarterly* 24:531–42.

———. 1973. A comparison of the voting preferences of likely voters and likely nonvoters. *Public Opinion Quarterly* 37:99–109.

———. 1979. Certain problems in election survey methodology. *Public Opinion Quarterly* 43:312–25.

Petrocik, J. 1991. An algorithm for estimating turnout as a guide to predicting elections. *Public Opinion Quarterly* 55:643–47.

Popkin, S. L., and M. P. McDonald. 1998. Who votes? *Blueprint: Ideas for a New Century* 1:28–29.

Presser, S., P. J. Lavrakas, M. W. Traugott, and V. Price.1998. Public opinion about polls: How people decide whether to believe survey results. Paper present at the 53rd annual conference of the American Association for Public Opinion Research, St. Louis, Mo.

Price, V. 1992. *Public opinion.* Newbury Park, Calif.: Sage Publications.

———, and P. Neijens. 1997. Opinion quality in public opinion research. *International Journal of Public Opinion Research* 9:336–60.

———, and P. Neijens, P. 1998. Deliberative polls: Toward improved measures of "informed" public opinion? *International Journal of Public Opinion Research* 10:145–76.

Raasch, C., and B. Tumulty. 1994. Gilman has reservations about GOP's "Contract with America." Gannett News Service, 27 September.

Rasinski, K. A., D. Mingay, and N. M. Bradburn. 1994. Do respondents really mark all that apply? *Public Opinion Quarterly* 58, no. 3:400–408.

Ready, T. 1996. Media's election project draws mixed reaction. *The News & Observer,* 9 December.

Renn, O., H. U. Stegelmann, G. Albrecht, U. Kotte, and H. P. Peters. 1984. An empirical investigation of citizens' preferences among four energy alternatives. *Technological Forecasting and Social Change* 26:11–46.

Rippey, J. 1980. Use of polls as a reporting tool. *Journalism Quarterly* 57, no. 4:642–46.

Robinson, C. E. 1932 *Straw votes.* New York: Columbia University Press.

Roll, C. W., and A. H. Cantril. 1980. *Polls: Their use and misuse in politics.* Cabin John, Md.: Seven Locks Press.

Roper Center Symposium. 1997. The tracking polls, how we did them. *Public Perspective* 8:1, 44–48.

Roper, B. 1986. Evaluating polls with poll data. *Public Opinion Quarterly* 50:10–16.

Rosen, J. 1991. Making journalism more public. *Communication* 12:267–84.

———. 1994. In public journalism: First principle. In *Public journalism: Theory and practice: An occasional paper of the Kettering Foundation.*

———. 1996. *Getting the connections right: Public journalism and the troubles of the press.* New York: Twentieth Century Fund.

———, and D. Merritt Jr. 1994. *Public journalism: Theory and practice.* Dayton, Ohio: Kettering Foundation.

Ross, L. 1977. The intuitive psychologist and his shortcomings: Distortions in the attribution process. In *Advances in experimental social psychology.* Edited by L. Berkowitz. Vol. 10. New York: Academic Press.

Ruth, D. 1996. Oh Mark? Interested in a volunteer? *Tampa Tribune,* 23 September.

Saad, L. K. 1997. An historical analysis: Presidential candidate preferences according to likelihood to vote: The Gallup poll, 1952–1996. Paper presented to the 52nd annual conference of the American Association for Public Opinion Research, Norfolk, Va., May.

Sabato, L., and G. Simpson. 1996a. *Dirty little secrets: The persistence of corruption in American politics.* New York: Times Books.

————, and G. Simpson. 1996b. When push comes to poll. *Washington Monthly*, 26–31 June.

Salmon, C. T., and T. L. Glasser. 1998. The politics of polling and the limits of consent. Pp. 4337–458 in *Public opinion and the communication of consent*. Edited by C. T. Salmon and T. L. Glasser. New York: Guilford Press.

Salwen, M. 1985. The reporting of public opinion polls during presidential years, 1968–1984. *Journalism Quarterly* 62:272–77.

————. 1987. Credibility of newspaper opinion polls: Source, source intent and precision. *Journalism Quarterly* 64:813–19.

Schell, J. 1987. *History in Sherman Park: An American family and the Reagan-Mondale election*. New York: Alfred A. Knopf.

Schleifer, S. 1986. Trends in attitudes toward and participation in survey research. *Public Opinion Quarterly* 50:17–26.

Schmitt, E. 1996. Half the electorate, perhaps satisfied or bored, sat out voting. *New York Times*, 7 November, p. B6.

Schneider, W. 1999. Lessons of '98: Cautions for 2000. *Election polling: 1999 Nebraska Symposium on Survey Research*. Lincoln: University of Nebraska Press and the Gallup Organization.

Schneider, W. 1999. Lessons of '98: Cautions for 2000. *Election polling: 1999 Nebraska Symposium on Survey Research*. Lincoln: University of Nebraska and the Gallup Organization.

Schudson, M. 1978. *Discovering the news*. New York: Basic Books.

Schuman, H., and S. Presser. 1981. *Questions and answers in attitude surveys: Experiments on question form, wording, and context*. New York: Academic Press.

Simpson, G. 1996. Dole campaign has paid over $1 million to firm that uses telemarketing to criticize opponents. *Wall Street Journal*, 12 March.

Smith, T. W., and F. D. Weil. 1990. Finding public opinion data: A guide to sources. *Public Opinion Quarterly*, 54:609–62.

Stein, R. M., and P. A. Garcia-Monet. 1997. Voting early, but not often. *Social Science Quarterly* 78:657–71.

Stephanopoulos, G. 1999. *All too human: A political education*. Boston: Little, Brown.

Taylor, H. 1997. Why most polls overestimated Clinton's margin. *Public Perspective* 8:2, 45–48.

Taylor, P. 1990. *See how they run*. New York: Knopf.

Teixeira, R. 1998. The real electorate. *The American Prospect* 37:82–85.

Tindale, R. S. 1996. Groups are unpredictably transformed by their internal dynamics. *Public Perspective*, 7, no. 1:9–20.

Tompson, T. N., and P. J. Lavrakas. 1997. Litmus test issues, voting intentions, and election polling. Paper presented at the 52nd annual conference of the American Association for Public Opinion Research, Norfolk, Va.

————, and P. J. Lavrakas. 1998. *"Litmus test" issues and voting intentions*. Montréal: International Society of Political Psychology.

Traugott, M. 1991. Public attitudes about news organizations, campaign coverage, and polls. Pp. 134–50 in *Polling and presidential election coverage*. Edited by P. Lavrakas and J. Holley. Newbury Park, Calif.: Sage Publications.

————. 1992. The impact of media polls on the public. Pp. 135–49 in *Media polls in American politics*. Edited by T. Mann and G. Orren. Washington, D.C.: Brookings Institution.

————. 1992. The "deliberative poll" is a well-intended but flawed idea. *Public Perspective*, 3, no. 3:27–29.

————. 1995. The use of focus groups to supplement campaign coverage." Pp. 51–66 in *Presidential polls and the news media*. Edited by P. J. Lavrakas, M. W. Traugott, and P. V. Miller. Boulder, Colo.: Westview Press.

————, and J. Means. 1995. Problems of character: Was it the candidate or the press? Pp. 193–208 in *Presidential polls and the news media*. Edited by P. J. Lavrakas, M. K. Traugott, and P. V. Miller. Boulder, Colo.: Westview Press.

————, and J. P. Katosh. 1979. Response validity in surveys of voting behavior. *Public Opinion Quarterly* 43:359–77.

————, and P. J. Lavrakas. 1996. *The voter's guide to election polls*. Chatham, N.J.: Chatham House Publishers.

————, and P. J. Lavrakas. 1999. *The voter's guide to election polls*. 2d ed. New York: Chatham House/Seven Bridges Press.

————, and C. Tucker. 1984. Strategies for predicting whether a citizen will vote and estimation of electoral outcomes. *Public Opinion Quarterly* 48:330–43.

Tringali, B. C. 1996. Experimenting with artificial democracy. *Public Perspective*, 7, no. 1:19–20.

Turner, D. 1994. GOP rally offers "pact" with voters; Paxon helps design campaign platform. *Buffalo News*, 28 September, p. 9.

Verba, S., and N. H. Nie. 1972. *Participation in America: Political democracy and social equality*. New York. Harper & Row.

Visser, P. S., J. A. Krosnick, J. F. Marquette, and M. F. Curtin. 1996. Mail surveys for election forecasting? An evaluation of the *Columbus Dispatch* poll. *Public Opinion Quarterly* 60:81–227.

Von Hoffman, N. 1980. Public opinion polls: Newspapers making their own news? *Public Opinion Quarterly* 44, no. 4:572–73.

Voss, D. S., A. Gelman, and G. King. 1995. Preelection survey methodology: Details from eight polling organizations, 1988 and 1992. *Public Opinion Quarterly* 59:98–132.

Walter, S. 1996. Push polls by telemarketers mar campaigns. *Milwaukee Journal Sentinel*, 27 October.

Weaver, D. H., and G. C. Wilhoit. 1986. *The American journalist: A portrait of U.S. news people and their work*. 2d ed. Bloomington: Indiana University Press.

Wilhoit, G. C., and D. H. Weaver. 1980. *Newsroom guide to polls and surveys*. Washington, D.C.: American Newspaper Publishers Association.

Will, G. 1994. Can Republicans move beyond minority status? *Times-Picayune*, 1 September, p. B7.

Willimack, D. K., H. Schuman, B. Pennell, and J. M. Lepkowski. 1995. Effects of a prepaid nonmonetary incentive on response rates and response quality in a face-to-face survey. *Public Opinion Quarterly* 59:78–92.

Winerip, M. 1994. *9 Highland Road*. New York: Pantheon Books.

————. 1996a. House debate hits home on jobs program. *New York Times*, 25 March.

————. 1996b. Model corporate citizen finds its trust in doubt over zoning issue. *New York Times*, 27 April.

Worcester, R. 1987. *Journalist's guide to the publication of opinion survey results*. London: Market and Opinion Research International.

———. 1993. A deliberate plan for confusing the issue. *MRS Research*, 1 November.

Wright, G. C. 1990. Misreports of voter choice in the 1988 NES Senate Election Study. *Legislative Studies Quarterly* 15:543–63.

———. 1992. Reported versus actual vote: There is a difference and it matters. *Legislative Studies Quarterly* 17:131–42.

———. 1993. Errors in measuring voter choice in the National Election Studies, 1952–1988. *American Journal of Political Science* 37:291–316.

Yankelovich, D. 1991. *Coming to public judgment: Making democracy work in a complex world*. Syracuse, N.Y.: Syracuse University Press.

Your voice, your vote: Results from a survey of registered voters in North Carolina. 1996. Frederick Schneiders Research. Washington, D.C., 9 December.

Zogby, J. 1996. The perils of polling: A look at why our polls are different. *Polling Report* 12, no. 22:1, 7.

Index